James

A Voyage to the Pacific Ocean

Discoveries in the Northern Hemisphere. Performed under the
Direction of Captains Cook, Clerke and Gore. In His Majesty's Ships
the Resolution and Discovery; in the Years 1776, 1777, 1778, 1779
and 1780.

Volume 2

SALZWASSER
VERLAG

James Cook & James King

A Voyage to the Pacific Ocean

Volume 2

HISTORISCHE
SCHIFFAHRT
SALZWASSERVERLAG

www.historische-schiffahrt.de

Cook, James & King, James

A Voyage to the Pacific Ocean

Volume 2

Reihe: Historische Schiffahrt, Band 62

1. Auflage 2009 | ISBN: 9783861950462

Salzwasser-Verlag (www.salzwasserverlag.de) ist ein Imprint der Europäischer Hochschulverlag GmbH & Co KG, Bremen. (www.ehverlag.de). Alle Rechte vorbehalten.

Die Deutsche Bibliothek verzeichnet diesen Titel in der Deutschen Nationalbibliografie.

Dieses Buch beruht auf einem alten Original. Der Verlag hat jedoch am ursprünglichen Text einige geringfügige Veränderungen vorgenommen, um die Übersichtlichkeit und Lesbarkeit zu verbessern.

A

VOYAGE

TO THE

PACIFIC OCEAN.

UNDERTAKEN,

BY THE COMMAND OF HIS MAJESTY,

FOR MAKING

Difcoveries in the Northern Hemifphere.

Performed under the Direction of Captains COOK, CLERKE, and GORE,
In His Majefty's Ships the *Refolution* and *Difcovery*; in the Years 1776, 1777, 1778, 1779, and 1780.

IN THREE VOLUMES.

VOL. I. and II. written by Captain JAMES COOK, F.R.S.
VOL. III. by Captain JAMES KING, LL.D. and F.R.S.

Publifhed by Order of the Lords Commiffioners of the Admiralty.

THE SECOND EDITION.

VOL. II.

LONDON:
PRINTED BY H. HUGHS,
FOR G. NICOL, BOOKSELLER TO HIS MAJESTY, IN THE STRAND;
AND T. CADELL, IN THE STRAND.
M.DCC.LXXXV.

CONTENTS

OF THE

SECOND VOLUME.

BOOK III.

TRANSACTIONS AT OTAHEITE, AND THE SOCIETY ISLANDS; AND PROSECUTION OF THE VOYAGE TO THE COAST OF NORTH AMERICA.

CHAP. I.

A   C H A P.

CONTENTS.

CHAP. II.

CHAP. III.

CHAP. IV.

CONTENTS.

A 2 *tions*

CONTENTS.

CHAP. VIII.

CHAP. IX.

CONTENTS.

CHAP.

CONTENTS.

CHAP. XII.

CHAP. XIII.

BOOK

CONTENTS.

BOOK IV.

TRANSACTIONS AMONGST THE NATIVES OF NORTH AME-
RICA; DISCOVERIES ALONG THAT COAST AND THE EAST-
ERN EXTREMITY OF ASIA, NORTHWARD TO ICY CAPE;
AND RETURN SOUTHWARD TO THE SANDWICH ISLANDS.

CHAP. I.

CHAP. II.

10

CONTENTS.

CHAP. III.

CHAP. IV.

CHAP. V.

CONTENTS.

CONTENTS.

CHAP. VIII.

CHAP. IX.

CHAP.

CONTENTS.

CHAP. X.

CHAP. XI.

I

CONTENTS.

CHAP. XII.

A VOY-

A VOYAGE TO THE PACIFIC OCEAN.

BOOK III.

TRANSACTIONS AT OTAHEITE, AND THE SOCIETY ISLANDS;
AND PROSECUTION OF THE VOYAGE TO THE
COAST OF NORTH AMERICA.

CHAP. I.

*An Eclipse of the Moon observed.—The Island Toobouai disco-
vered.—Its Situation, Extent, and Appearance.—Inter-
course with its Inhabitants.—Their Persons, Dresses, and
Canoes, described.—Arrival in Oheitepeha Bay at Otaheite.
—Omai's Reception and imprudent Conduct.—Account of
Spanish Ships twice visiting the Island.—Interview with the
Chief of this District.—The Olla, or God, of Bolabola.—A
mad Prophet.—Arrival in Matavai Bay.*

HAVING, as before related *, taken our final leave
of the Friendly Islands, I now resume my narrative of the voyage. In the evening of the 17th
of July, at eight o'clock, the body of Eaoo bore North East

1777.
July.

Thursday 17.

* See the conclusion of Chap. IX. Book II.

VOL. II.   B   by

by North, diftant three or four leagues. The wind was
now at Eaft, and blew a frefh gale. With it I ftood to the
South, till half an hour paft fix o'clock the next morning,
when a fudden fquall, from the fame direction, took our
fhip aback; and, before the fails could be trimmed, on the
other tack, the main-fail and the top-gallant fails were
much torn.

The wind kept between the South Weft, and South Eaft,
on the 19th and 20th; afterward, it veered to the Eaft,
North Eaft, and North. The night between the 20th and
21ft, an eclipfe of the moon was obferved as follows; being then in the latitude of 22° 57¼' South,

Apparent Time, A. M.
H. M. S.

Beginning, by Mr. King, at   o 32 50 ⎫
           Mr. Bligh, at   o 33 25 ⎬Mean long. 186° 57¼'.
           Myfelf, at   o 33 35 ⎭

End, by Mr. King, at   1 44 56 ⎫
        Mr. Bligh, at   1 44 6 ⎱Mean long. 186° 28¼'.
        Myfelf, at   1 44 56 ⎰Time keep. 186° 58¼'.

The latitude and longitude are thofe of the fhip, at 8ʰ 56ᵐ
A. M. being the time when the fun's altitude was taken for
finding the apparent time. At the beginning of the eclipfe,
the moon was in the zenith; fo that it was found moft convenient to make ufe of the fextants; and to make the obfervations by the reflected image, which was brought down
to a convenient altitude. The fame was done at the end;
except by Mr. King, who obferved with a night telefcope.
Although the greateft difference between our feveral obfervations, is no more than fifty feconds, it, neverthelefs,

3

appeared

appeared to me, that two obfervers might differ more than double that time, in both the beginning and end. And, though the times are noted to feconds, no fuch accuracy was pretended to. The odd feconds, fet down above, arofe by reducing the time, as given by the watch, to apparent time.

I continued to ftretch to the Eaft South Eaft, with the wind at North Eaft and North, without meeting with any thing worthy of note, till feven o'clock in the evening of the 29th; when we had a fudden and very heavy fquall of wind from the North. At this time, we were under fingle reefed topfails, courfes, and ftay-fails. Two of the latter were blown to pieces; and it was with difficulty that we faved the other fails. After this fquall, we obferved feveral lights moving about on board the Difcovery; by which we concluded, that fomething had given way; and, the next morning, we faw that her main-top-maft had been loft. Both wind and weather continued very unfettled till noon, this day, when the latter cleared up, and the former fettled in the North Weft quarter. At this time, we were in the latitude of 28° 6′ South, and our longitude was 198° 23′ Eaft. Here we faw fome pintado birds, being the firft fince we left the land.

On the 31ft, at noon, Captain Clerke made a fignal to fpeak with me. By the return of the boat, which I fent on board his fhip, he informed me, that the head of the main-maft had been juft difcovered to be fprung, in fuch a man-ner, as to render the rigging of another top-maft very dan-gerous; and that, therefore, he muft rig fomething lighter in its place. He alfo informed me, that he had loft his main-top-gallant-yard; and that he neither had another, nor a fpar to make one, on board. The Refolution's fprit-

fail

Friday 1. fail top-fail-yard, which I ſent him, ſupplied this want.
The next day, he got up a jury top-maſt, on which he ſet
a mizen-top-fail; and this enabled him to keep way with
the Reſolution.

The wind was fixed in the Weſtern board; that is, from
the North, round by the Weſt to South, and I ſteered Eaſt
North Eaſt, and North Eaſt, without meeting with any
thing remarkable, till eleven o'clock in the morning of
Friday 8. the 8th of Auguſt, when land was ſeen, bearing North
North Eaſt, nine or ten leagues diſtant. At firſt, it appeared in detached hills, like ſo many ſeparate iſlands;
but, as we drew nearer, we found, that they were all connected, and belonged to one and the ſame iſland. I ſteered
directly for it, with a fine gale at South Eaſt by South;
and, at half paſt ſix o'clock, in the afternoon, it extended
from North by Eaſt, to North North Eaſt ¼ Eaſt, diſtant
three or four leagues.

The night was ſpent ſtanding off and on; and, at day-
Saturday 9. break, the next morning, I ſteered for the North Weſt, or
lee ſide, of the iſland; and, as we ſtood round its South or
South Weſt part, we ſaw it every where guarded by a reef
of coral rock, extending, in ſome places, a full mile from
the land, and a high ſurf breaking upon it. Some thought
that they ſaw land to the Southward of this iſland; but, as
that was to the windward, it was left undetermined. As
we drew near, we ſaw people on ſeveral parts of the coaſt,
walking, or running along ſhore; and, in a little time,
after we had reached the lee-ſide of the iſland, we ſaw
them launch two canoes, into which above a dozen men
got, and paddled toward us.

I now ſhortened ſail, as well to give theſe canoes time to
come up with us, as to ſound for anchorage. At the diſtance
of

of about half a mile from the reef, we found from forty to thirty-five fathoms water, over a bottom of fine ſand. Nearer in, the bottom was ſtrewed with coral rocks. The canoes having advanced to about the diſtance of a piſtol-ſhot from the ſhip, there ſtopped. Omai was employed, as he uſually had been on ſuch occaſions, to uſe all his eloquence to prevail upon the men in them to come nearer; but no intreaties could induce them to truſt themſelves within our reach. They kept eagerly pointing to the ſhore, with their paddles, and calling to us to go thither; and ſeveral of their countrymen, who ſtood upon the beach, held up ſomething white, which we conſidered alſo as an invitation to land. We could very well have done this, as there was good anchorage without the reef, and a break or opening in it, from whence the canoes had come out, which had no ſurf upon it, and where, if there was not water for the ſhips, there was more than ſufficient for the boats. But I did not think proper to riſk loſing the advantage of a fair wind, for the ſake of examining an iſland, that appeared to be of little conſequence. We ſtood in no need of refreſhments, if I had been ſure of meeting with them there; and having already been ſo unexpectedly delayed in my progreſs to the Society Iſlands, I was deſirous of avoiding every poſſibility of farther retardment. For this reaſon, after making ſeveral unſucceſsful attempts to induce theſe people to come along-ſide, I made ſail to the North, and left them; but not without getting from them, during their vicinity to our ſhip, the name of their iſland, which they called Toobouai.

It is ſituated in the latitude of 23° 25′, South; and in 210° 37′, Eaſt longitude. Its greateſt extent, in any direction, excluſive of the reef, is not above five or ſix miles. On the

North

1777.
August.

North Weſt ſide, the reef appears in detached pieces, between which, the ſea ſeems to break upon the ſhore. Small
as the iſland is, there are hills in it of a conſiderable elevation. At the foot of the hills, is a narrow border of flat
land, running quite round it, edged with a white ſand
beach. The hills are covered with graſs, or ſome other her-
bage, except a few ſteep rocky cliffs at one part, with patches
of trees interſperſed to their ſummits. But the plantations
are more numerous, in ſome of the vallies; and the flat
border is quite covered with high, ſtrong trees, whoſe different kinds we could not diſcern, except ſome cocoa-palms,
and a few of the *etoa*. According to the information of the
men in the canoes, their iſland is ſtocked with hogs and
fowls; and produces the ſeveral fruits and roots that are
found at the other iſlands in this part of the Pacific Ocean.

We had an opportunity, from the converſation we had
with thoſe who came off to us, of ſatisfying ourſelves, that
the inhabitants of Toobouai ſpeak the Otaheite language;
a circumſtance that indubitably proves them to be of the
ſame nation. Thoſe of them whom we ſaw in the canoes,
were a ſtout copper-coloured people, with ſtraight black
hair, which ſome of them wore tied in a bunch on the
crown of the head, and others, flowing about the ſhoulders.
Their faces were ſomewhat round and full, but the features,
upon the whole, rather flat; and their countenances ſeemed
to expreſs ſome degree of natural ferocity. They had no
covering but a piece of narrow ſtuff wrapped about the
waiſt, and made to paſs between the thighs, to cover the
adjoining parts; but ſome of thoſe whom we ſaw upon
the beach, where about a hundred perſons had aſſembled,
were entirely clothed with a kind of white garment. We
could obſerve, that ſome of our viſiters, in the canoes, wore

pearl

1777.
Auguſt.

pearl ſhells, hung about the neck, as an ornament. One of them kept blowing a large conch-ſhell, to which a reed, near two feet long, was fixed; at firſt, with a continued tone of the ſame kind; but he, afterward, converted it into a kind of muſical inſtrument, perpetually repeating two or three notes, with the ſame ſtrength. What the blowing the conch portended, I cannot ſay; but I never found it the meſſenger of peace.

Their canoes appeared to be about thirty feet long, and two feet above the ſurface of the water, as they floated. The fore part projected a little, and had a notch cut acroſs, as if intended to repreſent the mouth of ſome animal. The after-part roſe, with a gentle curve, to the height of two or three feet, turning gradually ſmaller, and, as well as the upper part of the ſides, was carved all over. The reſt of the ſides, which were perpendicular, were curiouſly incruſt-ated with flat white ſhells, diſpoſed nearly in concentric ſemicircles, with the curve upward. One of the canoes carried ſeven, and the other eight men; and they were managed with ſmall paddles, whoſe blades were nearly round. Each of them had a pretty long outrigger; and they ſometimes paddled, with the two oppoſite ſides to-gether ſo cloſe, that they ſeemed to be one boat with two outriggers; the rowers turning their faces occaſionally to the ſtern, and pulling that way, without paddling the ca-noes round. When they ſaw us determined to leave them, they ſtood up in their canoes, and repeated ſomething, very loudly, in concert; but we could not tell, whether this was meant as a mark of their friendſhip or enmity. It is cer-tain, however, that they had no weapons with them; nor could we perceive, with our glaſſes, that thoſe on ſhore had any.

After

After leaving this iſland, from the diſcovery of which,
future navigators may poſſibly derive ſome advantage, I
ſteered to the North, with a freſh gale at Eaſt by South, and,
at day-break, in the morning of the 12th, we ſaw the iſland
of Maitea. Soon after, Otaheite made its appearance;
and, at noon, it extended from South Weſt by Weſt, to
Weſt North Weſt; the point of Oheitepeha bay bearing
Weſt, about four leagues diſtant. I ſteered for this bay,
intending to anchor there, in order to draw what refreſhments I could from the South Eaſt part of the iſland, before I went down to Matavai; from the neighbourhood of
which ſtation I expected my principal ſupply. We had a
freſh gale Eaſterly, till two o'clock in the afternoon; when,
being about a league from the bay, the wind ſuddenly died
away, and was ſucceeded by baffling, light airs, from
every direction, and calms, by turns. This laſted about
two hours. Then we had ſudden ſqualls, with rain, from
the Eaſt. Theſe carried us before the bay, where we got a
breeze from the land, and attempted, in vain, to work in,
to gain the anchoring-place. So that, at laſt, about nine
o'clock, we were obliged to ſtand out, and to ſpend the
night at ſea.

When we firſt drew near the iſland, ſeveral canoes came
off to the ſhip, each conducted by two or three men. But,
as they were common fellows, Omai took no particular notice of them, nor they of him. They did not, even, ſeem
to perceive, that he was one of their countrymen, although
they converſed with him for ſome time. At length, a Chief,
whom I had known before, named Ootee, and Omai's brother-in-law, who chanced to be now at this corner of the
iſland, and three or four more perſons, all of whom knew
Omai, before he embarked with Captain Furneaux, came

on

1777.
Auguſt.

on board. Yet there was nothing either tender or ſtriking in their meeting. On the contrary, there ſeemed to be a perfect indifference on both ſides, till Omai, having taken his brother down into the cabin, opened the drawer where he kept his red feathers, and gave him a few. This being preſently known, amongſt the reſt of the natives upon deck, the face of affairs was intirely turned, and Ootee, who would hardly ſpeak to Omai before, now begged, that they might be *tayos* *, and exchange names. Omai accepted of the honour, and confirmed it with a preſent of red feathers; and Ootee, by way of return, ſent aſhore for a hog. But it was evident to every one of us, that it was not the man, but his property, they were in love with. Had he not ſhewn to them his treaſure of red feathers, which is the commodity in greateſt eſtimation at the iſland, I queſtion much whether they would have beſtowed even a cocoa-nut upon him. Such was Omai's firſt reception amongſt his countrymen. I own, I never expected it would be otherwiſe; but, ſtill, I was in hopes, that the valuable cargo of preſents, with which the liberality of his friends in England had loaded him, would be the means of raiſing him into conſequence, and of making him reſpected, and even courted, by the firſt perſons throughout the extent of the Society Iſlands. This could not but have happened, had he conducted himſelf with any degree of prudence. But, inſtead of it, I am ſorry to ſay, that he paid too little regard to the repeated advice of thoſe who wiſhed him well, and ſuffered himſelf to be duped by every deſigning knave.

From the natives who came off to us, in the courſe of this day, we learnt, that two ſhips had twice been in Ohei-tepeha Bay, ſince my laſt viſit to this iſland in 1774, and

* Friends.

that

that they had left animals there, ſuch as we had on board.
But, on farther inquiry, we found they were only hogs,
dogs, goats, one bull, and the male of ſome other animal,
which, from the imperfect deſcription now given us, we
could not find out. They told us, that theſe ſhips had
come from a place called *Reema*; by which we gueſſed,
that Lima, the capital of Peru, was meant, and that theſe
late viſiters were Spaniards. We were informed, that the
firſt time they came, they built a houſe, and left four men
behind them, *viz.* two prieſts, a boy or ſervant, and a fourth
perſon, called Mateema, who was much ſpoken of at this
time; carrying away with them, when they ſailed, four of
the natives; that, in about ten months, the ſame two ſhips
returned, bringing back two of the iſlanders, the other two
having died at Lima; and that, after a ſhort ſtay, they took
away their own people; but that the houſe, which they had
built, was left ſtanding.

The important news, of red feathers being on board our
ſhips, having been conveyed on ſhore by Omai's friends,
day had no ſooner begun to break, next morning, than we
were ſurrounded by a multitude of canoes, crowded with
people, bringing hogs and fruits to market. At firſt, a
quantity of feathers, not greater than what might be got
from a tom-tit, would purchaſe a hog, of forty or fifty
pounds weight. But, as almoſt every body in the ſhips was
poſſeſſed of ſome of this precious article of trade, it fell, in
its value, above five hundred *per cent.* before night. However, even then, the balance was much in our favour;
and red feathers continued to preſerve their ſuperiority
over every other commodity. Some of the natives would
not part with a hog, unleſs they received an axe in exchange; but nails, and beads, and other trinkets, which,
                                                    during

during our former voyages, had ſo great a run at this iſland, were now ſo much deſpiſed, that few would deign ſo much as to look at them.

There being but little wind all the morning, it was nine o'clock before we could get to an anchor in the bay; where we moored with the two bowers. Soon after we had anchored, Omai's ſiſter came on board to ſee him. I was happy to obſerve, that, much to the honour of them both, their meeting was marked with expreſſions of the tendereſt affection, eaſier to be conceived than to be deſcribed.

This moving ſcene having cloſed, and the ſhip being properly moored, Omai and I went aſhore. My firſt object was to pay a viſit to a man whom my friend repreſented as a very extraordinary perſonage indeed, for he ſaid, that he was the god of Bolabola. We found him ſeated under one of thoſe ſmall awnings, which they uſually carry in their larger canoes. He was an elderly man, and had loſt the uſe of his limbs; ſo that he was carried from place to place upon a hand-barrow. Some called him *Olla*, or *Orra*, which is the name of the god of Bolabola; but his own proper name was Etary. From Omai's account of this perſon, I expected to have ſeen ſome religious adoration paid to him. But, excepting ſome young plantain trees that lay before him, and upon the awning under which he ſat, I could obſerve nothing by which he might be diſtinguiſhed from their other Chiefs. Omai preſented to him a tuft of red feathers, tied to the end of a ſmall ſtick; but, after a little converſation on indifferent matters with this Bolabola man, his attention was drawn to an old woman, the ſiſter of his mother. She was already at his feet, and had bedewed them plentifully with tears of joy.

I left him with the old lady, in the midſt of a number of

C 2   people,

people, who had gathered round him, and went to take a view of the houſe, ſaid to be built by the ſtrangers who had lately been here. I found it ſtanding at a ſmall diſtance from the beach. The wooden materials, of which it was compoſed, ſeemed to have been brought hither, ready prepared, to be ſet up occaſionally; for all the planks were numbered. It was divided into two ſmall rooms; and in the inner one were, a bedſtead, a table, a bench, ſome old hats, and other trifles, of which the natives ſeemed to be very careful, as alſo of the houſe itſelf, which had ſuffered no hurt from the weather, a ſhed having been built over it. There were ſcuttles all around, which ſerved as air holes; and, perhaps, they were alſo meant to fire from, with muſquets, if ever this ſhould have been found neceſſary. At a little diſtance from the front ſtood a wooden croſs, on the tranſverſe part of which was cut the following inſcription: *

Chriſtus vincit.

And, on the perpendicular part (which confirmed our conjecture, that the two ſhips were Spaniſh),

Carolus III. *imperat.* 1774.

On the other ſide of the poſt, I preſerved the memory of the prior viſits of the Engliſh, by inſcribing,

Georgius tertius Rex,

Annis 1767,

1769, 1773, 1774, & 1777.

The natives pointed out to us, near the foot of the croſs, the grave of the Commodore of the two ſhips, who had died here, while they lay in the bay, the firſt time. His name, as they pronounced it, was Oreede. Whatever the intentions of the Spaniards, in viſiting this iſland, might be, they ſeemed to have taken great pains to ingratiate them-

ſelves

ſelves with the inhabitants; who, upon every occaſion, mentioned them with the ſtrongeſt expreſſions of eſteem and veneration.

I met with no Chief of any conſiderable note on this occaſion, excepting the extraordinary perſonage above deſcribed. Waheiadooa, the ſovereign of Tiaraboo (as this part of the iſland is called), was now abſent; and, I afterward found, that he was not the ſame perſon, though of the ſame name with the Chief whom I had ſeen here during my laſt voyage; but his brother, a boy of about ten years of age, who had ſucceeded upon the death of the elder Waheiadooa, about twenty months before our arrival. We alſo learned, that the celebrated Oberea was dead; but that Otoo, and all our other friends, were living.

When I returned from viewing the houſe and croſs erected by the Spaniards, I found Omai holding forth to a large company; and it was with ſome difficulty that he could be got away to accompany me on board; where I had an important affair to ſettle.

As I knew that Otaheite, and the neighbouring iſlands, could furniſh us with a plentiful ſupply of cocoa-nuts, the liquor of which is an excellent *ſuccedaneum* for any artificial beverage, I was deſirous of prevailing upon my people to conſent to be abridged, during our ſtay here, of their ſtated allowance of ſpirits to mix with water. But as this ſtoppage of a favourite article, without aſſigning ſome reaſon, might have occaſioned a general murmur, I thought it moſt prudent to aſſemble the ſhip's company, and to make known to them the intent of the voyage, and the extent of our future operations. To induce them to undertake which, with cheerfulneſs and perſeverance, I took notice of the rewards offered by Parliament, to ſuch of his Majeſty's

jeſty's ſubjects as ſhall firſt diſcover a communication between the Atlantic and Pacific Oceans, in any direction
whatever, in the Northern hemiſphere; and alſo to ſuch as
ſhall firſt penetrate beyond the 89th degree of Northern
latitude. I made no doubt, I told them, that I ſhould find
them willing to co-operate with me in attempting, as far as
might be poſſible, to become intitled to one or both theſe
rewards; but, that to give us the beſt chance of ſucceeding,
it would be neceſſary to obſerve the utmoſt œconomy in
the expenditure of our ſtores and proviſions, particularly
the latter, as there was no probability of getting a ſupply,
any where, after leaving theſe iſlands. I ſtrengthened my
argument by reminding them, that our voyage muſt laſt at
leaſt a year longer than had been originally ſuppoſed, by
our having already loſt the opportunity of getting to the
North this ſummer. I begged them to conſider the various
obſtructions and difficulties we might ſtill meet with, and
the aggravated hardſhips they would labour under, if it
ſhould be found neceſſary to put them to ſhort allowance,
of any ſpecies of proviſions, in a cold climate. For theſe
very ſubſtantial reaſons, I ſubmitted to them, whether it
would not be better to be prudent in time, and rather
than to run the riſk of having no ſpirits left, when ſuch
a cordial would be moſt wanted, to conſent to be without their grog now, when we had ſo excellent a liquor as
that of cocoa-nuts to ſubſtitute in its place; but that,
after all, I left the determination entirely to their own
choice.

I had the ſatisfaction to find, that this propoſal did not
remain a ſingle moment under conſideration; being unanimouſly approved of, immediately, without any objection.
I ordered Captain Clerke to make the ſame propoſal to his
I
people;

people; which they alfo agreed to. Accordingly we ftopped ferving grog, except on Saturday nights; when the companies of both fhips had full allowance of it, that they might drink the healths of their female friends in England; left thefe, amongft the pretty girls of Otaheite, fhould be wholly forgotten.

The next day, we began fome neceffary operations; to infpect the provifions that were in the main and fore hold; to get the cafks of beef and pork, and the coals, out of the ground tier; and to put fome ballaft in their place. The caulkers were fet to work to caulk the fhip, which fhe ftood in great need of; having, at times, made much water on our paffage from the Friendly Iflands. I alfo put on fhore the bull, cows, horfes, and fheep, and appointed two men to look after them while grazing; for I did not intend to leave any of them, at this part of the ifland.

During the two following days, it hardly ever ceafed raining. The natives, neverthelefs, came to us from every quarter, the news of our arrival having rapidly fpread. Waheiadooa, though at a diftance, had been informed of it; and, in the afternoon of the 16th, a Chief, named Etorea, under whofe tutorage he was, brought me two hogs as a prefent from him; and acquainted me, that he himfelf would be with us the day after. And fo it proved; for I received a meffage from him the next morning, notifying his arrival, and defiring I would go afhore to meet him. Accordingly, Omai and I prepared to pay him a formal vifit. On this occafion, Omai, affifted by fome of his friends, dreffed himfelf; not after the Englifh fafhion, nor that of Otaheite, nor that of Tongataboo, nor in the drefs of any country upon earth; but in a ftrange medley of all that he was poffeffed of.

Thus

Thus equipped, on our landing, we firſt.viſited Etary;
who, carried on a hand-barrow, attended us to a large
houſe, where he was ſet down; and we ſeated ourſelves on
each ſide of him. I cauſed a piece of Tongataboo cloth to
be ſpread out before us, on which I laid the preſents I intended to make. Preſently the young Chief came, attended
by his mother, and ſeveral principal men, who all ſeated
themſelves, at the other end of the cloth, facing us. Then
a man, who ſat by me, made a ſpeech, conſiſting of ſhort
and ſeparate ſentences; part of which was dictated by thoſe
about him. He was anſwered by one from the oppoſite
ſide, near the Chief. Etary ſpoke next; then Omai; and
both of them were anſwered from the ſame quarter. Theſe
orations were entirely about my arrival, and connections
with them. The perſon who ſpoke laſt, told me, amongſt
other things, that the men of *Reema*, that is, the Spaniards,
had deſired them not to ſuffer me to come into Oheitepeha
Bay, if I ſhould return any more to the iſland, for that it
belonged to them; but that they were ſo far from paying
any regard to this requeſt, that he was authorized now to
make a formal ſurrender.of the province of Tiaraboo to me,
and of every thing in it; which marks very plainly, that
theſe people are no ſtrangers to the policy of accom-
modating themſelves to preſent circumſtances. At length,
the young Chief was directed, by his attendants, to come
and embrace me; and, by way of confirming this treaty of
friendſhip, we exchanged names. The ceremony being
cloſed, he and his friends accompanied me on board to
dinner.

Omai had prepared a *maro*, compoſed of red and yellow
feathers, which he intended for Otoo, the king of the whole
iſland; and, conſidering where we were, it was a preſent
of

of very great value. I faid all that I could to perfuade him
not to produce it now, wifhing him to keep it on board till
an opportunity fhould offer of prefenting it to Otoo, with
his own hands. But he had too good an opinion of the
honefty and fidelity of his countrymen to take my advice.
Nothing would ferve him, but to carry it afhore, on this occafion, and to give it to Waheiadooa, to be by him forward-
ed to Otoo, in order to its being added to the royal *maro*.
He thought, by this management, that he fhould oblige
both Chiefs ; whereas he highly difobliged the one, whofe
favour was of the moft confequence to him, without gaining any reward from the other. What I had forefeen happened. For Waheiadooa kept the *maro* for himfelf, and
only fent to Otoo a very fmall piece of feathers; not the
twentieth part of what belonged to the magnificent prefent.

On the 19th, this young Chief made me a prefent of ten
or a dozen hogs, a quantity of fruit, and fome cloth. In
the evening, we played off fome fireworks, which both
aftonifhed and entertained the numerous fpectators.

This day, fome of our gentlemen, in their walks, found,
what they were pleafed to call, a Roman Catholic chapel.
Indeed, from their account, this was not to be doubted; for
they defcribed the altar, and every other conftituent part of
fuch a place of worfhip. However, as they mentioned, at the
fame time, that two men, who had the care of it, would not
fuffer them to go in, I thought that they might be miftaken,
and had the curiofity to pay a vifit to it myfelf. The fuppofed chapel proved to be a *toopapaoo*, in which the remains
of the late Waheiadooa lay, as it were, in ftate. It was in a
pretty large houfe, which was inclofed with a low pallifade.
The *toopapaoo* was uncommonly neat, and refembled one

VOL. II.   D   of of those little houses, or awnings, belonging to their large canoes. Perhaps, it had originally been employed for that purpose. It was covered, and hung round, with cloth and mats of different colours, so as to have a pretty effect. There was one piece of scarlet broad-cloth, four or five yards in length, conspicuous amongst the other ornaments; which, no doubt, had been a present from the Spaniards. This cloth, and a few tassels of feathers, which our Gentlemen supposed to be silk, suggested to them the idea of a chapel; for whatever else was wanting to create a resemblance, their imagination supplied; and if they had not previously known, that there had been Spaniards lately here, they could not possibly have made the mistake. Small offerings of fruit and roots seemed to be daily made at this shrine, as some pieces were quite fresh. These were deposited upon a *whatta*, or altar, which stood without the pallisades; and within these we were not permitted to enter. Two men constantly attended, night and day, not only to watch over the place, but also to dress and undress the *toopapaoo*. For when I first went to survey it, the cloth and its appendages were all rolled up; but, at my request, the two attendants hung it out in order, first dressing themselves in clean white robes. They told me, that the Chief had been dead twenty months.

Friday 22. Having taken in a fresh supply of water, and finished all our other necessary operations, on the 22d, I brought off the cattle and sheep, which had been put on shore here to graze; and made ready for sea.

Saturday 23. In the morning of the 23d, while the ships were unmooring, Omai and I landed, to take leave of the young Chief. While we were with him, one of those enthusiastic persons, whom they call *Eatooas*, from a persuasion that they are

possessed

poſſeſſed with the ſpirit of the divinity, came and ſtood before us. He had all the appearance of a man not in his
right ſenſes; and his only dreſs was a large quantity of
plantain leaves, wrapped round his waiſt. He ſpoke in a
low, ſqueaking voice, ſo as hardly to be underſtood; at
leaſt, not by me. But Omai ſaid, that he comprehended
him perfectly, and that he was adwiſing Waheiadooa not to
go with me to Matavai; an expedition which I had never
heard that he intended, nor had I ever made ſuch a propoſal
to him. The *Eatooa* alſo foretold, that the ſhips would not
get to Matavai that day. But in this he was miſtaken;
though appearances now rather favoured his prediction,
there not being a breath of wind in any direction. While
he was propheſying, there fell a very heavy ſhower of rain,
which made every one run for ſhelter, but himſelf, who
ſeemed not to regard it. He remained ſqueaking, by us,
about half an hour, and then retired. No one paid any attention to what he uttered; though ſome laughed at him.
I aſked the Chief what he was, whether an *Earee*, or a *Toutou?* and the anſwer I received was, that he was *taata eno*;
that is, a bad man. And yet, notwithſtanding this, and the
little notice any of the natives ſeemed to take of the mad
prophet, ſuperſtition has ſo far got the better of their reaſon,
that they firmly believe ſuch perſons to be poſſeſſed with the
ſpirit of the *Eatooa*. Omai ſeemed to be very well inſtructed
about them. He ſaid, that, during the fits that come upon
them, they know nobody, not even their moſt intimate ac-
quaintances; and that, if any one of them happens to be a
man of property, he will very often give away every moveable he is poſſeſſed of, if his friends do not put them out of
his reach; and, when he recovers, will inquire what had
become of thoſe very things, which he had, but juſt before,

1777.
Auguſt.

D 2   diſtributed,

diſtributed, not ſeeming to have the leaſt remembrance of what he had done, while the fit was upon him.

As ſoon as I got on board, a light breeze ſpringing up at Eaſt, we got under ſail, and ſteered for Matavai Bay *; where the Reſolution anchored the ſame evening. But the Sunday 24. Diſcovery did not get in till the next morning; ſo that half of the man's prophecy was fulfilled.

* See a plan of this bay, in Hawkeſworth's Collection, Vol. ii. p. 248.

C H A P.

CHAP. II.

*Interview with Otoo, King of the Island.—Imprudent Con-
duct of Omai.—Employments on Shore.—European Animals
landed.—Particulars about a Native who had visited Lima.
—About Oedidee.—A Revolt in Eimeo.—War with that
Island determined upon, in a Council of Chiefs.—A human
Sacrifice on that Account.—A particular Relation of the
Ceremonies at the great Morai, where the Sacrifice was
offered.—Other barbarous Customs of this People.*

ABOUT nine o'clock in the morning, Otoo, the King
of the whole island, attended by a great number of
canoes full of people, came from Oparre, his place of re-
sidence, and having landed on Matavai Point, sent a message on board, expressing his desire to see me there. Accordingly I landed, accompanied by Omai, and some of
the officers. We found a prodigious number of people assembled on this occasion, and in the midst of them was the
king, attended by his father, his two brothers, and three
sisters. I went up, first, and saluted him, being followed by
Omai, who kneeled and embraced his legs. He had prepared himself for this ceremony, by dressing himself in his
very best suit of clothes, and behaved with a great deal of
respect and modesty. Nevertheless, very little notice was
taken of him. Perhaps, envy had some share in producing
this

1777.
August.
Sunday 24.

1777.
Auguſt.

this cold reception. He made the Chief a preſent of a large
piece of red feathers, and about two or three yards of gold
cloth; and I gave him a ſuit of fine linen, a gold-laced hat,
ſome tools, and, what was of more value than all the other
articles, a quantity of red feathers, and one of the bonnets
in uſe at the Friendly Iſlands.

After the hurry of this viſit was over, the king, and the
whole royal family, accompanied me on board, followed
by ſeveral canoes, laden with all kind of proviſions, in
quantity ſufficient to have ſerved the companies of both
ſhips for a week. Each of the family owned, or pretended
to own, a part; ſo that I had a preſent from every one of
them; and every one of them had a ſeparate preſent in return from me; which was the great object in view. Soon
after, the king's mother, who had not been preſent at the
firſt interview, came on board, bringing with her a quantity of proviſions and cloth, which ſhe divided between me
and Omai. For, although he was but little noticed, at firſt,
by his countrymen, they no ſooner gained the knowledge
of his riches, than they began to court his friendſhip. I encouraged this as much as I could; for it was my wiſh to fix
him with Otoo. As I intended to leave all my European
animals at this iſland, I thought he would be able to give
ſome inſtruction about the management of them, and about
their uſe. Beſides, I knew and ſaw, that the farther he was
from his native iſland, he would be the better reſpected.
But, unfortunately, poor Omai rejected my advice, and conducted himſelf in ſo imprudent a manner, that he ſoon loſt
the friendſhip of Otoo, and of every other perſon of note
in Otaheite. He aſſociated with none but vagabonds and
ſtrangers, whoſe ſole views were to plunder him. And, if
I had not interfered, they would not have left him a ſingle

3   article

article worth the carrying from the iſland. This neceſſa-
rily drew upon him the ill-will of the principal Chiefs;
who found that they could not procure, from any one in
the ſhips, ſuch valuable preſents as Omai beſtowed on the
loweſt of the people, his companions.

As ſoon as we had dined, a party of us accompanied Otoo
to Oparre, taking with us the poultry, with which we were
to ſtock the iſland. They conſiſted of a peacock and hen
(which Lord Beſborough was ſo kind as to ſend me, for
this purpoſe, a few days before I left London); a turkey
cock and hen; one gander, and three geeſe; a drake, and
four ducks. All theſe I left at Oparre, in the poſſeſſion of
Otoo; and the geeſe and ducks began to breed, before we
ſailed. We found there, a gander, which the natives told
us, was the ſame that Captain Wallis had given to Oberea
ten years before; ſeveral goats; and the Spaniſh bull,
whom they kept tied to a tree, near Otoo's houſe. I never
ſaw a finer animal of his kind. He was now the property
of Etary, and had been brought from Oheitepeha to this
place, in order to be ſhipped for Bolabola. But it paſſes my
comprehenſion, how they can contrive to carry him in one
of their canoes. If we had not arrived, it would have been
of little conſequence who had the property of him, as, without a cow, he could be of no uſe; and none had been left
with him. Though the natives told us, that there were
cows on board the Spaniſh ſhips, and that they took them
away with them, I cannot believe this; and ſhould rather
ſuppoſe, that they had died in the paſſage from Lima. The
next day, I ſent the three cows, that I had on board, to this Monday 25.
bull; and the bull, which I had brought, the horſe and
mare, and ſheep, I put aſhore at Matavai.

Having thus diſpoſed of theſe paſſengers, I found myſelf
lightened

lightened of a very heavy burthen. The trouble and vexation that attended the bringing this living cargo thus far,
is hardly to be conceived. But the ſatisfaction that I felt,
in having been ſo fortunate as to fulfil his Majeſty's humane deſign, in ſending ſuch valuable animals, to ſupply
the wants of two worthy nations, ſufficiently recompenſed
me for the many anxious hours I had paſſed, before this
ſubordinate object of my voyage could be carried into
execution.

As I intended to make ſome ſtay here, we ſet up the two
obſervatories on Matavai Point. Adjoining to them, two
tents were pitched, for the reception of a guard, and of ſuch
people as it might be neceſſary to leave on ſhore, in different
departments. At this ſtation, I intruſted the command to
Mr. King; who, at the ſame time, attended the obſervations,
for aſcertaining the going of the time-keeper, and other
purpoſes. During our ſtay, various neceſſary operations
employed the crews of both ſhips. The Diſcovery's main-
maſt was carried aſhore, and made as good as ever. Our
ſails and water-caſks were repaired; the ſhips were caulked;
and the rigging all overhauled. We alſo inſpected all the
bread that we had on board in caſks; and had the ſatisfaction to find, that but little of it was damaged.

Tueſday 26.　　On the 26th, I had a piece of ground cleared, for a
garden, and planted it with ſeveral articles; very few of
which, I believe, the natives will ever look after. Some
melons, potatoes, and two pine-apple plants, were in a fair
way of ſucceeding, before we left the place. I had brought,
from the Friendly Iſlands, ſeveral ſhaddock trees. Theſe I
alſo planted here; and they can hardly fail of ſucceſs, unleſs their growth ſhould be checked by the ſame premature
curioſity, which deſtroyed a vine planted by the Spaniards

at

at Oheitepeha. A number of the natives got together, to taſte the firſt fruit it bore; but, as the grapes were ſtill ſour, they conſidered it as little better than poiſon, and it was unanimouſly determined to tread it under foot. In that ſtate, Omai found it by chance, and was overjoyed at the diſcovery. For he had a full confidence, that, if he had but grapes, he could eaſily make wine. Accordingly, he had ſeveral ſlips cut off from the tree, to carry away with him; and we pruned, and put in order, the remains of it. Probably, grown wiſe by Omai's inſtructions, they may now ſuffer the fruit to grow to perfection, and not paſs ſo haſty a ſentence upon it again.

We had not been eight and forty hours at anchor in Matavai Bay, before we were viſited by all our old friends, whoſe names are recorded in the account of my laſt voyage. Not one of them came empty handed; ſo that we had more proviſions than we knew what to do with. What was ſtill more, we were under no apprehenſions of exhauſting the iſland, which preſented to our eyes every mark of the moſt exuberant plenty, in every article of refreſhment.

Soon after our arrival here, one of the natives, whom the Spaniards had carried with them to Lima, paid us a viſit; but, in his external appearance, he was not diſtinguiſhable from the reſt of his countrymen. However, he had not forgot ſome Spaniſh words which he had acquired, though he pronounced them badly. Amongſt them, the moſt frequent were, *ſi Sennor*; and, when a ſtranger was introduced to him, he did not fail to riſe up and accoſt him, as well as he could.

We alſo found here, the young man whom we called Oedidee, but whoſe real name is Heete-heete. I had carried him from Ulietea in 1773, and brought him back in 1774;

VOL. II.   E   after

after he had viſited the Friendly Iſlands, New Zealand, Eaſter Iſland, and the Marqueſes, and been on board my ſhip, in that extenſive navigation, about ſeven months. He was, at leaſt, as tenacious of his good breeding, as the man who had been at Lima; and *yes, Sir,* or *if you pleaſe, Sir,* were as frequently repeated by him, as *ſi Sennor,* was by the other. Heete-heete, who is a native of Bolabola, had arrived in Otaheite, about three months before, with no other intention, that we could learn, than to gratify his curioſity, or, perhaps, ſome other favourite paſſion; which are, very often, the only objects of the purſuit of other travelling gentlemen. It was evident, however, that he preferred the modes, and even garb, of his countrymen, to ours. For, though I gave him ſome clothes, which our Admiralty Board had been pleaſed to ſend for his uſe (to which I added a cheſt of tools, and a few other articles, as a preſent from myſelf), he declined wearing them, after a few days. This inſtance, and that of the perſon who had been at Lima, may be urged as a proof of the ſtrong propenſity natural to man, of returning to habits acquired at an early age, and only interrupted by accident. And, perhaps, it may be concluded, that even Omai, who had imbibed almoſt the whole Engliſh manners, will, in a very ſhort time after our leaving him, like Oedidee, and the viſiter of Lima, return to his own native garments.

In the morning of the 27th, a man came from Oheitepeha, and told us, that two Spaniſh ſhips had anchored in that bay the night before; and, in confirmation of this intelligence, he produced a piece of coarſe blue cloth, which, he ſaid, he got out of one of the ſhips; and which, indeed, to appearance, was almoſt quite new. He added, that Mateema

teema was in one of the ſhips; and that they were to come
down to Matavai in a day or two. Some other circumſtances which he mentioned, with the foregoing ones, gave
the ſtory ſo much the air of truth, that I diſpatched Lieutenant Williamſon in a boat, to look into Oheitepeha bay;
and, in the mean time, I put the ſhips into a proper poſture
of defence. For, though England and Spain were in peace
when I left Europe, for aught I knew, a different ſcene
might, by this time, have opened. However, on farther inquiry, we had reaſon to think that the fellow, who brought
the intelligence, had impoſed upon us; and this was put
beyond all doubt, when Mr. Williamſon returned next day;
who made his report to me, that he had been at Oheitepeha,
and found that no ſhips were there now, and that none had
been there ſince we left it. The people of this part of the
iſland, where we now were, indeed, told us, from the beginning, that it was a fiction invented by thoſe of Tiaraboo.
But what view they could have, we were at a loſs to conceive, unleſs they ſuppoſed, that the report would have
ſome effect in making us quit the iſland, and, by that means,
deprive the people of Otaheite-nooe of the advantages they
might reap from our ſhips continuing there; the inhabitants of the two parts of the iſland being inveterate enemies
to each other.

From the time of our arrival at Matavai, the weather had
been very unſettled, with more. or leſs rain every day, till
the 29th; before which we were not able to get equal altitudes of the ſun for aſcertaining the going of the time-
keeper. The ſame cauſe alſo retarded the caulking, and
other neceſſary repairs of the ſhips.

In the evening of this day, the natives made a precipitate
retreat, both from on board the ſhips, and from our ſtation

on

on fhore. For what reafon, we could not, at firft, learn; though, in general, we gueffed it arofe from their knowing that fome theft had been committed, and apprehending punifhment on that account. At length, I underftood what had happened. One of the furgeon's mates had been in the country to purchafe curiofities, and had taken with him four hatchets for that purpofe. Having employed one of the natives to carry them for him, the fellow took an opportunity to run off with fo valuable a prize. This was the caufe of the fudden flight, in which Otoo himfelf, and his whole family, had joined; and it was with difficulty that I ftopped them, after following them two or three miles. As I had refolved to take no meafures for the recovery of the hatchets, in order to put my people upon their guard againft fuch negligence for the future, I found no difficulty in bringing the natives back, and in reftoring every thing to its ufual tranquillity.

Hitherto, the attention of Otoo and his people had been confined to us; but, next morning, a new fcene of bufinefs opened, by the arrival of fome meffengers from Eimeo, or (as it is much oftener called by the natives) Morea *, with intelligence, that the people in that ifland were in arms; and that Otoo's partizans there had been worfted, and obliged to retreat to the mountains. The quarrel between the two iflands, which commenced in 1774, as mentioned in the account of my laft voyage, had, it feems, partly fubfifted ever fince. The formidable armament which I faw, at that time, and defcribed †, had failed foon after I then left Otaheite; but the malcontents of Eimeo had made fo

* Morea, according to Dr. Forfter, is a diftrict in Eimeo. See his *Obfervations*, p. 217.

† See Cook's Voyage, Vol. i. p. 347, &c.

ftout

ftout a refiftance, that the fleet had returned without effecting much; and now another expedition was neceffary.

On the arrival of thefe meffengers, all the Chiefs, who
happened to be at Matavai, affembled at Otoo's houfe, where
I actually was at the time, and had the honour to be admitted into their council. One of the meffengers opened
the bufinefs of the affembly, in a fpeech of confiderable
length. But I underftood little of it, befides its general
purport, which was to explain the fituation of affairs in
Eimeo; and to excite the affembled Chiefs of Otaheite to
arm on the occafion. This opinion was combated by others
who were againft commencing hoftilities; and the debate
was carried on with great order; no more than one man
fpeaking at a time. At laft, they became very noify, and
I expected that our meeting would have ended like a Polifh
diet. But the contending great men cooled as faft as they
grew warm, and order was foon reftored. At length, the
party for war prevailed; and it was determined, that a
ftrong force fhould be fent to affift their friends in Eimeo.
But this refolution was far from being unanimous. Otoo,
during the whole debate, remained filent; except that, now
and then, he addreffed a word or two to the fpeakers. Thofe
of the council, who were for profecuting the war, applied
to me for my affiftance; and all of them wanted to know
what part I would take. Omai was fent for to be my interpreter; but, as he could not be found, I was obliged to
fpeak for myfelf, and told them, as well as I could, that as
I was not thoroughly acquainted with the difpute, and as
the people of Eimeo had never offended me, I could not
think myfelf at liberty to engage in hoftilities againft them.
With this declaration they either were, or feemed, fatisfied.
The affembly then broke up; but, before I left them, Otoo
desired

defired me to come to him in the afternoon, and to bring Omai with me.

Accordingly, a party of us waited upon him at the appointed time; and we were conducted by him to his father, in whofe prefence the difpute with Eimeo was again talked over. Being very defirous of devifing fome method to bring about an accommodation, I founded the old Chief on that head. But we found him deaf to any fuch propofal, and fully determined to profecute the war. He repeated the folicitations which I had already refifted, about giving them my affiftance. On our inquiring into the caufe of the war, we were told, that, fome years ago, a brother of Waheia-dooa, of Tiaraboo, was fent to Eimeo, at the requeft of Maheine, a popular Chief of that ifland, to be their king; but that he had not been there a week before Maheine, having caufed him to be killed, fet up for himfelf, in oppofition to Tierataboonooe, his fifter's fon, who became the lawful heir; or elfe had been pitched upon, by the people of Ota-heite, to fucceed to the government on the death of the other.

Towha, who is a relation of Otoo, and Chief of the dif-trict of Tettaha, a man of much weight in the ifland, and who had been Commander in Chief of the armament fitted out againft Eimeo in 1774, happened not to be at Matavai at this time; and, confequently, was not prefent at any of thefe confultations. It, however, appeared that he was no ftranger to what was tranfacted; and that he entered with more fpirit into the affair than any other Chief. For, early in the morning of the 1ft of September, a meffenger arrived from him to acquaint Otoo, that he had killed a man to be facrificed to the *Eatooa*, to implore the affiftance of the God againft Eimeo. This act of worfhip was to be per-

formed

formed at the great *Morai* at Attahooroo; and Otoo's prefence, it feems, was abfolutely neceffary on that folemn
occafion.

That the offering of human facrifices is part of the religious inftitutions of this ifland, had been mentioned by
Monf. de Bougainville, on the authority of the native
whom he carried with him to France. During my laft
vifit to Otaheite, and while I had opportunities of converfing
with Omai on the fubjeſt, I had fatisfied myfelf, that there
was too much reafon to admit, that fuch a practice, however inconfiftent with the general humanity of the people,
was here adopted. But as this was one of thofe extraordinary facts, about which many are apt to retain doubts, unlefs the relater himfelf has had ocular proof to confirm
what he had heard from others, I thought this a good opportunity of obtaining the higheſt evidence of its certainty,
by being prefent myfelf at the folemnity; and, accordingly, propofed to Otoo that I might be allowed to accompany him. To this he readily confented; and we immediately fet out in my boat, with my old friend Potatou,
Mr. Anderfon, and Mr. Webber; Omai following in a
canoe.

In our way we landed upon a little ifland, which lies
off Tettaha, where we found Towha and his retinue. After
fome little converfation between the two Chiefs, on the
fubjeſt of the war, Towha addreffed himfelf to me, afking
my affiftance. When I excufed myfelf, he feemed angry;
thinking it ftrange, that I, who had always declared myfelf
to be the friend of their ifland, would not now go and
fight againſt its enemies. Before we parted, he gave to
Otoo two or three red feathers, tied up in a tuft; and a lean
half-ftarved dog was put into a canoe that was to accompany

pany us. We then embarked again, taking on board a prieſt who was to affiſt at the ſolemnity.

As ſoon as we landed at Attahooroo, which was about two o'clock in the afternoon, Otoo expreſſed his deſire that the ſeamen might be ordered to remain in the boat; and that Mr. Anderſon, Mr. Webber, and myſelf, might take off our hats, as ſoon as we ſhould come to the *morai*, to which we immediately proceeded, attended by a great many men, and ſome boys; but not one woman. We found four prieſts, and their attendants, or affiſtants, waiting for us. The dead body, or ſacrifice, was in a ſmall canoe that lay on the beach, and partly in the waſh of the ſea, fronting the *morai*. Two of the prieſts, with ſome of their attendants, were ſitting by the canoe; the others at the *morai*. Our company ſtopped about twenty or thirty paces from the prieſts. Here Otoo placed himſelf; we, and a few others, ſtanding by him; while the bulk of the people remained at a greater diſtance.

The ceremonies now began. One of the prieſt's attendants brought a young plantain-tree, and laid it down before Otoo. Another approached with a ſmall tuft of red feathers, twiſted on ſome fibres of the cocoa-nut huſk, with which he touched one of the king's feet, and then retired with it to his companions. One of the prieſts, ſeated at the *morai*, facing thoſe who were upon the beach, now began a long prayer; and, at certain times, ſent down young plantain-trees, which were laid upon the ſacrifice. During this prayer, a man, who ſtood by the officiating prieſt, held in his hands two bundles, ſeemingly of cloth. In one of them, as we afterward found, was the royal *maro*; and the other, if I may be allowed the expreſſion, was the ark of the *Eatooa*. As ſoon as the prayer was ended, the prieſts at the

morai,

morai, with their attendants, went and fat down by thofe
upon the beach, carrying with them the two bundles. Here
they renewed their prayers; during which the plantain-
trees were taken, one by one, at different times, from off
the facrifice ; which was partly wrapped up in cocoa leaves
and fmall branches. It was now taken out of the canoe,
and laid upon the beach, with the feet to the fea. The
priefts placed themfelves around it, fome fitting and others
ftanding ; and one, or more of them, repeated fentences for
about ten minutes. The dead body was now uncovered,
by removing the leaves and branches, and laid in a parallel direction with the fea-fhore. One of the priefts then
ftanding at the feet of it, pronounced a long prayer, in
which he was, at times, joined by the others ; each holding
in his hand a tuft of red feathers. In the courfe of this
prayer, fome hair was pulled off the head of the facrifice,
and the left eye taken out; both which were prefented
to Otoo, wrapped up in a green leaf. He did not, however,
touch it ; but gave, to the man who prefented it, the tuft
of feathers, which he had received from Towha. This,
with the hair and eye, was carried back to the priefts.
Soon after, Otoo fent to them another piece of feathers,
which he had given me in the morning to keep in my
pocket. During fome part of this laft ceremony, a king-
fifher making a noife in the trees, Otoo turned to me, faying, " That is the *Eatooa*;" and feemed to look upon it to
be a good omen.

The body was then carried a little way, with its head
toward the *morai*, and laid under a tree; near which were
fixed three broad thin pieces of wood, differently, but
rudely, carved. The bundles of cloth were laid on a part
of the *morai*; and the tufts of red feathers were placed at

VOL. II. F the

the feet of the sacrifice; round which the priests took their
stations; and we were now allowed to go as near as we
pleased. He who seemed to be the chief priest sat at a
small distance, and spoke for a quarter of an hour, but
with different tones and gestures; so that he seemed often
to expostulate with the dead person, to whom he constantly
addressed himself; and, sometimes, asked several questions,
seemingly with respect to the propriety of his having been
killed. At other times, he made several demands, as if the
deceased either now had power himself, or interest with
the Divinity, to engage him to comply with such requests.
Amongst which, we understood, he asked him to deliver
Eimeo, Maheine its chief, the hogs, women, and other
things of the island, into their hands; which was, indeed,
the express intention of the sacrifice. He then chanted a
prayer, which lasted near half an hour, in a whining, melancholy tone, accompanied by two other priests; and in
which Potatou, and some others, joined. In the course of
this prayer, some more hair was plucked by a priest from
the head of the corpse, and put upon one of the bundles.
After this, the chief priest prayed alone, holding in his
hand the feathers which came from Towha. When he
had finished, he gave them to another, who prayed in
like manner. Then all the tufts of feathers were laid upon
the bundles of cloth; which closed the ceremony at this
place.

The corpse was then carried up to the most conspicuous
part of the *morai*, with the feathers, the two bundles of
cloth, and the drums; the last of which beat flowly. The
feathers and bundles were laid against the pile of stones,
and the corpse at the foot of them. The priests having again
seated themselves round it, renewed their prayers; while
                                                    some

some of their attendants dug a hole about two feet deep, into which they threw the unhappy victim, and covered it over with earth and stones. While they were putting him into the grave, a boy squeaked aloud, and Omai said to me, that it was the *Eatooa.* During this time, a fire having been made, the dog, before mentioned, was produced, and killed, by twisting his neck, and suffocating him. The hair was singed off, and the entrails taken out, and thrown into the fire, where they were left to consume. But the heart, liver, and kidneys were only roasted, by being laid on hot stones for a few minutes; and the body of the dog, after being besmeared with the blood, which had been collected into a cocoa-nut shell, and dried over the fire, was, with the liver, *&c.* carried and laid down before the priests, who sat praying, round the grave. They continued their ejaculations over the dog, for some time, while two men, at intervals, beat on two drums very loud; and a boy screamed, as before, in a loud, shrill voice, three different times. This, as we were told, was to invite the *Eatooa* to feast on the banquet that they had prepared for him. As soon as the priests had ended their prayers, the carcase of the dog, with what belonged to it, were laid on a *whatta*, or scaffold, about six feet high, that stood close by, on which lay the remains of two other dogs, and of two pigs, which had lately been sacrificed, and, at this time, emitted an intolerable stench. This kept us at a greater distance, than would, otherwise, have been required of us. For, after the victim was removed from the sea-side toward the *morai*, we were allowed to approach as near as we pleased. Indeed, after that, neither seriousness nor attention were much observed by the spectators. When the dog was put upon the *whatta*, the priests and attendants

F 2   gave

gave a kind of fhout, which clofed the ceremonies for the
prefent. The day being now alfo clofed, we were conducted to a houfe belonging to Potatou, where we were
entertained, and lodged for the night. We had been told,
that the religious rites were to be renewed in the morning ; and I would not leave the place, while any thing remained to be feen.

Being unwilling to lofe any part of the folemnity, fome
of us repaired to the fcene of action pretty early, but found
nothing going forward. However, foon after, a pig was
facrificed, and laid upon the fame *whatta* with the others.
About eight o'clock, Otoo took us again to the *morai*, where
the priefts, and a great number of men, were, by this time,
affembled. The two bundles occupied the place in which
we had feen them depofited the preceding evening; the two
drums ftood in the front of the *morai*, but fomewhat nearer
it than before; and the priefts were beyond them. Otoo
placed himfelf between the two drums, and defired me to
ftand by him.

The ceremony began, as ufual, with bringing a young
plantain-tree, and laying it down at the king's feet. After
this a prayer was repeated by the priefts, who held in their
hands feveral tufts of red feathers, and alfo a plume of
oftrich feathers, which I had given to Otoo on my firft arrival, and had been confecrated to this ufe. When the
priefts had made an end of the prayer, they changed their
ftation, placing themfelves between us and the *morai* ; and
one of them, the fame perfon who had acted the principal
part the day before, began another prayer, which lafted
about half an hour. During the continuance of this, the
tufts of feathers were, one by one, carried and laid upon
the ark of the *Eatooa*.

Some

1777.
September.

Some little time after, four pigs were produced; one of
which was immediately killed; and the others were taken
to a fty, hard by, probably referved for fome future occafion of facrifice. One of the bundles was now untied; and
it was found, as I have before obferved, to contain the
maro, with which thefe people inveft their kings; and
which feems to anfwer, in fome degree, to the European
enfigns of royalty. It was carefully taken out of the
cloth, in which it had been wrapped up, and fpread, at
full length, upon the ground before the priefts. It is a
girdle, about five yards long, and fifteen inches broad;
and, from its name, feems to be put on in the fame manner
as is the common *maro*, or piece of cloth, ufed, by thefe
people, to wrap round the waift. It was ornamented with
red and yellow feathers; but moftly with the latter, taken
from a dove found upon the ifland. The one end was bor-
dered with eight pieces, each about the fize and fhape of
a horfe-fhoe, having their edges fringed with black feathers. The other end was forked, and the points were of
different lengths. The feathers were in fquare compartments, ranged in two rows, and, otherwife, fo difpofed as
to produce a pleafing effect. They had been firft pafted or
fixed upon fome of their own country cloth; and then
fewed to the upper end of the pendant which Captain
Wallis had difplayed, and left flying afhore, the firft time
that he landed at Matavai. This was what they told us;
and we had no reafon to doubt it, as we could eafily trace
the remains of an Englifh pendant. About fix or eight
inches fquare of the *maro* was unornamented; there being
no feathers upon that fpace, except a few that had been
fent by Waheiadooa, as already mentioned. The priefts
made a long prayer, relative to this part of the ceremony;
and,

and, if I miftook not, they called it the prayer of the *maro*. When it was finifhed, the badge of royalty was carefully folded up, put into the cloth, and depofited again upon the *morai*.

The other bundle, which I have diftinguifhed by the name of the ark, was next opened, at one end. But we were not allowed to go near enough to examine its myfterious contents. The information we received was, that the *Eatooa*, to whom they had been facrificing, and whofe name is *Ooro*, was concealed in it; or rather, what is fuppofed to reprefent him. This facred repofitory is made of the twifted fibres of the hufk of the cocoa-nut, fhaped fomewhat like a large fid, or fugar-loaf; that is, roundifh, with one end much thicker than the other. We had, very often, got fmall ones from different people, but never knew their ufe before.

By this time, the pig, that had been killed, was cleaned, and the entrails taken out. Thefe happened to have a confiderable fhare of thofe convulfive motions, which often appear, in different parts, after an animal is killed; and this was confidered by the fpectators as a very favourable omen to the expedition, on account of which the facrifices had been offered. After being expofed for fome time, that thofe who chofe, might examine their appearances, the entrails were carried to the priefts, and laid down before them. While one of their number prayed, another infpected the entrails more narrowly, and kept turning them gently with a ftick. When they had been fufficiently examined, they were thrown into the fire, and left to confume. The facrificed pig, and its liver, &c. were now put upon the *whatta*, where the dog had been depofited the day before; and then all the feathers, except the oftrich plume,

1777.
September.

plume, were inclofed with the *Eatooa*, in the ark ; and the folemnity finally clofed.

Four double canoes lay upon the beach, before the place of facrifice, all the morning. On the fore-part of each of thefe, was fixed a fmall platform, covered with palm-leaves, tied in myfterious knots; and this alfo is called a *morai*. Some cocoa-nuts, plantains, pieces of bread-fruit, fifh, and other things, lay upon each of thefe naval *morais*. We were told, that they belonged to the *Eatooa*; and that they were to attend the fleet defigned to go againft Eimeo.

The unhappy victim, offered to the object of their worfhip upon this occafion, feemed to be a middle-aged man ; and, as we were told, was a *toutou*; that is, one of the loweft clafs of the people. But, after all my inquiries, I could not learn, that he had been pitched upon, on account of any particular crime, committed by him, meriting death. It is certain, however, that they generally make choice of fuch guilty perfons for their facrifices ; or elfe of common, low, fellows, who ftroll about, from place to place, and from ifland to ifland, without having any fixed abode, or any vifible way of getting an honeft livelihood ; of which defcription of men, enough are to be met with at thefe iflands. Having had an opportunity of examining the appearance of the body of the poor fufferer, now offered up, I could obferve, that it was bloody about the head and face, and a good deal bruifed upon the right temple ; which marked the manner of his being killed. And we were told, that he had been privately knocked on the head with a ftone.

Thofe who are devoted to fuffer, in order to perform this bloody act of worfhip, are never apprized of their fate,

3   till

1777.
September.

till the blow is given that puts an end to their exiſtence. Whenever any one of the great Chiefs thinks a human ſacrifice neceſſary, on any particular emergency, he pitches upon the victim. Some of his truſty ſervants are then ſent, who fall upon him ſuddenly, and put him to death with a club, or by ſtoning him. The king is next acquainted with it, whoſe preſence, at the ſolemn rites that follow, is, as I was told, abſolutely neceſſary ; and, indeed, on the preſent occaſion, we could obſerve, that Otoo bore a principal part. The ſolemnity itſelf is called *Poore Eree*, or Chief's Prayer ; and the victim, who is offered up, *Taata-taboo*, or conſecrated man. This is the only inſtance where we have heard the word *taboo* uſed at this iſland, where it ſeems to have the ſame myſterious ſignification as at Tonga ; though it is there applied to all caſes where things are not to be touched. But at Otaheite, the word *raa* ſerves the ſame purpoſe, and is full as extenſive in its meaning.

The *morai* (which, undoubtedly, is a place of worſhip, ſacrifice, and burial, at the ſame time), where the ſacrifice was now offered, is that where the ſupreme Chief of the whole iſland is always buried, and is appropriated to his family, and ſome of the principal people. It differs little from the common ones, except in extent. Its principal part, is a large, oblong pile of ſtones, lying looſely upon each other, about twelve or fourteen feet high, contracted toward the top, with a ſquare area, on each ſide, looſely paved with pebble ſtones, under which the bones of the Chiefs are buried. At a little diſtance from the end neareſt the ſea, is the place where the ſacrifices are offered ; which, for a conſiderable extent, is alſo looſely paved. There is here a very large ſcaffold, or *whatta*, on which the

offerings

offerings of fruits, and other vegetables, are laid. But the
animals are depofited on a fmaller one, already mentioned,
and the human facrifices are buried under different parts of
the pavement. There are feveral other reliques which ignorant fuperftition had fcattered about this place; fuch as fmall
ftones, raifed in different parts of the pavement; fome with
bits of cloth tied round them; others covered with it; and
upon the fide of the large pile, which fronts the area, are
placed a great many pieces of carved wood, which are fuppofed to be fometimes the refidence of their divinities, and,
confequently, held facred. But one place, more particular
than the reft, is a heap of ftones, at one end of the large
whatta, before which the facrifice was offered, with a kind
of platform at one fide. On this are laid the fculls of all the
human facrifices, which are taken up after they have been
feveral months under ground. Juft above them, are placed
a great number of the pieces of wood; and it was alfo
here, where the *maro*, and the other bundle, fuppofed to
contain the god *Ooro* (and which I call the ark), were laid,
during the ceremony; a circumftance which denotes its
agreement with the altar of other nations.

It is much to be regretted, that a practice fo horrid in its
own nature, and fo deftructive of that inviolable right of
felf-prefervation, which every one is born with, fhould be
found ftill exifting; and (fuch is the power of fuperftition
to counteract the firft principles of humanity!) exifting
amongft a people, in many other refpects, emerged from
the brutal manners of favage life. What is ftill worfe, it is
probable, that thefe bloody rites of worfhip are prevalent
throughout all the wide-extended iflands of the Pacific
Ocean. The fimilarity of cuftoms and language, which
our late voyages have enabled us to trace, between the moft

VOL. II.   G   diftant

1777.
September.

diftant of thefe iflands, makes it not unlikely, that fome of the more important articles of their religious inftitutions fhould agree, And, indeed, we had the moft authentic in-formation, that human facrifices continue to be offered at the Friendly Iflands. When I defcribed the *Natche* at *Tonga-taboo*, I mentioned that, on the approaching fequel of that feftival, we had been told, that ten men were to be facri-ficed. This may give us an idea of the extent of this reli-gious maffacre in that ifland. And though we fhould fup-pofe, that never more than one perfon is facrificed, on any fingle occafion, at Otaheite, it is more than probable, that thefe occafions happen fo frequently, as to make a fhocking wafte of the human race ; for I counted no lefs than forty-nine fculls, of former victims, lying before the *morai*, where we faw one more added to the number. And as none of thofe fculls had, as yet, fuffered any confiderable change from the weather, it may hence be inferred, that no great length of time had elapfed, fince, at leaft, this confiderable number of unhappy wretches had been offered upon this altar of blood.

The cuftom, though no confideration can make it ceafe to be abominable, might be thought lefs detrimental, in fome refpects, if it ferved to imprefs any awe for the divi-nity, or reverence for religion, upon the minds of the mul-titude. But this is fo far from being the cafe, that though a great number of people had affembled at the *morai*, on this occafion, they did not feem to fhew any proper reve-rence for what was doing, or faying, during the celebration of the rites. And Omai happening to arrive, after they had begun, many of the fpectators flocked round him, and were engaged, the remainder of the time, in making him relate fome of his adventures, which they liftened to with

I   great

great attention, regardlefs of the folemn offices performing by their priefts. Indeed, the priefts themfelves, except the one who chiefly repeated the prayers, either from their being familiarized to fuch objects, or from want of confidence in the efficacy of their inftitutions, obferved very little of that folemnity, which is neceffary to give to religious performances their due weight. Their drefs was only an ordinary one; they converfed together, without fcruple; and the only attempt made by them to preferve any appearance of decency, was by exerting their authority, to prevent the people from coming upon the very fpot where the ceremonies were performed; and to fuffer us, as ftrangers, to advance a little forward. They were, however, very candid in their anfwers to any queftions that were put to them, concerning the inftitution. And, particularly, on being afked, what the intention of it was? they faid, that it was an old cuftom, and was agreeable to their god, who delighted in, or, in other words, came and fed upon the facrifices; in confequence of which, he complied with their petitions. Upon its being objected, that he could not feed on thefe, as he was neither feen to do it, nor were the bodies of the animals quickly confumed, and that as to the human victim, they prevented his feeding on him, by burying him. But to all this they anfwered, that he came in the night, but invifibly; and fed only on the foul, or immaterial part, which, according to their doctrine, remains about the place of facrifice, until the body of the victim be entirely wafted by putrefaction.

It were much to be wifhed, that this deluded people may learn to entertain the fame horror of murdering their fellow-creatures, in order to furnifh fuch an invifible banquet to their god, as they now have of feeding, corporeally, on

human

human flesh themselves. And, yet, we have great reason to believe, that there was a time when they were cannibals. We were told (and indeed partly saw it), that it is a necessary ceremony, when a poor wretch is sacrificed, for the priest to take out the left eye. This he presents to the king, holding it to his mouth, which he desires him to open; but, instead of putting it in, immediately withdraws it. This they call " eating the man," or " food for the Chief;" and, perhaps, we may observe here some traces of former times, when the dead body was really feasted upon.

But not to insist upon this : it is certain, that human sacrifices are not the only barbarous custom we find still prevailing amongst this benevolent, humane people. For, besides cutting out the jaw-bones of their enemies slain in battle, which they carry about as trophies, they, in some measure, offer their bodies as a sacrifice to the *Eatooa*. Soon after a battle, in which they have been victors, they collect all the dead that have fallen into their hands, and bring them to the *morai*, where, with a great deal of ceremony, they dig a hole, and bury them all in it, as so many offerings to the gods ; but their sculls are never after taken up.

Their own great Chiefs, that fall in battle, are treated in a different manner. We were informed, that their late king Tootaha, Tubourai-tamaide, and another Chief, who fell with them in the battle fought with those of Tiaraboo, were brought to this *morai*, at Attahooroo. There their bowels were cut out by the priests, before the great altar ; and the bodies afterward buried in three different places, which were pointed out to us, in the great pile of stones, that compose the most conspicuous part of this *morai*. And their common men, who also fell in this battle, were all
                                                                buried

buried in one hole, at the foot of the pile. This, Omai, who was prefent, told me, was done the day after the battle, with much pomp and ceremony, and in the midft of a great concourfe of people, as a thankfgiving offering to the *Eatooa*, for the victory they had obtained; while the vanquifhed had taken refuge in the mountains. There they remained a week, or ten days, till the fury of the victors was over, and a treaty fet on foot, by which it was agreed, that Otoo fhould be declared king of the whole ifland; and the folemnity of invefting him with the *maro*, was performed at the fame *morai*, with great pomp, in the prefence of all the principal men of the country.

CHAP.

CHAP. III.

Conference with Towha.—Heevas described.—Omai and Oedi-
dee give Dinners.—Fireworks exhibited.— A remarkable
- Present of Cloth.— Manner of preserving the Body of a
dead Chief.—Another human Sacrifice.—Riding on Horse-
back.—Otoo's Attention to supply Provisions, and prevent
Thefts.—Animals given to him.—Etary, and the Deputies
of a Chief, have Audiences.—A Mock-fight of Two War Ca-
noes.—Naval Strength of these Islands.—Manner of con-
ducting a War.

1777.
September.

Tuesday 2.

THE close of the very singular scene, exhibited at the
morai, which I have faithfully described in the last
Chapter, leaving us no other business in Attahooroo, we
embarked about noon, in order to return to Matavai; and,
in our way, visited Towha, who had remained on the little
island, where we met him the day before. Some conversation passed between Otoo and him, on the present posture of
public affairs; and then the latter solicited me, once more,
to join them in their war against Eimeo. By my positive re-
fusal I entirely lost the good graces of this Chief.

Before we parted, he asked us, if the solemnity, at which
we had been present, answered our expectations; what opinion we had of its efficacy; and whether we performed such
acts of worship in our own country? During the celebration of the horrid ceremony, we had preserved a profound
silence;

silence; but as soon as it was closed, had made no scruple
in expressing our sentiments very freely about it, to Otoo, and those who attended him; of course, therefore, I did not conceal my detestation of it, in this conversation with Towha. Besides the cruelty of the bloody custom, I strongly urged the unreasonableness of it; telling the Chief, that such a sacrifice, far from making the *Eatooa* propitious to their nation, as they ignorantly believed, would be the means of drawing down his vengeance; and that, from this very circumstance, I took upon me to judge, that their intended expedition against Maheine would be unsuccessful. This was venturing pretty far upon conjecture; but still, I thought, that there was little danger of being mistaken. For I found, that there were three parties in the island, with regard to this war; one extremely violent for it; another perfectly indifferent about the matter; and the third openly declaring themselves friends to Maheine, and his cause. Under these circumstances, of disunion distracting their councils, it was not likely that such a plan of military operations would be settled, as could insure even a probability of success. In conveying our sentiments to Towha, on the subject of the late sacrifice, Omai was made use of as our interpreter; and he entered into our arguments with so much spirit, that the Chief seemed to be in great wrath; especially when he was told, that if he had put a man to death in England, as he had done here, his rank would not have protected him from being hanged for it. Upon this, he exclaimed, *maeno! maeno!* [vile! vile!] and would not hear another word. During this debate, many of the natives were present, chiefly the attendants and servants of Towha himself; and when Omai began to explain the punishment that would be inflicted in England,

1777.
September.

England, upon the greateſt man, if he killed the meaneſt
ſervant, they ſeemed to liſten with great attention; and
were, probably, of a different opinion from that of their
maſter, on this ſubjeċt.

After leaving Towha, we proceeded to Oparre, where
Otoo preſſed us to ſpend the night. We landed in the
evening; and, on our road to his houſe, had an opportunity of obſerving in what manner theſe people amuſe
themſelves, in their private *heevas*. About a hundred of
them were found ſitting in a houſe; and in the midſt of
them were two women, with an old man behind each
of them, beating very gently upon a drum; and the women, at intervals, ſinging in a ſofter manner, than I ever
heard at their other diverſions. The aſſembly liſtened with
great attention; and were, ſeemingly, almoſt abſorbed in
the pleaſure the muſic gave them; for few took any notice
of us, and the performers never once ſtopped. It was almoſt dark before we reached Otoo's houſe, where we were
entertained with one of their public *heevas*, or plays, in
which his three ſiſters appeared as the principal charaċters.
This was what they call a *heeva raä*, which is of ſuch a nature, that nobody is to enter the houſe or area, where it is
exhibited. When the royal ſiſters are the performers, this
is always the caſe. Their dreſs, on this occaſion, was truly
piċtureſque and elegant; and they acquitted themſelves, in
their parts, in a very diſtinguiſhed manner; though ſome
comic interludes, performed by four men, ſeemed to yield
greater pleaſure to the audience, which was numerous.

Wedneſ. 3. The next morning we proceeded to Matavai, leaving Otoo
at Oparre; but his mother, ſiſters, and ſeveral other women, attended me on board, and Otoo himſelf followed ſoon
after.

                                                    While

While Otoo and I were abfent from the fhips, they had been but fparingly fupplied with fruit, and had few vifiters. After our return, we again overflowed with provifions, and with company.

On the 4th, a party of us dined afhore with Omai, who gave excellent fare, confifting of fifh, fowls, pork, and puddings. After dinner, I attended Otoo, who had been one of the party, back to his houfe, where I found all his fervants very bufy, getting a quantity of provifions ready for me. Amongft other articles, there was a large hog, which they killed in my prefence. The entrails were divided into eleven portions, in fuch a manner, that each of them contained a bit of every thing. Thefe portions were diftributed to the fervants, and fome dreffed theirs in the fame oven with the hog, while others carried off, undreffed, what had come to their fhare. There was alfo a large pudding, the whole procefs in making which, I faw. It was compofed of bread-fruit, ripe plantains, taro, and palm or pandanus nuts, each rafped, fcraped, or beat up fine, and baked by itfelf. A quantity of juice, expreffed from cocoa-nut kernels, was put into a large tray or wooden veffel. The other articles, hot from the oven, were depofited in this veffel; and a few hot ftones were alfo put in, to make the contents fimmer. Three or four men made ufe of fticks to ftir the feveral in-gredients, till they were incorporated one with another, and the juice of the cocoa-nut was turned to oil; fo that the whole mafs, at laft, became of the confiftency of a hafty-pudding. Some of thefe puddings are excellent; and few that we make in England equal them. I feldom, or never, dined without one, when I could get it, which was not al-ways the cafe. Otoo's hog being baked, and the pudding, which I have defcribed, being made, they, together with two living hogs, and a quantity of bread-fruit, and cocoa-nuts, were put into a canoe, and sent on board my ship, followed by myself, and all the royal family.

Friday 5.   The following evening, a young ram, of the Cape breed, that had been lambed, and, with great care, brought up on board the ship, was killed by a dog. Incidents are of more or less consequence, as connected with situation. In our present situation, desirous as I was to propagate this useful race, amongst these islands, the loss of the ram was a serious misfortune; as it was the only one I had of that breed; and I had only one of the English breed left.

Sunday 7.   In the evening of the 7th, we played off some fireworks before a great concourse of people. Some were highly entertained with the exhibition; but by far the greater number of spectators were terribly frightened; insomuch, that it was with difficulty we could prevail upon them to keep together, to see the end of the shew. A table-rocket was the last. It flew off the table, and dispersed the whole crowd in a moment; even the most resolute among them fled with precipitation.

Monday 8.   The next day, a party of us dined with our former shipmate, Oedidee, on fish and pork. The hog weighed about thirty pounds; and it may be worth mentioning, that it was alive, dressed, and brought upon the table, within the hour. We had but just dined, when Otoo came, and asked me, if my belly was full? On my answering in the affirmative, he said, " Then, come along with me." I, accordingly, went with him to his father's, where I found some people employed in dressing two girls with a prodigious quantity of fine cloth, after a very singular fashion. The one end of each piece of cloth, of which there were a good many, was held up over the heads of the girls, while the remainder was

wrapped

wrapped round their bodies, under the arm-pits. Then the upper ends were let fall, and hung down in folds to the ground, over the other, so as to bear some resemblance to a circular hoop-petticoat. Afterward, round the outside of all, were wrapped several pieces of differently-coloured cloth, which confiderably increafed the fize; fo that it was not lefs than five or fix yards in circuit, and the weight of this fingular attire was as much as the poor girls could fup-port. To each were hung two *taames*, or breaft-plates, by way of enriching the whole, and giving it a picturefque appearance. Thus equipped, they were conducted on board the ship, together with feveral hogs, and a quantity of fruit, which, with the cloth, was a prefent to me from Otoo's father. Perfons, of either fex, dreffed in this man-ner, are called *atee*; but, I believe, it is never practifed, ex-cept when large prefents of cloth are to be made. At leaft, I never faw it practifed upon any other occafion; nor, in-deed, had I ever fuch a prefent before; but both Captain Clerke and I had cloth given to us afterward, thus wrap-ped round the bearers. The next day, I had a prefent of *Tuefday 9.* five hogs, and fome fruit, from Otoo; and one hog, and fome fruit, from each of his fifters. Nor were other pro-vifions wanting. For two or three days, great quantities of mackerel had been caught by the natives, within the reef, in feines; fome of which they brought to the fhips and tents, and fold.

Otoo was not more attentive to fupply our wants, by a fucceffion of prefents, than he was to contribute to our amufement, by a fucceffion of diverfions. A party of us having gone down to Oparre, on the 10th, he treated us *Wednef. 10.* with what may be called a play. His three fifters were the actreffes; and the dreffes, that they appeared in, were new

H 2   and

and elegant; that is, more fo than we had ufually met with at any of thefe iflands. But the principal object I had in view, this day, in going to Oparre, was to take a view of an embalmed corpfe, which fome of our gentlemen had happened to meet with at that place, near the refidence of Otoo. On inquiry, I found it to be the remains of Tee, a Chief well known to me, when I was at this ifland, during my laft voyage. It was lying in a *toopapaoo*, more elegantly conftructed than their common ones, and in all refpects fimilar to that lately feen by us at Oheitepeha, in which the remains of Waheiadooa are depofited, embalmed in the fame manner. When we arrived at the place, the body was under cover, and wrapped up in cloth, within the *toopapaoo*; but, at my defire, the man who had the care of it, brought it out, and laid it upon a kind of bier, in fuch a manner, that we had as full a view of it as we could wifh; but we were not allowed to go within the pales that inclofed the *toopapaoo*. After he had thus exhibited the corpfe, he hung the place with mats and cloth, fo difpofed as to produce a very pretty effect. We found the body not only entire in every part; but, what furprized us much more, was, that putrefaction feemed fcarcely to be begun, as there was not the leaft difagreeable fmell proceeding from it; though the climate is one of the hotteft, and Tee had been dead above four months. The only remarkable alteration that had happened, was a fhrinking of the mufcular parts and eyes; but the hair and nails were in their original ftate, and ftill adhered firmly; and the feveral joints were quite pliable, or in that kind of relaxed ftate, which happens to perfons who faint fuddenly. Such were Mr. Anderfon's remarks to me, who alfo told me, that on his inquiring into the method of effecting this prefervation of their dead bodies, he had been informed, that,

foon

foon after their death, they are difembowelled, by drawing the inteftines, and other *vifcera*, out at the *anus*; and the whole cavity is then filled or ftuffed with cloth, introduced through the fame part; that when any moifture appeared on the fkin, it was carefully dried up, and the bodies afterward rubbed all over, with a large quantity of perfumed cocoa-nut oil; which, being frequently repeated, preferved them a great many months; but that, at laft, they gradually moulder away. This was the information Mr. Anderfon received; for my own part, I could not learn any more about their mode of operation, than what Omai told me, who faid, that they made ufe of the juice of a plant which grows amongft the mountains; of cocoa-nut oil; and of frequent wafhing with fea-water. I was alfo told, that the bodies of all their great men, who die a natural death, are preferved in this manner; and that they expofe them to public view for a very confiderable time after. At firft, they are laid out every day, when it does not rain; afterward, the intervals become greater and greater; and, at laft, they are feldom to be feen.

In the evening, we returned from Oparre, where we left Otoo, and all the royal family; and I faw none of them till the 12th; when all, but the Chief himfelf, paid me a vifit. He, as they told me, was gone to Attahooroo, to affift, this day, at another human facrifice, which the Chief of Tiaraboo had fent thither to be offered up at the *morai*. This fecond inftance, within the courfe of a few days, was too melancholy a proof, how numerous the victims of this bloody fuperftition are amongft this humane people. I would have been prefent at this facrifice too, had I known of it in time; for, now, it was too late. From the very fame caufe, I miffed being prefent at a public tranfaction, which

which had paffed at Oparre the preceding day, when Otoo,
with all the folemnities obferved on fuch occafions, reftored
to the friends and followers of the late king Tootaha, the
lands and poffeffions, which had been withheld from them
ever fince his death. Probably, the new facrifice was the
concluding ceremony of what may be called the reverfal of
attainder.

Saturday 13. · The following evening, Otoo returned from exercifing
this moft difagreeable of all his duties as fovereign; and, the
Sunday 14. next day, being now honoured with his company, Captain
Clerke and I, mounted on horfeback, took a ride round the
plain of Matavai, to the very great furprize of a great train
of people who attended on the occafion, gazing upon us,
with as much aftonifhment as if we had been centaurs.
Omai, indeed, had, once or twice before this, attempted to
get on horfeback; but he had as often been thrown off,
before he could contrive to feat himfelf; fo that this was
the firft time they had feen any body ride a horfe. What
Captain Clerke and I began, was, after this, repeated every
day, while we ftaid, by one or another of our people. And
yet the curiofity of the natives continued ftill unabated.
They were exceedingly delighted with thefe animals, after
they had feen the ufe that was made of them; and, as far
as I could judge, they conveyed to them a better idea of the
greatnefs of other nations, than all the other novelties, put
together, that their European vifiters had carried amongft
them. Both the horfe and mare were in good cafe, and
looked extremely well.

Monday 15. The next day, Etary, or Olla, the god of Bolabola, who
had, for feveral days paft, been in the neighbourhood of
Matavai, removed to Oparre, attended by feveral failing canoes. We were told, that Otoo did not approve of his being

fo

fo near our ftation, where his people could more eafily invade our property. I muft do Otoo the juftice to fay, that
he took every method prudence could fuggeft to prevent
thefts and robberies; and it was more owing to his regulations, than to our own circumfpection, that fo few were
committed. He had taken care to erect a little houfe or two,
on the other fide of the river, behind our poft; and two
others, clofe to our tents, on the bank between the river and
the fea. In all thefe places fome of his own people conftantly kept watch; and his father generally refided on
Matavai point; fo that we were, in a manner, furrounded
by them. Thus ftationed, they not only guarded us in the
night from thieves, but could obferve every thing that
paffed in the day; and were ready to collect contributions
from fuch girls as had private connections with our people; which was generally done every morning. So that the
meafures adopted by him to fecure our fafety, at the fame
time ferved the more effential purpofe of enlarging his own
profits.

Otoo informing me, that his prefence was neceffary at
Oparre, where he was to give audience to the great per-
fonage from Bolabola; and afking me to accompany him,
I readily confented, in hopes of meeting with fomething
worth our notice. Accordingly I went with him, in the
morning of the 16th, attended by Mr. Anderfon. Nothing,
however, occurred on this occafion, that was either interefting or curious. We faw Etary and his followers prefent
fome coarfe cloth and hogs to Otoo; and each article was
delivered with fome ceremony, and a fet fpeech. After
this, they, and fome other Chiefs, held a confultation about
the expedition to Eimeo. Etary, at firft, feemed to difap-
prove of it; but, at laft, his objections were over-ruled.

I   Indeed,

Indeed, it appeared, next day, that it was too late to deliberate about this meafure; and that Towha, Potatou, and another Chief, had already gone upon the expedition with the fleet of Attahooroo. For a meffenger arrived in the evening, with intelligence that they had reached Eimeo, and that there had been fome fkirmifhes, without much lofs or advantage on either fide.

In the morning of the 18th, Mr. Anderfon, myfelf, and Omai, went again with Otoo to Oparre, and took with us the fheep which I intended to leave upon the ifland, confifting of an Englifh ram and ewe, and three Cape ewes; all which I gave to Otoo. As all the three cows had taken the bull, I thought I might venture to divide them, and carry fome to Ulietea. With this view, I had them brought before us, and propofed to Etary, that if he would leave his bull with Otoo, he fhould have mine, and one of the three cows; adding, that I would carry them for him to Ulietea; for I was afraid to remove the Spanifh bull, left fome accident fhould happen to him, as he was a bulky fpirited beaft. To this propofal of mine, Etary, at firft, made fome objections; but, at laft, agreed to it; partly through the perfuafion of Omai. However, juft as the cattle were putting into the boat, one of Etary's followers valiantly oppofed any exchange whatever being made. Finding this, and fufpecting that Etary had only confented to the propofed arrangement, for the prefent moment, to pleafe me; and that, after I was gone, he might take away his bull, and then Otoo would not have one, I thought it beft to drop the idea of an exchange, as it could not be made with the mutual confent of both parties; and finally determined to leave them all with Otoo, ftrictly injoining him never to fuffer them to be removed from Oparre, not even the Spanifh
bull,

bull, nor any of the fheep, till he fhould get a ftock of young ones; which he might then difpofe of to his friends, and fend to the neighbouring iflands.

This being fettled, we left Etary and his party to ruminate upon their folly, and attended Otoo to another place, hard by, where we found the fervants of a Chief, whofe name I forgot to afk, waiting with a hog, a pig, and a dog, as a prefent from their mafter to the fovereign. Thefe were delivered with the ufual ceremonies, and with an harangue in form, in which the fpeaker, in his mafter's name, inquired after the health of Otoo, and of all the principal people about him. This compliment was echoed back in the name of Otoo, by one of his minifters; and then the difpute with Eimeo was difcuffed, with many arguments for and againft it. The deputies of this Chief were for profecuting the war with vigour, and advifed Otoo to offer a human facrifice. On the other hand, a Chief, who was in conftant attendance on Otoo's perfon, oppofed it, feemingly, with great ftrength of argument. This confirmed me in the opinion, that Otoo himfelf never entered heartily into the fpirit of this war. He now received repeated meffages from Towha, ftrongly foliciting him to haften to his affiftance. We were told, that his fleet was, in a manner, furrounded by that of Maheine; but that neither the one, nor the other, durft hazard an engagement.

After dining with Otoo, we returned to Matavai, leaving him at Oparre. This day, and alfo the 19th, we were very fparingly fupplied with fruit. Otoo hearing of this, he and his brother, who had attached himfelf to Captain Clerke, came from Oparre, between nine and ten o'clock in the evening, with a large fupply for both fhips. This marked his humane attention more ftrongly, than any thing he had

VOL. II.   I   hitherto

hitherto done for us. The next day, all the royal family
came with prefents; fo that our wants were not only relieved, but we had more provifions than we could confume.

Having got all our water on board, the fhips being caulked, the rigging overhauled, and every thing put in order, I
began to think of leaving the ifland, that I might have fufficient time to fpare for vifiting the others in this neighbourhood. With this view, we removed from the fhore our
obfervatories and inftruments, and bent the fails. Early
Sunday 21. the next morning, Otoo came on board to acquaint me, that
all the war canoes of Matavai, and of three other diftricts
adjoining, were going to Oparre, to join thofe belonging to
that part of the ifland; and that there would be a general
review there. Soon after, the fquadron of Matavai was all
in motion; and, after parading awhile about the bay, affembled afhore, near the middle of it. I now went in my
boat to take a view of them.

Of thofe with ftages, on which they fight, or what they
call their war canoes, there were about fixty; with near as
many more of a fmaller fize. I was ready to have attended
them to Oparre; but, foon after, a refolution was taken by
the Chiefs, that they fhould not move till the next day. I
looked upon this to be a fortunate delay, as it afforded me a
good opportunity to get fome infight into their manner of
fighting. With this view, I expreffed my wifh to Otoo, that
he would order fome of them to go through the neceffary
manœuvres. Two were, accordingly, ordered out into the
bay; in one of which, Otoo, Mr. King, and myfelf embarked;
and Omai went on board the other. When we had got fufficient fea-room, we faced, and advanced upon each other,
and retreated by turns, as quick as our rowers could paddle.
During this, the warriors on the ftages flourifhed their

3   weapons,

weapons, and played a hundred antic tricks, which could anfwer no other end, in my judgment, than to work up their paffions, and prepare them for fighting. Otoo ftood by the fide of our ftage, and gave the neceffary orders, when to advance, and when to retreat. In this, great judgment and a quick eye, combined together, feemed requifite, to feize every advantage that might offer, and to avoid giving any advantage to the adverfary. At laft, after advancing and retreating to and from each other, at leaft a dozen of times, the two canoes clofed, head to head, or ftage to ftage; and, after a fhort conflict, the troops on our ftage were fuppofed to be all killed, and we were boarded by Omai and his affociates. At that very inftant, Otoo, and all our paddlers leaped over-board, as if reduced to the neceffity of endeavouring to fave their lives by fwimming.

If Omai's information is to be depended upon, their naval engagements are not always conducted in this manner. He told me, that they fometimes begin with lafhing the two veffels together, head to head, and then fight till all the warriors are killed, on one fide or the other. But this clofe combat, I apprehend, is never practifed, but when they are determined to conquer or die. Indeed, one or the other muft happen; for all agree, that they never give quarter, unlefs it be to referve their prifoners for a more cruel death the next day.

The power and ftrength of thefe iflands lie entirely in their navies. I never heard of a general engagement on land; and all their decifive battles are fought on the water. If the time and place of conflict are fixed upon by both parties, the preceding day and night are fpent in diverfions and feafting. Toward morning, they launch the canoes, put every thing in order, and, with the day, begin the

battle;

battle; the fate of which generally decides the difpute. The vanquifhed fave themfelves by a precipitate flight; and fuch as reach the fhóre fly, with their friends, to the mountains; for the victors, while their fury lafts, fpare neither the aged, nor women, nor children. The next day, they affemble at the *morai*, to return thanks to the *Eatooa* for the victory, and to offer up the flain as facrifices, and the prifoners alfo, if they have any. After this, a treaty is fet on foot; and the conquerors, for the moft part, obtain their own terms; by which particular diftricts of land, and, fometimes, whole iflands, change their owners. Omai told us, that he was once taken a prifoner by the men of Bolabola, and carried to that ifland, where he and fome others would have been put to death the next day, if they had not found means to efcape in the night.

As foon as this mock-fight was over, Omai put on his fuit of armour, mounted a ftage in one of the canoes, and was paddled all along the fhore of the bay; fo that every one had a full view of him. His coat of mail did not draw the attention of his countrymen fo much as might have been expected. Some of them, indeed, had feen a part of it before; and there were others, again, who had taken fuch a diflike to Omai, from his imprudent conduct at this place, that they would hardly look at any thing, however fingular, that was exhibited by him.

C H A P.

C H A P. IV.

The Day of sailing fixed.—Peace made with Eimeo.—Debates about it, and Otoo's Conduct blamed.—A Solemnity at the Morai on the Occasion, described by Mr. King.—Observations upon it.—Instance of Otoo's Art.—Omai's War Canoe, and Remarks upon his Behaviour.—Otoo's Present, and Message to the King of Great Britain.—Reflections on our Manner of Traffic, and on the good Treatment we met with at Otaheite.—Account of the Expedition of the Spaniards.— Their Fictions to depreciate the English.—Wishes expressed that no Settlement may be made.—Omai's Jealousy of another Traveller.

EARLY in the morning of the 22d, Otoo and his father came on board, to know when I proposed sailing. For, having been informed, that there was a good harbour at Eimeo, I had told them, that I should visit that island on my way to Huaheine; and they were desirous of taking a passage with me, and of their fleet sailing, at the time, to reinforce Towha. As I was ready to take my departure, I left it to them to name the day; and the Wednesday following was fixed upon; when I was to take on board Otoo, his father, mother, and, in short, the whole family. These points being settled, I proposed setting out immediately for Oparre, where all the fleet, fitted out for the expedition, was to assemble this day, and to be reviewed.

1777.
September.
Monday 22.

I had

I had but juſt time to get into my boat, when news was brought, that Towha had concluded a treaty with Maheine, and had returned with his fleet to Attahooroo. This unexpected event made all further proceedings, in the military way, quite unneceſſary; and the war canoes, inſtead of rendezvouſing at Oparre, were ordered home to their reſpective diſtricts. This alteration, however, did not hinder me from following Otoo to Oparre, accompanied by Mr. King and Omai. Soon after our arrival, and while dinner was preparing, a meſſenger arrived from Eimeo, and related the conditions of the peace; or rather of the truce, it being only for a limited time. The terms were diſadvantageous to Otaheite; and much blame was thrown upon Otoo, whoſe delay, in ſending reinforcements, had obliged Towha to ſubmit to a diſgraceful accommodation. It was even currently reported, that Towha, reſenting his not being ſupported, had declared, that, as ſoon as I ſhould leave the iſland, he would join his forces to thoſe of Tiaraboo, and attack Otoo at Matavai, or Oparre. This called upon me to declare, in the moſt public manner, that I was determined to eſpouſe the intereſt of my friend, againſt any ſuch combination; and that whoever preſumed to attack him, ſhould feel the weight of my heavy diſpleaſure, when I returned again to their iſland. My declaration, probably, had the deſired effect; and, if Towha had any ſuch hoſtile intention at firſt, we ſoon heard no more of the report. Whappai, Otoo's father, highly diſapproved of the peace, and blamed Towha very much for concluding it. This ſenſible old man wiſely judged, that my going down with them to Eimeo muſt have been of ſingular ſervice to their cauſe, though I ſhould take no other part whatever in the quarrel. And it was upon this that he

built

built all his arguments, and maintained, that Otoo had acted properly by waiting for me; though this had prevented his giving affiftance to Towha fo foon as he expected.

Our debates at Oparre, on this fubject, were hardly ended, before a meffenger arrived from Towha, defiring Otoo's attendance, the next day, at the *morai* in Attahooroo, to give thanks to the Gods for the peace he had concluded; at leaft, fuch was Omai's account to me, of the object of this folemnity. I was afked to go; but being much out of order, was obliged to decline it. Defirous, however, of knowing what ceremonies might be obferved on fo memorable an occafion, I fent Mr. King, and Omai, and returned on board my fhip, attended by Otoo's mother, his three fifters, and eight more women. At firft, I thought that this numerous train of females came into my boat with no other view than to get a paffage to Matavai. But when we arrived at the fhip, they told me, they intended paffing the night on board, for the exprefs purpofe of undertaking the cure of the diforder I complained of; which was a pain of the rheumatic kind, extending from the hip to the foot. I accepted the friendly offer, had a bed fpread for them upon the cabin floor, and fubmitted myfelf to their directions. I was defired to lay myfelf down amongft them. Then, as many of them as could get round me, began to fqueeze me with both hands, from head to foot, but more particularly on the parts where the pain was lodged, till they made my bones crack, and my flefh became a perfect mummy. In fhort, after undergoing this difcipline about a quarter of an hour, I was glad to get away from them. However, the operation gave me immediate relief, which encouraged me to fubmit to another rubbing-down before I went to bed;

1777.
September.
Tuefday 23.

Wednef. 24.

Thurfday 25.

bed; and it was fo effectual, that I found myfelf pretty eafy all the night after. My female phyficians repeated their prefcription the next morning, before they went afhore, and again, in the evening, when they returned on board; after which, I found the pains entirely removed; and the cure being perfected, they took their leave of me the following morning. This they call *romee*; an operation which, in my opinion, far exceeds the flefh-brufh, or any thing of the kind that we make ufe of externally. It is univerfally practifed amongft thefe iflanders; being fometimes performed by the men, but more generally by the women. If, at any time, one appears languid and tired, and fits down by any of them, they immediately begin to practife the *romee* upon his legs; and I have always found it to have an exceedingly good effect *.

In the morning of the 25th, Otoo, Mr. King, and Omai, returned from Attahooroo; and Mr. King gave me the following account of what he had feen:

" Soon after you left me, a fecond meffenger came from Towha to Otoo, with a plantain-tree. It was fun-fet when we embarked in a canoe and left Oparre. About nine o'clock we landed at Tettaha, at that extremity which joins to Attahooroo. Before we landed, the people called to us from the fhore; probably, to tell us that Towha was there. The meeting of Otoo and this Chief, I expected, would afford fome incident worthy of obfervation. Otoo, and his attendants, went and feated themfelves on the beach, clofe to the canoe in which Towha was. He was then afleep; but his fervants having awakened him, and mentioning Otoo's name, immediately a plantain-tree and a dog, were laid at

---

* See Captain Wallis's account of the fame operation performed on himfelf, and his firft Lieutenant, in *Hawkefworth's Collection*, Vol. i. p. 243.

Otoo's

Otoo's feet; and many of Towha's people came and talked
with him, as I conceived, about their expedition to Eimeo.
After I had, for some time, remained seated close to Otoo,
Towha neither stirring from his canoe, nor holding any
conversation with us, I went to him. He asked me if *Toote*
was angry with him. I answered, No: that he was his *taio*;
and that he had ordered me to go to Attahooroo to tell him
so. Omai now had a long conversation with this Chief;
but I could gather no information of any kind from him.
On my returning to Otoo, he seemed desirous, that I should
go to eat, and then to sleep. Accordingly, Omai and I left
him. On questioning Omai, he said, the reason of Towha's
not stirring from his canoe, was his being lame; but that,
presently, Otoo and he would converse together in private.
This seemed true; for in a little time, those we left with
Otoo came to us; and, about ten minutes after, Otoo himself arrived, and we all went to sleep in his canoe.

The next morning, the *ava* was in great plenty. One
man drank so much that he lost his senses. I should have
supposed him to be in a fit, from the convulsions that agi-
tated him. Two men held him, and kept plucking off his
hair by the roots. I left this spectacle to see another that
was more affecting. This was the meeting of Towha and
his wife, and a young girl, whom I understood to be his
daughter. After the ceremony of cutting their heads, and
discharging a tolerable quantity of blood and tears, they
washed, embraced the Chief, and seemed unconcerned. But
the young girl's sufferings were not yet come to an end.
Terridiri * arrived; and she went, with great composure,
to repeat the same ceremonies to him, which she had just

* Terridiri is Oberea's son. See an account of the royal family of Otaheite, in
Hawkesworth's Collection, Vol. ii. p. 154.

1777.
September.
performed on meeting her father. Towha had brought a large war canoe from Eimeo. I inquired if he had killed the people belonging to her; and was told, that there was no man in her when fhe was captured.

We left Tettaha, about ten or eleven o'clock, and landed, clofe to the *morai* of Attahooroo, a little after noon. There lay three canoes, hauled upon the beach, oppofite the *morai*, with three hogs expofed in each: their fheds, or awnings, had fomething under them which I could not difcern. We expected the folemnity to be performed the fame afternoon; but as neither Towha nor Potatou had joined us, nothing was done.

A Chief from Eimeo came with a fmall pig, and a plantain-tree, and placed them at Otoo's feet. They talked fome time together; and the Eimeo Chief often repeating the words, *Warry, warry,* " falfe," I fuppofed that Otoo was relating to him what he had heard, and that the other denied it.

The next day (Wednefday) Towha, and Potatou, with about eight large canoes, arrived, and landed near the *morai*. Many plantain-trees were brought, on the part of different Chiefs, to Otoo. Towha did not ftir from his canoe. The ceremony began by the principal prieft bringing out the *maro*, wrapped up; and a bundle, fhaped like a large fugar-loaf. Thefe were placed at the head of what I underftood to be a grave. Then three priefts came, and fat down oppofite, that is, at the other end of the grave; bringing with them a plantain-teee, the branch of fome other tree, and the fheath of the flower of the cocoa-nut tree.

The priefts, with thefe things in their hands, feparately repeated fentences; and, at intervals, two, and fometimes all three fung a melancholy ditty, little attended to by the

I   people.

people. This praying and finging continued for an hour. 1777. September. Then, after a fhort prayer, the principal prieft uncovered the *maro*; and Otoo rofe up, and wrapped it about him, holding, at the fame time, in his hand, a cap or bonnet, compofed of the red feathers of the tail of the tropic bird, mixed with other feathers of a dark colour. He ftood in the middle fpace, facing the three priefts, who continued their prayers for about ten minutes; when a man, ftarting from the crowd, faid fomething which ended with the word *beiva!* and the crowd echoed back to him, three times, *Earee!* This, as I had been told before, was the principal part of the folemnity.

The company now moved to the oppofite fide of the great pile of ftones, where is, what they call, the king's *morai*; which is not unlike a large grave. Here the fame ceremony was performed over again, and ended in three cheers. The *maro* was now wrapped up, and increafed in its fplendor by the addition of a fmall piece of red feathers, which one of the priefts gave Otoo when he had it on, and which he ftuck into it.

From this place, the people went to a large hut, clofe by the *morai*, where they feated themfelves in much greater order than is ufual among them. A man of Tiaraboo, then made an oration, which lafted about ten minutes. He was followed by an Attahooroo man; afterward Potatou fpoke with much greater fluency and grace than any of them; for, in general, they fpoke in fhort, broken fentences, with a motion of the hand that was rather awkward. Tooteo, Otoo's orator, fpoke next; and, after him, a man from Eimeo. Two or three more fpeeches were made; but not much attended to. Omai told me, that the fpeeches declared, that they fhould not fight, but all be friends. As

K 2   many

1777.
September.
 many of the fpeakers expreffed themfelves with warmth,
poffibly there were fome recriminations and proteftations of
their good intentions. In the midft of their fpeaking, a man
of Attahooroo got up, with a fling faftened to his waift, and
a large ftone placed upon his fhoulder. After parading near
a quarter of an hour, in the open fpace, repeating fomething in a finging tone, he threw the ftone down. This
ftone, and a plantain tree that lay at Otoo's feet, were, after the
fpeeches ended, carried to the *morai*; and one of the priefts,
and Otoo with him, faid fomething upon the occafion.

On our return to Oparre, the fea breeze having fet in, we
were obliged to land; and had a pleafant walk through almoft the whole extent of Tettaha to Oparre. A tree, with
two bundles of dried leaves fufpended upon it, marked the
boundary of the two diftricts. The man who had performed the ceremony of the ftone and fling came with us.
With him, Otoo's father had a long converfation. He
feemed very angry. I underftood, he was enraged at the
part Towha had taken in the Eimeo bufinefs."

From what I can judge of this folemnity, as thus defcribed by Mr. King, it had not been wholly a thankfgiving,
as Omai told us; but rather a confirmation of the treaty;
or, perhaps, both. The grave, which Mr. King fpeaks of,
feems to be the very fpot where the celebration of the rites
began, when the human facrifice, at which I was prefent,
was offered, and before which the victim was laid, after being removed from the fea fide. It is at this part of the *morai*,
alfo, that they firft inveft their kings with the *maro*. Omai,
who had been prefent when Otoo was made king, defcribed
to me the whole ceremony, when we were here; and I find
it to be almoft the fame, as this that Mr. King has now defcribed, though we underftood it to be upon a very different
occafion.

occafion. The plantain tree, fo often mentioned, is always the firft thing introduced, not only in all their religious ceremonies, but in all their debates, whether of a public or private nature. It is alfo ufed on other occafions; perhaps many more than we know of. While Towha was at Eimeo, one or more meffengers came from him to Otoo every day. The meffenger always came with a young plantain tree in his hand, which he laid down at Otoo's feet, before he fpoke a word; then feated himfelf before him, and related what he was charged with. I have feen two men in fuch high difpute that I expected they would proceed to blows; yet, on one laying a plantain tree before the other, they have both become cool, and carried on the argument without farther animofity. In fhort, it is, upon all occafions, the olive-branch of thefe people.

The war with Eimeo, and the folemn rites which were the confequence of it, being thus finally clofed, all our friends paid us a vifit on the 26th; and, as they knew that we were upon the point of failing, brought with them more hogs than we could take off their hands. For, having no falt left, to preferve any, we wanted no more than for prefent ufe.

The next day, I accompanied Otoo to Oparre; and, before I left it, I looked at the cattle and poultry, which I had configned to my friend's care, at that place. Every thing was in a promifing way; and properly attended unto. Two of the geefe, and two of the ducks were fitting; but the pea and turkey hens had not begun to lay. I got from Otoo four goats; two of which I intended to leave at Ulietea, where none had as yet been introduced; and the other two, I propofed to referve for the ufe of any other iflands I might meet with, in my paffage to the North.

A circum-

A circumſtance which I ſhall now mention of Otoo, will ſhew, that theſe people are capable of much addreſs and art, to gain their purpoſes. Amongſt other things, which, at different times, I had given to this Chief, was a ſpying-glaſs. After having it in his poſſeſſion two or three days, tired of its novelty, and probably finding it of no uſe to him, he carried it privately to Captain Clerke, and told him, that, as he had been his very good friend, he had got a pre-ſent for him, which he knew would be agreeable. " But, ſays Otoo, you muſt not let *Toote* know it, becauſe he wants it, and I would not let him have it." He then put the glaſs into Captain Clerke's hands; at the ſame time, aſſuring him, that he came honeſtly by it. Captain Clerke, at firſt, de-clined accepting it; but Otoo inſiſted upon it, and left it with him. Some days after, he put Captain Clerke in mind of the glaſs; who, though he did not want it, was yet de-ſirous of obliging Otoo; and thinking, that a few axes would be of more uſe at this iſland, produced four to give him in return. Otoo no ſooner ſaw this, than he ſaid, " *Toote* offered me five for it." " Well, ſays Captain Clerke, if that be the caſe, your friendſhip for me ſhall not make you a loſer, and you ſhall have ſix axes." Theſe he accepted; but deſired again, that I might not be told what he had done.

Our friend Omai got one good thing, at this iſland, for the many good things he gave away. This was a very fine double ſailing canoe, completely equipped, and fit for the ſea. Some time before, I had made up for him, a ſuit of Engliſh colours; but he thought theſe too valuable to be uſed at this time; and patched up a parcel of colours, ſuch as flags and pendants, to the number of ten or a dozen, which he ſpread on different parts of his veſſel, all at the

fame

1777.
September.

fame time; and drew together as many people to look at her, as a man of war would, dreffed, in a European port. Thefe ftreamers of Omai were a mixture of Englifh, French, Spanifh, and Dutch, which were all the European colours that he had feen. When I was laft at this ifland, I gave to Otoo an Englifh jack and pendant, and to Towha a pendant; which I now found they had preferved with the greateft care.

Omai had alfo provided himfelf with a good ftock of cloth and cocoa-nut oil, which are not only in greater plenty, but much better, at Otaheite, than at any of the Society Iflands; infomuch, that they are articles of trade. Omai would not have behaved fo inconfiftently, and fo much unlike himfelf, as he did, in many inftances, but for his fifter and brother-in-law, who, together with a few more of their acquaintance, engroffed him entirely to themfelves, with no other view than to ftrip him of every thing he had got. And they would, undoubtedly, have fucceeded in their fcheme, if I had not put a ftop to it in time, by taking the moft ufeful articles of his property into my pof-feffion. But even this would not have faved Omai from ruin, if I had fuffered thefe relations of his to have gone with, or to have followed us to, his intended place of fettle-ment, Huaheine. This they had intended; but I difap-pointed their farther views of plunder, by forbidding them to fhew themfelves in that ifland, while I remained in the neighbourhood; and they knew me too well not to comply.

On the 28th, Otoo came on board, and informed me, that he had got a canoe, which he defired I would take with me, and carry home, as a prefent from him to the *Earee rahie no Pretane*; it being the only thing, he faid, that he could fend

Sunday 28.

fend worth his Majefty's acceptance. I was not a little pleafed with Otoo, for this mark of his gratitude. It was a thought entirely his own, not one of us having given him the leaft hint about it; and it fhewed, that he fully under-ftood to whom he was indebted for the moft valuable pre-fents that he had received. At firft, I thought, that this canoe had been a model of one of their veffels of war; but I foon found, that it was a fmall *Evaa*, about fixteen feet long. It was double, and feemed to have been built for the purpofe; and was decorated with all thofe pieces of carved work, which they ufually fix upon their ca-noes. As it was too large for me to take on board, I could only thank him for his good intention; but it would have pleafed him much better, if his prefent could have been accepted.

We were detained here fome days longer than I expected, by light breezes from the Weft, and calms by turns; fo that we could not get out of the bay. During this time, the fhips were crowded with our friends, and furrounded by a multitude of canoes; for not one would leave the place, till we were gone. At length, at three o'clock in the
afternoon of the 29th, the wind came at Eaft, and we weigh-ed anchor.

As foon as the fhips were under fail, at the requeft of Otoo, and to gratify the curiofity of his people, I fired feven guns, loaded with fhot; after which, all our friends, ex-cept him, and two or three more, left us with fuch marks of affection and grief, as fufficiently fhewed how much they regretted our departure. Otoo being defirous of fee-ing the fhip fail, I made a ftretch out to fea, and then in again; when he alfo bid us farewell, and went afhore in his canoe.

The

The frequent vifits we had lately paid to this ifland, feem to have created a full perfuafion, that the intercourfe will not be difcontinued. It was ftrictly enjoined to me by Otoo, to requeft, in his name, the *Earee rabie no Pretane*, to fend him, by the next fhips, red feathers, and the birds that produce them; axes; half a dozen mufquets, with powder and fhot; and, by no means, to forget horfes.

I have occafionally mentioned my receiving confiderable prefents from Otoo, and the reft of the family, without fpecifying what returns I made. It is cuftomary for thefe people, when they make a prefent, to let us know what they expect in return; and we find it neceffary to gratify them; fo that, what we get by way of prefent, comes dearer than what we get by barter. But as we were fometimes preffed by occafional fcarcity, we could have recourfe to our friends for a prefent, or fupply, when we could not get our wants relieved by any other method; and, therefore, upon the whole, this way of traffic was full as advantageous to us as to the natives. For the moft part, I paid for each feparate article as I received it, except in my intercourfe with Otoo. His prefents, generally, came fo faft upon me, that no account was kept between us. Whatever he afked for, that I could fpare, he had whenever he afked for it; and I always found him moderate in his demands.

If I could have prevailed upon Omai to fix himfelf at Otaheite, I fhould not have left it fo foon as I did. For there was not a probability of our being better or cheaper fupplied with refrefhments at any other place, than we continued to be here, even at the time of our leaving it. Befides, fuch a cordial friendfhip and confidence fubfifted between us and the inhabitants, as could hardly be expected any where elfe; and, it was a little extraordinary, that this friendly intercourfe had never once been fufpended, by any untoward accident; nor had there been a theft committed that deferves to be mentioned. Not that I believe their morals, in this refpect, to be much mended; but am rather of opinion, that their regularity of conduct was owing to the fear, the Chiefs were under, of interrupting a traffic which they might confider as the means of fecuring to themfelves a more confiderable fhare of our commodities, than could have been got by plunder or pilfering. Indeed, this point I fettled at the firft interview with their Chiefs, after my arrival. For, obferving the great plenty that was in the ifland, and the eagernefs of the natives to poffefs our various articles of trade, I refolved to make the moft of thefe two favourable circumftances, and explained myfelf, in the moft decifive terms, that I would not fuffer them to rob us, as they had done upon many former occafions. In this, Omai was of great ufe, as I inftructed him to point out to them the good confequences of their honeft conduct; and the fatal mifchiefs they muft expect to fuffer by deviating from it.

It is not always in the power of the Chiefs to prevent robberies; they are frequently robbed themfelves; and complain of it as a great evil. Otoo left the moft valuable things he had from me, in my poffeffion, till the day before we failed; and the reafon he gave for it was, that they were no where fo fafe. Since the bringing in of new riches, the inducements to pilfering muft have increafed. The Chiefs, fenfible of this, are now extremely defirous of chefts. They feemed to fet much value upon a few that the Spaniards had left amongft them; and they were continually afking us for fome. I had one made for Otoo, the dimenfions of

3   which,

which, according to his own directions, were eight feet in length, five in breadth, and about three in depth. Locks and bolts were not a sufficient security; but it must be large enough for two people to sleep upon, by way of guarding it in the night.

It will appear a little extraordinary, that we, who had a smattering of their language, and Omai, besides, for an interpreter, could never get any clear account of the time when the Spaniards arrived, how long they stayed, and when they departed. The more we inquired into this matter, the more we were convinced of the inability of most of these people to remember, or note the time, when past events happened; especially if it exceeded ten or twenty months. It, however, appeared, by the date of the inscription upon the cross, and by the information we received from the most intelligent of the natives, that two ships arrived at Oheitepeha in 1774, soon after I left Matavai, which was in May, the same year. They brought with them the house and live stock, before mentioned. Some said, that, after landing these things, and some men, they failed in quest of me, and returned in about ten days. But I have some doubt of the truth of this, as they were never seen, either at Huaheine, or at Ulietea. The live stock they left here, consisted of one bull, some goats, hogs, and dogs, and the male of some other animal; which we afterward found to be a ram, and, at this time, was at Bolabola, whither the bull was also to have been transported.

The hogs are of a large kind; have already greatly improved the breed originally found by us upon the island; and, at the time of our late arrival, were very numerous. Goats are, also, in tolerable plenty, there being hardly a Chief of any note who has not got some. As to the dogs

that

that the Spaniards put afhore, which are of two or three
forts, I think they would have done the ifland a great deal
more fervice, if they had hanged them all, inftead of leaving them upon it. It was to one of them, that my young
ram fell a victim.

When thefe fhips left the ifland, four Spaniards remained
behind. Two were priefts, one a fervant, and the fourth
made himfelf very popular among the natives, who diftinguifh him by the name of Mateema. He feems to have
been a perfon who had ftudied their language; or, at leaft,
to have fpoken it fo as to be underftood; and to have taken
uncommon pains to imprefs the minds of the iflanders with
the moft exalted ideas of the greatnefs of the Spanifh nation, and to make them think meanly of the Englifh. He
even went fo far as to affure them, that we no longer exifted as an independent nation; that *Pretane* was only a
fmall ifland, which they, the Spaniards, had entirely deftroyed; and, for me, that they had met with me at fea,
and, with a few fhot, had fent my fhip, and every foul in
her, to the bottom; fo that my vifiting Otaheite, at this
time, was, of courfe, very unexpected. All this, and many
other improbable falfehoods, did this Spaniard make thefe
people believe. If Spain had no other views, in this expedition, but to depreciate the Englifh, they had better have
kept their fhips at home; for my returning again to Otaheite, was confidered as a complete confutation of all that
Mateema had faid.

With what defign the priefts ftayed, we can only guefs.
If it was to convert the natives to the catholic faith, they
have not fucceeded in any one inftance. But it does not appear, that they ever attempted it; for, if the natives are to
be believed, they never converfed with them, either on this,

or

or on any other fubject. The priefts refided conftantly in the houfe at Oheitepeha; but Mateema roved about, vifiting moft parts of the ifland. At length, after he and his companions had ftayed ten months, two fhips came to Oheitepeha, took them on board, and failed again in five days. This hafty departure fhews, that, whatever defign the Spaniards might have had upon this ifland, they had now laid it afide. And yet, as I was informed by Otoo, and many others, before they went away, they would have the natives believe, that they ftill meant to return, and to bring with them houfes, all kinds of animals, and men and women who were to fettle, live, and die, on the ifland. Otoo, when he told me this, added, that if the Spaniards fhould return, he would not let them come to Matavai Fort, which, he faid, was ours. It was eafy to fee, that the idea pleafed him; little thinking, that the completion of it would, at once, deprive him of his kingdom, and the people of their liberties. This fhews with what facility a fettlement might be made at Otaheite; which, grateful as I am for repeated good offices, I hope will never happen. Our occafional vifits may, in fome refpects, have benefited its inhabitants; but a permanent eftablifhment amongft them, conducted as moft European eftablifhments amongft Indian nations have unfortunately been, would, I fear, give them juft caufe to lament, that our fhips had ever found them out. Indeed, it is very unlikely, that any meafure of this kind fhould ever be ferioufly thought of, as it can neither ferve the purpofes of public ambition, nor of private avarice; and, without fuch inducements, I may pronounce, that it will never be undertaken.

I have already mentioned the vifit that I had from one of the two natives of this ifland, who had been carried by the

Spaniards

Spaniards to Lima. I never faw him afterward; which I rather wondered at, as I had received him with uncommon civility. I believe, however, that Omai had kept him at a diftance from me, by fome rough ufage; jealous, that there fhould be another traveller upon the ifland, who might vie with himfelf. Our touching at Teneriffe was a fortunate circumftance for Omai; as he prided himfelf in having vifited a place belonging to Spain, as well as this man. I did not meet with the other, who had returned from Lima; but Captain Clerke, who had feen him, fpoke of him as a low fellow, and as a little out of his fenfes. His own countrymen, I found, agreed in the fame account of him. In fhort, thefe two adventurers feemed to be held in no efteem. They had not, indeed, been fo fortunate as to return home with fuch valuable acquifitions of pro- perty, as we had beftowed upon Omai; and, with the ad- vantages he reaped from his voyage to England, it muft be his own fault, if he fhould fink into the fame ftate of infignificance.

C H A P.

CHAP. V.

Arrival at Eimeo.—Two Harbours there, and an Account of them.—Vifit from Maheine, Chief of the Ifland.—His Perfon defcribed.—A Goat ftolen, and fent back with the Thief.—Another Goat ftolen and fecreted—Meafures taken on the Occafion.—Expedition crofs the Ifland.—Houfes and Canoes burnt.—The Goat delivered up, and Peace reftored. —Some Account of the Ifland, &c.

AS I did not give up my defign of touching at Eimeo, at day-break, in the morning of the 30th, after leaving Otaheite, I ftood for the North end of the ifland; the harbour, which I wifhed to examine, being at that part of it. Omai, in his canoe, having arrived there long before us, had taken fome neceffary meafures to fhew us the place. However, we were not without pilots, having feveral men of Otaheite on board, and not a few women. Not caring to truft entirely to thefe guides, I fent two boats to examine the harbour; and on their making the fignal for fafe anchorage, we ftood in with the fhips, and anchored clofe up to the head of the inlet, in ten fathoms water, over a bottom of foft mud, and moored with a hawfer faft to the fhore.

This harbour, which is called Taloo, is fituated upon the North fide of the ifland, in the diftrict of Oboonohoo, or

Poonohoo.

Poonohoo. It runs in South, or South by Eaſt, between
the hills, above two miles. For ſecurity, and goodneſs of
its bottom, it is not inferior to any harbour that I have met
with at any of the iſlands in this ocean; and it has this advantage over moſt of them, that a ſhip can ſail in and out,
with the reigning trade wind; ſo that the acceſs and receſs
are equally eaſy. There are ſeveral rivulets that fall into it.
The one, at the head, is ſo conſiderable as to admit boats to
go a quarter of a mile up, where we found the water perfectly freſh. Its banks are covered with the *pooroo* tree, as
it is called by the natives, which makes good firing, and
which they ſet no value upon; ſo that wood and water are
to be got here with great facility.

On the ſame ſide of the iſland, and about two miles to
the Eaſtward, is the harbour of Parowroah, much larger
within than that of Taloo; but the entrance, or opening
in the reef (for the whole iſland is ſurrounded by a reef
of coral rock) is conſiderably narrower, and lies to leeward of the harbour. Theſe two defects are ſo ſtriking,
that the harbour of Taloo muſt always have a decided
preference. It is a little extraordinary, that I ſhould have
been three times at Otaheite before, and have once ſent a
boat to Eimeo, and yet not know, till now, that there
was a harbour in it. On the contrary, I always underſtood, there was not. Whereas, there are not only the
two above mentioned, but one or two more, on the South
ſide of the iſland. But theſe laſt are not ſo conſiderable as
the two we have juſt deſcribed, and of which a ſketch has
been made, for the uſe of thoſe who may follow us in ſuch
a voyage.

We had no ſooner anchored, than the ſhips were crowded with the inhabitants, whom curioſity alone brought on
                                               board;

board; for they had nothing with them for the purpofes of
barter. But, the next morning, this deficiency was fupplied; feveral canoes then arriving from more diftant parts,
which brought with them abundance of bread-fruit, cocoa-
nuts, and a few hogs. Thefe they exchanged for hatchets,
nails, and beads; for red feathers were not fo much fought
after here as at Otaheite. The fhip being a good deal peft-
ered with rats, I hauled her within thirty yards of the fhore,
as near as the depth of water would allow, and made a
path for them to get to the land, by faftening hawfers to
the trees. It is faid, that this experiment has fometimes
fucceeded; but, I believe, we got clear of very few, if any,
of the numerous tribe that haunted us.

In the morning of the 2d, Maheine, the Chief of the
ifland, paid me a vifit. He approached the fhip with great
caution, and it required fome perfuafion to get him on
board. Probably, he was under fome apprehenfions of mifchief from us, as friends of the Otaheiteans; thefe people
not being able to comprehend, how we can be friends with
any one, without adopting, at the fame time, his caufe
againft his enemies. Maheine was accompanied by his
wife, who, as I was informed, is fifter to Oamo, of Otaheite,
of whofe death we had an account, while we were at this
ifland. I made prefents to both of them, of fuch things as
they feemed to fet the higheft value upon; and after a ftay
of about half an hour, they went away. Not long after,
they returned with a large hog, which they meant as a return for my prefent; but I made them another prefent to
the full value of it. After this, they paid a vifit to Captain Clerke.

This Chief, who, with a few followers, has made himfelf,
in a manner, independent of Otaheite, is between forty and

Vol. II.   M   fifty

fifty years old. He is bald-headed; which is rather an
uncommon appearance in thefe iflands, at that age. He
wore a kind of turban, and feemed afhamed to fhew his
head. But, whether they themfelves confidered this deficiency of hair as a mark of difgrace, or whether they entertained a notion of our confidering it as fuch, I cannot fay.
We judged that the latter fuppofition was the truth, from
this circumftance, that they had feen us fhave the head of
one of their people, whom we had caught ftealing. They,
therefore, concluded, that this was the punifhment ufually
inflicted by us upon all thieves; and one or two of our
gentlemen, whofe heads were not over-burth'ened with
hair, we could obferve, lay under violent fufpicions of
being *tetos*.

In the evening, Omai and I mounted on horfeback, and
took a ride along the fhore to the Eaftward. Our train was
not very numerous, as Omai had forbid the natives to follow us; and many complied; the fear of giving offence,
getting the better of their curiofity. Towha had ftationed
his fleet in this harbour; and though the war lafted but a
few days, the marks of its devaftation were every where
to be feen. The trees were ftripped of their fruit; and all
the houfes in the neighbourhood had been pulled down
or burnt.

Having employed two or three days in getting up all our
fpirit cafks, to tar their heads, which we found neceffary, to
fave them from the efforts of a fmall infect to deftroy them,
we hauled the fhip off into the ftream, on the 6th in the
morning, intending to put to fea the next day; but an accident happened that prevented it, and gave me a good deal
of trouble. We had fent our goats afhore, in the day time,
to graze, with two men to look after them; notwithftanding
which

which precaution, the natives had contrived to fteal one of
them this evening. The lofs of this goat would have been
of little confequence, if it had not interfered with my
views of ftocking other iflands with thefe animals; but
this being the cafe, it became neceffary to recover it, if poffible. The next morning, we got intelligence, that it had
been carried to Maheine, the Chief, who was, at this time,
at Parowroah harbour. Two old men offered to conduct
any of my people, whom I might think proper to fend to
him, to bring back the goat. Accordingly, I difpatched
them in a boat, charged with a threatening meffage to
Maheine, if the goat was not immediately given up to me,
and alfo the thief.

It was only the day before, that this Chief had requefted
me to give him two goats. But, as I could not fpare them,
unlefs at the expence of other iflands, that might never
have another opportunity to get any, and had, befides,
heard that there were already two upon this ifland, I did
not gratify him. However, to fhew my inclination to affift
his views in this refpect, I defired Tidooa, an Otaheite Chief,
who was prefent, to beg Otoo, in my name, to fend two of
thefe animals to Maheine; and, by way of infuring a com-
pliance with this requeft, I fent to Otoo, by this Chief, a
large piece of red feathers, equal to the value of the two
goats that I required. I expected that this arrangement
would have been fatisfactory to Maheine, and all the other
Chiefs of the ifland; but the event fhewed that I was miftaken.

Not thinking, that any one would dare to fteal a fecond,
at the very time I was taking meafures to recover the firft,
the goats were put afhore again this morning; and in the
evening a boat was fent to bring them on board. As our

people

people were getting them into the boat, one was carried off undifcovered. It being immediately miffed, I made no doubt of recovering it without much trouble, as there had not been time to carry it to any confiderable diftance. Ten or twelve of the natives fet out, foon after, different ways, to bring it back, or to look for it; for not one of them would own that it was ftolen, but all tried to perfuade us, that it had ftrayed into the woods; and, indeed, I thought fo myfelf. I was convinced to the contrary, however, when I found that not one of thofe who went in purfuit of it, returned; fo that their only view was to amufe me, till their prize was beyond my reach; and night coming on, put a ftop to all farther fearch. About this time, the boat returned with the other goat, bringing alfo one of the men who had ftolen it; the firft inftance of the kind that I had met with amongft thefe iflands.

Wednef. 8.
The next morning, I found that moft of the inhabitants in the neighbourhood had moved off; carrying with them a corpfe which lay on a *toopapaoo* oppofite the fhip; and that Maheine himfelf had retired to the moft diftant part of the ifland. It feemed now no longer doubtful, that a plan had been laid to fteal what I had refufed to give; and that, though they had reftored one, they were refolved to keep the other; which was a fhe-goat, and big with kid. I was equally fixed in my refolution that they fhould not keep it. I, therefore, applied to the two old men who had been inftrumental in getting back the firft. They told me, that this had been carried to Watea, a diftrict on the South fide of the ifland, by Hamoa, the Chief of that place; but that, if I would fend any body for it, it would be delivered up. They offered to conduct fome of my people crofs the ifland; but on my learning from them, that a boat might go and return
turn

turn the fame day, I fent one, with two petty officers, Mr. Roberts and Mr. Shuttleworth; one to remain with the boat, in cafe fhe could not get to the place, while the other fhould go with the guides, and one or two of our people.

Late in the evening, the boat returned, and the officers informed me, that after proceeding as far in the boat as rocks and fhoals would permit, Mr. Shuttleworth, with two marines, and one of the guides, landed and travelled to Watea, to the houfe of Hamoa, where the people of the place amufed them for fome time, by telling them, that the goat would foon be brought, and pretended they had fent for it. It however never came; and the approach of night obliged Mr. Shuttleworth to return to the boat without it.

I was now very forry, that I had proceeded fo far; as I could not retreat with any tolerable credit, and without giving encouragement to the people of the other iflands we had yet to vifit, to rob us with impunity. I afked Omai and the two old men, what methods I fhould next take; and they, without hefitation, advifed me to go with a party of men into the country, and fhoot every foul I fhould meet with. This bloody counfel I could not follow; but I refolved to march a party of men crofs the ifland; and, at day-break the next morning, fet out with thirty-five of my people, accompanied by one of the old men, by Omai, and three or four of his attendants. At the fame time, I ordered Lieutenant Williamfon, with three armed boats, round the Weftern part of the ifland, to meet us.

I had no fooner landed with my party, than the few natives who ftill remained in the neighbourhood, fled before us. The firft man that we met with upon our march,

run

run fome rifk of his life; for Omai, the moment he faw
him, afked me if he fhould fhoot him; fo fully was he
perfuaded, that I was going to carry his advice into execution. I immediately ordered both him and our guide to
make it known, that I did not intend to hurt, much lefs
to kill, a fingle native. Thefe glad tidings flew before us
like lightning, and ftopped the flight of the inhabitants;
fo that no one quitted his houfe, or employment, afterward.

As we began to afcend the ridge of hills over which lay
our road, we got intelligence, that the goat had been carried that way before us; and, as we underftood, could not,
as yet, have paffed the hills; fo that we marched up, in
great filence, in hopes of furprizing the party who were
bearing off the prize. But when we had got to the upper-
moft plantation on the fide of the ridge, the people there
told us, that what we were in fearch of had, indeed, been
kept there the firft night, but had been carried, the next
morning, to Watea, by Hamoa. We then croffed the ridge
without making any further inquiry, till we came within
fight of Watea, where fome people fhewed us Hamoa's
houfe, and told us, that the goat was there; fo that I made
no doubt of getting it immediately upon my arrival. But
when I reached the houfe, to my very great furprize, the
few people we met with denied that they had ever feen it,
or knew any thing about it; even Hamoa himfelf came,
and made the fame declaration.

On our firft coming to the place, I obferved feveral men
running to and fro in the woods, with clubs and bundles of
darts in their hands; and Omai, who followed them, had
fome ftones thrown at him; fo that it feemed as if they had
intended to oppofe any ftep I fhould take, by force; but on

I   feeing

seeing my party was too strong, had dropped the design. I was confirmed in this notion, by observing, that all their houses were empty. After getting a few of the people of the place together, I desired Omai to expostulate with them on the absurdity of the conduct they were pursuing; and to tell them, that, from the testimony of many on whom I could depend, I was well assured, that the goat was in their possession; and, therefore, insisted upon its being delivered up, otherwise I would burn their houses and canoes. But, notwithstanding all that I or Omai could say, they continued to deny their having any knowledge of it. The consequence was, that I set fire to six or eight houses, which were presently consumed, with two or three war-canoes that lay contiguous to them. This done, I marched off to join the boats, which were about seven or eight miles from us; and, in our way, we burnt six more war-canoes, without any one attempting to oppose us; on the contrary, many assisted, though, probably, more out of fear than good-will. In one place, Omai, who had advanced a little before, came back with information, that a great many men were getting together to attack us. We made ready to receive them; but, instead of enemies, we found petitioners with plantain-trees in their hands, which they laid down at my feet, and begged that I would spare a canoe that lay close by; which I readily complied with.

At length, about four in the afternoon, we got to the boats, that were waiting at Wharrarade, the district belonging to Tiarataboonoue; but this Chief, as well as all the principal people of the place, had fled to the hills; though I touched not a single thing that was their property, as they were the friends of Otoo. After resting ourselves here about an hour, we set out for the ships, where

where we arrived about eight o'clock in the evening. At that time, no account of the goat had been received; fo that the operations of this day had not produced the defired effect.

Friday 10.
Early next morning, I difpatched one of Omai's men to Maheine, with this peremptory meffage, that, if he perfifted in his refufal, I would not leave him a fingle canoe upon the ifland, and that he might expect a continuation of hoftilities as long as the ftolen animal remained in his poffeffion. And, that the meffenger might fee that I was in earneft, before he left me, I fent the carpenter to break up three or four canoes that lay afhore at the head of the harbour. The plank was carried on board, as materials for building a houfe for Omai, at the place where he intended to fettle. I afterward went, properly accompanied, to the next harbour, where we broke up three or four more canoes, and burnt an equal number; and then returned on board about feven in the evening. On my arrival, I found that the goat had been brought back, about half an hour before; and, on inquiry, it appeared that it had come from the very place where I had been told, the day before, by the inhabitants, that they knew nothing of it. But in confequence of the meffage I fent to the Chief in the morning, it was judged prudent to trifle with me no longer.

Thus ended this troublefome, and rather unfortunate, bufinefs; which could not be more regretted on the part of the natives, than it was on mine. And it grieved me to reflect, that, after refufing the preffing folicitations of my friends at Otaheite to favour their invafion of this ifland, I fhould, fo foon, find myfelf reduced to the neceffity of engaging in hoftilities againft its inhabitants, which, perhaps, did them
more

more mifchief than they had fuffered from Towha's expedition.

The next morning, our intercourfe with the natives was
renewed; and feveral canoes brought, to the fhips, bread-
fruit and cocoa-nuts to barter; from whence it was natural
for me to draw this conclufion, that they were confcious it
was their own fault, if I had treated them with feverity;
and that the caufe of my difpleafure being removed, they
had a full confidence that no further mifchief would enfue.
About nine o'clock, we weighed with a breeze down the
harbour; but it proved fo faint and variable, that it was noon
before we got out to fea, when I fteered for Huaheine, attended by Omai in his canoe. He did not depend entirely
upon his own judgment, but had got on board a pilot. I
obferved, that they fhaped as direct a courfe for the ifland
as I could do.

At Eimeo we abundantly fupplied the fhips with fire-
wood. We had not taken in any at Otaheite, where the
procuring this article would have been very inconvenient;
there not being a tree at Matavai, but what is ufeful to the
inhabitants. We alfo got here good ftore of refrefhments;
both in hogs and vegetables; that is, bread-fruit and cocoa-
nuts; little elfe being in feafon. I do not know that there
is any difference between the produce of this ifland and of
Otaheite; but there is a very ftriking difference in their women, that I can by no means account for. Thofe of Eimeo
are of low ftature, have a dark hue; and, in general, forbidding features. If we met with a fine woman amongft them,
we were fure, upon inquiry, to find that fhe had come from
fome other ifland.

The general appearance of Eimeo is very different from
that of Otaheite. The latter rifing in one fteep hilly body,

VOL. II.   N   has

has little low land, except fome deep valleys ; and the flat border that furrounds the greateft part of it, toward the fea. Eimeo, on the contrary, has hills running in different directions, which are very fteep and rugged, leaving, in the interfpaces, very large valleys, and gently-rifing grounds about their fides. Thefe hills, though of a rocky difpofition, are, in general, covered, almoft to their tops, with trees; but the lower parts, on the fides, frequently only with fern. At the bottom of the harbour, where we lay, the ground rifes gently to the foot of the hills, which run acrofs nearly in the middle of the ifland; but its flat border, on each fide, at a very fmall diftance from the fea, becomes quite fteep. This gives it a romantic caft, which renders it a profpect fuperior to any thing we faw at Otaheite. The foil, about the low grounds, is a yellowifh and pretty ftiff mould; but, upon the lower hills, it is blacker and more loofe: and the ftone that compofes the hills is, when broken, of a blueifh colour, but not very compact texture, with fome particles of *glimmer* interfperfed. Thefe particulars feem worthy of obfervation. Perhaps the reader will think differently of my judgment, when I add, that, near the ftation of our fhips, were two large ftones, or rather rocks, concerning which the natives have fome fuperftitious notions. They confider them as *Eatooas*, or Divinities; faying, that they are brother and fifter, and that they came, by fome fupernatural means, from Ulietea.

C H A P.

CHAP. VI.

Arrival at Huaheine.—Council of the Chiefs.—Omai's Offerings, and Speech to the Chiefs.—His Establishment in this Island agreed to.— A House built, and Garden planted for him.—Singularity of his Situation.—Measures taken to insure his Safety.—Damage done by Cock-roaches on board the Ships.— A Thief detected and punished.—Fireworks exhibited.—Animals left with Omai.—His Family.—Weapons.—Inscription on his House.— His Behaviour on the Ships leaving the Island.—Summary View of his Conduct and Character.—Account of the two New Zealand Youths.

HAVING left Eimeo, with a gentle breeze and fine weather, at day-break, the next morning, we saw Huaheine, extending from South West by West, half West, to West by North.   At noon, we anchored at the North entrance of Owharre harbour *, which is on the West side of the island.   The whole afternoon was spent in warping the ships into a proper birth, and mooring.   Omai entered the harbour just before us, in his canoe, but did not land. Nor did he take much notice of any of his countrymen, though many crowded to see him; but far more of them came off to the ships, insomuch that we could hardly work on account of their numbers.   Our passengers pre-

1777.
October.
Sunday 12.

* See a plan of this harbour in Hawkesworth's Collection, Vol. ii. p. 248.

N 2

sently

fently acquainted them with what we had done at Eimeo,
and multiplied the number of houfes and canoes that we
had deftroyed, by ten at leaft.   I was not forry for this exaggerated account; as I faw, that it made a great impreffion upon all who heard it; fo that I had hopes it would
induce the inhabitants of this ifland to behave better to us,
than they had done during my former vifits.

While I was at Otaheite, I had learned that my old friend
Oree was no longer the Chief of Huaheine; and that, at
this time, he refided at Ulietea.   Indeed, he never had been
more than regent during the minority of Taireetareea, the
prefent *Earee rahie*; but he did not give up the regency, till
he was forced.   His two fons, Opoony and Towha, were the
firft who paid me a vifit, coming on board before the fhip
was well in the harbour, and bringing a prefent with
them.

Our arrival brought all the principal people of the ifland
to our fhips, on the next morning, being the 13th.   This
was juft what I wifhed, as it was high time to think of fettling Omai; and the prefence of thefe Chiefs, I guefled,
would enable me to do it in the moft fatisfactory manner.
He now feemed to have an inclination to eftablifh himfelf
at Ulietea; and if he and I could have agreed about the
mode of bringing that plan to bear, I fhould have had no
objection to adopt it.   His father had been difpoffeffed by
the men of Bolabola, when they conquered Ulietea, of fome
land in that ifland; and I made no doubt of being able to
get it reftored to the fon in an amicable manner.   For that
purpofe it was neceflary, that he fhould be upon good terms
with thofe who now were mafters of the ifland; but he was
too great a patriot to liften to any fuch thing; and was
vain enough to fuppofe, that I would reinftate him in his
                                                    forfeited

forfeited lands by force. This made it impoffible to fix him
at Ulietea, and pointed out to me Huaheine as the proper
place. I, therefore, refolved to avail myfelf of the prefence
of the chief men of the ifland, and to make this propofal
to them.

After the hurry of the morning was over, we got ready
to pay a formal vifit to Taireetareea, meaning then to introduce this bufinefs. Omai dreffed himfelf very properly on
the occafion ; and prepared a handfome prefent for the
Chief himfelf, and another for his *Eatooa*. Indeed, after
he had got clear of the gang that furrounded him at
Otaheite, he behaved with fuch prudence as to gain refpect. Our landing drew moft of our vifiters from the fhips ;
and they, as well as thofe that were on fhore, affembled in
a large houfe. The concourfe of people, on this occafion,
was very great ; and, amongft them, there appeared to be a
greater proportion of perfonable men and women than we
had ever feen in one affembly at any of thefe new iflands.
Not only the bulk of the people feemed, in general, much
ftouter and fairer than thofe of Otaheite, but there was alfo
a much greater number of men who appeared to be of
confequence, in proportion to the extent of the ifland ; moft
of whom had exactly the corpulent appearance of the Chiefs
of Wateeoo. We waited fome time for Taireetareea, as I
would do nothing till the *Earee rahie* came ; but when he
appeared I found that his prefence might have been dif-
penfed with, as he was not above eight or ten years of age.
Omai, who ftood at a little diftance from this circle of great
men, began with making his offering to the Gods, confifting of red feathers, cloth, &c. Then followed another offering, which was to be given to the Gods by the Chief ;
and, after that, feveral other fmall pieces and tufts of red
feathers

feathers were prefented. Each article was laid before one
of the company, who, I underftood, was a prieft, and was
delivered with a fet fpeech or prayer, fpoken by one of
Omai's friends, who fat by him, but moftly dictated by
himfelf. In thefe prayers, he did not forget his friends in
England, nor thofe who had brought him fafe back. The
Earee rabie no Pretane, Lord Sandwich, *Toote*, *Tatee* *, were
mentioned in every one of them. When Omai's offerings
and prayers were finifhed, the prieft took each article, in
the fame order in which it had been laid before him, and
after repeating a prayer, fent it to the *morai*; which, as
Omai told us, was at a great diftance, otherwife the offerings would have been made there.

Thefe religious ceremonies having been performed, Omai
fat down by me, and we entered upon bufinefs, by giving
the young Chief my prefent, and receiving his in return;
and, all things confidered, they were liberal enough, on
both fides. Some arrangements were next agreed upon, as
to the manner of carrying on the intercourfe betwixt us;
and I pointed out the mifchievous confequences that would
attend their robbing us, as they had done during my former
vifits. Omai's eftablifhment was then propofed to the affembled Chiefs.

He acquainted them, " That he had been carried by us,
into our country, where he was well received by the great
King and his *Earees*, and treated with every mark of regard
and affection, while he ftaid amongft us; that he had been
brought back again, enriched, by our liberality, with a variety of articles, which would prove very ufeful to his
countrymen; and that, befides the two horfes which were
to remain with him, feveral other new and valuable animals

---

* Cook and Clerke.

had

had been left at Otaheite, which would foon multiply, and furnifh a fufficient number for the ufe of all the iflands in the neighbourhood. He then fignified to them, that it was my earneft requeft, in return for all my friendly offices, that they would give him a piece of land, to build a houfe upon, and to raife provifions for himfelf and fervants; adding, that, if this could not be obtained for him in Huaheine, either by gift or by purchafe, I was determined to carry him to Ulietea, and fix him there."

Perhaps I have here made a better fpeech for my friend, than he actually delivered; but thefe were the topics I dictated to him. I obferved, that what he concluded with, about carrying him to Ulietea, feemed to meet with the approbation of all the Chiefs; and I inftantly faw the reafon. Omai had, as I have already mentioned, vainly flattered himfelf, that I meant to ufe force in reftoring him to his father's lands in Ulietea, and he had talked idly, and without any authority from me, on this fubject, to fome of the prefent affembly; who dreamed of nothing lefs than a hoftile invafion of Ulietea, and of being affifted by me to drive the Bolabola men out of that ifland. It was of confequence, therefore, that I fhould undeceive them; and, in order to this, I fignified, in the moft peremptory manner, that I neither would affift them in fuch an enterprize, nor fuffer it to be put in execution, while I was in their feas; and that, if Omai fixed himfelf in Ulietea, he muft be introduced as a friend, and not forced upon the Bolabola men as their conqueror.

This declaration gave a new turn to the fentiments of the council. One of the Chiefs immediately expreffed himfelf to this effect: " That the whole ifland of Huaheine, and every thing in it, were mine; and that, therefore, I might

3   give

give what portion of it I pleafed to my friend." Omai, who, like the reft of his countrymen, feldom fees things beyond the prefent moment, was greatly pleafed to hear this; thinking, no doubt, that I fhould be very liberal, and give him enough. But to offer what it would have been improper to accept, I confidered as offering nothing at all; and, therefore, I now defired, that they would not only affign the particular fpot, but alfo the exact quantity of land, which they would allot for the fettlement. Upon this, fome Chiefs, who had already left the affembly, were fent for ; and, after a fhort confultation among themfelves, my requeft was granted by general confent; and the ground immediately pitched upon, adjoining to the houfe where our meeting was held. The extent, along the fhore of the harbour, was about two hundred yards ; and its depth, to the foot of the hill, fomewhat more; but a proportional part of the hill was included in the grant.

This bufinefs being fettled to the fatisfaction of all parties, I fet up a tent afhore, eftablifhed a poft, and erected the obfervatories. The carpenters of both fhips were alfo fet to work, to build a fmall houfe for Omai, in which he might fecure the European commodities that were his property. At the fame time, fome hands were employed in making a garden for his ufe, planting fhaddocks, vines, pine-apples, melons, and the feeds of feveral other vegetable articles; all of which I had the fatisfaction of obferving to be in a flourifhing ftate before I left the ifland.

Omai now began ferioufly to attend to his own affairs, and repented heartily of his ill-judged prodigality while at Otaheite. He found at Huaheine, a brother, a fifter, and a brother-in-law ; the fifter being married. But thefe did not plunder him, as he had lately been by his other relations.

1777.
October.

tions. I was forry, however, to difcover, that, though they were too honeft to do him any injury, they were of too little confequence in the ifland to do him any pofitive good. They had neither authority nor influence to protect his perfon, or his property; and, in that helplefs fituation, I had reafon to apprehend, that he run great rifk of being ftripped of every thing he had got from us, as foon as he fhould ceafe to have us within his reach, to enforce the good behaviour of his countrymen, by an immediate appeal to our irrefiftible power.

A man who is richer than his neighbours is fure to be envied, by numbers who wifh to fee him brought down to their own level. But in countries where civilization, law, and religion, impofe their reftraints, the rich have a reafonable ground of fecurity. And, befides, there being, in all fuch communities, a diffufion of property, no fingle individual need fear, that the efforts of all the poorer fort can ever be united to injure him, exclufively of others who are equally the objects of envy. It was very different with Omai. He was to live amongft thofe who are ftrangers, in a great meafure, to any other principle of action befides the immediate impulfe of their natural feelings. But, what was his principal danger, he was to be placed in the very fingular fituation, of being the only rich man in the community to which he was to belong. And having, by a fortunate connection with us, got into his poffeffion an accumulated quantity of a fpecies of treafure which none of his countrymen could create by any art or induftry of their own; while all coveted a fhare of this envied wealth, it was natural to apprehend that all would be ready to join in attempting to ftrip its fole proprietor.

VOL. II.   O   To

To prevent this, if poffible, I advifed him to make a proper diftribution of fome of his moveables, to two or three
of the principal Chiefs; who, being thus gratified themfelves, might be induced to take him under their patronage,
and protect him from the injuries of others. He promifed
to follow my advice; and I heard, with fatisfaction, before
I failed, that this very prudent ftep had been taken. Not
trufting, however, entirely to the operations of gratitude, I
had recourfe to the more forcible motive of intimidation.
With this view, I took every opportunity of notifying to
the inhabitants, that it was my intention to return to their
ifland again, after being abfent the ufual time; and that, if
I did not find Omai in the fame ftate of fecurity in which I
was now to leave him, all thofe whom I fhould then difcover to have been his enemies, might expect to feel the
weight of my refentment. This threatening declaration
will, probably, have no inconfiderable effect. For our fucceffive vifits of late years have taught thefe people to believe, that our fhips are to return at certain periods; and
while they continue to be imprefied with fuch a notion,
which I thought it a fair ftratagem to confirm, Omai has
fome profpect of being permitted to thrive upon his new
plantation.

While we lay in this harbour, we carried afhore the
bread remaining in the bread-room, to clear it of vermin.
The number of cock-roaches that infefted the fhip, at this
time, is incredible. The damage they did us was very
confiderable; and every method devifed by us to deftroy
them proved ineffectual. Thefe animals, which, at firft,
were a nuifance, like all other infects, had now become
a real peft; and fo deftructive, that few things were free
from their ravages. If food of any kind was expofed,
only

1777.
October.

only for a few minutes, it was covered with them; and they foon pierced it full of holes, refembling a honey-comb. They were particularly deftructive to birds, which had been ftuffed and preferved as curiofities; and, what was worfe, were uncommonly fond of ink; fo that the writing on the labels, faftened to different articles, was quite eaten out; and the only thing that preferved books from them, was the clofenefs of the binding, which pre-vented thefe devourers getting between the leaves. Ac-cording to Mr. Anderfon's obfervations, they were of two forts, the *blatta orientalis*, and *germanica*. The firft of thefe had been carried home in the fhip from her former voyage, where they withftood the feverity of the hard winter in 1776, though fhe was in dock all the time. The others had only made their appearance fince our leaving New Zealand; but had increafed fo faft, that they now not only did all the mifchief mentioned above, but had even got amongft the rigging; fo that when a fail was loofened, thoufands of them fell upon the decks. The *orientales*, though in infinite numbers, fcarcely came out but in the night, when they made every thing in the cabins feem as if in motion, from the particular noife in crawling about. And, befides their difagreeable appearance, they did great mifchief to our bread, which was fo befpattered with their excrement, that it would have been badly re-lifhed by delicate feeders.

The intercourfe of trade, and friendly offices, was carried on, between us and the natives, without being difturbed by any one accident, till the evening of the 22d, when a man found means to get into Mr. Bayly's obfervatory, and to carry off a fextant, unobferved. As foon as I was made ac-quainted with the theft, I went afhore, and got Omai to ap-

Wednef. 22.

ply

ply to the Chiefs, to procure reſtitution. He did ſo; but they took no ſteps toward it, being more attentive to a *beeva*, that was then acting, till I ordered the performers of the exhibition to deſiſt. They were now convinced, that I was in earneſt, and began to make ſome inquiry after the thief, who was ſitting in the midſt of them, quite unconcerned, inſomuch that I was in great doubt of his being the guilty perſon; eſpecially as he denied it. Omai, however, aſſuring me that he was the man, I ſent him on board the ſhip, and there confined him. This raiſed a general ferment amongſt the aſſembled natives; and the whole body fled, in ſpite of all my endeavours to ſtop them. Having employed Omai to examine the priſoner, with ſome difficulty he was brought to confeſs where he had hid the ſextant; but, as it was now dark, we could not find it till day-light

Thurſday 23. the next morning, when it was brought back unhurt. After this, the natives recovered from their fright, and began to gather about us as uſual. And, as to the thief, he appearing to be a hardened ſcoundrel, I puniſhed him more ſeverely than I had ever done any one culprit before. Beſides having his head and beard ſhaved, I ordered both his ears to be cut off, and then diſmiſſed him.

This, however, did not deter him from giving us farther
Saturday 25. trouble; for, in the night between the 24th and 25th, a general alarm was ſpread, occaſioned, as was ſaid, by one of our goats being ſtolen by this very man. On examination, we found, that all was ſafe in that quarter. Probably, the goats were ſo well guarded, that he could not put his deſign in execution. But his hoſtilities had ſucceeded againſt another object; and it appeared, that he had deſtroyed and carried off ſeveral vines and cabbage-plants in Omai's grounds; and he publicly threatened to kill him, and to burn

3

burn his houfe, as foon as we fhould leave the ifland. To prevent the fellow's doing me and Omai any more mifchief, I had him feized, and confined again on board the fhip, with a view of carrying him off the ifland; and it feemed to give general fatisfaction to the Chiefs, that I meant thus to difpofe of him. He was from Bolabola; but there were too many of the natives here ready to affift him in any of his defigns, whenever he fhould think of executing them. I had always met with more troublefome people in Huaheine, than in any other of the neighbouring iflands; and it was only fear, and the want of opportunities, that induced them to behave better now. Anarchy feemed to prevail amongft them. Their nominal fovereign the *Earee rahie*, as I have before obferved, was but a child; and I did not find, that there was any one man, or fet of men, who managed the government for him; fo that, whenever any mifunderftanding happened between us, I never knew, with fufficient precifion, where to make application, in order to bring about an accommodation, or to procure redrefs. The young Chief's mother would, indeed, fometimes exert herfelf; but I did not perceive that fhe had greater authority than many others.

Omai's houfe being nearly finifhed, many of his moveables were carried afhore on the 26th. Amongft a variety of other ufelefs articles was a box of toys, which, when expofed to public view, feemed greatly to pleafe the gazing multitude. But, as to his pots, kettles, difhes, plates, drinking-mugs, glaffes, and the whole train of our domeftic accommodations, hardly any one of his countrymen would fo much as look at them. Omai himfelf now began to think that they were of no manner of ufe to him; that a baked hog was more favory food than a boiled one; that a plantain-tain-leaf made as good a difh or plate as pewter; and that a cocoa-nut fhell was as convenient a goblet as a black-jack. And, therefore, he very wifely difpofed of as many of thefe articles of Englifh furniture for the kitchen and pantry, as he could find purchafers for, amongft the people of the fhips; receiving from them, in return, hatchets, and other iron tools, which had a more intrinfic value in this part of the world, and added more to his diftinguifhing fuperiority over thofe with whom he was to pafs the remainder of his days.

Tuefday 28.   In the long lift of the prefents beftowed upon him in England, fire-works had not been forgot. Some of thefe we exhibited, in the evening of the 28th, before a great concourfe of people, who beheld them with a mixture of pleafure and fear. What remained, after the evening's entertainment, were put in order, and left with Omai, agreeably to their original deftination. Perhaps we need not lament it as a ferious misfortune, that the far greater fhare of this part of his cargo, had been already expended in exhibitions at other iflands, or rendered ufelefs by being kept fo long.

Thurfday 30.   Between midnight and four in the morning of the 30th, the Bolabola man, whom I had in confinement, found means to make his efcape out of the fhip. He carried with him the fhackle of the bilboo-bolt that was about his leg, which was taken from him, as foon as he got on fhore, by one of the Chiefs, and given to Omai; who came on board, very early in the morning, to acquaint me that his mortal enemy was again let loofe upon him. Upon inquiry, it appeared, that not only the fentry placed over the prifoner, but the whole watch, upon the quarter deck where he was confined, had laid themfelves down to fleep. He feized the opportunity

nity to take the key of the irons out of the binnacle-drawer, where he had feen it put, and fet himfelf at liberty. This efcape convinced me, that my people had been very remifs in their night-duty; which made it neceffary to punifh thofe who were now in fault, and to eftablifh fome new regulations to prevent the like negligence for the future. I was not a little pleafed to hear, afterward, that the fellow who efcaped, had tranfported himfelf to Ulietea; in this, feconding my views of putting him a fecond time in irons.

As foon as Omai was fettled in his new habitation, I began to think of leaving the ifland; and got every thing off from the fhore, this evening, except the horfe and mare, and a goat big with kid; which were left in the poffeffion of our friend, with whom we were now finally to part. I alfo gave him a boar and two fows of the Englifh breed; and he had got a fow or two of his own. The horfe covered the mare while we were at Otaheite; fo that I confider the introduction of a breed of horfes into thefe iflands, as likely to have fucceeded, by this valuable prefent.

The hiftory of Omai will, perhaps, intereft a very numerous clafs of readers, more than any other occurrence of a voyage, the objects of which do not, in general, promife much entertainment. Every circumftance, therefore, which may ferve to convey a fatisfactory account of the exact fituation in which he was left, will be thought worth preferving; and the following particulars are added, to complete the view of his domeftic eftablifhment. He had picked up at Otaheite four or five *Toutous*; the two New Zealand youths remained with him; and his brother, and fome others, joined him at Huaheine: fo that his family confifted already of eight or ten perfons; if that can be called a family, to

which

which not a single female, as yet, belonged; nor, I doubt, was likely to belong, unless its master became less volatile. At present, Omai did not seem at all disposed to take unto himself a wife.

The house which we erected for him was twenty-four feet by eighteen; and ten feet high. It was composed of boards, the spoils of our military operations at Eimeo; and, in building it, as few nails, as possible, were used, that there might be no inducement, from the love of iron, to pull it down. It was settled, that immediately after our departure, he should begin to build a large house after the fashion of his country; one end of which was to be brought over that which we had erected, so as to inclose it entirely for greater security. In this work, some of the Chiefs promised to assist him; and, if the intended building should cover the ground which he marked out, it will be as large as most upon the island.

His European weapons consisted of a musquet, bayonet, and cartouch box; a fowling-piece; two pair of pistols; and two or three swords or cutlasses. The possession of these made him quite happy; which was my only view in giving him such presents. For I was always of opinion, that he would have been happier without fire-arms, and other European weapons, than with them; as such implements of war, in the hands of one, whose prudent use of them I had some grounds for mistrusting, would rather increase his dangers than establish his superiority. After he had got on shore every thing that belonged to him, and was settled in his house, he had most of the officers of both ships, two or three times, to dinner; and his table was always well supplied with the very best provisions that the island produced.

Before

Before I failed, I had the following infcription cut upon the outfide of his houfe:

Georgius Tertius, Rex, 2 *Novembris,* 1777.
Naves { *Refolution, Jac. Cook,* Pr.
{ *Difcovery, Car. Clerke,* Pr.

On the fecond of November, at four in the afternoon, I took the advantage of a breeze, which then fprung up at Eaft, and failed out of the harbour. Moft of our friends remained on board till the fhips were under fail; when, to gratify their curiofity, I ordered five guns to be fired. They then all took their leave, except Omai, who remained till we were at fea. We had come to fail by a hawfer faftened to the fhore. In cafting the fhip, it parted, being cut by the rocks, and the outer end was left behind, as thofe who caft it off did not perceive that it was broken; fo that it became neceffary to fend a boat to bring it on board. In this boat, Omai went afhore, after taking a very affectionate farewel of all the officers. He fuftained himfelf with a manly refolution, till he came to me. Then his utmoft efforts to conceal his tears failed; and Mr. King, who went in the boat, told me, that he wept all the time in going afhore.

It was no fmall fatisfaction to reflect, that we had brought him fafe back to the very fpot from which he was taken. And, yet, fuch is the ftrange nature of human affairs, that it is probable we left him in a lefs defirable fituation, than he was in before his connexion with us. I do not, by this, mean, that, becaufe he has tafted the fweets of civilized life, he muft become more miferable from being obliged to abandon all thoughts of continuing them. I confine myfelf to this single disagreeable circumstance, that the advantages he received from us, have placed him in a more hazardous situation, with respect to his personal safety. Omai, from being much caressed in England, lost sight of his original condition; and never considered in what manner his acquisitions, either of knowledge or of riches, would be estimated by his countrymen, at his return; which were the only things he could have to recommend him to them now, more than before, and on which he could build either his future greatness or happiness. He seemed even to have mistaken their genius in this respect; and, in some measure, to have forgotten their customs; otherwise he must have known the extreme difficulty there would be in getting himself admitted as a person of rank, where there is, perhaps, no instance of a man's being raised from an inferior station by the greatest merit. Rank seems to be the very foundation of all distinction here, and, of its attendant, power; and so pertinaciously, or rather blindly adhered to, that, unless a person has some degree of it, he will certainly be despised and hated, if he assumes the appearance of exercising any authority. This was really the case, in some measure, with Omai; though his countrymen were pretty cautious of expressing their sentiments while we remained amongst them. Had he made a proper use of the presents he brought with him from England, this, with the knowledge he had acquired by travelling so far, might have enabled him to form the most useful connections. But we have given too many instances, in the course of our narrative, of his childish inattention to this obvious means of advancing his interest. His schemes seemed to be of a higher, though ridiculous nature; indeed, I might say, meaner; for revenge, rather than a

I

desire

1777.
November.

desire of becoming great, appeared to actuate him from the beginning. This, however, may be excused, if we consider that it is common to his countrymen. His father was, doubtless, a man of considerable property in Ulietea, when that island was conquered by those of Bolabola; and, with many others, sought refuge in Huaheine, where he died, and left Omai, with some other children; who, by that means, became totally dependent. In this situation he was taken up by Captain Furneaux, and carried to England. Whether he really expected, from his treatment there, that any assistance would be given him against the enemies of his father and his country; or whether he imagined that his own personal courage, and superiority of knowledge, would be sufficient to dispossess the conquerors of Ulietea, is uncertain; but from the beginning of the voyage, this was his constant theme. He would not listen to our remonstrances on so wild a determination; but flew into a passion, if more moderate and reasonable counsels were proposed for his advantage. Nay, so infatuated and attached to his favourite scheme was he, that he affected to believe these people would certainly quit the conquered island, as soon as they should hear of his arrival in Otaheite. As we advanced, however, on our voyage, he became more sensible of his error; and, by the time we reached the Friendly Islands, had even such apprehensions of his reception at home, that, as I have mentioned in my journal, he would fain have staid behind at Tongataboo, under Feenou's protection. At these islands, he squandered away much of his European treasure very unnecessarily; and he was equally imprudent, as I also took notice of above, at Tiaraboo, where he could have no view of making friends, as he had not any intention of remaining there. At Matavai, he continued the same inconsiderate

fiderate behaviour, till I abfolutely put a ftop to his profu-
fion ; and he formed fuch improper connections there, that
Otoo, who was, at firft, much difpofed to countenance him,
afterward openly expreffed his diflike of him, on account of
his conduct. It was not, however, too late to recover his
favour; and he might have fettled, to great advantage, in
Otaheite, as he had formerly lived feveral years there, and
was now a good deal noticed by Towha, whofe valuable
prefent, of a very large double canoe, we have feen above.
The objection to admitting him to fome rank would have
alfo been much leffened, if he had fixed at Otaheite; as a
native will always find it more difficult to accomplifh fuch
a change of ftate amongft his countrymen, than a ftranger,
who naturally claims refpect. But Omai remained undetermined to the laft, and would not, I believe, have adopted
my plan of fettlement in Huaheine, if I had not fo explicitly refufed to employ force in reftoring him to his father's
poffeffions. Whether the remains of his European wealth,
which, after all his improvident wafte, was ftill confiderable, will be more prudently adminiftered by him, or whether the fteps I took, as already explained, to infure him
protection in Huaheine, fhall have proved effectual, muft be
left to the decifion of future navigators of this Ocean; with
whom it cannot but be a principal object of curiofity to trace
the future fortunes of our traveller. At prefent, I can only
conjecture, that his greateft danger will arife from the very
impolitic declarations of his antipathy to the inhabitants of
Bolabola. For thefe people, from a principle of jealoufy,
will, no doubt, endeavour to render him obnoxious to thofe
of Huaheine; as they are at peace with that ifland at prefent, and may eafily effect their defigns, many of them
living there. This is a circumftance, which, of all others,

he

he might, the moſt eaſily, have avoided. For they were not only free from any averſion to him, but the perſon, mentioned before, whom we found at Tiaraboo as an ambaſſador, prieſt, or God, abſolutely offered to reinſtate him in the property that was formerly his father's. But he refuſed this peremptorily; and, to the very laſt, continued determined to take the firſt opportunity that offered of ſatisfying his revenge in battle. To this, I gueſs, he is not a little ſpurred by the coat of mail he brought from England; clothed in which, and in poſſeſſion of ſome fire-arms, he fancies that he ſhall be invincible.

Whatever faults belonged to Omai's character, they were more than overbalanced by his great good-nature and docile diſpoſition. During the whole time he was with me, I very ſeldom had reaſon to·be ſeriouſly diſpleaſed with his general conduct. His grateful heart always retained the higheſt ſenſe of the favours he had received in England; nor will he ever forget thoſe who honoured him with their protection and friendſhip, during his ſtay there. He had a tolerable ſhare of underſtanding, but wanted application and perſeverance to exert it; ſo that his knowledge of things was very general, and, in many inſtances, imperfect. He was not a man of much obſervation. There were many uſeful arts, as well as elegant amuſements, amongſt the people of the Friendly Iſlands, which he might have conveyed to his own; where they probably would have been readily adopted, as being ſo much in their own way. But I never found that he uſed the leaſt endeavour to make himſelf maſter of any one. This kind of indifference is, indeed, the characteriſtic foible of his nation. Europeans have viſited them, at times, for theſe ten years paſt; yet we could not diſcover the ſlighteſt trace of any attempt to profit

profit by this intercourfe; nor have they hitherto copied after us in any one thing. We are not, therefore, to expect that Omai will be able to introduce many of our arts and cuftoms amongft them, or much improve thofe to which they have been long habituated. I am confident, however, that he will endeavour to bring to perfection the various fruits and vegetables we planted, which will be no fmall acquifition. But the greateft benefit thefe iflands are likely to receive from Omai's travels, will be in the animals that have been left upon them; which, probably, they never would have got, had he not come to England. When thefe multiply, of which I think there is little doubt, Otaheite, and the Society Iflands, will equal, if not exceed, any place in the known world, for provifions.

Omai's return, and the fubftantial proofs he brought back with him of our liberality, encouraged many to offer them- felves as volunteers to attend me to *Pretane*. I took every opportunity of expreffing my determination to reject all fuch applications. But, notwithftanding this, Omai, who was very ambitious of remaining the only great traveller, being afraid left I might be prevailed upon to put others in a fituation of rivalling him, frequently put me in mind, that Lord Sandwich had told him, no others of his country- men were to come to England.

If there had been the moft diftant probability of any fhip being again fent to New Zealand, I would have brought the two youths of that country home with me; as both of them were very defirous of continuing with us. Tiarooa, the eldeft, was an exceedingly well difpofed young man, with ftrong natural fenfe, and capable of receiving any in- ftruction. He feemed to be fully fenfible of the inferiority of his own country to thefe iflands, and refigned himfelf,

though

though perhaps with reluctance, to end his days, in eafe and plenty, in Huaheine. But the other was fo ftrongly attached to us, that he was taken out of the fhip, and carried afhore by force. He was a witty, fmart boy ; and, on that account, much noticed on board.

CHAP.

CHAP. VII.

Arrival at Ulietea.—Aſtronomical Obſervations.—A Marine
deſerts, and is delivered up.—Intelligence from Omai.—In-
ſtructions to Captain Clerke.—Another Deſertion of a Mid-
ſhipman and a Seaman.—Three of the chief Perſons of the
Iſland confined on that Account.—A Deſign to ſeize Cap-
tains Cook and Clerke, diſcovered.—The two Deſerters
brought back, and the Priſoners releaſed.—The Ships ſail.
—Refreſhments received at Ulietea.—Preſent and former
State of that Iſland.—Account of its dethroned King, and
of the late Regent of Huaheine.

1777.
November.

THE boat which carried Omai aſhore, never to join
us again, having returned to the ſhip, with the remainder of the hawſer, we hoiſted her in, and immediately ſtood over for Ulietea, where I intended to touch
next. At ten o'clock at night, we brought to, till four the
next morning, when we made ſail round the South end of
the iſland, for the harbour of Ohamaneno *. We met
with calms and light airs of wind, from different directions, by turns; ſo that, at noon, we were ſtill a league
from the entrance of the harbour. While we were thus
detained, my old friend Oreo, Chief of the iſland, with
his ſon, and Pootoe, his ſon-in-law, came off to viſit us.

* See a plan of this harbour, in Hawkeſworth's Collection, Vol. ii. p. 248.

Being

Being refolved to pufh for the harbour, I ordered all the boats to be hoifted out, and fent them a-head to tow, being affifted by a flight breeze from the Southward. This breeze failed too foon, and being fucceeded by one from the Eaft, which blew right out of the harbour, we were obliged to come to an anchor, at its entrance, at two o'clock, and to warp in, which employed us till night fet in. As foon as we were within the harbour, the fhips were furrounded with canoes filled with people, who brought hogs and fruit to barter with us for our commodities; fo that, wherever we went, we found plenty.

Next morning, being the 4th, I moored the fhip, head and ftern, clofe to the North fhore, at the head of the harbour; hauled up the cables on deck; and opened one of the ballaft-ports. From this a flight ftage was made to the land, being at the diftance of about twenty feet, with a view to get clear of fome of the rats that continued to infeft us. The Difcovery moored along-fide the South fhore for the fame purpofe. While this work was going forward, I returned Oreo's vifit. The prefent I made him, on the occafion, confifted of a linen gown, a fhirt, a red-feathered cap from Tongataboo, and other things of lefs value. I then brought him, and fome of his friends, on board to dinner.

On the 6th, we fet up the obfervatories, and got the neceffary inftruments on fhore. The two following days, we obferved the fun's azimuths, both on board and afhore, with all the compaffes, in order to find the variation; and in the night of the latter, obferved an occultation of ϛ *Capricorni*, by the moon's dark limb. Mr. Bayly and I agreed in fixing the time of its happening, at fix minutes and fifty-four feconds and a half, paft ten o'clock. Mr.

VOL. II.   Q   King

King made it half a fecond fooner. Mr. Bayly obferved with the achromatic telefcope belonging to the Board of Longitude; Mr. King, with the reflector belonging alfo to the Board; and I made ufe of my own reflector, of eighteen inches. There was alfo an immerfion of π *Capricorni* behind the moon's dark limb, fome time before; but it was obferved by Mr. Bayly alone. I attempted to trace it, with a fmall achromatic; but found its magnifying power not fufficient.

Nothing worthy of note happened, till the night between the 12th and 13th, when John Harrifon, a marine, who was fentinel at the obfervatory, deferted; carrying with him his mufquet and accoutrements. Having in the morning got intelligence which way he had moved off, a party was fent after him; but they returned in the evening, after an inef-
fectual inquiry and fearch. The next day, I applied to the Chief to intereft himfelf in this matter. He promifed to fend a party of his men after him, and gave me hopes that he fhould be brought back the fame day. But this did not happen; and I had reafon to fufpect, that no fteps had been taken by him. We had, at this time, a great number of the natives about the fhips, and fome thefts were committed; the confequence of which being dreaded by them, very few
vifiters came near us the next morning. The Chief himfelf joined in the alarm, and he and his whole family fled. I thought this a good opportunity to oblige them to deliver up the deferter; and having got intelligence that he was at a place called Hamoa, on the other fide of the ifland, I went thither with two armed boats, accompanied by one of the natives; and, in our way, we found the Chief, who alfo embarked with me. I landed about a mile and a half from the place, with a few people, and marched brifkly up to it,

I   left

left the fight of the boats fhould give the alarm, and allow the man time to efcape to the mountains. But this precaution was unneceffary; for the natives there had got information of my coming, and were prepared to deliver him up.

I found Harrifon, with the mufquet lying before him, fitting between two women, who, the moment that I entered the houfe, rofe up to plead in his behalf. As it was highly proper to difcourage fuch proceedings, I frowned upon them, and bid them begone. Upon this they burft into tears, and walked off. Paha, the Chief of the diftrict, now came with a plantain tree, and a fucking pig, which he would have prefented to me, as a peace-offering. I rejected it, and ordered him out of my fight; and having embarked, with the deferter, on board the firft boat that arrived, returned to the fhips. After this, harmony was again reftored. The fellow had nothing to fay in his defence, but that the natives had enticed him away; and this might in part be true, as it was certain, that Paha, and alfo the two women above-mentioned, had been at the fhip the day before he deferted. As it appeared, that he had remained upon his poft, till within a few minutes of the time when he was to have been relieved, the punifhment that I inflicted upon him was not very fevere.

Though we had feparated from Omai, we were ftill near enough to have intelligence of his proceedings; and I had defired to hear from him. Accordingly, about a fortnight after our arrival at Ulietea, he fent two of his people in a canoe; who brought me the fatisfactory intelligence, that he remained undifturbed by the people of the ifland, and that every thing went well with him, except that his goat had died in kidding. He accompanied this

Q 2   intelligence,

intelligence, with a requeſt, that I would ſend him another goat, and two axes. Being happy to have this additional opportunity of ſerving him, the meſſengers were
ſent back to Huaheine, on the 18th, with the axes, and
two kids, male and female, which were ſpared for him out
of the Diſcovery.

The next day, I delivered to Captain Clerke inſtructions
how to proceed, in caſe of being ſeparated from me, after
leaving theſe iſlands; and it may not be improper to give
them a place here.

*By Captain James Cook, Commander of his Majeſty's
Sloop the Reſolution.*

" WHEREAS the paſſage from the Society Iſlands, to
the Northern coaſt of America, is of conſiderable length,
both in diſtance and in time, and as a part of it muſt be
performed in the very depth of winter, when gales of wind
and bad weather muſt be expected, and may, poſſibly, occaſion a ſeparation, you are to take all imaginable care to
prevent this. But if, notwithſtanding all our endeavours
to keep company, you ſhould be ſeparated from me, you
are firſt to look for me where you laſt ſaw me. Not ſeeing
me in five days, you are to proceed (as directed by the inſtructions of their Lordſhips, a copy of which you have
already received) for the coaſt of New Albion; endeavouring to fall in with it in the latitude of 45°.

In that latitude, and at a convenient diſtance from the
land, you are to cruize for me ten days. Not ſeeing me in
that time, you are to put into the firſt convenient port, in
or to the North of that latitude, to recruit your wood and
water, and to procure refreſhments.

During

During your ſtay in port, you are conſtantly to keep a good look-out for me. It will be neceſſary, therefore, to make choice of a ſtation, ſituated as near the ſea-coaſt as is poſſible, the better to enable you to ſee me, when I ſhall appear in the offing.

If I do not join you before the 1ſt of next April, you are to put to ſea, and proceed Northward to the latitude 56°; in which latitude, and at a convenient diſtance from the coaſt, never exceeding fifteen leagues, you are to cruize for me till the 10th of May.

Not ſeeing me in that time, you are to proceed North-ward, and endeavour to find a paſſage into the Atlantic Ocean, through Hudſon's or Baffin's Bays, as directed by the above-mentioned inſtructions.

But if you ſhould fail in finding a paſſage through either of the ſaid bays, or by any other way, as the ſeaſon of the year may render it unſafe for you to remain in high lati-tudes, you are to repair to the harbour of St. Peter and St. Paul, in Kamtſchatka, in order to refreſh your people, and to paſs the winter.

But, neverthelefs, if you find, that you cannot procure the neceſſary refreſhments at the ſaid port, you are at li-berty to go where you ſhall judge moſt proper; taking care, before you depart, to leave with the Governor an account of your intended deſtination, to be delivered to me upon my arrival: And in the ſpring of the enſuing year, 1779, you are to repair back to the above-mentioned port, endeavouring to be there by the 10th of May, or ſooner.

If, on your arrival, you receive no orders from, or ac-count of me, ſo as to juſtify your purſuing any other mea-ſures than what are pointed out in the before-mentioned
inſtructions,

inftruc̈tions, your future proceedings are to be governed by them.

You are alfo to comply with fuch parts of faid inftruc̈tions, as have not been executed, and are not contrary to thefe orders.   And in cafe of your inability, by ficknefs or otherwife, to carry thefe, and the inftruc̈tions of their Lordfhips, into execution, you are to be careful to leave them with the next officer in command, who is hereby required to execute them in the beft manner he can.

Given under my hand, on board the Refolution, at Ulietea, the 18th Day of November 1777.

J. COOK."

" *To Captain Charles Clerke, Commander of his Majefty's Sloop, the Difcovery.*"

While we lay moored to the fhore, we heeled, and fcrubbed both fides of the bottoms of the fhips.   At the fame time, we fixed fome tin-plates under the binds; firft taking off the old fheathing, and putting in a piece unfilled, over which the plates were nailed.   Thefe plates I had from the ingenious Mr. Pelham, Secretary to the Commiffioners for Vic̈tualling his Majefty's Navy; with a view of trying whether tin would anfwer the fame end as copper, oh the bottoms of fhips.

Monday 24.   On the 24th in the morning, I was informed that a midfhipman, and a feaman, both belonging to the Difcovery, were miffing.   Soon after, we learnt from the natives, that they went away in a canoe the preceding evening, and were, at this time, at the other end of the ifland.   As the midfhipman was known to have expreffed a defire to remain at thefe iflands, it feemed pretty certain, that he and his

companion

companion had gone off with this intention; and Captain Clerke set out in quest of them with two armed boats, and a party of marines. His expedition proved fruitless; for he returned in the evening, without having got any certain intelligence where they were. From the conduct of the natives, Captain Clerke seemed to think, that they intended to conceal the deserters; and, with that view, had amused him with false information the whole day, and directed him to search for them in places where they were not to be found. The Captain judged right; for, the next morning, we were told, that our runaways were at Otaha. As these two were not the only persons in the ships who wished to end their days at these favourite islands, in order to put a stop to any further desertion, it was necessary to get them back at all events; and, that the natives might be convinced that I was in earnest, I resolved to go after them myself; having observed, from repeated instances, that they seldom offered to deceive me with false information.

Accordingly, I set out, the next morning, with two armed boats; being accompanied by the Chief himself. I proceeded, as he directed, without stopping any where, till we came to the middle of the East side of Otaha. There we put ashore; and Oreo dispatched a man before us, with orders to seize the deserters, and keep them till we should arrive with the boats. But when we got to the place where we expected to find them, we were told, that they had quitted this island, and gone over to Bolabola the day before. I did not think proper to follow them thither; but returned to the ships; fully determined, however, to have recourse to a measure, which, I guessed, would oblige the natives to bring them back.

In

In the night, Mr. Bayly, Mr. King, and myfelf, obferved an immerfion of Jupiter's third fatellite. It happened, by the obfervation of

Mr. Bayly, at 2ʰ 37ᵐ 54ˢ ⎫
Mr. King, at 2 37 24 ⎬ in the morning.
Myfelf, at 2 37 44 ⎭

Mr. Bayly and Mr. King obferved, with Dollond's three and a half feet achromatic telefcope, and with the greateft magnifying power. I obferved, with a two-feet Gregorian reflector, made by Bird.

Soon after day-break, the Chief, his fon, daughter, and fon-in-law, came on board the Refolution. The three laft I refolved to detain, till the two deferters fhould be brought back. With this view, Captain Clerke invited them to go on board his fhip; and as foon as they arrived there, confined them in his cabin. The Chief was with me when the news reached him. He immediately acquainted me with it, fuppofing that this ftep had been taken without my knowledge, and confequently without my approbation. I inftantly undeceived him; and then he began to have apprehenfions as to his own fituation, and his looks expreffed the utmoft perturbation of mind. But I foon made him eafy as to this, by telling him, that he was at liberty to leave the fhip whenever he pleafed, and to take fuch meafures as he fhould judge beft calculated to get our two men back; that, if he fucceeded, his friends on board the Difcovery fhould be delivered up; if not, that I was determined to carry them away with me. I added, that his own conduct, as well as that of many of his people, in not only affifting thefe two men to efcape, but in being, even at this very time, affi-

duous

duous in enticing others to follow them, would juftify any
ftep I could take to put a ftop to fuch proceedings.

This explanation of the motives upon which I acted, and which we found means to make Oreo and his people, who were prefent, fully comprehend, feemed to recover them, in a great meafure, from that general confternation into which they were at firft thrown. But, if relieved from apprehenfions about their own fafety, they continued under the deepeft concern for thofe who were prifoners. Many of them went under the Difcovery's ftern in canoes, to bewail their captivity, which they did with long and loud exclamations. *Poedooa!* for fo the Chief's daughter was called, refounded from every quarter; and the women feemed to vie with each other in mourning her fate, with more fignificant expreffions of their grief than tears and cries; for there were many bloody heads upon the occafion.

Oreo himfelf did not give way to unavailing lamentations, but, inftantly, began his exertions to recover our deferters, by difpatching a canoe to Bolabola, with a meffage to Opoony, the fovereign of that ifland, acquainting him with what had happened, and requefting him to feize the two fugitives, and fend them back. The meffenger, who was no lefs a man than the father of Pootoe, Oreo's fon-in-law, before he fet out, came to receive my commands. I ftrictly enjoined him not to return without the deferters; and to tell Opoony, from me, that, if they had left Bolabola, he muft fend canoes to bring them back; for I fufpected that they would not long remain in one place.

The confequence, however, of the prifoners was fo great, that the natives did not think proper to truft to the return of our people for their releafe; or, at leaft, their impatience was fo great, that it hurried them to meditate an attempt which might have involved them in ftill greater diftrefs, had it not been fortunately prevented. Between five and fix o'clock in the evening, I obferved that all their canoes, in and about the harbour, began to move off, as if fome fudden panic had feized them. I was afhore, abreaft of the fhip, at the time, and inquired, in vain, to find out the caufe; till our people called to us from the Difcovery, and told us, that a party of the natives had feized Captain Clerke and Mr. Gore, who had walked out a little way from the fhips. Struck with the boldnefs of this plan of retaliation, which feemed to counteraft me fo effeftually in my own way, there was no time to deliberate. I inftantly ordered the people to arm; and, in lefs than five minutes, a ftrong party, under the command of Mr. King, was fent to refcue our two gentlemen. At the fame time, two armed boats, and a party under Mr. Williamfon, went after the flying canoes, to cut off their retreat to the fhore. Thefe feveral detachments were hardly out of fight, before an account arrived that we had been mifinformed; upon which I fent, and called them all in.

It was evident, however, from feveral corroborating circumftances, that the defign of feizing Captain Clerke had really been in agitation amongft the natives. Nay, they made no fecret in fpeaking of it the next day. But their firft and great plan of operations was to have laid hold of me. It was my cuftom, every evening, to bathe in the frefh water. Very often I went alone; and always without arms. Expefting me to go, as ufual, this evening, they had determined to feize me, and Captain Clerke too, if he had accompanied me. But I had, after confining Oreo's family,

3

thought

thought it prudent to avoid putting myself in their power; and had cautioned Captain Clerke, and the officers, not to go far from the ships. In the courfe of the afternoon, the Chief afked me, three feveral times, if I would not go to the bathing-place; and when he found, at laft, that I could not be prevailed upon, he went off, with the reft of his people, in fpite of all that I could do or fay to ftop him. But as I had no fufpicion, at this time, of their defign, I imagined that fome fudden fright had feized them, which would, as ufual, foon be over. Finding themfelves difappointed as to me, they fixed on thofe who were more in their power. It was fortunate, for all parties, that they did not fucceed; and not lefs fortunate, that no mifchief was done on the occafion. For not a mufquet was fired, except two or three, to ftop the canoes. To that firing, perhaps, Meffrs. Clerke and Gore owed their fafety *; for, at that very inftant, a party of the natives, armed with clubs, were advancing toward them; and on hearing the report of the mufquets, they difperfed.

This confpiracy, as it may be called, was firft difcovered by a girl, whom one of the officers had brought from Huaheine. She, overhearing fome of the Ulieteans fay, that they would feize Captain Clerke and Mr. Gore, ran to acquaint the firft of our people that fhe met with. Thofe who were charged with the execution of the defign threatened to kill her as foon as we fhould leave the ifland, for difappointing them. Being aware of this, we contrived that her friends fhould come, fome days after, and

* Perhaps they owed their fafety, principally, to Captain Clerke's walking with a piftol in his hand, which he once fired. This circumftance is omitted both in Captain Cook's and in Mr. Anderfon's journal; but it is here mentioned on the authority of Captain King.

take

take her out of the fhip, to convey her to a place of fafety, where fhe might lie concealed, till they fhould have an opportunity of fending her back to Huaheine.

Thurfday 27.   On the 27th, our obfervatories were taken down, and every thing we had afhore carried on board; the moorings of the fhips were caft off; and we tranfported them a little way down the harbour, where they came to an anchor again. Toward the afternoon, the natives began to fhake off their fears, gathering round, and on board, the fhips, as ufual; and the awkward tranfaction of the day before feemed to be forgotten on both fides.

Friday 28.   The following night the wind blew in hard fqualls from South to Eaft, attended with heavy fhowers of rain. In one of the fqualls, the cable, by which the Refolution was riding, parted, juft without the hawfe. We had another anchor ready to let go; fo that the fhip was, prefently, brought up again. In the afternoon the wind became moderate; and we hooked the end of the beft fmall bower cable, and got it again into the hawfe.

Oreo, the Chief, being uneafy, as well as myfelf, that no account had been received from Bolabola, fet out, this evening, for that ifland, and defired me to follow down, the next day, with the fhips. This was my intention; but the wind would not admit of our getting to fea. But the fame wind which kept us in the harbour, brought Oreo back from Bolabola, with the two deferters. They had reached Otaha the fame night they deferted; but, finding it impoffible to get to any of the iflands to the Eaft-ward (which was their intention), for want of wind, they had proceeded to Bolabola, and from thence to the fmall ifland Toobaee, where they were taken by the father of Pootoe, in confequence of the firft meffage fent to Opoony.

As

As foon as they were on board, the three prifoners were re-
leafed. Thus ended an affair, which had given me much
trouble and vexation. Nor would I have exerted myfelf fo
refolutely on the occafion, but for the reafon before mentioned, and to fave the fon of a brother officer from being
loft to his country.

The wind continued conftantly between the North and
Weft, and confined us in the harbour, till eight o'clock in
the morning of the 7th of December; when we took the
advantage of a light breeze which then fprung up at North
Eaft, and, with the affiftance of all the boats, got out to fea
with the Difcovery in company.

During the laft week, we had been vifited by people from
all parts of the ifland, who furnifhed us with a large ftock
of hogs and green plantains. So that the time we lay wind-
bound in the harbour was not entirely loft; green plantains
being an excellent fubftitute for bread, as they will keep
good a fortnight, or three weeks. Befides this fupply of
provifions, we alfo completed our wood and water.

The inhabitants of Ulietea feemed, in general, fmaller
and blacker than thofe of the other neighbouring iflands;
and appeared alfo lefs orderly, which, perhaps, may be confidered as the confequence of their having become fubject
to the natives of Bolabola. Oreo, their Chief, is only a fort
of deputy of the fovereign of that ifland; and the conqueft
feems to have leffened the number of fubordinate Chiefs
refident among them; fo that they are lefs immediately
under the infpection of thofe whofe intereft it is to enforce
due obedience to authority. Ulietea, though now reduced
to this humiliating ftate, was formerly, as we were told,
the moft eminent of this clufter of iflands; and, probably,
the firft feat of government; for they fay, that the prefent

royal

royal family of Otaheite is defcended from that which
reigned here, before the late revolution. Ooroo, the dethroned monarch of Ulietea, was ftill alive, when we were
at Huaheine, where he refides, a royal wanderer, furnifhing, in his perfon, an inftance of the inftability of power;
but, what is more remarkable, of the refpect paid by thefe
people to particular families, and to the cuftoms which have
once conferred fovereignty; for they fuffer Ooroo to preferve all the enfigns which they appropriate to majefty,
though he has loft his dominions.

We faw a fimilar inftance of this while we were at Ulietea.
One of the occafional vifiters I now had, was my old friend
Oree, the late Chief of Huaheine. He ftill preferved his
confequence; came always at the head of a numerous body
of attendants; and was always provided with fuch prefents
as were very acceptable. This Chief looked much better
now than I had ever feen him, during either of my former
voyages *. I could account for his improving in health as
he grew older, only from his drinking lefs copioufly of the
awa in his prefent ftation as a private gentleman, than he
had been accuftomed to do when he was regent.

---

* Captain Cook had feen Oree in 1769, when he commanded the Endeavour; alfo,
twice, during his fecond voyage, in 1772.

CHAP.

C H A P. VIII.

Arrival at Bolabola.—Interview with Opoony.—Reasons for purchasing Monsieur de Bougainville's Anchor.—Departure from the Society Islands.—Particulars about Bolabola.— History of the Conquest of Otaha and Ulietea.—High Reputation of the Bolabola Men.—Animals left there, and at Ulietea.—Plentiful Supply of Provisions, and Manner of salting Pork on board.—Various Reflections relative to Otaheite, and the Society Islands.—Astronomical and nautical Observations made there.

A S soon as we had got clear of the harbour, we took our leave of Ulietea, and steered for Bolabola. The chief if not sole object I had in view, by visiting that island, was, to procure from its monarch, Opoony, one of the anchors which Monsieur de Bougainville had lost at Otaheite. This having afterward been taken up by the natives there, had, as they informed me, been sent by them as a present to that Chief. My desire to get possession of it did not arise from our being in want of anchors. But having expended all the hatchets, and other iron tools, which we had brought from England, in purchasing refreshments, we were now reduced to the necessity of creating a fresh assortment of trading articles, by fabricating them out of the spare iron we had on board; and, in such conversions, and in the occasional

1777.
December.

cafional ufes of the fhips, great part of that had been already expended. I thought that Mr. de Bougainville's anchor would fupply our want of this ufeful material; and I made no doubt that I fhould be able to tempt Opoony to part with it.

Oreo, and fix or eight men more from Ulietea, took a paffage with us to Bolabola. Indeed, moft of the natives in general, except the Chief himfelf, would have gladly taken a paffage with us to England. At funfet, being the length of the South point of Bolabola, we fhortened fail, and fpent the night making fhort boards. At day-break,

on the 8th, we made fail for the harbour, which is on the Weft fide of the ifland. The wind was fcant, fo that we had to ply up, and it was nine o'clock before we got near enough to fend away a boat to found the entrance. For I had thoughts of running the fhips in, and anchoring for a day or two.

When the boat returned, the Mafter, who was in her, reported, that though at the entrance of the harbour the bottom was rocky, there was good ground within, and the depth of water twenty-feven and twenty-five fathoms; and that there was room to turn the fhips in, the channel being one third of a mile broad. In confequence of this report, we attempted to work the fhips in. But the tide, as well as the wind, being againft us, after making two or three trips, I found that it could not be done, till the tide fhould turn in our favour. Upon this, I gave up the defign of carrying the fhips into the harbour; and having ordered the boats to be got ready, I embarked in one of them, accompanied by Oreo and his companions; and was rowed in for the ifland.

We landed where the natives directed us; and, foon after,
I was

I was introduced to Opoony, in the midſt of a great con-
courſe of people. Having no time to loſe, as ſoon as the
neceſſary formality of compliments was over, I aſked the
Chief to give me the anchor, and produced the preſent I
had prepared for him, conſiſting of a linen night-gown, a
ſhirt, ſome gauze handkerchiefs, a looking-glaſs, ſome
beads, and other toys; and ſix axes. At the ſight of theſe
laſt, there was a general outcry. I could only gueſs the
cauſe, by Opoony's abſolutely refuſing to receive my preſent till I ſhould get the anchor. He ordered three men to
go and deliver it to me; and, as I underſtood, I was to ſend,
by them, what I thought proper in return. With theſe
meſſengers, we ſet out in our boats for an iſland, lying at
the North ſide of the entrance into the harbour, where the
anchor had been depoſited. I found it to be neither ſo large,
nor ſo perfect, as I expected. It had originally weighed ſeven hundred pounds, according to the mark that was upon
it; but the ring, with part of the ſhank, and the two palms,
were now wanting. I was no longer at a loſs to gueſs the
reaſon of Opoony's refuſing my preſent. He, doubtleſs,
thought that it ſo much exceeded the value of the anchor in
its preſent ſtate, that I ſhould be diſpleaſed when I ſaw it.
Be this as it may, I took the anchor as I found it, and ſent
him every article of the preſent that I at firſt intended.
Having thus completed my negociation, I returned on
board; and having hoiſted in the boats, made ſail from the
iſland to the North.

While the boats were hoiſting in, ſome of the natives
came off, in three or four canoes, to ſee the ſhips, as they
ſaid. They brought with them a few cocoa-nuts, and one
pig, which was the only one we got at the iſland. I make
no doubt, however, that, if we had ſtayed till the next day,

VOL. II.   S   we

we fhould have been plentifully fupplied with provifions;
and, I think, the natives would feel themfelves difappointed, when they found that we were gone. But, as we had
already a very good ftock both of hogs and of fruit on board,
and very little of any thing left to purchafe more, I could
have no inducement to defer, any longer, the profecution
of our voyage.

The harbour of Bolabola, called Oteavanooa, fituated on
the Weft fide of the ifland, is one of the moft capacious that
I ever met with; and though we did not enter it, it was a
fatisfaction to me, that I had an opportunity of employing
my people to afcertain its being a very proper place for the
reception of fhips *.

The high double-peaked mountain, which is in the
middle of the ifland, appeared to be barren on the Eaft
fide; but, on the Weft fide, has trees or bufhes on its moft
craggy parts. The lower grounds, all round, toward the
fea, are covered with cocoa-palms and bread-fruit trees, like
the other iflands of this ocean; and the many little iflots
that furround it on the infide of the reef, add both to the
amount of its vegetable productions, and to the number of
its inhabitants.

But, ftill, when we confider its very fmall extent, being
not more than eight leagues in compafs, it is rather remarkable, that its people fhould have attempted, or have
been able to atchieve the conqueft of Ulietea and Otaha, the
former of which iflands is, of itfelf, at leaft double its fize.
In each of my three voyages, we had heard much of the
war that produced this great revolution. The refult of our

* See a chart of the ifland of Bolabola, in *Hawkefworth's Collection*, Vol. ii. p. 249.
Though we have no particular drawing of the harbour, its fituation is there diftinctly reprefented.

inquiries,

inquiries, as to the circumftances attending it, may amufe the reader; and I give it as a fpecimen of the hiftory of our friends, in this part of the world, as related to us * by themfelves.

Ulietea and Otaha, which adjoins it, lived long in friend-fhip, or, as the natives exprefs it, were confidered as two brothers, infeparable by any interefted views. They alfo admitted the ifland of Huaheine as their friend, though not fo intimate. Otaha, however, like a traitor, leagued with Bolabola, and they refolved jointly to attack Ulietea; whofe people called in their friends of Huaheine, to affift them againft thefe two powers. The men of Bolabola were en-couraged by a prieftefs, or rather prophetefs, who foretold, that they fhould be fuccefsful; and, as a proof of the cer-tainty of her prediction, fhe defired, that a man might be fent to the fea, at a particular place, where, from a great depth, a ftone would afcend. He went, accordingly, in a ca-noe to the place mentioned; and was going to dive to fee where this ftone lay, when, behold, it ftarted up to the fur-face fpontaneoufly into his hand! The people were afto-nifhed at the fight: the ftone was depofited as facred in the houfe of the *Eatooa*; and is ftill preferved at Bolabola, as a proof of this woman's influence with the divinity. Their fpirits being thus elevated with the hopes of victory, the canoes of Bolabola fet out to engage thofe of Ulietea and Huaheine, which being ftrongly faftened together with ropes, the encounter lafted long, and would probably, not-withftanding the prediction and the miracle, have ended in the overthrow of the Bolabola fleet, if that of Otaha had not, in the critical moment, arrived. This turned the fortune

* For this, as for many other particulars about thefe people, we are indebted to Mr. Anderfon.

of

of the day, and their enemies were defeated with great
flaughter. The men of Bolabola, profecuting their victory,
invaded Huaheine two days after, which they knew muft be
weakly defended, as moft of its warriors were abfent. Accordingly, they made themfelves mafters of that ifland.
But many of its fugitives having got to Otaheite, there told
their lamentable ftory; which fo grieved thofe of their
countrymen, and of Ulietea, whom they met with in that
ifland, that they obtained fome affiftance from them. They
were equipped with only ten fighting canoes ; but, though
their force was fo inconfiderable, they conducted the expedition with fo much prudence, that they landed at Huaheine at night, when dark, and falling upon the Bolabola
men by furprize, killed many of them, forcing the reft to
fly. So that, by this means, they got poffeffion of their
ifland again, which now remains independent, under the
government of its own Chiefs. Immediately after the de-
feat of the united fleets of Ulietea and Huaheine, a propofal
was made to the Bolabola men by their allies of Otaha, to
be admitted to an equal fhare of the conquefts. The refufal
of this broke the alliance ; and in the courfe of the war,
Otaha itfelf, as well as Ulietea, was conquered; and both
now remain fubject to Bolabola; the Chiefs who govern
them, being only deputies of Opoony, the fovereign of that
ifland. In the reduction of the two iflands, five battles were
fought, at different places, in which great numbers were
flain on both fides.

Such was the account we received. I have more than
once remarked, how very imperfectly thefe people recollect
the exact dates of paft events. And with regard to this war,
though it happened not many years ago, we could only
guefs at the time of its commencement and its conclufion,

from

1777.
December.

from collateral circumftances, furnifhed by our own obfervation, as the natives could not fatisfy our inquiries with any precifion. The final conqueft of Ulietea, which clofed the war, we know, had been made before I was there in the Endeavour, in 1769; but we may infer, that peace had not been very long reftored, as we could then fee marks of recent hoftilities * having been committed upon that ifland. Some additional light may be thrown upon this inquiry, by attending to the age of Teereetareea, the prefent Chief of Huaheine. His looks fhewed, that he was not above ten or twelve years old; and we were informed, that his father had been killed in one of the battles. As to the time when the war began, we had no better rule for judging, than this, that the young people of about twenty years of age, of whom we made inquiries, could fcarcely remember the firft battles; and I have already mentioned, that Omai's countrymen, whom we found at Wateeoo, knew nothing of this war; fo that its commencement was fubfequent to their voyage.

Ever fince the conqueft of Ulietea and Otaha, the Bolabola men have been confidered, by their neighbours, as invincible; and fuch is the extent of their fame, that even at Otaheite, which is almoft out of their reach, if they are not dreaded, they are, at leaft, refpected for their valour. It is faid, that they never fly in battle, and that they always beat an equal number of the other iflanders. But, befides thefe advantages, their neighbours feem to afcribe a great deal to the fuperiority of their god, who, they believed, detained us at Ulietea by contrary winds, as being unwilling that we fhould vifit an ifland under his fpecial protection.

---

* Thefe are taken notice of in *Hawkefworth's Collection*, Vol. ii. p. 256, &c.

How

How high the Bolabola men are now in eſtimation at Otaheite, may be inferred from Monſieur de Bougainville's anchor having been conveyed to them. To the ſame cauſe we
muſt aſcribe the intention of tranſporting to their iſland the
Spaniſh bull. And they had already got poſſeſſion of a third
European curioſity, the male of another animal, brought
to Otaheite by the Spaniards. We had been much puzzled,
by the imperfect deſcription of the natives, to gueſs what
this could be. But Captain Clerke's deſerters, when brought
back from Bolabola, told me, that the animal had been
there ſhewn to them, and that it was a ram. It ſeldom happens, but that ſome good ariſes out of evil; and if our two
men had not deſerted, I ſhould not have known this. In
conſequence of their information, at the ſame time that I
landed to meet Opoony, I carried aſhore a ewe, which we
had brought from the Cape of Good Hope; and I hope that,
by this preſent, I have laid the foundation for a breed of
ſheep at Bolabola. I alſo left at Ulietea, under the care of
Oreo, an Engliſh boar and ſow, and two goats. So that, not
only Otaheite, but all the neighbouring iſlands, will, in a
few years, have their race of hogs conſiderably improved;
and, probably, be ſtocked with all the valuable animals
which have been tranſported hither by their European
viſiters.

When once this comes to paſs, no part of the world will
equal theſe iſlands in variety and abundance of refreſhments for navigators. Indeed, even in their preſent ſtate, I
know no place that excels them. After repeated trials, in
the courſe of ſeveral voyages, we find, when they are not
diſturbed by inteſtine broils, but live in amity with one
another, which has been the caſe for ſome years paſt;
that their productions are in the greateſt plenty; and,
                                        particularly,

particularly, the moſt valuable of all the articles, their hogs.

If we had had a larger aſſortment of goods, and a ſuffi-cient quantity of ſalt on board, I make no doubt that we might have ſalted as much pork as would have ſerved both ſhips near twelve months. But our viſiting the Friendly Iſlands, and our long ſtay at Otaheite and the neighbour-hood, quite exhauſted our trading commodities; particu-larly our axes, with which alone hogs, in general, were to be purchaſed. And we had hardly ſalt enough to cure fif-teen puncheons of meat. Of theſe, five were added to our ſtock of proviſions, at the Friendly Iſlands, and the other ten at Otaheite. Captain Clerke alſo ſalted a proportionable quantity for his ſhip.

The proceſs was the ſame that had been adopted by me in my laſt voyage; and it may be worth while to deſcribe it again. The hogs were killed in the evening; as ſoon as they were cleaned, they were cut up, the bone taken out, and the meat ſalted when it was hot. It was then laid in ſuch a poſition as to permit the juices to drain from it, till the next morning, when it was again ſalted, packed into a caſk, and covered with pickle. Here it remained for four or five days, or a week; after which it was taken out and examined, piece by piece, and if there was any found to be in the leaſt tainted, as ſometimes happened, it was ſeparated from the reſt, which was repacked into another caſk, headed up, and filled with good pickle. In about eight or ten days time, it underwent a ſecond examination; but this ſeemed unneceſſary, as the whole was generally found to be per-fectly cured. A mixture of bay and of white ſalt anſwers the beſt; but either of them will do alone. Great care ſhould be taken, that none of the large blood-veſſels remain

I

in

in the meat; nor muſt too great a quantity be packed together at the firſt ſalting, left the pieces in the middle ſhould
heat, and, by that means, prevent the ſalt from penetrating
them, This once happened to us, when we killed a larger
quantity than uſual. Rainy, ſultry weather, is unfavourable for ſalting meat in tropical climates.

Perhaps, the frequent viſits Europeans have lately made
to theſe iſlanders, may be one great inducement to their
keeping up a large ſtock of hogs, as they have had experience enough to know, that, whenever we come, they may
be ſure of getting from us what they eſteem a valuable conſideration for them. At Otaheite, they expect the return of
the Spaniards every day; and they will look for the Engliſh, two or three years hence, not only there, but at the
other iſlands. It is to no purpoſe to tell them, that you
will not return. They think you muſt; though not one of
them knows, or will give himſelf the trouble to inquire,
the reaſon of your coming.

I own, I cannot avoid expreſſing it as my real opinion,
that it would have been far better for theſe poor people,
never to have known our ſuperiority in the accommodations
and arts that make life comfortable, than, after once knowing it, to be again left and abandoned to their original inca-
pacity of improvement. Indeed, they cannot be reſtored to
that happy mediocrity in which they lived before we diſcovered them, if the intercourſe between us ſhould be diſcon-
tinued. It ſeems to me, that it has become, in a manner,
incumbent on the Europeans to viſit them once in three or
four years, in order to ſupply them with thoſe convenien-
cies which we have introduced among them, and have
given them a predilection for. The want of ſuch occaſional
ſupplies will, probably, be felt very heavily by them, when

it

it may be too late to go back to their old lefs perfect con-
trivances, which they now defpife, and have difcontinued,
fince the introduction of ours. For by the time that the
iron tools, of which they are now poffeffed, are worn out,
they will have almoft loft the knowledge of their own. A
ftone hatchet is, at prefent, as rare a thing amongft them,
as an iron one was eight years ago; and a chiffel of bone,
or ftone, is not to be feen. Spike nails have fupplied the
place of thefe laft; and they are weak enough to fancy, that
they have got an inexhauftible ftore of them; for thefe were
not now at all fought after. Sometimes, however, nails,
much fmaller than a fpike, would ftill be taken in exchange
for fruit. Knives happened, at prefent, to be in great efteem
at Ulietea; and axes and hatchets remained unrivalled by
any other of our commodities, at all the iflands. With refpect to articles of mere ornament, thefe people are as
changeable as any of the polifhed nations of Europe; fo
that what pleafes their fancy, while a fafhion is in vogue,
may be rejected, when another whim has fupplanted it.
But our iron tools, are fo ftrikingly ufeful, that they will,
we may confidently pronounce, continue to prize them
highly; and be completely miferable, if, neither poffeffing
the materials, nor trained up to the art of fabricating them,
they fhould ceafe to receive fupplies of what may now be
confidered as having become neceffary to their comfortable
exiftence.

Otaheite, though not comprehended in the number of
what we have called the Society Iflands, being inhabited by
the fame race of men, agreeing in the fame leading features of character and manners, it was fortunate, that we
happened to difcover this principal ifland before the others;
as the friendly and hofpitable reception we there met with,

VOL. II.   T   of

of courfe, led us to make it the principal place of refort, in our fucceffive vifits to this part of the Pacific Ocean. By the frequency of this intercourfe, we have had better opportuni- ties of knowing fomething about it and its inhabitants, than about the other fimilar, but lefs confiderable, iflands in its vicinity. Of thefe, however, we have feen enough to fatisfy us, that all that we obferved and have related of Otaheite, may, with trifling variations, be applied to them.

Too much feems to have been already known, and pub- lifhed in our former relations, about fome of the modes of life, that made Otaheite fo agreeable an abode to many on board our fhips; and, if I could now add any finifhing ftrokes to a picture, the outlines of which have been al- ready drawn with fufficient accuracy, I fhould ftill have he- fitated to make this journal the place for exhibiting a view of licentious manners, which could only ferve to difguft thofe for whofe information I write. There are, however, many parts of the domeftic, political, and religious inftitu- tions of thefe people, which, after all our vifits to them, are but imperfectly underftood. The foregoing narrative of the incidents that happened during our ftay, will, probably, be thought to throw fome additional light; and, for farther fa- tisfaction, I refer to Mr. Anderfon's remarks.

Amidft our various fubordinate employments, while at thefe iflands, the great objects of our duty were always at- tended to. No opportunity was loft of making aftronomical and nautical obfervations; from which the following table was drawn up:

Place.	Latitude. South.	Longitude. East.	Variation of the Compafs.	Dip of the Needle.
Matavai Point, Otaheite	17° 29¼′	210° 22′ 28″	5° 34′ Eaft	29° 12′
Owharre Harbour, Huaheine	16° 42¾′	208° 52′ 24″	5° 13¾′Eaft	28° 28′
Ohamaneno Harbour, Ulietea	16° 45¼′	208° 25′ 22″	6° 19′ Eaft	29° 5′

The

The longitude of the three feveral places is deduced from the mean of 145 fets of obfervations made on fhore; fome at one place, and fome at another; and carried on to each of the ftations, by the time-keeper. As the fituation of thefe places was very accurately fettled, during my former voyages, the above obfervations were now made chiefly with a view of determining how far a number of lunar obfervations might be depended upon, and how near they would agree with thofe made upon the fame fpot in 1769, which fixed Matavai Point to be in 210° 27′ 30″. The difference, it appears, is only of 5′ 2″; and, perhaps, no other method could have produced a more perfect agreement. Without pretending to fay which of the two computations is the neareft the truth, the longitude of 210° 22′ 28″, or, which is the fame thing, 208° 25′ 22″, will be the longitude we fhall reckon from with the time-keeper, allowing it to be lofing, on mean time, 1,″69 each day, as found by the mean of all the obfervations made at thefe iflands, for that purpofe.

On our arrival at Otaheite, the error of the time-keeper in longitude was,

by { Greenwich rate,   1° 18′ 58″
     { Tongataboo rate   0° 16′ 40″

Some obfervations were alfo made on the tide; particularly at Otaheite and Ulietea; with a view of afcertaining its greateft rife at the firft place. When we were there, in my fecond voyage, Mr. Wales thought he had difcovered, that it rofe higher than I had obferved it to do, when I firft vifited Otaheite in 1769. But the obfervations we now made, proved that it did not; that is, that it never rofe higher than twelve or fourteen inches at moft. And it was obferved to be high-water nearly at noon, as well at the quadratures, as at the full and change of the moon.

T 2   To

To verify this, the following obfervations were made at Ulietea:

Day of the Month.	Water at a ftand, from	to	Mean Time of High Water.	Perpendicular rife. Inches.
November 6.	$11^h 15^m$ to	$12^h 20^m$	$11^h 48^m$	5, 5
7.	11 40	1 00	12 20	5, 2
8.	11 35	12 50	12 12	5, 0
9.	11 40	1 16	12 28	5, 5
10.	11 25	1 10	12 18	6, 5
11.	12 00	1 40	12 20	5, 0
12.	11 00	1 05	12 02	5, 7
13.	9 30	11 40	10 35	8, 0
14.	11 10	12 50	12 00	8, 0
15.	9 20	11 30	10 25	9, 2
16.	10 00	12 00	11 00	9, 0
17.	10 45	12 15	11 30	8, 5
18.	10 25	12 10	11 18	9, 0
19.	11 00	1 00	12 00	8, 0
20.	11 30	2 00	12 45	7, 0
21.	11 00	1 00	12 00	8, 0
22.	11 30	1 07	12 18	8, 0
23.	12 00	1 30	12 45	6, 5
24.	11 30	1 40	12 35	5, 5
25.	11 40	1 50	12 45	4, 7
26.	11 00	1 30	12 15	5, 2

Having now finifhed all that occurs to me, with regard to thefe iflands, which make fo confpicuous a figure in the lift of our difcoveries, the Reader will permit me to fufpend the profecution of my Journal, while he perufes the following Chapter, for which I am indebted to Mr. Anderfon.

CHAP.

CHAP. IX.

*Accounts of Otaheite still imperfect.—The prevailing Winds.
—Beauty of the Country.—Cultivation.—Natural Curiosi-
ties.—The Persons of the Natives.—Diseases.—General Character.—Love of Pleasure.—Language.—Surgery and Phy-
sic.—Articles of Food.—Effects of drinking Ava.—Times and
Manner of Eating.—Connections with the Females.—Cir-
cumcision.—System of Religion.—Notions about the Soul and
a future Life.—Various Superstitions.—Traditions about the
Creation.—An historical Legend.—Honours paid to the
King.—Distinction of Ranks.—Punishment of Crimes.—
Peculiarities of the neighbouring Islands.—Names of their
Gods.—Names of Islands they visit.—Extent of their Navigation.*

" TO what has been said of Otaheite, in the accounts
of the successive voyages of Captain Wallis, Monf.
de Bougainville, and Captain Cook, it would, at first sight,
seem superfluous to add any thing; as it might be supposed, that little could be now produced, but a repetition
of what has been told before. I am, however, far from
being of that opinion; and will venture to affirm, though
a very accurate description of the country, and of the most
obvious customs of its inhabitants, has been already given,
especially by Captain Cook, that much still remains un-
touched; that, in some instances, mistakes have been
made,

1777.
December.

made, which later and repeated obfervation has been able to rectify ; and that, even now, we are ftrangers to many of the moft important inftitutions that prevail amongft thefe people. The truth is, our vifits, though frequent, have been but tranfient ; many of us had no inclination to make inquiries ; more of us were unable to direct our inquiries properly ; and we all laboured, though not to the fame degree, under the difadvantages attending an imperfect knowledge of the language of thofe, from whom alone we could receive any information. The Spaniards had it more in their power to furmount this bar to inftruction ; fome of them having refided at Otaheite much longer than any other European vifiters. As, with their fuperior advantages, they could not but have had an opportunity of obtaining the fulleft information on moft fubjects relating to this ifland, their account of it would, probably, convey more authentic and accurate intelligence, than, with our beft endeavours, any of us could poffibly obtain. But, as I look upon it to be very uncertain, if not very unlikely, that we fhall ever have any communication from that quarter, I have here put together what additional intelligence, about Otaheite, and its neighbouring iflands, I was able to procure, either from Omai, while on board the fhip, or by converfing with the other natives, while we remained amongft them.

The wind, for the greateft part of the year, blows from between Eaft South Eaft, and Eaft North Eaft. This is the true trade wind, or what the natives call *Maaraee* ; and it fometimes blows with confiderable force. When this is the cafe, the weather is often cloudy, with fhowers of rain ; but when the wind is more moderate, it is clear, fettled, and ferene. If the wind fhould veer farther to the

Southward,

Southward, and become South East, or South South East, it then blows more gently, with a smooth sea, and is called *Maoai*. In those months, when the sun is nearly vertical, that is, in December and January, the winds and weather are both very variable; but it frequently blows from West North West, or North West. This wind is what they call *Toerou*; and is generally attended by dark, cloudy weather, and frequently by rain. It sometimes blows strong, though generally moderate; but seldom lasts longer than five or six days without interruption; and is the only wind in which the people of the islands to leeward come to this, in their canoes. If it happens to be still more Northerly, it blows with less strength, and has the different appellation of *Era-potaia*; which they feign to be the wife of the *Toerou*; who, according to their mythology, is a male.

The wind from South West, and West South West, is still more frequent than the former; and though it is, in general, gentle, and interrupted by calms, or breezes from the Eastward, yet it sometimes blows in brisk squalls. The weather attending it is commonly dark, cloudy, and rainy, with a close, hot air; and often accompanied by a great deal of lightning and thunder. It is called *Etoa*, and often succeeds the *Toerou*; as does also the *Farooa*, which is still more Southerly; and, from its violence, blows down houses and trees, especially the cocoa-palms, from their loftiness; but it is only of a short duration.

The natives seem not to have a very accurate knowledge of these changes, and yet pretend to have drawn some general conclusions from their effects: for they say, when the sea has a hollow sound, and dashes slowly on the shore, or rather on the reef without, that it por-

I
tends

tends good weather; but, if it has a sharp sound, and the waves succeed each other fast, that the reverse will happen.

Perhaps there is scarcely a spot in the universe that affords a more luxuriant prospect than the South East part of Otaheite. The hills are high and steep; and, in many places, craggy. But they are covered to the very summits with trees and shrubs, in such a manner, that the spectator can scarcely help thinking, that the very rocks possess the property of producing and supporting their verdant clothing. The flat land which bounds those hills toward the sea, and the interjacent valleys also, teem with various productions that grow with the most exuberant vigour; and, at once, fill the mind of the beholder with the idea, that no place upon earth can outdo this, in the strength and beauty of vegetation. Nature has been no less liberal in distributing rivulets, which are found in every valley; and as they approach the sea, often divide into two or three branches, fertilizing the flat lands through which they run. The habitations of the natives are scattered, without order, upon these flats; and many of them appearing toward the shore, presented a delightful scene, viewed from our ships; especially as the sea, within the reef, which bounds the coast, is perfectly still, and affords a safe navigation, at all times, for the inhabitants; who are often seen paddling in their canoes indolently along, in passing from place to place, or in going to fish. On viewing these charming scenes, I have often regretted my inability to transmit to those who have had no opportunity of seeing them, such a description as might, in some measure, convey an impression similar to what must be felt by every one who has been fortunate enough to be upon the spot.

It

It is, doubtlefs, the natural fertility of the country, combined with the mildnefs and ferenity of the climate, that renders the natives' fo carelefs in their cultivation, that, in many places, though overflowing with the richeft productions, the fmalleft traces of it cannot be obferved. The cloth plant, which is raifed by feeds brought from the mountains, and the *ava*, or intoxicating pepper, which they defend from the fun when very young, by covering them with leaves of the bread-fruit-tree, are almoft the only things to which they feem to pay any attention; and thefe they keep very clean.

I have inquired very carefully into their manner of cultivating the bread-fruit-tree; but was always anfwered, that they never planted it. This, indeed, muft be evident to every one who will examine the places where the young trees come up. It will be always obferved, that they fpring from the roots of the old ones; which run along near the furface of the ground. So that the bread-fruit-trees may be reckoned thofe that would naturally cover the plains, even fuppofing that the ifland was not inhabited; in the fame manner that the white-barked trees, found at Van Diemen's Land, conftitute the forefts there. And from this we may obferve, that the inhabitant of Otaheite, inftead of being obliged to plant his bread, will rather be under a neceffity of preventing its progrefs; which, I fuppofe, is fometimes done, to give room for trees of another fort, to afford him fome variety in his food.

The chief of thefe are the cocoa-nut and plantain; the firft of which can give no trouble, after it has raifed itfelf a foot or two above the ground; but the plantain requires a little more care. For, after it is planted, it fhoots up, and, in about three months, begins to bear fruit; during which time it gives young fhoots, which fupply a fucceffion of fruit. For the old ftocks are cut down, as the fruit is taken off.

The products of the ifland, however, are not fo remarkable for their variety, as great abundance; and curiofities of any kind are not numerous. Amongft thefe we may reckon a pond or lake of frefh water, at the top of one of the higheft mountains, to go to, and to return from which, takes three or four days. It is remarkable for its depth; and has eels of an enormous fize in it; which are fometimes caught by the natives, who go upon this water in little floats of two or three wild plantain-trees faftened together. This is efteemed one of the greateft natural curiofities of the country; infomuch, that travellers, who come from the other iflands, are commonly afked, amongft the firft things, by their friends, at their return, if they have feen it? There is alfo a fort of water, of which there is only one fmall pond upon the ifland, as far diftant as the lake, and to appearance very good, with a yellow fediment at the bottom: but it has a bad tafte, and proves fatal to thofe who drink any quantity; or makes them break out in blotches, if they bathe in it.

Nothing could make a ftronger impreffion, at firft fight, on our arrival here, than the remarkable contraft between the robuft make and dark colour of the people of Tongataboo, and a fort of delicacy and whitenefs, which diftinguifh the inhabitants of Otaheite. It was even fome time before that difference could preponderate in favour of the Otaheiteans; and then only, perhaps, becaufe we became accuftomed to them, the marks which had recommended the others began to be forgotten. Their women, however,

ftruck

struck us as superior in every respect; and as possessing all those delicate characteristics, which distinguish them from the other sex in many countries. The beard which the men here wear long, and the hair which is not cut so short, as is the fashion at Tongataboo, made also a great difference; and we could not help thinking, that, on every occasion, they shewed a greater degree of timidity and fickleness. The muscular appearance, so common amongst the Friendly Islanders, and which seems a consequence of their being accustomed to much action, is lost here, where the superior fertility of their country enables the inhabitants to lead a more indolent life; and its place is supplied by a plumpness and smoothness of the skin; which, though, perhaps, more consonant with our ideas of beauty, is no real advantage; as it seems attended with a kind of languor in all their motions, not observable in the others. This observation is fully verified, in their boxing and wrestling, which may be called little better than the feeble efforts of children, if compared to the vigour with which these exercises are performed at the Friendly Islands.

Personal endowments being in great esteem amongst them, they have recourse to several methods of improving them, according to their notions of beauty. In particular, it is a practice, especially amongst the *Erreoes*, or unmarried men of some consequence, to undergo a kind of physical operation to render them fair. This is done by remaining a month or two in the house; during which time they wear a great quantity of clothes, eat nothing but bread-fruit, to which they ascribe a remarkable property in whitening them. They also speak, as if their corpulence and colour, at other times, depended upon their

food;

food; as they are obliged, from the change of seasons, to use different sorts at different times.

Their common diet is made up of, at least, nine-tenths of vegetable food; and, I believe, more particularly, the *mahee*, or fermented bread-fruit, which enters almost every meal, has a remarkable effect upon them, preventing a costive habit, and producing a very sensible coolness about them, which could not be perceived in us who fed on animal food. And it is, perhaps, owing to this temperate course of life that they have so few diseases among them.

They only reckon five or six, which might be called chronic, or national disorders; amongst which are the dropsy, and the *fefai*, or indolent swellings before mentioned, as frequent at Tongataboo. But this was before the arrival of the Europeans; for we have added to this short catalogue, a disease which abundantly supplies the place of all the others; and is now almost universal. For this they seem to have no effectual remedy. The priests, indeed, sometimes give them a medley of simples; but they own that it never cures them. And yet, they allow, that, in a few cases, nature, without the assistance of a physician, exterminates the poison of this fatal disease, and a perfect recovery is produced. They say, that if a man is infected with it, he will often communicate it to others in the same house, by feeding out of the same utensils, or handling them; and that, in this case, they frequently die, while he recovers; though we see no reason why this should happen.

Their behaviour, on all occasions, seems to indicate a great openness and generosity of disposition. Omai, indeed, who, as their countryman, should be supposed rather
willing

willing to conceal any of their defects, has often said, that they are fometimes cruel in punifhing their enemies. According to his reprefentation, they torment them very deliberately; at one time, tearing out fmall pieces of flefh from different parts; at another, taking out the eyes; then cutting off the nofe; and laftly, killing them by opening the belly. But this only happens on particular occafions. If cheerfulnefs argues a confcious innocence, one would fuppofe that their life is feldom fullied by crimes. This, however, I rather impute to their feelings, which, though lively, feem in no cafe permanent; for I never faw them, in any misfortune, labour under the appearance of anxiety, after the critical moment was paft. Neither does care ever feem to wrinkle their brow. On the contrary, even the approach of death does not appear to alter their ufual vivacity. I have feen them, when brought to the brink of the grave by difeafe, and when preparing to go to battle; but, in neither cafe, ever obferved their countenances overclouded with melancholy, or ferious reflection.

Such a difpofition, leads them to direct all their aims only to what can give them pleafure and eafe. Their amufements all tend to excite and continue their amorous paffions; and their fongs, of which they are immoderately fond, anfwer the fame purpofe. But as a conftant fucceffion of fenfual enjoyments muft cloy, we found, that they frequently varied them to more refined fubjects, and had much pleafure in chanting their triumphs in war, and their occupations in peace; their travels to other iflands, and adventures there; and the peculiar beauties, and fuperior advantages of their own ifland over the reft, or of different parts of it over other lefs favourite diftricts. This marks, that they receive great delight from mufic; and though they rather expreffed

preffed a diflike to our complicated compofitions, yet were they always delighted with the more melodious founds produced fingly on our inftruments, as approaching nearer to the fimplicity of their own.

Neither are they ftrangers to the foothing effects produced by particular forts of motion; which, in fome cafes, feem to allay any perturbation of mind, with as much fuccefs as mufic. Of this, I met with a remarkable inftance. For on walking, one day, about Matavai Point, where our tents were erected, I faw a man paddling, in a fmall canoe, fo quickly, and looking about with fuch eagernefs, on each fide, as to command all my attention. At firft, I imagined that he had ftolen fomething from one of the fhips, and was purfued; but, on waiting patiently, faw him repeat his amufement. He went out from the fhore, till he was near the place where the fwell begins to take its rife; and, watching its firft motion very attentively, paddled before it, with great quicknefs, till he found that it overtook him, and had acquired fufficient force to carry his canoe before it, without paffing underneath. He then fat motionlefs, and was carried along, at the fame fwift rate as the wave, till it landed him upon the beach. Then he ftarted out, emptied his canoe, and went in fearch of another fwell. I could not help concluding, that this man felt the moft fupreme pleafure, while he was driven on, fo faft and fo fmoothly, by the fea; efpecially as, though the tents and fhips were fo near, he did not feem, in the leaft, to envy, or even to take any notice of, the crowds of his countrymen collected to view them as objects which were rare and curious. During my ftay, two or three of the natives came up, who feemed to fhare his felicity, and always called out, when there was an appearance of a favourable fwell, as he fometimes miffed

ed it, by his back being turned, and looking about for it.
By them I underſtood, that this exerciſe, which is called
eborooe, was frequent amongſt them; and they have probably more amuſements of this ſort, which afford them at
leaſt as much pleaſure as ſkaiting, which is the only one of
ours, with whoſe effects I could compare it.

The language of Otaheite, though doubtleſs radically the
ſame with that of New Zealand and the Friendly Iſlands, is
deſtitute of that guttural pronunciation, and of ſome con-
ſonants, with which thoſe latter dialects abound. The ſpecimens we have already given, are ſufficient to mark
wherein the variation chiefly conſiſts, and to ſhew, that,
like the manners of the inhabitants, it has become ſoft and
ſoothing. During the former voyage, I had collected a copious vocabulary, which enabled me the better to compare
this dialect with that of the other iſlands; and, during this
voyage, I took every opportunity of improving my acquaintance with it, by converſing with Omai, before we arrived, and by my daily intercourſe with the natives, while we
now remained there *. It abounds with beautiful and figu-
rative expreſſions, which, were it perfectly known, would, I
have no doubt, put it upon a level with many of the languages that are moſt in eſteem for their warm and bold
images. For inſtance; the Otaheiteans expreſs their notions
of death very emphatically, by ſaying, " That the ſoul goes
into darkneſs; or rather into night." And, if you ſeem to
entertain any doubt, in aſking the queſtion, " if ſuch a perſon is their mother?" they immediately reply, with fur-

* See this vocabulary, at the end of the ſecond volume of Captain Cook's ſecond
voyage. Many corrections, and additions to it, were now made by this indefatigable in-
quirer; but the ſpecimens of the language of Otaheite, already in the hands of the Public,
ſeem ſufficient for every uſeful purpoſe.

prize,

prize, " Yes, the mother that bore me." They have one expreffion, that correfponds exactly with the phrafeology of the fcriptures, where we read of the " yearning of the bowels." They ufe it on all occafions, when the paffions give them uneafinefs; as they conftantly refer pain from grief, anxious defire, and other affections, to the bowels, as its feat; where they likewife fuppofe all operations of the mind are performed. Their language admits of that inverted arrangement of words, which fo much diftinguifhes the Latin and Greek from moft of our modern European tongues, whofe imperfections require a more orderly conftruction, to prevent ambiguities. It is fo copious, that for the bread-fruit alone, in its different ftates, they have above twenty names; as many for the *taro* root; and about ten for the cocoa-nut. Add to this, that, befides the common dialect, they often expoftulate, in a kind of ftanza or recitative, which is anfwered in the fame manner.

Their arts are few and fimple; yet, if we may credit them, they perform cures in furgery, which our extenfive knowledge in that branch has not, as yet, enabled us to imitate. In fimple fractures, they bind them up with fplints; but if part of the fubftance of the bone be loft, they infert a piece of wood, between the fractured ends, made hollow like the deficient part. In five or fix days, the *rapaoo*, or furgeon, infpects the wound, and finds the wood partly covered with the growing flefh. In as many more days, it is generally entirely covered; after which, when the patient has acquired fome ftrength, he bathes in the water, and recovers. We know that wounds will heal over leaden bullets; and fometimes, though rarely, over other extraneous bodies. But what makes me entertain fome doubt of the truth of fo extraordinary fkill, as in the above inftance, is, that in

other

other cafes which fell under my own obfervation, they are far from being fo dexterous. I have feen the ftump of an arm, which was taken off, after being fhattered by a fall from a tree, that bore no marks of fkilful operation, though fome allowance be made for their defective inftruments. And I met with a man going about with a diflocated fhoulder, fome months after the accident, from their being ignorant of a method to reduce it; though this be confider-ed as one of the fimpleft operations of our furgery. They know that fractures or luxations of the fpine are mortal, but not fractures of the fcull; and they likewife know, from experience, in what parts of the body wounds prove fatal. They have fometimes pointed out thofe inflicted by fpears, which, if made in the direction they mentioned, would certainly have been pronounced deadly by us; and yet thefe people have recovered.

Their phyfical knowledge feems more confined; and that, probably, becaufe their difeafes are fewer than their accidents. The priefts, however, adminifter the juices of herbs in fome cafes; and women who are troubled with after-pains, or other diforders after child-bearing, ufe a remedy which one would think needlefs in a hot coun-try. They firft heat ftones, as when they bake their food; then they lay a thick cloth over them, upon which is put a quantity of a fmall plant of the muftard kind; and thefe are covered with another cloth. Upon this they feat themfelves, and fweat plentifully, to obtain a cure. The men have practifed the fame method for the ve-nereal *lues*, but find it ineffectual. They have no emetic medicines.

Notwithftanding the extreme fertility of the ifland, a fa-mine frequently happens, in which, it is faid, many perifh.

VOL. II.   X   Whether

Whether this be owing to the failure of some seasons, to over-population, which must sometimes almost necessarily happen, or to wars, I have not been able to determine; though the truth of the fact may fairly be inferred, from the great œconomy that they observe with respect to their food, even when there is plenty. In times of scarcity, after their bread-fruit and yams are consumed, they have recourse to various roots, which grow, without cultivation, upon the mountains. The *patarra*, which is found in vast quantities, is what they use first. It is not unlike a very large potatoe or yam, and good when in its growing state; but, when old, is full of hard stringy fibres. They then eat two other roots; one not unlike *taro*; and, lastly, the *eboee*. This is of two forts; one of them possessing deleterious qualities, which obliges them to slice and macerate it in water, a night before they bake and eat it. In this respect, it resembles the *cassava* root of the West-Indies; but it forms a very insipid, moist paste, in the manner they dress it. However, I have seen them eat it at times when no such scarcity reigned. Both this and the *patarra* are creeping plants; the last, with ternate leaves.

Of animal food, a very small portion falls, at any time, to the share of the lower class of people; and then it is either fish, sea-eggs, or other marine productions; for they seldom or ever eat pork. The *Eree de boi* * alone, is able to furnish pork every day; and inferior Chiefs, according to their riches, once a week, fortnight, or month. Sometimes, they are not even allowed that; for, when the island is impoverished by war, or other causes, the Chief prohibits his

* Mr. Anderson invariably, in his manuscript, writes *Eree de boi*. According to Captain Cook's mode, it is *Eree rabie*. This is one of the numerous instances that perpetually occur, of our people's representing the same word differently.

subjects

subjects to kill any hogs; and this prohibition, we were told, is in force, sometimes, for several months, or even for a year or two. During that reſtraint, the hogs multiply ſo faſt, that there are inſtances of their changing their domeſtic ſtate, and turning wild. When it is thought proper to take off the prohibition, all the Chiefs aſſemble at the king's place of abode; and each brings with him a preſênt of hogs. The king then orders ſome of them to be killed, on which they feaſt; and, after that, every one returns home with liberty to kill what he pleaſes for his own uſe. Such a prohibition was actually in force, on our laſt arrival here; at leaſt, in all thoſe diſtricts of the iſland, that are immediately under the direction of Otoo. And, leſt it ſhould have prevented our going to Matavai after leaving Oheitepeha, he ſent a meſſage to aſſure us, that it ſhould be taken off, as ſoon as the ſhips arrived there. With reſpect to us, we found it ſo; but we made ſuch a conſumption of them, that, I have no doubt, it would be laid on again, as ſoon as we ſailed. A ſimilar prohibition is alſo, ſometimes, extended to fowls.

It is alſo amongſt the better ſort, that the *ava* is chiefly uſed. But this beverage is prepared ſomewhat differently, from that which we ſaw ſo much of at the Friendly Iſlands. For they pour a very ſmall quantity of water upon the root here; and ſometimes roaſt or bake, and bruiſe the ſtalks, without chewing it previouſly to its infuſion. They alſo uſe the leaves of the plant here, which are bruiſed, and water poured upon them, as upon the root. Large companies do not aſſemble to drink it, in that ſociable way which is practiſed at Tongataboo. But its pernicious effects are more obvious here; perhaps, owing to the manner of preparing it; as we often ſaw inſtances of its intoxicating, or

X 2   rather

rather ftupifying powers. Some of us, who had been at thefe iflands before, were furprized to find many people, who, when we faw them laft, were remarkable for their fize and corpulency, now almoft reduced to fkeletons ; and, upon inquiring into the caufe of this alteration, it was univerfally allowed to be the ufe of the *ava*. The fkins of thefe people were rough, dry, and covered with fcales; which, they fay, every now and then, fall off, and their fkin is, as it were, renewed. As an excufe for a practice fo deftructive, they allege, that it is adopted to prevent their growing too fat; but it evidently enervates them ; and, in all probability, fhortens their days. As its effects had not been fo vifible, during our former vifits, it is not unlikely that this article of luxury had never been fo much abufed as at this time. If it continues to be fo fafhionable, it bids fair to deftroy great numbers.

The times of eating, at Otaheite, are very frequent. Their firft meal, or (as it may rather be called) their laft, as they go to fleep after it, is about two o'clock in the morning ; and the next is at eight. At eleven, they dine ; and again, as Omai expreffed it, at two, and at five ; and fup at eight. In this article of domeftic life, they have adopted fome cuftoms which are exceedingly whimfical. The women, for inftance, have not only the mortification of being obliged to eat by themfelves, and in a different part of the houfe from the men; but, by a ftrange kind of policy, are excluded from a fhare of moft of the better forts of food. They dare not tafte turtle, nor fifh of the tunny kind, which is much efteemed ; nor fome particular forts of the beft plantains ; and it is very feldom that even thofe of the firft rank are fuffered to eat pork. The children of each fex alfo eat apart ; and the women, generally, ferve up their own victuals ;

tuals; for they would certainly ftarve, before any grown man would do them fuch an office. In this, as well as in fome other cuftoms relative to their eating, there is a myf-terious conduct, which we could never thoroughly compre-hend. When we inquired into the reafons of it, we could get no other anfwer, but that it is right and neceffary that it fhould be fo.

In other cuftoms refpecting the females, there feems to be no fuch obfcurity; efpecially as to their connections with the men. If a young man and woman, from mutual choice, cohabit, the man gives the father of the girl fuch things as are neceffary in common life; as hogs, cloth, or canoes, in proportion to the time they are together; and if he thinks that he has not been fufficiently paid for his daughter, he makes no fcruple of forcing her to leave her friend, and to cohabit with another perfon who may be more liberal. The man, on his part, is always at liberty to make a new choice; but, fhould his confort become preg-nant, he may kill the child; and, after that, either continue his connection with the mother, or leave her. But if he fhould adopt the child, and fuffer it to live, the parties are then confidered as in the married ftate, and they commonly live together ever after. However, it is thought no crime in the man to join a more youthful partner to his firft wife, and to live with both. The cuftom of changing their con-nections is, however, much more general than this laft; and it is a thing fo common, that they fpeak of it with great indifference. The *Erreoes* are only thofe of the better fort, who, from their ficklenefs, and their poffeffing the means of purchafing a fucceffion of frefh connections, are con-ftantly roaming about; and, from having no particular at-tachment, feldom adopt the more fettled method mentioned
above.

above. And fo agreeable is this licentious plan of life to
their difpofition, that the moft beautiful of both fexes thus
commonly fpend their youthful days, habituated to the
practice of enormities which would difgrace the moft favage
tribes ; but are peculiarly fhocking amongft a people whofe
general character, in other refpects, has evident traces of
the prevalence of humane and tender feelings *. When an
Erreoe

* That the Caroline Iflands are inhabited by the fame tribe or nation, whom Captain
Cook found, at fuch immenfe diftances, fpread throughout the South Pacific Ocean, has
been fatisfactorily eftablifhed in fome preceding notes. The fituation of the Ladrones,
or Marianne Iflands, ftill farther North than the Carolines, but at no great diftance from
them, is favourable, at firft fight, to the conjecture, that the fame race alfo peopled that
clufter ; and, on looking into Father le Gobien's Hiftory of them, this conjecture appears
to be actually confirmed by direct evidence. One of the greateft fingularities of the Otaheite manners, is the exiftence of the fociety of young men, called *Erreoes*, of whom fome
account is given in the preceding paragraph. Now we learn from Father le Gobien,
that fuch a fociety exifts alfo amongft the inhabitants of the Ladrones. His words are ;
*Les Urritoes font parmi eux les jeuns gens qui vivent avec des maitreffes, fans vouloir s'engager
dans les liens du mariage.* That there fhould be young men in the Ladrones, as well as in
Otaheite, *who live with miftreffes, without being inclined to enter into the married ftate,*
would not, indeed, furnifh the fhadow of any peculiar refemblance between them. But
that the young men in the Ladrones, and in Otaheite, whofe manners are thus licentious,
fhould be confidered as a diftinct confraternity, called by a particular name ; and that this
name fhould be the fame in both places : this fingular coincidence of cuftom, confirmed
by that of language, feems to furnifh an irrefragable proof of the inhabitants of both places
being the fame nation. We know, that it is the general property of the Otaheite dialect,
to foften the pronunciation of its words. And, it is obfervable, that, by the omiffion of
one fingle letter (the confonant *t*), our *Arreoys* (as fpelled in Hawkefworth's Collection),
or *Erreoes* (according to Mr. Anderfon's orthography), and the *Urritoes* of the Ladrones,
are brought to fuch a fimilitude of found (the only rule of comparing two unwritten languages), that we may pronounce them to be the fame word, without expofing ourfelves
to the fneers of fupercilious criticifm.

One or two more fuch proofs, drawn from fimilarity of language, in very fignificant
words, may be affigned. Le Gobien tells us, that the people of the Ladrones worfhip
their dead, whom they call *Anitis*. Here, again, by dropping the confonant *n*, we have a
word that bears a ftrong refemblance to that which fo often occurs in Captain Cook's

Erreoe woman is delivered of a child, a piece of cloth, dipped in water, is applied to the mouth and nofe, which fuffocates it.

As

Voyages, when fpeaking of the Divinities of his iflands, whom he calls *Eatooas*. And it may be matter of curiofity to remark, that what is called an *Aniti*, at the Ladrones, is, as we learn from Cantova [*Lettres Edifiantes et Curieufes*, Tom. xv. p. 309, 310.], at the Caroline Iflands, where dead Chiefs are alfo worfhipped, called a *Tahutup*; and that, by foftening or finking the ftrong founding letters, at the beginning and at the end of this latter word, the *Ahutu* of the Carolines, the *Aiti* of the Ladrones, and the *Eatooa* of the South Pacific Iflands, affume fuch a fimilarity in pronunciation (for we can have no other guide), as ftrongly marks one common original. Once more; we learn from Le Gobien, that the Marianne people call their Chiefs *Chamorris*, or *Chamoris*. And, by foftening the afpirate *Ch* into *T*, and the harfhnefs of *r* into *l* (of which the vocabularies of the different iflands give us repeated inftances), we have the *Tamole* of the Caroline Iflands, and the *Tamolao*, or *Tamaha*, of the Friendly ones.

If thefe fpecimens of affinity of language fhould be thought too fcanty, fome very remarkable inftances of fimilarity of cuftoms and inftitutions will go far to remove every doubt. 1. A divifion into three claffes, of nobles, a middle rank, and the common people, or fervants, was found, by Captain Cook, to prevail both at the Friendly and the Society Iflands. Father le Gobien exprefsly tells us, that the fame diftinction prevails at the Ladrones: *Il y a trois états, parmi les infulaires, la nobleffe, le moyen, et le menu.* 2. Numberlefs inftances occur in Captain Cook's voyage to prove the great fubjection under which the people of his iflands are to their Chiefs. We learn from Le Gobien,. that it is fo alfo at the Ladrones—*La nobleffe eft d'un fierté incroyable, et tien le peuple dans un abaifement qu'on ne pourroit imaginer en Europe*, &c. 3. The diverfions of the natives at Wateeoo, the Friendly, and the Society Iflands, have been copioufly defcribed by Captain Cook. How fimilar are thofe which Le Gobien mentions in the following words, as prevailing at the Ladrones! *Ils fe divertiffent à danfer, courir, fautir, lutter, pour s'exercer, et éprouver leur forces. Ils prennent grand plaifir à raconter les avantures de leurs ancêtres, et à reciter des vers de leurs poëtes.* 4. The principal fhare fuftained by the women, in the entertainments at Captain Cook's iflands, appears fufficiently from a variety of inftances in this work; and we cannot read what Le Gobien fays, of the practice at the Ladrones, without tracing the ftrongeft refemblance.—*Dans leurs affemblées elles fe mettent doux ou trieze femmes en rond, debout, fans fe remuer. Dans cette attitude elles chantent les vers fabuleux de leurs poëtes avec un agrément, et une jufteffe qui plairoit en Europe. L'accord de leur voix eft admirable, et ne cede en rien à la mufique canceriée. Elles ont dans les mains de petits coquilles, dont elles fe fervent avec beaucoup de precifion. Elles*

foutiennent

As in such a life, their women muft contribute a very large fhare of its happinefs, it is rather furprizing, befides the humiliating reftraints they are laid under with regard to food,

foutiennent leur voix, et animent leur chants avec une aɛtion fi vive, et des geftes fi expreffives, qu'elles charment ceux qui les voient, et qui les entendent. 5. We read, in Hawkefworth's account of Captain Cook's firft voyage [Vol. ii. p. 235.] that at Otaheite garlands of the fruit of the palm-tree and cocoa-leaves, with other things particularly confecrated to funeral folemnities, are depofited about the places where they lay their dead ; and that provifions and water are alfo left at a little diftance. How conformable to this is the praɛtice at the Ladrones, as defcribed by Le Gobien ! *Ils font quelques repas autour du tombeau ; car on en eleve toujours un fur le lieu où le corps eft enterré, ou dans le voifinage ; on le charge de fleurs, de branches de palmiers, de coquillages, et de tout ce qu'ils ont de plus precieux.* 6. It is the cuftom at Otaheite [fee Hawkefworth, Vol. ii. p. 236.] not to bury the fculls of the Chiefs, with the reft of the bones, but to put them into boxes made for that purpofe. Here again, we find the fame ftrange cuftom prevailing at the Ladrones ; for Le Gobien exprefsly tells us, *qu'ils gardent les crânes en leur maifons,* that they put thefe fculls into little bafkets *(petites corbeilles) ;* and that thefe dead Chiefs are the *Anitis,* to whom their priefts addrefs their invocations. 7. The people of Otaheite, as we learn from Captain Cook, in his account of Tee's embalmed corpfe, make ufe of cocoa-nut oil, and other ingredients, in rubbing the dead bodies. The people of the Ladrones, Father Le Gobien tells us, fometimes do the fame—*D'autres frottent les morts d'huile odoriferante.* 8. The inhabitants of Otaheite [fee Hawkefworth, Vol. ii. p. 239, 240.] believe the immortality of the foul ; and that there are two fituations after death, fomewhat analogous to our heaven and hell ; but they do not fuppofe, that their aɛtions here in the leaft influence their future ftate. And in the account given in this voyage [Vol. i. p. 403.] of the religious opinions entertained at the Friendly Iflands, we find there, exaɛtly the fame doɛtrine. It is very obfervable, how conformable to this is the belief of the inhabitants of the Ladrones—*Ils font perfuadés* (fays Le Gobien) *de l'immortalité de l'âme. Ils reconnoiffent même un Paradis et un Enfer, dont ils fe forment des idées affez bizarres. Ce n'eft point, felon eux, la vertu ni le crime, qui conduit dans ces lieux là ; les bonnes ou les mauvaifes aɛtions n'y fervent de rien.* 9. One more very fingular inftance of agreement, fhall clofe this long lift. In Captain Cook's account of the New Zealanders [Vol. i. p. 138.], we find, that, according to them, the foul of the man who is killed, and whofe flefh is devoured, is doomed to a perpetual fire ; while the fouls of all who die a natural death, afcend to the habitations of the Gods. And, from Le Gobien, we learn, that this very notion is adopted by his iflanders—*Si on a le malheur de mourir de mort violente, on a l'enfer pour leur partage.*

Surely, fuch a concurrence of very charaɛteriftic conformities cannot be the refult of mere

food, to find them often treated with a degree of harſhneſs, or rather brutality, which one would ſcarcely ſuppoſe a man would beſtow, on an object for whom he had the leaſt affection. Nothing, however, is more common, than to ſee the men beat them without mercy; and, unleſs this treatment is the effect of jealouſy, which both ſexes, at leaſt, pretend to be ſometimes infected with, it will be difficult to account for it. It will be leſs difficult to admit this as the motive, as I have ſeen ſeveral inſtances where the women have preferred perſonal beauty to intereſt; though I muſt own, that, even in theſe caſes, they ſeem ſcarcely ſuſceptible of thoſe delicate ſentiments that are the reſult of mutual affection; and, I believe, that there is leſs Platonic love in Otaheite than in any other country.

Cutting or inciding the fore-ſkin ſhould be mentioned here as a practice adopted amongſt them, from a notion of cleanlineſs; and they have a reproachful epithet in their language, for thoſe who do not obſerve that cuſtom. When there are five or ſix lads pretty well grown up in a neighbourhood, the father of one of them goes to a *Tahoua,* or man of knowledge, and lets him know. He goes with the lads to the top of the hills, attended by a ſervant; and,

mere accident; and, when combined with the ſpecimens of affinity of language mentioned at the beginning of this note, it ſhould ſeem, that we are fully warranted, from premiſes thus unexceptionable, to draw a certain concluſion, that the inhabitants of the various iſlands diſcovered or viſited by Captain Cook, in the South Pacific Ocean, and thoſe whom the Spaniards found ſettled upon the Ladrones or Mariannes, in the Northern hemiſphere, carried the ſame language, cuſtoms, and opinions, from one common centre, from which they had emigrated; and that, therefore, they may be conſidered as ſcattered members of the ſame nation.

See Pere le Gobien's *Hiſtoire des Iſles Mariannes,* Book ii. or the ſummary of it in *Hiſtoire des Navigations aux Terres Auſtrales,* T. ii. p. 492—512, from which the materials for this note have been extracted.

feating one of them properly, introduces a piece of wood
underneath the forefkin, and defires him to look afide at
fomething he pretends is coming. Having thus engaged the
young man's attention to another object, he cuts through
the fkin upon the wood, with a fhark's tooth, generally at
one ftroke. He then feparates, or rather turns back the divided parts; and, having put on a bandage, proceeds to
perform the fame operation on the other lads. At the end
of five days they bathe, and the bandages being taken off,
the matter is cleaned away. At the end of five days more,
they bathe again, and are well; but a thicknefs of the
prepuce, where it was cut, remaining, they go again to the
mountains with the *Taboua* and fervant; and a fire being
prepared, and fome ftones heated, the *Taboua* puts the prepuce between two of them, and fqueezes it gently, which
removes the thicknefs. They then return home, having
their heads, and other parts of their bodies, adorned with
odoriferous flowers; and the *Taboua* is rewarded for his fer-
vices by their fathers, in proportion to their feveral abilities, with prefents of hogs and cloth; and if they be poor,
their relations are liberal on the occafion.

Their religious fyftem is extenfive, and, in many inftances,
fingular; but few of the common people have a perfect
knowledge of it; that being confined chiefly to their priefts,
who are pretty numerous. They do not feem to pay refpect
to one God as poffeffing pre-eminence; but believe in a
plurality of divinities, who are all very powerful; and, in
this cafe, as different parts of the ifland, and the other iflands
in the neighbourhood, have different ones, the inhabitants
of each, no doubt, think that they have chofen the moft
eminent, or, at leaft, one who is invefted with power fufficient to protect them, and to fupply all their wants. If he
fhould

should not anfwer their expectations, they think it no impiety to change; as has very lately happened in Tiaraboo, where, in the room of the two divinities formerly honoured there, Oraa *, God of Bolabola, has been adopted, I fhould fuppofe, becaufe he is the protector of a people who have been victorious in war; and as, fince they have made this change, they have been very fuccefsful themfelves againft the inhabitants of *Otaheite-nooe*, they impute it entirely to *Oraa*, who, as they literally fay, fights their battles.

Their affiduity in ferving their Gods is remarkably confpicuous. Not only the *whattas*, or offering-places of the *morais*, are commonly loaded with fruits and animals; but there are few houfes where you do not meet with a fmall place of the fame fort near them. Many of them are fo rigidly fcrupulous, that they will not begin a meal, without firft laying afide a morfel for the *Eatooa*; and we had an opportunity, during this voyage, of feeing their fuperftitious zeal carried to a moft pernicious height, in the inftance of human facrifices; the occafions of offering which, I doubt, are too frequent. Perhaps, they have recourfe to them when misfortunes occur; for they afked, if one of our men, who happened to be confined, when we were detained by a contrary wind, was *taboo?* Their prayers are alfo very frequent, which they chant, much after the manner of the fongs in their feftive entertainments. And the women, as in other cafes, are alfo obliged to fhew their inferiority in religious obfervances; for it is required of them, that they fhould partly uncover themfelves, as they pafs the *morais*; or take a confiderable circuit to avoid them. Though they have no notion, that their God muft always be conferring

* We have another inftance of the fame word being differently pronounced by our people. Captain Cook, as appears above, fpeaks of *Olla*, as the Bolabola God.

benefits,

benefits, without fometimes forgetting them, or fuffering evil to befall them, they feem to regard this lefs than the attempts of fome more inaufpicious being to hurt them. They tell us, that *Etee* is an evil fpirit, who fometimes does them mifchief; and to whom, as well as to their God, they make offerings. But the mifchiefs they apprehend from any fuperior invifible beings, are confined to things merely temporal.

They believe the foul to be both immaterial and immortal. They fay, that it keeps fluttering about the lips during the pangs of death; and that then it afcends, and mixes with, or, as they exprefs it, is eaten by the Deity. In this ftate it remains for fome time; after which, it departs to a certain place deftined for the reception of the fouls of men, where it exifts in eternal night; or, as they fometimes fay, in twilight, or dawn. They have no idea of any permanent punifhment after death, for crimes that they have committed on earth; for the fouls of good and of bad men are eat indifcriminately by God. But they certainly confider this coalition with the Deity as a kind of purification neceffary to be undergone before they enter a ftate of blifs. For, according to their doctrine, if a man refrain from all connection with women fome months before death, he paffes immediately into his eternal manfion, without fuch a previous union; as if already, by this abftinence, he were pure enough to be exempted from the general lot.

They are, however, far from entertaining thofe fublime conceptions of happinefs, which our religion, and, indeed, reafon, gives us room to expect hereafter. The only great privilege they feem to think they fhall acquire by death, is immortality; for they fpeak of fpirits being, in fome meafure, not totally divefted of thofe paffions which actuated them

them when combined with material vehicles. Thus, if souls, who were formerly enemies, fhould meet, they have many conflicts; though, it fhould feem, to no purpofe, as they are accounted invulnerable in this invifible ftate. There is a fimilar reafoning with regard to the meeting of man and wife. If the hufband dies firft, the foul of his wife is known to him on its arrival in the land of fpirits. They refume their former acquaintance, in a fpacious houfe, called *Tourooa*, where the fouls of the deceafed affemble to recreate themfelves with the Gods. She then retires with him to his feparate habitation, where they remain for ever, and have an offspring; which, however, is entirely fpiritual; as they are neither married, nor are their embraces fuppofed to be the fame as with corporeal beings.

Some of their notions about the Deity, are extravagantly abfurd. They believe, that he is fubject to the power of thofe very fpirits to whom he has given exiftence; and that, in their turn, they frequently eat or devour him, though he poffefs the power of re-creating himfelf. They, doubtlefs, ufe this mode of expreffion, as they feem incapable of converfing about immaterial things, without conftantly referring to material objects to convey their meaning. And in this manner they continue the account, by faying, that, in the *tourooa*, the Deity inquires, if they intend, or not, to deftroy him? And that he is not able to alter their determination. This is known to the inhabitants on earth, as well as to the fpirits; for when the moon is in its wane, it is faid, that they are then devouring their *Eatooa*; and that, as it increafes, he is renewing himfelf. And to this accident, not only the inferior, but the moft eminent Gods are liable. They alfo believe, that there are other places for the reception of fouls at death. Thus, thofe who are drowned in

the

the fea, remain there; where they think that there is a fine country, houfes, and every thing that can make them happy. But what is more fingular, they maintain, that not only all other animals, but trees, fruit, and even ftones, have fouls, which at death, or upon being confumed or broken, afcend to the divinity, with whom they firft mix, and afterwards pafs into the manfion allotted to each.

They imagine, that their punctual performance of religious offices procures for them every temporal blefling. And as they believe, that the animating and powerful influence of the divine fpirit is every where diffufed, it is no wonder that they join to this many fuperftitious opinions about its operations. Accordingly, they believe that fudden deaths, and all other accidents, are effected by the immediate action of fome divinity. If a man only ftumble againft a ftone, and hurt his toe, they impute it to an *Eatooa*; fo that they may be literally faid, agreeably to their fyftem, to tread enchanted ground. They are ftartled, in the night, on approaching a *toopapaoo*, where the dead are expofed, in the fame manner that many of our ignorant and fuperftitious people are with the apprehenfions of ghofts, and at the fight of a church-yard; and they have an equal confidence in dreams, which they fuppofe to be communications either from their God, or from the fpirits of their departed friends, enabling thofe favoured with them to foretell future events; but this kind of knowledge is confined to particular people. Omai pretended to have this gift. He told us, that the foul of his father had intimated to him in a dream, on the 26th of July 1776, that he fhould go on fhore, at fome place, within three days; but he was unfortunate in this firft attempt to perfuade us, that he was a prophet; for it was the 1ft of Auguft before we

got

got into Teneriffe. Amongſt them, however, the dreamers poſſeſs a reputation little inferior to that of their inſpired prieſts and prieſteſſes, whoſe predictions they implicitly believe, and are determined by them in all undertakings of conſequence. The prieſteſs who perſuaded Opoony to invade Ulietea, is much reſpected by him; and he never goes to war, without conſulting her. They alſo, in ſome degree, maintain our old doctrine of planetary influence; at leaſt, they are ſometimes regulated, in their public counſels, by certain appearances of the moon; particularly, when lying horizontally, or much inclined on the convex part, on its firſt appearance after the change, they are encouraged to engage in war, with confidence of ſucceſs.

They have traditions concerning the creation, which, as might be expected, are complex, and clouded with obſcurity. They ſay, that a goddeſs, having a lump or maſs of earth ſuſpended in a cord, gave it a ſwing, and ſcattered about pieces of land, thus conſtituting Otaheite and the neighbouring iſlands, which were all peopled by a man and woman originally fixed at Otaheite. This, however, only reſpects their own immediate creation; for they have notions of an univerſal one before this; and of lands, of which they have now no other knowledge than what is mentioned in the tradition. Their moſt remote account reaches to Tatooma and Tapuppa, male and female ſtones or rocks, who ſupport the congeries of land and water, or our globe underneath. Theſe produced Totorro, who was killed, and divided into land; and, after him, Otaia and Oroo were begotten, who were afterward married, and produced, firſt land, and then a race of Gods. Otaia is killed, and Oroo marries a God, her ſon, called Teorraha, whom ſhe orders to create more land, the animals, and all ſorts of food

1777.
December.

food found upon the earth; as alfo the fky, which is fupported by men called Teeferei. The fpots obferved in the
moon, are fuppofed to be groves of a fort of trees which
once grew in Otaheite, and, being deftroyed by fome accident, their feeds were carried up thither by doves, where
they now flourifh.

They have alfo many legends, both religious and hifto-
rical; one of which latter, relative to the practice of eating
human flefh, I fhall give the fubftance of, as a fpecimen of
their method. A long time fince, there lived in Otaheite
two men called *Taheeai*; the only name they yet have for
cannibals. None knew from whence they came, or in
what manner they arrived at the ifland. Their habitation
was in the mountains, from whence they ufed to iffue, and
kill many of the natives, whom they afterward devoured,
and, by that means, prevented the progrefs of population.
Two brothers, determined to rid their country of fuch a formidable enemy, ufed a ftratagem for their deftruction, with
fuccefs. Thefe ftill lived farther upward than the *Taheeai*,
and in fuch a fituation, that they could fpeak with them,
without greatly hazarding their own fafety. They invited
them to accept of an entertainment, that fhould be provided
for them, to which thefe readily confented. The brothers
then taking fome ftones, heated them in a fire, and thrufting
them into pieces of *mahee*, defired one of the *Taheeai* to open
his mouth. On which, one of thefe pieces was dropped in,
and fome water poured down, which made a boiling or hiff-
ing noife, in quenching the ftone, and killed him. They
intreated the other to do the fame; but he declined it, reprefenting the confequences of his companion's eating. However, they affured him, that the food was excellent, and its
effects only temporary; for that the other would foon recover.

cover. His credulity was fuch, that he fwallowed the bait, and fhared the fate of the firft. The natives then cut them in pieces, which they buried; and conferred the government of the ifland on the brothers, as a reward for delivering them from fuch monfters. Their refidence was in the diftrict called Whapaeenoo; and, to this day, there remains a bread-fruit tree, once the property of the *Taheeais*. They had alfo a woman, who lived with them, and had two teeth of a prodigious fize. After they were killed, fhe lived at the ifland Otaha, and, when dead, was ranked amongft their deities. She did not eat human flefh, as the men; but, from the fize of her teeth, the natives ftill call any animal that has a fierce appearance, or is reprefented with large tufks, *Taheeai*.

Every one muft allow, that this ftory is juft as natural as that of Hercules deftroying the Hydra, or the more modern one of Jack the giant-killer. But I do not find, that there is any moral couched under it, any more than under moft old fables of the fame kind, which have been received as truths only during the prevalence of the fame ignorance that marked the character of the ages in which they were invented. It, however, has not been improperly introduced, as ferving to exprefs the horror and deteftation entertained here, againft thofe who feed upon human flefh. And yet, from fome circumftances, I have been led to think, that the natives of thefe ifles were formerly cannibals. Upon afking Omai, he denied it ftoutly; yet mentioned a fact, within his own knowledge, which almoft confirms fuch an opinion. When the people of Bolabola, one time, defeated thofe of Huaheine, a great number of his kinfmen were flain. But one of his relations had, afterward, an opportunity of revenging himfelf, when the Bolabola men were worfted in

VOL. II.   Z   their

their turn, and cutting a piece out of the thigh of one of his enemies, he broiled and eat it. I have, alfo, frequently confidered the offering of the perfon's eye, who is facrificed, to the Chief, as a veftige of a cuftom which once really exifted to a greater extent, and is ftill commemorated by this emblematical ceremony.

The being invefted with the *maro*, and the prefiding at human facrifices, feem to be the peculiar characteriftics of the fovereign. To thefe, perhaps, may be added the blowing a conch-fhell, which produces a very loud found. On hearing it, all his fubjects are obliged to bring food of every fort to his royal refidence, in proportion to their abilities. On fome other occafions, they carry their veneration for his very name, to an extravagant and very deftructive pitch. For if, on his acceffion to the *maro*, any words in their language be found to have a refemblance to it in found, they are changed for others; and if any man be bold enough not to comply, and continue to ufe thofe words, not only he, but all his relations, are immediately put to death. The fame feverity is exercifed toward thofe who fhall prefume to apply this facred name to any animal. And, agreeably to this cuftom of his countrymen, Omai ufed to exprefs his indignation, that the Englifh fhould give the names of Prince or Princefs to their favourite horfes or dogs. But while·death is the punifhment for making free with the name of their fovereign, if abufe be only levelled at his government, the offender efcapes with the forfeiture of land and houfes.

The king never enters the houfe of any of his fubjects; but has, in every diftrict, where he vifits, houfes belonging to himfelf. And if, at any time, he fhould be obliged by accident to deviate from this rule, the houfe thus honoured with his prefence, and every part of its furniture, is burnt.

I   His

His fubjects not only uncover to him, when prefent, down to the waift; but if he be at any particular place, a pole, having a piece of cloth tied to it, is fet up fomewhere near, to which they pay the fame honours. His brothers are alfo intitled to the firft part of the ceremony; but the women only uncover to the females of the royal family. In fhort, they feem even fuperftitious in their refpect to him, and efteem his perfon little lefs than facred. And it is, perhaps, to thefe circumftances, that he owes the quiet poffeffion of his dominions. For even the people of Tiaraboo allow him the fame honours as his right; though, at the fame time, they look upon their own Chief as more powerful; and fay, that he would fucceed to the government of the whole ifland, fhould the prefent reigning family become extinct. This is the more likely, as Waheiadooa not only poffeffes Tiaraboo, but many diftricts of Opooreanoo. His territories, therefore, are almoft equal, in extent, to thofe of Otoo; and he has, befides, the advantage of a more populous and fertile part of the ifland. His fubjects, alfo, have given proofs of their fuperiority, by frequent victories over thofe of Otaheite-nooe, whom they affect to fpeak of as contemptible warriors, eafily to be worfted, if, at any time, their Chief fhould wifh to put it to the teft.

The ranks of people, befides the *Eree de hoi*, and his family, are the *Erees*, or powerful Chiefs; the *Manahoone*, or vaffals; and the *Teou*, or *Toutou*, fervants, or rather flaves. The men of each of thefe, according to the regular inftitution, form their connections with women of their refpective ranks; but if with any inferior one, which frequently happens, and a child be born, it is preferved, and has the rank of the father, unlefs he happens to be an *Eree*, in which cafe it is killed. If a woman of condition fhould choofe

Z 2

an

1777.
December.

an inferior perſon to officiate as a huſband, the children he
has by her are killed. And if a *Teou* be caught in an in-
trigue with a woman of the blood-royal, he is put to death.
The ſon of the *Eree de hoi* ſucceeds his father in title and
honours, as ſoon as he is born; but if he ſhould have no
children, the brother aſſumes the government at his death.
In other families, poſſeſſions always deſcend to the eldeſt
ſon; but he is obliged to maintain his brothers and ſiſters,
who are allowed houſes on his eſtates.

The boundaries of the ſeveral diſtricts, into which Otaheite is divided, are, generally, either rivulets, or low hills,
which, in many places, jut out into the ſea. But the ſub-
diviſions into particular property, are marked by large ſtones,
which have remained from one generation to another. The
removal of any of theſe gives riſe to quarrels, which are decided by arms; each party bringing his friends into the
field. But if any one complain to the *Eree de hoi*, he terminates the difference amicably. This is an offence, however, not common; and long cuſtom ſeems to ſecure property here as effectually, as the moſt ſevere laws do in other
countries. In conformity alſo to ancient practice eſtabliſhed
amongſt them, crimes of a leſs general nature are left to be
puniſhed by the ſufferer, without referring them to a ſuperior. In this caſe, they ſeem to think, that the injured perſon will judge as equitably as thoſe who are totally unconcerned; and, as long cuſtom has allotted certain puniſh-
ments for crimes of different ſorts, he is allowed to inflict
them, without being amenable to any other perſon. Thus,
if any one be caught ſtealing, which is commonly done in
the night, the proprietor of the goods may put the thief inſtantly to death; and if any one ſhould inquire of him
after the deceaſed, it is ſufficient to acquit him, if he only
inform

inform them of the provocation he had to kill him. But so fevere a punifhment is feldom inflicted, unlefs the articles that are ftolen be reckoned very valuable; fuch as breaft-plates, and plaited hair. If only cloth, or even hogs be ftolen, and the thief efcape, upon his being afterward dif-covered, if he promife to return the fame number of pieces of cloth, or of hogs, no farther punifhment is inflicted. Sometimes, after keeping out of the way for a few days, he is forgiven, or, at moft, gets a flight beating. If a perfon kill another in a quarrel, the friends of the deceafed af-femble, and engage the furvivor and his adherents. If they conquer, they take poffeffion of the houfe, lands, and goods of the other party; but if conquered, the reverfe takes place. If a *Manaboone* kill the *Toutou*, or flave of a Chief, the latter fends people to take poffeffion of the lands and houfe of the former, who flies either to fome other part of the ifland, or to fome of the neighbouring iflands. After fome months he returns, and finding his ftock of hogs much increafed, he offers a large prefent of thefe, with fome red feathers, and other valuable articles, to the *Toutou*'s mafter, who generally accepts the compenfation, and permits him to repoffefs his houfe and lands. This practice is the height of venality and injuftice; and the flayer of the flave feems to be under no farther neceffity of abfcond-ing, than to impofe upon the lower clafs of people, who are the fufferers. For it does not appear, that the Chief has the leaft power to punifh this *Manaboone*; but the whole ma-nagement marks a collufion between him and his fuperior, to gratify the revenge of the former, and the avarice of the latter. Indeed, we need not wonder that the killing of a man fhould be confidered as fo venial an offence, amongft a people who do not confider it as any crime at all, to murder

their

their own children. When, talking to them about such instances of unnatural cruelty, and asking, whether the Chiefs or principal people were not angry, and did not punish them? I was told, that the Chief neither could nor would interfere in such cases; and that every one had a right to do with his own child what he pleased.

Though the productions, the people, and the customs and manners of all the islands in the neighbourhood, may, in general, be reckoned the same as at Otaheite, there are a few differences which should be mentioned; as this may lead to an inquiry about more material ones hereafter, if such there be, of which we are now ignorant.

With regard to the little island Mataia, or Ofnaburgh Island, which lies twenty leagues East of Otaheite, and belongs to a Chief of that place, who gets from thence a kind of tribute; a different dialect from that of Otaheite, is there spoken. The men of Mataia also wear their hair very long; and, when they fight, cover their arms with a substance which is beset with sharks teeth, and their bodies with a sort of shagreen, being skin of fishes. At the same time, they are ornamented with polished pearl shells, which make a prodigious glittering in the sun; and they have a very large one, that covers them before, like a shield or breast-plate.

The language of Otaheite has many words, and even phrases, quite unlike those of the islands to the Westward of it, which all agree; and this island is remarkable for producing great quantities of that delicious fruit we called apples, which are found in none of the others, except Eimeo. It has also the advantage of producing an odoriferous wood, called *eaboi*, which is highly valued at the other isles, where there is none; nor even in the South East peninsula, or Tiaraboo, though joining it. Huaheine and Eimeo, again, are remarkable

markable for producing greater quantities of yams than the other iflands. And at Mourooa, there is a particular bird, found upon the hills, much efteemed for its white feathers; at which place there is alfo faid to be fome of the apples, though it be the moft remote of the Society Iflands from Otaheite and Eimeo, where they are produced.

Though the religion of all the iflands be the fame, each of them has its particular, or tutelar God; whofe names, according to the beft information I could receive, are fet down in the following lift:

Gods of the Ifles.

Huaheine,	*Tanne.*
Ulietea,	*Ooro.*
Otaha,	*Tanne.*
Bolabola,	*Oraa,*
Mourooa,	*Otoo, ee weiaboo.*
Toobaee,	*Tamouee.*
Tabooymanoo, or Saunders's Ifland, which is fubject to Huaheine,	*Taroa.*
Eimeo,	*Oroo badoo.*
Otaheite, { Otaheite-nooe,	*Ooroo.*
Tiaraboo, { *Opoonooa,* and *Whatooteeree,* { whom they have lately changed for Oraa, God of Bolabola.
Mataia, or Ofnaburgh Ifland,	*Tooboo, toobooai, Ry maraiva,*
The low ifles, Eaftward,	*Tammaree.*

Befides

1777.
December.

Befides the clufter of high iflands from Mataia to Mourooa inclufive, the people of Otaheite are acquainted with
a low uninhabited ifland, which they name Mopeeha, and
feems to be Howe's Ifland, laid down to the Weftward of
Mourooa in our late charts of this ocean. To this the inhabitants of the moft leeward iflands fometimes go. There
are alfo feveral low iflands, to the North Eaftward of Otaheite, which they have fometimes vifited, but not conftantly; and are faid to be only at the diftance of two days fail
with a fair wind. They were thus named to me:

Mataeeva,

Oanaa, { called Oannah in Dalrymple's Letter to
        {   Hawkefworth.

Taboohoe,

Awehee,

Kaoora,

Orootooa,

Otavaoo, where are large pearls.

The inhabitants of thefe ifles come more frequently to
Otaheite, and the other neighbouring high iflands, from
whofe natives they differ in being of a darker colour, with
a fiercer afpect, and differently punctured. I was informed,
that at Mataeeva, and others of them, it is a cuftom for the
men to give their daughters to ftrangers who arrive amongft
them; but the pairs muft be five nights lying near each
other, without prefuming to proceed farther. On the fixth
evening, the father of the young woman treats his gueft
with food, and informs his daughter, that fhe muft, that
night, receive him as her hufband. The ftranger, however, muft not offer to exprefs the leaft diflike, though the
bed-

bed-fellow allotted to him fhould be ever fo difagreeable; for this is confidered as an unpardonable affront, and is punifhed with death. Forty men of Bolabola, who, incited by curiofity, had róamed as far as Mataeeva in a canoe, were treated in this manner; one of them having incautioufly mentioned his diflike of the woman who fell to his lot, in the hearing of a boy, who informed her father. In confequence of this, the Mateevans fell upon them; but thefe warlike people killed three times their own number; though with the lofs of all their party, except five. Thefe hid themfelves in the woods, and took an opportunity, when the others were burying their dead, to enter fome houfes, where, having provided themfelves with victuals and water, they carried them on board a canoe, in which they made their efcape; and, after paffing Mataia, at which they would not touch, at laft arrived fafe at Eimeo. The Bolabolans, however, were fenfible enough that their travellers had been to blame; for a canoe from Mateeva, arriving fome time after at Bolabola, fo far were they from retaliating upon them for the death of their countrymen, that they acknowledged they had deferved their fate, and treated their vifiters kindly.

Thefe low ifles are, doubtlefs, the fartheft navigation, which thofe of Otaheite, and the Society Iflands, perform at prefent. It feems to be a groundlefs fuppofition, made by Monf. de Bougainville, that they made voyages of the prodigious extent * he mentions; for I found, that it is reckoned a fort of a prodigy, that a canoe, once driven by a ftorm from Otaheite, fhould have fallen in with Mopeeha, or Howe's Ifland, though fo near, and directly to leeward. The

---

* See *Bougainville's Voyage autour du Monde*, p. 228, where we are told, that thefe people fometimes navigate at the diftance of more than three hundred leagues.

knowledge they have of other diftant iflands is, no doubt, traditional; and has been communicated to them by the natives of thofe iflands, driven accidentally upon their coafts, who, befides giving them the names, could eafily inform them of the direction in which the places lie from whence they came, and of the number of days they had been upon the fea. In this manner, it may be fuppofed, that the natives of Wateeoo have increafed their catalogue by the addition of Otaheite and its neighbouring ifles, from the people we met with there, and alfo of the other iflands thefe had heard of. We may thus account for that extenfive knowledge attributed, by the gentlemen of the Endeavour *, to Tupia, in fuch matters. And, with all due deference to his veracity, I prefume that it was, by the fame means of information, that he was able to direct the fhip to Oheteroa, without having ever been there himfelf, as he pretended; which, on many accounts, is very improbable."

* Hawkefworth's Collection, Vol. ii. p. 278.

CHAP.

CHAP. X.

Progress of the Voyage, after leaving the Society Islands.— Christmas Island discovered, and Station of the Ships there. —Boats sent ashore.—Great Success in catching Turtle.—An Eclipse of the Sun observed.—Distress of two Seamen who had lost their Way.—Inscription left in a Bottle.—Account of the Island.—Its Soil.—Trees and Plants.—Birds.—Its Size.—Form.—Situation.—Anchoring Ground.

AFTER leaving Bolabola, I steered to the Northward, close-hauled, with the wind between North East and East; hardly ever having it to the Southward of East, till after we had crossed the line, and had got into North latitudes. So that our course, made good, was always to the West of North, and, sometimes, no better than North West.

Though seventeen months had now elapsed since our departure from England, during which, we had not, upon the whole, been unprofitably employed, I was sensible that, with regard to the principal object of my instructions, our voyage was, at this time, only beginning; and, therefore, my attention to every circumstance that might contribute toward our safety, and our ultimate success, was now to be called forth anew. With this view I had examined into the state of our provisions at the last islands; and, as soon as I had left them, and got beyond the extent of my former

1777.
December.

Monday 8.

A a 2   discoveries,

difcoveries, I ordered a furvey to be taken of all the boatfwain's and carpenter's ftores that were in the ships, that I
might be fully informed of the quantity, ftate, and condition of every article; and, by that means, know how to
ufe them to the greateft advantage.

Before I failed from the Society Iflands, I loft no opportunity of inquiring of the inhabitants, if there were any
iflands in a North or a North Weft direction from them;
but I did not find that they knew of any. Nor did we
meet with any thing that indicated the vicinity of land, till
we came to about the latitude of 8° South, where we began
to fee birds; fuch as boobies, tropic and men-of-war-birds,
tern, and fome other forts. At this time our longitude
was 205° Eaft. Mendana, in his firft voyage in 1568 *,
difcovered an ifland which he named Ifla de Jefus, in latitude 6° 45′ South, and 1450 leagues from Callao, which
is 200° Eaft longitude from Greenwich. We croffed this
latitude near a hundred leagues to the Eaftward of this
longitude, and faw there many of the above-mentioned
birds; which are feldom known to go very far from land.

Monday 22.   In the night, between the 22d and 23d, we croffed the
Tuefday 23. line in the longitude of 203° 15′ Eaft. Here the variation
of the compafs was 6° 30′ Eaft, nearly.

Wednef. 24.   On the 24th, about half an hour after day-break, land
was difcovered bearing North Eaft by Eaft, half Eaft. Upon
a nearer approach, it was found to be one of thofe low
iflands fo common in this ocean; that is, a narrow bank of
land inclofing the fea within. A few cocoa-nut trees were
feen in two or three places; but, in general, the land had
a very barren appearance. At noon, it extended from North
Eaft by Eaft, to South by Eaft, half Eaft, about four miles

* See Dalrymple's Collection, Vol. i. p. 45.

diftant.

distant. The wind was at Eaft South Eaft; fo that we were under a neceffity of making a few boards, to get up to the lee, or Weft fide; where we found from forty to twenty and fourteen fathoms water, over a bottom of fine fand; the leaft depth about half a mile from the breakers, and the greateft about one mile. The meeting with foundings determined me to anchor, with a view to try to get fome turtles; for the ifland feemed to be a likely place to meet with them, and to be without inhabitants. Accordingly, we dropped anchor in thirty fathoms; and then a boat was difpatched to examine whether it was practicable to land; of which I had fome doubt, as the fea broke in a dreadful furf all along the fhore. When the boat returned, the officer, whom I had intrufted with this examination, reported to me, that he could fee no place where a boat could land; but that there was great abundance of fifh in the fhoal water, without the breakers.

At day-break, the next morning, I fent two boats, one from each fhip, to fearch more accurately for a landing-place; and, at the fame time, two others, to fifh at a grappling near the fhore. Thefe laft returned about eight o'clock, with upward of two hundred weight of fifh. Encouraged by this fuccefs, they were difpatched again after breakfaft; and I then went in another boat, to take a view of the coaft, and attempt landing; but this I found to be wholly impracticable. Toward noon, the two boats, fent on the fame fearch, returned. The mafter, who was in that belonging to the Refolution, reported to me, that, about a league and a half to the North, was a break in the land, and a channel into the *lagoon*, confequently, that there was a fit place for landing; and that he had found the fame foundings off this entrance, as we had where we now lay. In
consequence

A VOYAGE TO

consequence of this report the ships weighed anchor, and, after two or three trips, came to again in twenty fathoms water, over a bottom of fine dark sand, before a small island that lies at the entrance of the *lagoon*; and on each side of which there is a channel leading into it; but only fit for boats. The water in the *lagoon* itself is all very shallow.

Friday 26.
On the 26th, in the morning, I ordered Captain Clerke to send a boat, with an officer, to the South East part of the *lagoon*, to look for turtles; and Mr. King and I went each in a boat to the North East part. I intended to have gone to the most Easterly extremity; but the wind blew too fresh to allow it, and obliged us to land more to leeward, on a sandy flat, where we caught one turtle; the only one that we saw in the *lagoon*. We walked, or rather waded, through the water, to an island; where finding nothing but a few birds, I left it, and proceeded to the land that bounds the sea to the North West, leaving Mr. King to observe the sun's meridian altitude. I found this land to be even more barren than the island I had been upon; but walking over to the sea-coast, I saw five turtles close to the shore. One of these we caught, and the rest made their escape. Not seeing any more, I returned on board, as did Mr. King soon after, without having seen one turtle. We, however, did not despair of getting a supply; for some of Captain Clerke's officers, who had been ashore on the land to the Southward of the channel leading into the *lagoon*, had been more fortunate, and caught several there.

Saturday 27.
In the morning of the 27th, the pinnace and cutter, under the command of Mr. King, were sent to the South East part of the island, within the *lagoon*; and the small cutter to the Northward, where I had been the day before; both parties being ordered upon the same service, to catch turtles.

tles. Captain Clerke having had fome of his people on fhore all night, they had been fo fortunate as to turn between forty and fifty on the fand, which were brought on board, with all expedition, this day. And in the afternoon, the party I had fent Northward returned with fix. They were fent back again, and remained there till we left the ifland; having in general pretty good fuccefs.

On the 28th, I landed, in company with Mr. Bayly, on the ifland which lies between the two channels into the *lagoon*, to prepare the telefcopes for obferving the approaching eclipfe of the fun; which was one great inducement to my anchoring here. About noon, Mr. King returned with one boat, and eight turtles; leaving feven behind to be brought by the other boat, whofe people were employed in catching more; and, in the evening, the fame boat was fent with water and provifions for them. Mr. Williamfon now went to fuperintend this duty in the room of Mr. King, who remained on board, to attend the obfervation of the eclipfe.

The next day, Mr. Williamfon difpatched the two boats back to the fhip, laden with turtles. At the fame time, he fent me a meffage, defiring, that the boats might be ordered round by fea, as he had found a landing-place on the South Eaft fide of the ifland, where moft of the turtles were caught; fo that, by fending the boats thither, the trouble would be faved of carrying them over the land to the infide of the *lagoon*, as had been hitherto done. The boats were, accordingly, difpatched to the place which he pointed out.

On the morning of the 30th, the day when the eclipfe was to happen, Mr. King, Mr. Bayly, and myfelf, went afhore, on the fmall ifland above-mentioned, to attend the obfervation. The fky was over-caft, till paft nine o'clock, when

when the clouds about the fun difperfed long enough to take its altitude, to rectify the time by the watch we made ufe of. After this, it was again obfcured, till about thirty minutes paft nine; and then we found, that the eclipfe was begun. We now fixed the micrometers to the tele-fcopes, and obferved, or meafured, the uneclipfed part of the fun's difk. At thefe obfervations I continued about three-quarters of an hour before the end, when I left off; being, in fact, unable to continue them longer, on account of the great heat of the fun, increafed by the reflection from the fand.

The fun was clouded at times; but it was clear, when the eclipfe ended, the time of which was obferved as follows :

		H. M. S.	
	Mr. Bayly	0 26 3	
By	Mr. King	at 0 26 1	Apparent Time P. M.
	Myfelf	0 25 37	

Mr. Bayly and I obferved with the large achromatic tele-fcopes; and Mr. King with a reflector. As Mr. Bayly's tele-fcope and mine were of the fame magnifying power, I ought not to have differed fo much from him as I did. Per-haps, it was, in part, if not wholly, owing to a protube-rance in the moon, which efcaped my notice, but was feen by both the other gentlemen.

In the afternoon, the boats and turtling party, at the South Eaft part of the ifland, all returned on board, except a feaman belonging to the Difcovery, who had been miffing two days. There were two of them at firft, who had loft their way; but difagreeing about the moft probable track to bring them back to their companions, they had feparated; and

and one of them joined the party, after having been abfent twenty-four hours, and been in great diftrefs. Not a
drop of frefh water could be had, for there is none upon
the whole ifland; nor was there a fingle cocoa-nut tree on
that part of it. In order to allay his thirft, he had recourfe
to the fingular expedient of killing turtles, and drinking
their blood. His mode of refrefhing himfelf, when weary,
of which he faid he felt the good effects, was equally whimfical. He undreffed himfelf, and lay down for fome time
in the fhallow water upon the beach.

It was a matter of furprize to every one, how thefe two
men could contrive to lofe themfelves. The land over which
they had to travel, from the fea-coaft to the *lagoon*, where
the boats lay, was not more than three miles acrofs; nor
was there any thing to obftruct their view; for the country
was a flat, with a few fhrubs fcattered upon it; and, from
many parts of it, the mafts of the fhips could eafily be feen.
But this was a rule of direction they never once thought of;
nor did they recollect in what quarter of the ifland the fhips
had anchored; and they were as much at a lofs how to get
back to them, or to the party they had ftraggled from, as if
they had but juft dropped from the clouds. Confidering
how ftrange a fet of beings the generality of feamen are,
when on fhore, inftead of being furprized that thefe two
men fhould thus lofe their way, it is rather to be wondered
at, that no more of the party were miffing. Indeed, one
of thofe who landed with me, was in a fimilar fituation; but
he had fagacity enough to know that the fhips were to leeward, and got on board almoft as foon as it was difcovered
that he had been left behind.

As foon as Captain Clerke knew, that one of the ftragglers
was ftill in this awkward fituation, he fent a party in fearch

of him; but neither the man nor the party having come
back, the next morning, I ordered two boats into the *lagoon*,
to go different ways, in profecution of the fearch. Not long
after, Captain Clerke's party returned with their loft companion; and my boats having now no object left, I called
them back by fignal. This poor fellow muft have fuffered
far greater diftrefs than the other ftraggler; not only as
having been loft a longer time, but as we found that he
was too fqueamifh to drink turtle's blood.

Having fome cocoa-nuts and yams on board, in a ftate of
vegetation, I ordered them to be planted on the little ifland
where we had obferved the eclipfe; and fome melon-feeds
were fown in another place. I alfo left, on the little ifland,
a bottle containing this infcription:

Georgius Tertius, Rex, 31 *Decembris*, 1777.
Naves { *Refolution, Jac. Cook, Pr.*
{ *Difcovery, Car. Clerke, Pr.*

On the 1ft of January 1778, I fent boats to bring on board
all our parties from the land, and the turtles they had
caught. Before this was completed, it was late in the afternoon; fo that I did not think proper to fail till next morning. We got at this ifland, to both fhips, about three hundred turtles, weighing, one with another, about ninety or a
hundred pounds. They were all of the green kind; and
perhaps as good as any in the world. We alfo caught, with
hook and line, as much fifh as we could confume, during
our ftay. They confifted principally of cavallies, of different fizes; large and fmall fnappers; and a few of two
forts of rock-fifh; one with numerous fpots of blue, and
the other with whitifh ftreaks fcattered about.

The

The foil of this ifland, in fome places, is light and black, evidently compofed of decayed vegetables, the dung of birds, and fand. There are other places again, where nothing but marine productions, fuch as broken coral ftones, and fhells, are to be feen. Thefe are depofited in long, narrow ridges, lying in a parallel direction with the fea-coaft, not unlike a ploughed field; and muft have been thrown up by the waves, though, at this time, they do not reach within a mile of fome of thefe places. This feems to furnifh an inconteftable proof, that the ifland has been produced by acceffions from the fea, and is in a ftate of increafe; for not only the broken pieces of coral, but many of the fhells, are too heavy and large to have been brought by any birds, from the beach, to the places where they now lie. Not a drop of frefh water was any where found, though frequently dug for. We met with feveral ponds of falt water, which had no vifible communication with the fea, and muft, therefore, in all probability, be filled by the water filtrating through the fand, in high tides. One of the loft men found fome falt on the South Eaft part of the ifland. But, though this was an article of which we were in want, a man who could lofe himfelf, as he did, and not know whether he was travelling Eaft, Weft, North, or South, was not to be depended upon as a fit guide to conduct us to the place.

There were not the fmalleft traces of any human being having ever been here before us; and, indeed, fhould any one be fo unfortunate as to be accidentally driven upon the ifland, or left there, it is hard to fay, that he could be able to prolong exiftence. There is, indeed, abundance of birds and fifh; but no vifible means of allaying thirft, nor any vegetable that could fupply the place of bread, or correct

B b 2   the

the bad effects of an animal diet; which, in all probability, would soon prove fatal alone. On the few cocoa-trees upon the island, the number of which did not exceed thirty, very little fruit was found; and, in general, what was found, was either not fully grown, or had the juice salt, or brackish. So that a ship touching here, must expect nothing but fish and turtles; and of these an abundant supply may be depended upon.

On some parts of the land were a few low trees. Mr. Anderson gave me an account, also, of two small shrubs, and of two or three small plants; all which we had seen on Palmerston's Island, and Otakootaia. There was also a species of *sida*, or Indian mallow; a sort of purslain; and another small plant, that seemed, from its leaves, a *mesembryanthemum*; with two species of grass. But each of these vegetable productions was in so small a quantity, and grew with so much languor, that one is almost surprized that the species do not become extinct.

Under the low trees above-mentioned, sat infinite numbers of a new species of tern, or egg-bird. These are black above, and white below, with a white arch on the forehead; and are rather larger than the common noddy. Most of them had lately hatched their young; which lay under old ones, upon the bare ground. The rest had eggs; of which they only lay one, larger than that of a pigeon, bluish and speckled with black. There were also a good many common boobies; a sort that are almost like a gannet; and a sooty, or chocolate-coloured one, with a white belly. To this list we must add men-of-war-birds; tropic-birds; curlews; sand-pipers; a small land-bird like a hedge-sparrow; land-crabs; small lizards; and rats.

As we kept our Christmas here, I called this discovery
Christmas

Chriſtmas Iſland. I judge it to be about fifteen or twenty
leagues in circumference. It ſeemed to be of a ſemicir-cular form; or like the moon in the laſt quarter, the two horns being the North and South points; which bear from each other nearly North by Eaſt, and South by Weſt, four or five leagues diſtant. This Weſt ſide, or the little iſle at the entrance into the *lagoon,* upon which we obſerved the eclipſe, lies in the latitude of 1° 59′ North, and in the lon-gitude of 202° 30′ Eaſt, determined by a conſiderable num-ber of lunar obſervations, which differed only 7′ from the time-keeper; it being ſo much leſs. The variation of the compaſs was 6° 22¼′ Eaſt; and the dip of the North end of the needle 11° 54′.

Chriſtmas Iſland, like moſt others in this ocean, is bound-ed by a reef of coral rocks, which extends but a little way from the ſhore. Farther out than this reef, on the Weſt ſide, is a bank of fine ſand, extending a mile into the ſea. On this bank is good anchorage, in any depth between eighteen and thirty fathoms. In leſs than the firſt-men-tioned depth, the reef would be too near; and in more than the laſt, the edge of the bank would not be at a ſufficient diſtance. During the time we lay here, the wind blew, conſtantly, a freſh gale at Eaſt, or Eaſt by South, except one or two days. We had, always, a great ſwell from the Northward, which broke upon the reef, in a prodigious ſurf. We had found this ſwell before we came to the iſland; and it continued for ſome days after we left it.

CHAP.

CHAP. XI.

Some Iſlands diſcovered.—Account of the Natives of Atooi, who come off to the Ships, and their Behaviour on going on board.—One of them killed.—Precautions uſed to prevent Intercourſe with the Females.—A watering-place found.— Reception upon landing.—Excurſion into the Country.—A Morai viſited and deſcribed.—Graves of the Chiefs, and of the human Sacrifices, there buried.—Another Iſland, called Oneeheow, viſited.—Ceremonies performed by the Natives, who go off to the Ships.—Reaſons for believing that they are Cannibals.—A Party ſent aſhore, who remain two Nights.— Account of what paſſed on landing.—The Ships leave the Iſlands, and proceed to the North.

1778.
January.
Friday 2.

ON the 2d of January, at day-break, we weighed anchor, and reſumed our courſe to the North; having fine weather, and a gentle breeze at Eaſt, and Eaſt South Eaſt, till we got into the latitude of 7° 45′ North, and the longitude of 205° Eaſt, where we had one calm day. This was ſucceeded by a North Eaſt by Eaſt, and Eaſt North Eaſt wind. At firſt it blew faint, but freſhened as we advanced to the North. We continued to ſee birds every day, of the ſorts laſt mentioned; ſometimes in greater numbers than others; and between the latitude of 10° and 11°, we ſaw ſeveral turtles. All theſe are looked upon as ſigns of the vicinity of land. However, we diſcovered none till daybreak,

break, in the morning of the 18th, when an ifland made its
appearance, bearing North Eaft by Eaft; and, foon after, we
faw more land bearing North, and entirely detached from
the former. Both had the appearance of being high land.
At noon, the firft bore North Eaft by Eaft, half Eaft, by eftim-
mation about eight or nine leagues diftant; and an elevated
hill, near the Eaft end of the other, bore North, half Weft.
Our latitude, at this time, was 21° 12′, North; and longitude 200° 41′, Eaft. We had now light airs and calms, by
turns; fo that, at funfet, we were not lefs than nine or ten
leagues from the neareft land.

On the 19th, at fun-rife, the ifland firft feen, bore Eaft,
feveral leagues diftant. This being directly to windward,
which prevented our getting near it, I ftood for the other,
which we could reach; and, not long after, difcovered a
third ifland in the direction of Weft North Weft, as far diftant as land could be feen. We had now a fine breeze at
Eaft by North; and I fteered for the Eaft end of the fecond
ifland; which, at noon, extended from North, half Eaft, to
Weft North Weft, a quarter Weft, the neareft part being
about two leagues diftant. At this time, we were in fome
doubt whether or no the land before us was inhabited;
but this doubt was foon cleared up, by feeing fome canoes
coming off from the fhore, toward the fhips. I immediately brought to, to give them time to join us. They had
from three to fix men each; and, on their approach, we
were agreeably furprized to find, that they fpoke the language of Otaheite, and of the other iflands we had lately
vifited. It required but very little addrefs, to get them to
come along-fide; but no intreaties could prevail upon any
of them to come on board. I tied fome brafs medals to a
rope, and gave them to thofe in one of the canoes, who, in

3   return,

1778.
January.

return, tied some small mackerel to the rope, as an equivalent.   This was repeated; and some small nails, or bits
of iron, which they valued more than any other article,
were given them.   For these they exchanged more fish, and
a sweet potatoe; a sure sign that they had some notion of
bartering; or, at least, of returning one present for another.
They had nothing else in their canoes, except some large
gourd shells, and a kind of fishing-net; but one of them
offered for sale the piece of stuff that he wore round his
waist, after the manner of the other islands.   These people
were of a brown colour; and, though of the common size,
were stoutly made.   There was little difference in the
casts of their colour, but a considerable variation in their
features; some of their visages not being very unlike those
of Europeans.   The hair of most of them was cropt pretty
short; others had it flowing loose; and, with a few, it was
tied in a bunch on the crown of the head.   In all, it seemed
to be naturally black; but most of them had stained it, as
is the practice of the Friendly Islanders, with some stuff
which gave it a brown or burnt colour.   In general, they
wore their beards.   They had no ornaments about their
persons, nor did we observe that their ears were perforated; but some were punctured on the hands, or near
the groin, though in a small degree; and the bits of cloth,
which they wore, were curiously stained with red, black,
and white colours.   They seemed very mild; and had no
arms of any kind, if we except some small stones, which
they had evidently brought for their own defence; and
these they threw overboard when they found that they
were not wanted.

Seeing no signs of an anchoring-place at this Eastern
extreme of the island, I bore away to leeward, and ranged
along

along the South Eaſt ſide, at the diſtance of half a league from the ſhore. As ſoon as we made ſail, the canoes left us; but others came off, as we proceeded along the coaſt, bringing with them roaſting-pigs, and ſome very fine potatoes, which they exchanged, as the others had done, for whatever was offered to them. Several ſmall pigs were purchaſed for a ſixpenny nail; ſo that we again found ourſelves in a land of plenty; and juſt at the time when the turtles, which we had ſo fortunately procured at Chriſtmas Iſland, were nearly expended. We paſſed ſeveral villages; ſome ſeated near the ſea, and others farther up the country. The inhabitants of all of them crowded to the ſhore, and collected themſelves on the elevated places to view the ſhips. The land upon this ſide of the iſland riſes, in a gentle ſlope, from the ſea to the foot of the mountains, which occupy the centre of the country, except at one place near the Eaſt end, where they riſe directly from the ſea, and ſeemed to be formed of nothing but ſtone, or rocks lying in horizontal *ſtrata*. We ſaw no wood, but what was up in the interior part of the iſland, except a few trees about the villages; near which, alſo, we could obſerve ſeveral plantations of plantains and ſugar-canes, and ſpots that ſeemed cultivated for roots.

We continued to ſound, without ſtriking ground with a line of fifty fathoms, till we came abreaſt of a low point, which is about the middle of this ſide of the iſland, or rather nearer the North Weſt end. Here we met with twelve and fourteen fathoms, over a rocky bottom. Being paſt this point, from which the coaſt trended more Northerly, we had twenty, then ſixteen, twelve, and, at laſt, five fathoms over a ſandy bottom. The laſt ſoundings were about a mile from the ſhore. Night now put a ſtop to any farther re-

VOL. II.   C c   ſearches;

fearches; and we fpent it ftanding off and on. The next morning, we ftood in for the land, and were met with feveral canoes filled with people; fome of whom took courage, and ventured on board.

In the courfe of my feveral voyages, I never before met with the natives of any place fo much aftonifhed, as thefe people were, upon entering a fhip. Their eyes were continually flying from object to object; the wildnefs of their looks and geftures fully expreffing their entire ignorance about every thing they faw, and ftrongly marking to us, that, till now, they had never been vifited by Europeans, nor been acquainted with any of our commodities, except iron; which, however, it was plain, they had only heard of, or had known it in fome fmall quantity, brought to them at fome diftant period. They feemed only to underftand, that it was a fubftance, much better adapted to the purpofes of cutting, or of boring of holes, than any thing their own country produced. They afked for it by the name of *hamaite*, probably referring to fome inftrument, in the making of which iron could be ufefully employed; for they applied that name to the blade of a knife, though we could be certain that they had no idea of that particular inftrument; nor could they, at all, handle it properly. For the fame reafon, they frequently called iron by the name of *toe*, which, in their language, fignifies a hatchet, or rather a kind of adze. On afking them what iron was, they immediately anfwered, "We do not know; you know what it is, and we only underftand it as *toe*, or *hamaite*." When we fhewed them fome beads, they afked firft, "What they were; and then, whether they fhould eat them." But on their being told, that they were to be hung in their ears, they returned them as ufelefs. They were equally indifferent

ferent as to a looking-glafs, which was offered them, and returned it, for the fame reafon; but fufficiently expreffed their defire for *bamaite* and *toe*, which they wifhed might be very large. Plates of earthen-ware, china-cups, and other fuch things, were fo new to them, that they afked if they were made of wood; but wifhed to have fome, that they might carry them to be looked at on fhore. They were, in fome refpects, naturally well bred; or, at leaft, fearful of giving offence, afking, whether they fhould fit down, whether they might fpit upon the deck, and the like. Some of them repeated a long prayer before they came on board; and others, afterward, fung and made motions with their hands, fuch as we had been accuftomed to fee in the dances of the iflands we had lately vifited. There was another circumftance, in which they alfo perfectly refembled thofe other iflanders. At firft, on their entering the fhip, they endeavoured to fteal every thing they came near; or rather to take it openly, as what we either fhould not refent, or not hinder. We foon convinced them of their miftake; and if they, after fome time, became lefs active in appropriating to themfelves whatever they took a fancy to, it was becaufe they found that we kept a watchful eye over them.

At nine o'clock, being pretty near the fhore, I fent three armed boats, under the command of Lieutenant Williamfon, to look for a landing-place, and for frefh water. I ordered him, that if he fhould find it neceffary to land in fearch of the latter, not to fuffer more than one man to go with him out of the boats. Juft as they were putting off from the fhip, one of the natives having ftolen the butcher's cleaver, leaped overboard, got into his canoe, and haftened to the fhore, the boats purfuing him in vain.

The order not to permit the crews of the boats to go on

fhore

shore was issued, that I might do every thing in my power to prevent the importation of a fatal disease into this island, which I knew some of our men now laboured under, and which, unfortunately, had been already communicated by us to other islands in these seas. With the same view, I ordered all female visiters to be excluded from the ships. Many of them had come off in the canoes. Their size, colour, and features did not differ much from those of the men; and though their countenances were remarkably open and agreeable, there were few traces of delicacy to be seen, either in their faces, or other proportions. The only difference in their dress, was their having a piece of cloth about the body, reaching from near the middle, to half-way down the thighs, instead of the *maro* worn by the other sex. They would as readily have favoured us with their company on board as the men; but I wished to prevent all connection, which might, too probably, convey an irreparable injury to themselves, and, through their means, to the whole nation. Another necessary precaution was taken, by strictly enjoining, that no person, known to be capable of propagating the infection, should be sent upon duty out of the ships.

Whether these regulations, dictated by humanity, had the desired effect, or no, time only can discover. I had been equally attentive to the same object, when I first visited the Friendly Islands; yet I afterward found, with real concern, that I had not succeeded. And I am much afraid, that this will always be the case, in such voyages as ours, whenever it is necessary to have a number of people on shore. The opportunities and inducements to an intercourse between the sexes are then too numerous to be guarded against; and however confident we may be of the health of our men, we are often undeceived too late. It is even

a matter

a matter of doubt with me, if it be always in the power of the moſt ſkilful of the faculty to pronounce, with any certainty, whether a perſon who has been under their care, in certain ſtages of this malady, is ſo effectually cured, as to leave no poſſibility of his being ſtill capable of communicating the taint. I think I could mention ſome inſtances which juſtify my preſuming to hazard this opinion. It is, likewiſe, well known, that, amongſt a number of men, there are, generally, to be found ſome ſo baſhful as to endeavour to conceal their labouring under any ſymptoms of this diſorder. And there are others, again, ſo profligate, as not to care to whom they communicate it. Of this laſt, we had an inſtance at Tongataboo, in the gunner of the Diſcovery, who had been ſtationed on ſhore to manage the trade for that ſhip. After he knew that he had contracted this diſeaſe, he continued to have connections with different women, who were ſuppoſed not to have already contracted it. His companions expoſtulated with him without effect, till Captain Clerke, hearing of this dangerous irregularity of conduct, ordered him on board.

While the boats were occupied in examining the coaſt, we ſtood on and off with the ſhips, waiting for their return. About noon, Mr. Williamſon came back, and reported, that he had ſeen a large pond behind a beach near one of the villages, which the natives told him contained freſh water; and that there was anchoring-ground before it. He alſo reported, that he had attempted to land in another place, but was prevented by the natives, who, coming down to the boats in great numbers, attempted to take away the oars, muſquets, and, in ſhort, every thing that they could lay hold of; and preſſed ſo thick upon him, that he was obliged to fire, by which one man was killed. But this unhappy

happy circumftance I did not know till after we had left the
ifland; fo that all my meafures were directed as if nothing
of the kind had happened. Mr. Williamfon told me, that,
after the man fell, his countrymen took him up, carried
him off, and then retired from the boat; but ftill they made
fignals for our people to land, which he declined. It did
not appear to Mr. Williamfon, that the natives had any defign to kill, or even to hurt, any of his party; but they
feemed excited by mere curiofity, to get from them what
they had, being, at the fame time, ready to give, in return,
any thing of their own.

After the boats were on board, I difpatched one of them
to lie in the beft anchoring-ground; and as foon as fhe had
got to this ftation, I bore down with the fhips, and anchored
in twenty-five fathoms water; the bottom a fine grey fand.
The Eaft point of the road, which was the low point before mentioned, bore South 51° Eaft; the Weft point, North
65° Weft; and the village, behind which the water was faid
to be, North Eaft by Eaft, diftant one mile. But, little more
than a quarter of a mile from us, there were breakers, which
I did not fee till after the Refolution was placed. The Difcovery anchored to the Eaftward of us, and farther from
the land. The fhips being thus ftationed, between three
and four o'clock, I went afhore with three armed boats, and
twelve marines, to examine the water, and to try the difpofition of the inhabitants, feveral hundred of whom were
affembled on a fandy beach before the village; behind it
was a narrow valley, the bottom of which was occupied by
the piece of water.

The very inftant I leaped on fhore, the collected body of
the natives all fell flat upon their faces, and remained in
that very humble pofture, till, by expreffive figns, I prevailed

3   upon

upon them to rife. They then brought a great many fmall
pigs, which they prefented to me, with plantain-trees, ufing much the fame ceremonies that we had feen practifed, on fuch occafions, at the Society and other iflands; and a long prayer being fpoken by a fingle perfon, in which others of the affembly fometimes joined. I expreffed my acceptance of their proffered friendfhip, by giving them, in return, fuch prefents as I had brought with me from the fhip for that purpofe. When this introductory bufinefs was finifhed, I ftationed a guard upon the beach, and got fome of the natives to conduct me to the water, which proved to be very good, and in a proper fituation for our purpofe. It was fo confiderable, that it may be called a lake; and it extended farther up the country than we could fee. Having fatisfied myfelf about this very effential point, and about the peaceable difpofition of the natives, I returned on board; and then gave orders that every thing fhould be in readinefs for landing and filling our water-cafks in the morning; when I went afhore with the people employed in that fervice, having a party of marines with us for a guard, who were ftationed on the beach.

As foon as we landed, a trade was fet on foot for hogs and potatoes, which the people of the ifland gave us in exchange for nails and pieces of iron, formed into fomething like chiffels. We met with no obftruction in watering; on the contrary, the natives affifted our men in rolling the cafks to and from the pool; and readily performed whatever we required. Every thing thus going on to my fatisfaction, and confidering my prefence on the fpot as unneceffary, I left the command to Mr. Williamfon, who had landed with me, and made an excurfion into the country, up the valley, accompanied by Mr. Anderfon and Mr. Webber;

the

the former of whom was as well qualified to defcribe with the pen, as the latter was to reprefent with his pencil, every thing we might meet with worthy of obfervation. A numerous train of natives followed us; and one of them, whom I had diftinguifhed for his activity in keeping the reft in order, I made choice of as our guide. This man, from time to time, proclaimed our approach; and every one, whom we met, fell proftrate upon the ground, and remained in that pofition till we had paffed. This, as I afterward underftood, is the mode of paying their refpect to their own great Chiefs. As we ranged down the coaft from the Eaft, in the fhips, we had obferved at every village one or more elevated white objects, like pyramids or rather obelifks; and one of thefe, which I gueffed to be at leaft fifty feet high, was very confpicuous from the fhip's anchoring ftation, and feemed to be at no great diftance up this valley. To have a nearer infpection of it, was the principal object of my walk. Our guide perfectly underftood that we wifhed to be conducted to it. But it happened to be fo placed, that we could not get at it, being feparated from us by the pool of water. However, there being another of the fame kind within our reach, about half a mile off, upon our fide of the valley, we fet out to vifit that. The moment we got to it, we faw that it ftood in a burying-ground, or *morai*; the refemblance of which, in many refpects, to thofe we were fo well acquainted with at other iflands in this ocean, and particularly Otaheite, could not but ftrike us; and we alfo foon found, that the feveral parts that compofe it, were called by the fame names. It was an oblong fpace, of confiderable extent, furrounded by a wall of ftone, about four feet high. The fpace inclofed was loofely paved with fmaller ftones; and at one end of it, ftood what I call the pyramid,

1778.
January.

mid, but, in the language of the island, is named *hena-nanoo*; which appeared evidently to be an exact model of the larger one, obferved by us from the fhips. It was about four feet fquare at the bafe, and about twenty feet high. The four fides were compofed of fmall poles interwoven with twigs and branches, thus forming an indifferent wicker-work, hollow or open within, from bottom to top. It feemed to be rather in a ruinous ftate; but there were fufficient remaining marks, to fhew, that it had originally been covered with a thin, light, grey cloth; which thefe people, it fhould feem, confecrate to religious purpofes; as we could fee a good deal of it hanging in different parts of the *morai*; and fome of it had been forced upon me when I firft landed. On each fide of the pyramid were long pieces of wicker-work, called *hereanee*, in the fame ruinous condition; with two flender poles, inclining to each other, at one corner, where fome plantains were laid upon a board, fixed at the height of five or fix feet. This they called *herairemy*; and informed us, that the fruit was an offering to their God, which makes it agree exactly with the *whatta* of Otaheite. Before the *henananoo* were a few pieces of wood, carved into fomething like human figures, which, with a ftone near two feet high, covered with pieces of cloth, called *hoho*, and confecrated to *Tongarooa*, who is the God of thefe people, ftill more and more reminded us of what we ufed to meet with in the *morais* of the iflands we had lately left *. Adjoining to thefe, on the outfide of the *morai*, was a fmall fhed, no bigger than a dog-kennel, which they called *ha-*

* See the defcription of the *morai*, in Otaheite, where the human facrifice was offered, at which Captain Cook was prefent.

reepahoo; and before it was a grave, where, as we were told, the remains of a woman lay.

On the farther fide of the area of the *morai*, ftood a houfe or fhed, about forty feet long; ten broad in the middle, each end being narrower, and about ten feet high. This, which, though much longer, was lower than their common dwelling-places, we were informed, was called *hemanaa*. The entrance into it was at the middle of the fide, which was in the *morai*. On the farther fide of this houfe, oppofite the entrance, ftood two wooden images, cut out of one piece, with pedeftals, in all about three feet high; neither very indifferently defigned nor executed. Thefe were faid to be *Eatooa no Veheina*, or reprefentations of goddeffes. On the head of one of them was a carved helmet, not unlike thofe worn by the ancient warriors; and on that of the other, a cylindrical cap, refembling the head-drefs at Otaheite, called *tomou*; and both of them had pieces of cloth, tied about the loins, and hanging a confiderable way down. At the fide of each, was alfo a piece of carved wood, with bits of the cloth hung on them, in the fame manner: and between, or before, the pedeftals, lay a quantity of fern, in a heap. It was obvious, that this had been depofited there, piece by piece, and at different times; for there was of it, in all ftates, from what was quite decayed, to what was ftill frefh and green.

In the middle of the houfe, and before the two images, was an oblong fpace, inclofed by a low edging of ftone, and covered with fhreds of the cloth fo often mentioned. This, on inquiry, we found, was the grave of feven Chiefs, whofe names were enumerated, and the place was called *Heneene*. We had met already with fo many ftriking inftances of refemblance,

femblance, between the burying-place we were now vifiting, and thofe of the iflands we had lately come from in the South Pacific, that we had little doubt in our minds, that the refemblance exifted alfo, in the ceremonies practifed here, and particularly in the horrid one of offering human facrifices. Our fufpicions were too foon confirmed, by direct evidence. For, on coming out of the houfe, juft on one fide of the entrance, we faw a fmall fquare place, and another ftill lefs, near it; and on afking, what thefe were? Our guide immediately informed us, that in the one was buried a man who had been facrificed; a *Taata (Tanata* or *Tangata,* in this country) *taboo (tafoo,* as here pronounced); and in the other, a hog, which had alfo been made an offering to the divinity. At a little diftance from thefe, near the middle of the *morai,* were three more of thefe fquare, inclofed places, with two pieces of carved wood at each, and upon them a heap of fern. Thefe, we were told, were the graves of three Chiefs; and before them, was an oblong, inclofed fpace, to which our conductor alfo gave the name of *Tangata-taboo;* telling us, fo explicitly, that we could not miftake his meaning, that three human facrifices had been buried there; that is, one at the funeral of each Chief. It was with moft fincere concern, that I could trace, on fuch undoubted evidence, the prevalence of thefe bloody-rites, throughout this immenfe ocean, amongft people disjoined by fuch a diftance, and even ignorant of each other's exiftence, though fo ftrongly marked as originally of the fame nation. It was no fmall addition to this concern, to reflect, that every appearance led us to believe, that the barbarous practice was very general here. The ifland feemed to abound with fuch places of facrifice as this which we were now vifiting, and which appeared to be one of the moft inconfiderable of

them;

them; being far lefs confpicuous than feveral others which
we had feen, as we failed along the coaft, and particularly
than that on the oppofite fide of the water, in this valley,
the white *henananoo*, or pyramid, of which, we were now
almoft fure, derived its colour only from pieces of the confecrated cloth laid over it.   In feveral parts, within the in-
clofure of this burying-ground, were planted trees of the
cordia febeftina; fome of the *morinda citrifolia*; and feveral
plants of the *etee*, or *jeejee*, of Tongataboo, with the leaves
of which the *hemanaa* was thatched ; and, as I obferved,
that this plant was not made ufe of in thatching their
dwelling-houfes, probably it is referved entirely for religious purpofes.

Our road to and from the *morai*, which I have defcribed,
lay through the plantations.   The greateft part of the
ground was quite flat, with ditches full of water interfect-
ing different parts, and roads that feemed artificially raifed
to fome height.   The interfpaces were, in general, planted
with *taro*, which grows here with great ftrength, as the fields
are funk below the common level, fo as to contain the water
neceffary to nourifh the roots.   This water probably comes
from the fame fource, which fupplies the large pool from
which we filled our cafks.   On the drier fpaces were feveral
fpots, where the cloth-mulberry was planted, in regular rows;
alfo growing vigoroufly, and kept very clean.   The cocoa-
trees were not in fo thriving a ftate, and were all low; but
the plantain-trees made a better appearance ; though they
were not large.   In general, the trees round this village,
and which were feen at many of thofe which we paffed before we anchored, are the *cordia febeftina* ; but of a more di-
minutive fize than the product of the Southern ifles.   The
greateft part of the village ftands near the beach, and confifts

1778.
January.

sists of above sixty houses there; but, perhaps, about forty more stand scattered about, farther up the country, toward the burying-place.

After we had examined, very carefully, every thing that was to be seen about the *morai*, and Mr. Webber had taken drawings of it, and of the adjoining country, we returned by a different route. I found a great crowd assembled at the beach; and a brisk trade for pigs, fowls, and roots, going on there, with the greatest good order; though I did not observe any particular person, who took the lead amongst the rest of his countrymen. At noon, I went on board to dinner, and then sent Mr. King, to command the party ashore. He was to have gone upon that service in the morning, but was then detained in the ship, to make lunar observations. In the afternoon, I landed again, accompanied by Captain Clerke, with a view to make another excursion up the country. But, before this could be put in execution, the day was too far spent; so that I laid aside my intention for the present; and it so happened, that I had not another opportunity. At sun-set, I brought every body on board; having procured, in the course of the day, nine tons of water; and, by exchanges, chiefly for nails and pieces of iron, about seventy or eighty pigs, a few fowls, a quantity of potatoes, and a few plantains, and *taro* roots. These people merited our best commendations, in this commercial intercourse, never once attempting to cheat us, either ashore, or along-side the ships. Some of them, indeed, as already mentioned, at first betrayed a thievish disposition; or rather, they thought, that they had a right to every thing they could lay their hands upon; but they soon laid aside a conduct, which, we convinced them, they could not persevere in with impunity.

Amongst

Amongſt the articles which they brought to barter, this day, we could not help taking notice of a particular ſort of cloak and cap, which, even in countries where dreſs is more particularly attended to, might be reckoned elegant. The firſt, are nearly of the ſize and ſhape of the ſhort cloaks worn by the women in England, and by the men in Spain, reaching to the middle of the back, and tied looſely before. The ground of them is a net-work, upon which the moſt beautiful red and yellow feathers are ſo cloſely fixed, that the ſurface might be compared to the thickeſt and richeſt velvet, which they reſemble, both as to the feel, and the gloſſy appearance. The manner of varying the mixture is very different; ſome having triangular ſpaces of red and yellow, alternately; others, a kind of creſcent; and ſome that were entirely red, had a broad yellow border, which made them appear, at ſome diſtance, exactly like a ſcarlet cloak edged with gold lace. The brilliant colours of the feathers, in thoſe that happened to be new, added not a little to their fine appearance; and we found, that they were in high eſtimation with their owners; for they would not, at firſt, part with one of them, for any thing that we offered, aſking no leſs a price than a muſquet. However, ſome were afterward purchaſed for very large nails. Such of them as were of the beſt ſort, were ſcarce; and it ſhould ſeem, that they are only uſed on the occaſion of ſome particular cere-mony, or diverſion; for the people who had them, always made ſome geſticulations, which we had ſeen uſed before by thoſe who ſung.

The cap is made almoſt exactly like a helmet, with the middle part, or creſt, ſometimes of a hand's breadth; and it fits very cloſe upon the head, having notches to admit the ears. It is a frame of twigs and oſiers, covered with a net-
work,

work, into which are wrought feathers, in the fame manner as upon the cloaks, though rather clofer, and lefs diverfified; the greater part being red, with fome black, yellow, or green ftripes, on the fides, following the curve direction of the creft. Thefe, probably, complete the drefs, with the cloaks; for the natives, fometimes, appeared in both together.

We were at a lofs to guefs from whence they could get fuch a quantity of thefe beautiful feathers; but were foon informed, as to one fort; for they afterward brought great numbers of fkins of fmall red birds for fale, which were often tied up in bunches of twenty or more, or had a fmall wooden fkewer run through their noftrils. At the firft, thofe that were bought, confifted only of the fkin from behind the wings forward; but we, afterward, got many with the hind part, including the tail and feet. The firft, however, ftruck us, at once, with the origin of the fable formerly adopted, of the birds of paradife wanting legs; and fufficiently explained that circumftance. Probably the people of the iflands Eaft of the Moluccas, from whence the fkins of the birds of paradife are brought, cut off their feet, for the very reafon affigned by the people of Atooi, for the like practice; which was, that they hereby can preferve them with greater eafe, without lofing any part which they reckon valuable. The red-bird of our ifland, was judged by Mr. Anderfon to be a fpecies of *merops*, about the fize of a fparrow; of a beautiful fcarlet colour, with a black tail and wings; and an arched bill, twice the length of the head, which, with the feet, was alfo of a reddifh colour. The contents of the heads were taken out, as in the birds of paradife; but it did not appear, that they ufed any other method to preferve them, than by fimple drying; for the

3   fkins,

ſkins, though moiſt, had neither a taſte nor ſmell that could give room to ſuſpect the uſe of antiputreſcent ſubſtances *.

In the night, and all the morning, on the 22d, it rained almoſt continually. The wind was at South Eaſt, South South Eaſt, and South; which brought in a ſhort, chopping ſea; and as there were breakers little more than two cables length from the ſtern of our ſhip, her ſituation was none of the ſafeſt. The ſurf broke ſo high againſt the ſhore, that we could not land in our boats; but the day was not wholly loſt; for the natives ventured in their canoes, to bring off to the ſhips hogs and roots, which they bartered as before. One of our viſiters, on this occaſion, who offered ſome fiſhhooks to ſale, was obſerved to have a very ſmall parcel, tied

---

* It is matter of real curioſity to obſerve, how very extenſively the predilection for red feathers is ſpread throughout all the iſlands of the Pacific Ocean: and the additional circumſtance, mentioned in this paragraph, will, probably, be looked upon, by thoſe who amuſe themſelves in tracing the wonderful migrations of the ſame family, or tribe, as a confirmation of that hypotheſis (built indeed on other inſtances of reſemblance), which conſiders New Guinea, and its neighbouring Eaſt India iſlands, from whence the Dutch bring their birds of paradiſe, as originally peopled by the ſame race, which Captain Cook found at every iſland from New Zealand to this new group, to which Atooi belongs. What Mr. Sonnerat tells us, about the bird of paradiſe, agrees perfectly with the account here given of the preſerved red-birds. Speaking of the *Papous*, he proceeds thus: " Ils nous préſenterent pluſieurs eſpeces d'oiſeaux, auſſi élégants par leur forme, que " brillants par l'éclat de leur couleur. La dépouille des oiſeaux ſert à la parure des " Chefs, qui la portent attachée à leurs bonnets en forme d'aigrettes. *Mais en préparant* " *les peaux, ils coupent les pieds.* Les Hollandois, qui trafiquent ſur ces cotes, y achetent " de ces peaux ainſi préparées, les tranſportent en Perſe, à Surate, dans les Indes, où ils " les vendent fort chère aux habitans riches, qui en font des aigrettes pour leurs turbans, " et pour le caſque des guerriers, et qui en parent leur chevaux. C'eſt de là qu'eſt ve- " nue l'opinion, qu'une de ces eſpeces d'oiſeaux (l'oiſeau de paradis) *n'a point de pattes.* " Les Hollandois ont accrédité ces fables, qui, en jetant du merveilleux ſur l'objet dont " ils traffiquoient, étoient propres à le rendre plus précieux, et à en rechauſſer la valeur." *Voyage à la Nouvelle Guinée*, p. 154.

to

to the string of one of them, which he separated with great care, and reserved for himself, when he parted with the hook. Being asked, what it was? He pointed to his belly, and spoke something of its being dead; at the same time saying, it was bad; as if he did not wish to answer any more questions about it. On seeing him so anxious to conceal the contents of this parcel, he was requested to open it, which he did with great reluctance, and some difficulty; as it was wrapped up in many folds of cloth. We found, that it contained a thin bit of flesh, about two inches long, which, to appearance, had been dried, but was now wet with salt water. It struck us, that it might be human flesh, and that these people might, perhaps, eat their enemies; as we knew, that this was the practice of some of the natives of the South Sea islands. The question being put to the person who produced it, he answered, that the flesh was part of a man. Another of his countrymen, who stood by him, was then asked, whether it was their custom to eat those killed in battle? and he immediately answered in the affirmative.

There were some intervals of fair weather in the afternoon; and the wind then inclined to the East and North East; but, in the evening, it veered back again to South South East, and the rain also returned, and continued all night. Very luckily, it was not attended with much wind. We had, however, prepared for the worst, by dropping the small bower anchor; and striking our top-gallant-yards.

At seven o'clock, the next morning, a breeze of wind *Friday 23.* springing up at North East, I took up the anchors, with a view of removing the ship farther out. The moment that the last anchor was up, the wind veered to the East, which

VOL. II.   E e   made

made it neceſſary to ſet all the ſail we could, in order to clear the ſhore; ſo that, before we had tolerable ſea-room, we were driven ſome diſtance to leeward. We made a ſtretch off, with a view to regain the road; but having very little wind, and a ſtrong current againſt us, I found, that this was not to be effected. I therefore diſpatched Meſſrs. King and Williamſon aſhore, with three boats, for water, and to trade for refreſhments. At the ſame time, I ſent an order to Captain Clerke, to put to ſea after me, if he ſhould ſee that I could not recover the road. Being in hopes of finding one, or perhaps a harbour, at the Weſt end of the iſland, I was the leſs anxious about getting back to my former ſtation. But as I had ſent the boats thither, we kept to windward as much as poſſible; notwithſtanding which, at noon, we were three leagues to leeward. As we drew near the Weſt end of the iſland, we found the coaſt to round gradually to the North Eaſt, without forming a creek, or cove, to ſhelter a veſſel from the force of the ſwell, which rolled in from the North, and broke upon the ſhore in a prodigious ſurf; ſo that all hopes of finding a harbour here vaniſhed

Several canoes came off in the morning, and followed us as we ſtood out to ſea, bartering their roots and other articles. Being very averſe to believe theſe people to be cannibals, notwithſtanding the ſuſpicious circumſtance which had happened the day before, we took occaſion now to make ſome more inquiries about this. A ſmall wooden inſtrument, beſet with ſharks teeth, had been purchaſed; and from its reſemblance to the ſaw or knife uſed by the New Zealanders, to diſſect the bodies of their enemies, it was ſuſpected to have the ſame uſe here. One of the natives being aſked about this, immediately gave the name of the inſtrument, and told us, that it was uſed to cut out the

flefhy

flefhy part of the belly, when any perfon was killed. This explained and confirmed the circumftance above-mentioned, of the perfon pointing to his belly. The man, however, from whom we now had this information, being afked, if his countrymen eat the part thus cut out? denied it ftrongly; but, upon the queftion being repeated, fhewed fome degree of fear, and fwam to his canoe. Juft before he reached it, he made figns, as he had done before, expreffive of the ufe of the inftrument. And an old man, who fat foremoft in the canoe, being then afked, whether they eat the flefh? anfwered in the affirmative, and laughed, feemingly at the fimplicity of fuch a queftion. He affirmed the fact, on being afked again; and alfo faid, it was excellent food, or, as he expreffed it, " favoury eating."

At feven o'clock in the evening, the boats returned, with two tons of water, a few hogs, a quantity of plantains, and fome roots. Mr. King informed me, that a great number of the inhabitants were at the watering or landing place. He fuppofed, that they had come from all parts of the ifland. They had brought with them a great many fine fat hogs, to barter; but my people had not commodities with them equal to the purchafe. This, however, was no great lofs; for we had already got as many on board, as we could well manage for immediate ufe; and, wanting the materials, we could not have falted them. Mr. King alfo told me, that a great deal of rain had fallen afhore, whereas, out at fea, we had only a few fhowers; and that the furf had run fo high, that it was with great difficulty our men landed, and got back into the boats.

We had light airs and calms, by turns, with fhowers of rain, all night; and at day-break, in the morning of the 24th, we found, that the currents had carried the fhip to Saturday 24.

E e 2   the

the North Weſt and North; ſo that the Weſt end of the
iſland, upon which we had been, called Atooi by the natives, bore Eaſt, one league diſtant; another iſland, called
Oreehoua, Weſt by South; and the high land of a third
iſland, called Oneeheow, from South Weſt by Weſt, to Weſt
South Weſt. Soon after, a breeze ſprung up at North; and,
as I expected that this would bring the Diſcovery to ſea, I
ſteered for Oneeheow, in order to take a nearer view of it,
and to anchor there, if I ſhould find a convenient place. I
continued to ſteer for it, till paſt eleven o'clock, at which
time we were about two leagues from it. But not ſeeing the
Diſcovery, and being doubtful whether they could ſee us, I
was fearful leſt ſome ill conſequence might attend our ſepa-
rating ſo far. I, therefore, gave up the deſign of viſiting
Oneeheow for the preſent, and ſtood back to Atooi, with
an intent to anchor again in the road, to complete our
water. At two o'clock in the afternoon, the Northerly wind
died away, and was ſucceeded by variable light airs and
calms, that continued till eleven at night, with which we
ſtretched to the South Eaſt, till day-break in the morning
Sunday 25. of the 25th, when we tacked and ſtood in for Atooi road,
which bore about North from us; and, ſoon after, we were
joined by the Diſcovery.

We fetched in with the land about two leagues to leeward
of the road, which, though ſo near, we never could recover;
for what we gained at one time, we loſt at another; ſo that,
Thurſday 29. by the morning of the 29th, the currents had carried us
Weſtward, within three leagues of Oneeheow. Being tired
with plying ſo unſucceſsfully, I gave up all thoughts of
getting back to Atooi, and came to the reſolution of trying,
whether we could not procure what we wanted at the other
iſland, which was within our reach. With this view, I ſent
the

the Master in a boat, to sound the coast; to look out for a landing-place; and, if he should find one, to examine if fresh water could be conveniently got in its neighbourhood. To give him time to execute his commission, we followed, under an easy sail, with the ships. As soon as we were abreast, or to the Westward of the South point of Oneeheow, we found thirty, twenty-five, and twenty fathoms water, over a bottom of coral sand, a mile from the shore.

At ten o'clock, the Master returned, and reported, that he had landed in one place, but could find no fresh water; and that there was anchorage all along the coast. Seeing a village a little farther to leeward; and some of the islanders, who had come off to the ships, informing us, that fresh water might be got there, I ran down, and came to an anchor before it, in twenty-six fathoms water, about three quarters of a mile from the shore. The South East point of the island bore South, 65° East, three miles distant; the other extreme of the island bore North by East, about two or three miles distant; a peaked hill, inland, North East, a quarter East; and another island, called Tahoora, which was discovered the preceding evening, bore South, 61° West, distant seven leagues.

Six or seven canoes had come off to us, before we anchored, bringing some small pigs and potatoes, and a good many yams and mats. The people in them resembled those of Atooi; and seemed to be equally well acquainted with the use of iron, which they asked for also by the names of *hamaite* and *toe*; parting readily with all their commodities for pieces of this precious metal. Several more canoes soon reached the ships, after they had anchored; but the natives in these seemed to have no other object, than to pay us a formal visit. Many of them came readily on board,

crouching

crouching down upon the deck, and not quitting that humble posture, till they were desired to get up. They had brought several females with them, who remained along-side in the canoes, behaving with far less modesty than their countrywomen of Atooi; and, at times, all joining in a song, not remarkable for its melody, though performed in very exact concert, by beating time upon their breasts with their hands. The men who had come on board did not stay long; and before they departed, some of them requested our per-mission to lay down, on the deck, locks of their hair.

These visiters furnished us with an opportunity of agitat-ing again, this day, the curious inquiry, whether they were cannibals; and the subject did not take its rise from any questions of ours, but from a circumstance that seemed to remove all ambiguity. One of the islanders, who wanted to get in at the gun-room port, was refused; and, at the same time, asked, whether, if he should come in, we would kill and eat him? accompanying this question with signs so ex-pressive, that there could be no doubt about his meaning. This gave a proper opening to retort the question as to this practice; and a person behind the other, in the canoe, who paid great attention to what was passing, immediately an-swered, that if we were killed on shore, they would cer-tainly eat us. He spoke with so little emotion, that it ap-peared plainly to be his meaning, that they would not de-stroy us for that purpose; but that their eating us would be the consequence of our being at enmity with them. I have availed myself of Mr. Anderson's collections for the decision of this matter; and am sorry to say, that I cannot see the least reason to hesitate in pronouncing it to be cer-tain, that the horrid banquet of human flesh is as much re-lished here, amidst plenty, as it is in New Zealand.

In

In the afternoon, I fent Lieutenant Gore, with three armed boats, to look for the moft convenient landing-place; and, when on fhore, to fearch for frefh water. In the evening he returned, having landed at the village above mentioned, and acquainted me, that he had been conducted to a well half a mile up the country; but, by his account, the quantity of water it contained was too inconfiderable for our purpofe, and the road leading to it exceedingly bad.

On the 30th, I fent Mr. Gore afhore again, with a guard of marines, and a party to trade with the natives for refrefhments. I intended to have followed foon after, and went from the fhip with that defign. But the furf had increafed fo much, by this time, that I was fearful, if I got afhore, I fhould not be able to get off again. This really happened to our people who had landed with Mr. Gore, the communication between them and the fhips, by our own boats, being foon ftopped. In the evening, they made a fignal for the boats, which were fent accordingly; and, not long after, they returned with a few yams and fome falt. A tolerable quantity of both had been procured in the courfe of the day; but the furf was fo great, that the greateft part of both thefe articles had been loft in conveying them to the boats. The officer and twenty men, deterred by the danger of coming off, were left afhore all night; and, by this unfortunate circumftance, the very thing happened, which, as I have already mentioned, I wifhed fo heartily to prevent, and vainly imagined I had effectually guarded againft. The violence of the furf, which our own boats could not act againft, did not hinder the natives from coming off to the fhips in their canoes. They brought refrefhments with them, which were purchafed in exchange for nails, and

pieces

pieces of iron hoops; and I diftributed a good many pieces of ribbon, and fome buttons, as bracelets, amongft the women in the canoes. One of the men had the figure of a lizard punctured upon his breaft, and upon thofe of others were the figures of men badly imitated. Thefe vifiters informed us, that there was no Chief, or *Hairee*, of this ifland; but that it was fubject to Teneooneoo, a Chief of Atooi; which ifland, they faid, was not governed by a fingle Chief, but that there were many to whom they paid the honour of *moe*, or proftration; and, amongft others, they named Otaeaio and Terarotoa. Among other things, which thefe people now brought off, was a fmall drum, almoft like thofe of Otaheite.

About ten or eleven o'clock at night, the wind veered to the South, and the fky feemed to forebode a ftorm. With fuch appearances, thinking that we were rather too near the fhore, I ordered the anchors to be taken up, and, having carried the fhips into forty-two fathoms, came to again in that fafer ftation. The precaution, however, proved to be unneceffary; for the wind, foon after, veered to North North Eaft, from which quarter it blew a frefh gale, with fqualls, attended with very heavy fhowers of rain.

This weather continued all the next day; and the fea ran fo high, that we had no manner of communication with our party on fhore; and even the natives themfelves durft not venture out to the fhips in their canoes. In the evening, I fent the Mafter in a boat up to the South Eaft head, or point of the ifland, to try if he could land under it. He returned with a favourable report; but it was too late, now, to fend for our party till the next morning; and thus they had another night to improve their intercourfe with the natives.

Encouraged

Encouraged by the Mafter's report, I fent a boat to the South Eaft point, as foon as day-light returned, with an order to Mr. Gore, that, if he could not embark his people from the fpot where they now were, to march them up to the point. As the boat could not get to the beach, one of the crew fwam afhore, and carried the order. On the return of the boat, I went myfelf with the pinnace and launch up to the point, to bring the party on board; taking with me a ram-goat and two ewes, a boar and fow pig of the Englifh breed; and the feeds of melons, pumpkins, and onions; being very defirous of benefiting thefe poor people, by furnifhing them with fome additional articles of food. I landed with the greateft eafe, under the Weft fide of the point, and found my party already there, with fome of the natives in company. To one of them, whom Mr. Gore had obferved affuming fome command over the reft, I gave the goats, pigs, and feeds. I fhould have left thefe well-intended prefents at Atooi, had we not been fo unexpectedly driven from it.

While the people were engaged in filling four watercafks, from a fmall ftream occafioned by the late rain, I walked a little way up the country, attended by the man above-mentioned, and followed by two others carrying the two pigs. As foon as we got upon a rifing ground, I ftopped to look round me; and obferved a woman, on the oppofite fide of the valley where I landed, calling to her countrymen who attended me. Upon this, the Chief began to mutter fomething which I fuppofed was a prayer; and the two men, who carried the pigs, continued to walk round me all the time, making, at leaft, a dozen circuits before the other had finifhed his oraifon. This ceremony being performed, we proceeded; and, prefently, met people

VOL. II.   F f   coming

coming from all parts, who, on being called to by my attendants, threw themfelves proftrate on their faces, till I was out of fight. The ground, through which I paffed, was in a ftate of nature, very ftony, and the foil feemed poor. It was, however, covered with fhrubs and plants, fome of which perfumed the air, with a more delicious fragrancy than I had met with at any other of the iflands vifited by us in this ocean. Our people, who had been obliged to remain fo long on fhore, gave me the fame account of thofe parts of the ifland which they had traverfed. They met with feveral falt ponds, fome of which had a little water remaining, but others had none; and the falt that was left in them was fo thin, that no great quantity could have been procured. There was no appearance of any running ftream; and though they found fome fmall wells, in which the frefh water was tolerably good, it feemed fcarce. The habitations of the natives were thinly fcattered about; and it was fuppofed, that there could not be more than five hundred people upon the ifland, as the greateft part were feen at the marketing-place of our party, and few found about the houfes by thofe who walked up the country. They had an opportunity of obferving the method of living amongft the natives, and it appeared to be decent and cleanly. They did not, however, fee any inftance of the men and women eating together; and the latter feemed generally affociated in companies by themfelves. It was found, that they burnt here the oily nuts of the *dooe dooe* for lights in the night, as at Otaheite; and that they baked their hogs in ovens; but, contrary to the practice of the Society and Friendly Iflands, fplit the carcafes through their whole length. They met with a pofitive proof of the exiftence of the *taboo* (or as they pronounce it the *tafoo*),

for

for one woman fed another who was under that interdiction. They alfo obferved fome other myfterious ceremonies; one of which was performed by a woman, who took a fmall pig, and threw it into the furf, till it was drowned, and then tied up a bundle of wood, which fhe alfo difpofed of in the fame manner. The fame woman, at another time, beat with a ftick upon a man's fhoulders, who fat down for that purpofe. A particular veneration feemed to be paid here to owls, which they have very tame; and it was obferved to be a pretty general practice, amongft them, to pull out one of their teeth *; for which odd cuftom, when afked the reafon, the only anfwer that could be got was, that it was *teeba*, which was alfo the reafon affigned for another of their practices, the giving a lock of their hair.

After the water-cafks had been filled and conveyed into the boat, and we had purchafed from the natives a few roots, a little falt, and fome falted fifh, I returned on board with all the people, intending to vifit the ifland the next day. But, about feven o'clock in the evening, the anchor of the Refolution ftarted, and fhe drove off the bank. As we had a whole cable out, it was fome time before the anchor was at the bows; and then we had the launch to hoift up along-fide, before we could make fail. By this unlucky accident, we found ourfelves, at day-break next morning, three leagues to the leeward of our laft ftation; and forefeeing that it would require more time to recover it than I chofe to fpend, I made the fignal for the Difcovery

* It is very remarkable, that, in this cuftom, which one would think is fo unnatural, as not to be adopted by two different tribes, originally unconnected, the people of this ifland, and Dampier's natives on the Weft fide of New Holland, at fuch an immenfe diftance, fhould be found to agree.

to weigh and join us. This was done about noon; and we immediately ftood away to the Northward, in profecution of our voyage. Thus, after fpending more time about thefe iflands than was neceffary to have anfwered all our pur-pofes, we were obliged to leave them before we had com-pleted our water, and got from them fuch a quantity of re-frefhments as their inhabitants were both able and willing to have fupplied us with. But, as it was, our fhip pro-cured from them provifions, fufficient for three weeks at leaft; and Captain Clerke, more fortunate than us, got, of their vegetable productions, a fupply that lafted his people upward of two months. The obfervations I was enabled to make, combined with thofe of Mr. Anderfon, who was a very ufeful affiftant on all fuch occafions, will furnifh ma-terials for the next chapter.

C H A P.

CHAP. XII.

The Situation of the Iſlands now diſcovered.—Their Names.—
Called the Sandwich Iſlands.—Atooi deſcribed.—The Soil.—
Climate.—Vegetable Productions.—Birds.—Fiſh.—Domeſtic
Animals.—Perſons of the Inhabitants.—Their Diſpoſition.—
Dreſs. — Ornaments. — Habitations. — Food. — Cookery.—
Amuſements. — Manufactures. — Working-tools. — Know-
ledge of Iron accounted for.—Canoes.—Agriculture.—Ac-
count of one of their Chiefs.—Weapons.—Cuſtoms agreeing
with thoſe of Tongataboo and Otaheite.—Their Language
the ſame.—Extent of this Nation throughout the Pacific
Ocean.—Reflections on the uſeful Situation of the Sandwich
Iſlands.

I T is worthy of obſervation, that the iſlands in the Pacific Ocean, which our late voyages have added to the
geography of the globe, have been generally found lying
in groups or cluſters; the ſingle intermediate iſlands, as yet
diſcovered, being few in proportion to the others; though,
probably, there are many more of them ſtill unknown,
which ſerve as ſteps between the ſeveral cluſters. Of what
number this newly-diſcovered Archipelago conſiſts, muſt
be left for future inveſtigation. We ſaw five of them, whoſe
names, as given to us by the natives, are Woahoo, Atooi,
Oneeheow, Oreehoua, and Tahoora. The laſt is a ſmall
elevated iſland, lying four or five leagues from the South

1778.
February.

Eaſt

Eaſt point of Oneeheow, in the direction of South, 69° Weſt.
We were told, that it abounds with birds, which are its
only inhabitants. We alſo got ſome information of the
exiſtence of a low uninhabited iſland in the neighbourhood, whoſe name is Tammata pappa. Beſides theſe ſix,
which we can diſtinguiſh by their names, it appeared, that
the inhabitants of thoſe with whom we had intercourſe,
were acquainted with ſome other iſlands both to the Eaſtward and Weſtward. I named the whole group the
Sandwich Iſlands, in honour of the Earl of Sandwich.
Thoſe that I ſaw, are ſituated between the latitude of 21° 30',
and 22° 15' North, and between the longitude of 199° 20',
and 201° 30' Eaſt.

Of Woahoo, the moſt Eaſterly of theſe iſlands, ſeen by
us, which lies in the latitude of 21° 36', we could get no
other intelligence, but that it is high land, and is inhabited.

We had opportunities of knowing ſome particulars about
Oneeheow, which have been mentioned already. It lies
ſeven leagues to the Weſtward of our anchoring-place at
Atooi; and is not above fifteen leagues in circuit. Its chief
vegetable produce is yams; if we may judge from what
was brought to us by the natives. They have ſalt, which
they call *patai*; and is produced in ſalt ponds. With it they
cure both fiſh and pork; and ſome ſalt fiſh, which we got
from them, kept very well, and were found to be very good.
This iſland is moſtly low land, except the part facing Atooi,
which riſes directly from the ſea to a good height; as does
alſo the South Eaſt point of it, which terminates in a round
hill. It was on the Weſt ſide of this point where our ſhips
anchored.

Of Oreehoua we know nothing more than that it is
a ſmall

a fmall elevated ifland, lying clofe to the North fide of Oneeheow.

Atooi, which is the largeft, being the principal fcene of our operations, I fhall now proceed to lay before my readers what information I was able to collect about it, either from actual obfervation, while on fhore, or from converfation with its inhabitants, who were perpetually on board the fhips while we lay at anchor; and who, in general, could be tolerably well underftood, by thofe of us who had acquired an acquaintance with the dialects of the South Pacific Iflands. It is, however, to be regretted, that we fhould have been obliged, fo foon, to leave a place, which, as far as our opportunities of knowing reached, feemed to be highly worthy of a more accurate examination.

Atooi, from what we faw of it, is, at leaft, ten leagues in length from Eaft to Weft; from whence its circuit may nearly be guefled, though it appears to be much broader at the Eaft than at the Weft point, if we may judge from the double range of hills which appeared there. The road, or anchoring-place, which we occupied, is on the South Weft fide of the ifland, about fix miles from the Weft end, before a village which has the name of Wymoa. As far as we founded, we found, that the bank has a fine grey fand at the bottom, and is free from rocks; except a little to the Eaftward of the village, where there fpits out a fhoal, on which are fome rocks and breakers; but they are not far from the fhore. This road would be entirely fheltered from the trade wind, if the height of the land, over which it blows, did not alter its direction, and make it follow that of the coaft; fo that it blows at North Eaft, on one fide of the ifland, and at Eaft South Eaft, or South Eaft, on the other, falling obliquely upon the fhore. Thus the road, though

I   fituated

fituated on the lee fide of the ifland, is a little expofed to the trade wind; but, notwithftanding this defect, is far from being a bad ftation, and much fuperior to thofe which neceffity obliges fhips daily to ufe, in regions where the winds are both more variable and more boifterous; as at Teneriffe, Madeira, the Azores, and elfewhere. The landing too is more eafy than at moft of thofe places; and, unlefs in very bad weather, always practicable. The water to be got in the neighbourhood is excellent, and eafy to be conveyed to the boats. But no wood can be cut at any diftance, convenient enough to bring it from, unlefs the natives could be prevailed upon to part with the few *etooa* trees (for fo they call the *cordia febaftina*), that grow about their villages, or a fort called *dooe dooe*, that grow farther up the country.

The land, as to its general appearance, does not, in the leaft, refemble any of the iflands we have hitherto vifited within the tropic, on the South fide of the *equator*; if we except its hills near the centre, which are high, but flope gently to the fea, or lower lands. Though it be deftitute of the delightful borders of Otaheite, and of the luxuriant plains of Tongataboo, covered with trees, which at once afford a friendly fhelter from the fcorching fun, and an enchanting profpect to the eye, and food for the natives, which may be truly faid to drop from the trees into their mouths, without the laborious tafk of rearing; though, I fay, Atooi be deftitute of thefe advantages, its poffeffing a greater quantity of gently-rifing land, renders it, in fome meafure, fuperior to the above favourite iflands, as being more capable of improvement.

The height of the land within, the quantity of clouds which we faw, during the whole time we ftaid, hanging

over

over it, and frequently on the other parts, feems to put it beyond all doubt, that there is a fufficient fupply of water; and that there are fome running ftreams which we did not fee, efpecially in the deep valleys, at the entrance of which the villages commonly ftand. From the wooded part to the fea, the ground is covered with an excellent fort of grafs, about two feet high, which grows fometimes in tufts, and, though not very thick at the place where we were, feemed capable of being converted into plentiful crops of fine hay. But not even a fhrub grows naturally on this extenfive fpace.

In the break, or narrow valley, through which we had our road to the *morai*, the foil is of a brownifh black colour, fomewhat loofe; but as we advanced upon the high ground, it changed to a reddifh brown, more ftiff and clayey, though, at this time, brittle from its drynefs. It is moft probably the fame all over the cultivated parts; for what adhered to moft of the potatoes, bought by us, which, no doubt, came from very different fpots, was of this fort. Its quality, however, may be better underftood from its products, than from its appearance. For the vale, or moift ground, produces *taro*, of a much larger fize than any we had ever feen; and the higher ground furnifhes fweet potatoes, that often weigh ten, and fometimes twelve or fourteen pounds; very few being under two or three.

The temperature of the climate may be eafily gueffed from the fituation of the ifland. Were we to judge of it from our experience, it might be faid to be very variable; for, according to the generally-received opinion, it was now the feafon of the year, when the weather is fuppofed to be moft fettled, the fun being at his greateft annual diftance. The heat was, at this time, very moderate; and

VOL. II.   G g   few

few of thofe inconveniences, which many tropical countries
are fubject to, either from heat or moifture, feem to be
experienced here, as the habitations of the natives are quite
clofe; and they falt both fifh and pork, which keep well,
contrary to what has ufually been obferved to be the cafe,
when this operation is attempted in hot countries. Neither
did we find any dews of confequence, which may, in fome
meafure, be accounted for, by the lower part of the country
being deftitute of trees.

  The rock that forms the fides of the valley, and which
feems to be the fame with that feen by us at different
parts of the coaft, is a greyifh black, ponderous ftone; but
honey-combed, with fome very minute fhining particles,
and fome fpots of a rufty colour interfperfed. The laft gives
it often a reddifh caft, when at a diftance. It is of an immenfe depth, but feems divided into *ftrata,* though nothing
is interpofed. For the large pieces always broke off to a
determinate thicknefs, without appearing to have adhered
to thofe below them. Other ftones are probably much
more various, than in the Southern iflands. For, during
our fhort ftay, befides the *lapis lydius,* which feems common all over the South Sea, we found a fpecies of cream-
coloured whetftone, fometimes variegated with blacker or
whiter veins, as marble; or in pieces, as *brecciæ*; and common writing flate, as well as a coarfer fort; but we faw none
of them in their natural ftate; and the natives brought
fome pieces of a coarfe whitifh pumice-ftone. We got
alfo a brown fort of *hæmatites,* which, from being ftrongly
attracted by the magnet, difcovered the quantity of metal
that it contained, and feems to belong to the fecond fpecies
of Cronftedt, though Linnæus has placed it amongft his *in-
tractabilia.* But its variety could not be difcovered; for
                                                    what

what we faw of it, as well as the flates and whetftones, was cut artificially.

Befides the vegetable articles, bought by us as refrefhments, amongft which were, at leaft, five or fix varieties of plantains, the ifland produces bread-fruit; though it feems to be fcarce, as we faw only one tree, which was large, and had fome fruit upon it. There are alfo a few cocoa-palms; yams, as we were told, for we faw none; the *kappe* of the Friendly Iflands, or Virginian *arum*; the *etooa* tree, and fweet fmelling *gardenia*, or *cape jafmine*. We faw feveral trees of the *dooe dooe*, fo ufeful at Otaheite, as bearing the oily nuts, which are ftuck upon a kind of fkewer, and burnt as candles. Our people faw them ufed, in the fame manner, at Oneeheow. We were not on fhore at Atooi but in the day-time, and then we faw the natives wearing thefe nuts, hung on ftrings, round the neck. There is a fpecies of *fida*, or Indian mallow, fomewhat altered, by the climate, from what we faw at Chriftmas Ifland; the *morinda citrifolia*, which is called *none*; a fpecies of *convolvulus*; the *ava*, or intoxicating pepper; and great numbers of gourds. Thefe laft grow to a very large fize, and are of a vaft variety of fhapes, which probably is effected by art. Upon the dry fand, about the village, grew a plant, that we had never feen in thefe feas, of the fize of a common thiftle, and prickly, like that; but bearing a fine flower, almoft refembling a white poppy. This, with another fmall one, were the only uncommon plants, which our fhort excurfion gave us an opportunity of obferving.

The fcarlet birds, already defcribed, which were brought for fale, were never met with alive; but we faw a fingle fmall one, about the fize of a canary-bird, of a deep crimfon colour; a large owl; two large brown hawks, or kites; and a

Gg 2

wild

wild duck. The natives mentioned the names of several other birds; amongft which we knew the *otoo*, or blueifh heron; and the *torata*, a fort of whimbrel, which are known by the fame names at Otaheite; and it is probable, that there are a great many forts, judging by the quantity of fine yellow, green, and very fmall, velvet-like, black feathers ufed upon the cloaks, and other ornaments, worn by the inhabitants.

Fifh, and other marine productions, were, to appearance, not various; as, befides the fmall mackerel, we only faw common mullets; a fort of a dead white, or chalky colour; a fmall, brownifh rock-fifh, fpotted with blue; a turtle, which was penned up in a pond; and three or four forts of fifh falted. The few fhell-fifh, that we faw, were chiefly converted into ornaments, though they neither had beauty nor novelty to recommend them.

The hogs, dogs, and fowls, which were the only tame or domeftic animals that we found here, were all of the fame kind that we met with at the South Pacific iflands. There were alfo fmall lizards; and fome rats, refembling thofe feen at every ifland at which we had, as yet, touched.

The inhabitants are of a middling ftature, firmly made, with fome exceptions, neither remarkable for a beautiful fhape, nor for ftriking features, which rather exprefs an opennefs and good-nature, than a keen, intelligent difpofition. Their vifage, efpecially amongft the women, is fometimes round; but others have it long; nor can we fay, that they are diftinguifhed, as a nation, by any general caft of countenance. Their colour is nearly of a nut brown; and it may be difficult to make a nearer comparifon, if we take in all the different hues of that colour; but fome individuals are darker. The women have been already mentioned, as
being

being little more delicate than the men, in their formation;
and I may fay, that, with a very few exceptions, they have little claim to thofe peculiarities that diftinguifh the fex, in other countries. There is, indeed, a more remarkable equality in the fize, colour, and figure of both fexes, than in moft places I have vifited. However, upon the whole, they are far from being ugly, and appear to have few natural deformities of any kind. Their fkin is not very foft, nor fhining; perhaps for want of oiling, which is practifed at the Southern iflands; but their eyes and teeth are, in general, very tolerable. The hair, for the greateft part, is ftraight, though, in fome, frizzling; and though its natural colour be, commonly, black, it is ftained, as at the Friendly and other iflands. We faw but few inftances of corpulence; and thefe oftener amongft the women than the men; but it was chiefly amongft the latter that perfonal defects were obferved, though, if any of them can claim a fhare of beauty, it was moft confpicuous amongft the young men.

They are vigorous, active, and moft expert fwimmers; leaving their canoes upon the moft trifling occafion; diving under them; and fwimming to others though at a great diftance. It was very common to fee women, with infants at the breaft, when the furf was fo high, that they could not land in the canoes, leap overboard, and, without endangering their little ones, fwim to the fhore, through a fea that looked dreadful.

They feem to be bleft with a frank, cheerful difpofition; and were I to draw any comparifons, fhould fay, that they are equally free from the fickle levity which diftinguifhes the natives of Otaheite, and the fedate caft obfervable amongft many of thofe of Tongataboo. They feem to live

very

very fociably in their intercourfe with one another; and, except the propenfity to thieving, which feems innate in moft of the people we have vifited in this ocean, they were exceedingly friendly to us. And it does their fenfibility no little credit, without flattering ourfelves, that when they faw the various articles of our European manufacture, they could not help expreffing their furprize, by a mixture of joy and concern, that feemed to apply the cafe, as a leffon of humility to themfelves; and, on all occafions, they appeared deeply impreffed with a confcioufnefs of their own inferiority; a behaviour which equally exempts their national character from the prepofterous pride of the more polifhed Japanefe, and of the ruder Greenlander. It was a pleafure to obferve with how much affection the women managed their infants, and how readily the men lent their affiftance to fuch a tender office; thus fufficiently diftinguifhing themfelves from thofe favages, who efteem a wife and child as things rather neceffary, than defirable, or worthy of their notice.

From the numbers which we faw collected at every village, as we failed paft, it may be fuppofed, that the inhabitants of this ifland are pretty numerous. Any computation, that we make, can be only conjectural. But, that fome notion may be formed, which fhall not greatly err on either fide, I would fuppofe, that, including the ftraggling houfes, there might be, upon the whole ifland, fixty fuch villages, as that before which we anchored; and that, allowing five perfons to each houfe, there would be, in every village, five hundred; or thirty thoufand upon the ifland. This number is, certainly, not exaggerated; for we had fometimes three thoufand perfons, at leaft, upon the beach; when it could not be fup-

3   pofed,

pofed, that above a tenth part of the inhabitants were prefent.

The common drefs, both of the women and of the men, has been already defcribed. The firft have often much larger pieces of cloth wrapped round them, reaching from juft below the breafts to the hams, or lower; and feveral were feen with pieces thrown loofely about the fhoulders, which covered the greateft part of the body; but the children, when very young, are quite naked. They wear nothing upon the head; but the hair, in both fexes, is cut in different forms; and the general fafhion, efpecially among the women, is, to have it long before, and fhort behind. The men often had it cut, or fhaved, on each fide, in fuch a manner, that the remaining part, in fome meafure, refembles the creft of their caps or helmets, formerly defcribed. Both fexes, however, feem very carelefs about their hair, and have nothing like combs to drefs it with. Inftances of wearing it, in a fingular manner, were fometimes met with among the men, who twift it into a number of feparate parcels, like the tails of a wig, each about the thicknefs of a finger; though the greateft part of thefe, which are fo long that they reach far down the back, we obferved, were artificially fixed upon the head, over their own hair *.

It is remarkable, that, contrary to the general practice of the iflands we had hitherto difcovered in the Pacific Ocean, the people of the Sandwich Iflands have not their ears perforated; nor have they the leaft idea of wearing ornaments

* The print of Horn Ifland, which we meet with in Mr. Dalrymple's account of Le Maire and Schouten's voyage, reprefents fome of the natives of that ifland with fuch long tails, hanging from their heads, as are here defcribed. See *Dalrymple's Voyages to the South Pacific*, Vol. ii. p. 58.

in them. Both fexes, neverthelefs, adorn themfelves with necklaces made of bunches of fmall black cord, like our hat-ftring, often above a hundred-fold; exactly like thofe of Wateeoo; only, that, inftead of the two little balls, on the middle before, they fix a fmall bit of wood, ftone, or fhell, about two inches long, with a broad hook, turning forward at its lower part, well polifhed. They have, like-wife, necklaces of many ftrings of very fmall fhells, or of the dried flowers of the Indian mallow. And, fometimes, a fmall human image of bone, about three inches long, neatly polifhed, is hung round the neck. The women alfo wear bracelets of a fingle fhell, pieces of black wood, with bits of ivory interfperfed, and well polifhed, fixed by a ftring drawn very clofely through them; or others of hogs teeth, laid parallel to each other, with the concave part outward, and the points cut off, faftened together as the former; fome of which, made only of large boars' tufks, are very elegant *. The men, fometimes, wear plumes of the tropic birds feathers, ftuck in their heads; or thofe of cocks, faft-ened round neat polifhed fticks, two feet long, commonly decorated, at the lower part, with *oora*; and, for the fame purpofe, the fkin of a white dog's tail is fewed over a ftick, with its tuft at the end. They alfo, frequently, wear on the head a kind of ornament, of a finger's thicknefs, or more, covered with red and yellow feathers, curioufly va-ried, and tied behind; and on the arm, above the elbow, a kind of broad fhell-work, grounded upon net-work.

The men are frequently punctured, though not in any particular part, as the Otaheiteans, and thofe of Tongataboo. Sometimes there are a few marks upon their hands, or arms, and near the groin; but frequently we could obferve

* See Plate, N° LXVII.

none at all; though a few individuals had more of this fort of ornament, than we had ufually feen at other places, and ingenioufly executed in a great variety of lines and figures, on the arms and fore-part of the body ; on which latter, fome of them had the figure of the *taame,* or breaft-plate, of Otaheite, though we did not meet with the thing itfelf amongft them. Contrary to the cuftom of the Society and Friendly Iflands, they do not flit, or cut off, part of the *prepuce*; but have it, univerfally, drawn over the *glans,* and tied with a ftring, as practifed by fome of the natives of New Zealand.

Though they feem to have adopted the mode of living in villages, there is no appearance of defence, or fortification, near any of them; and the houfes are fcattered about, without any order, either with refpect to their diftances from each other, or their pofition in any particular direction. Neither is there any proportion as to their fize; fome being large and commodious, from forty to fifty feet long, and twenty or thirty broad, while others of them are mere hovels. Their figure is not unlike oblong corn, or hay-ftacks; or, perhaps, a better idea may be conceived of them, if we fuppofe the roof of a barn placed on the ground, in fuch a manner, as to form a high, acute ridge, with two very low fides, hardly difcernible at a diftance. The gable, at each end, correfponding to the fides, makes thefe habitations perfectly clofe all round; and they are well thatched with long grafs, which is laid on flender poles, difpofed with fome regularity. The entrance is made indifferently in the end or fide, and is an oblong hole, fo low, that one muft rather creep than walk in; and is often fhut up by a board of planks, faftened together, which ferves as a door, but having no hinges, muft be removed occafionally. No light

enters the houfe, but by this opening; and though fuch
clofe habitations may afford a comfortable retreat in bad
weather, they feem but ill-adapted to the warmth of the
climate. They are, however, kept remarkably clean; and
their floors are covered with a large quantity of dried grafs,
over which they fpread mats to fit and fleep upon. At one
end ftands a kind of bench, about three feet high, on
which their houfehold utenfils are placed. The catalogue
is not long. It confifts of gourd-fhells, which they convert
into veffels that ferve as bottles to hold water, and as bafkets to contain their victuals, and other things, with covers
of the fame; and of a few wooden bowls and trenchers, of
different fizes. Judging from what we faw growing, and
from what was brought to market, there can be no doubt,
that the greateft part of their vegetable food confifts of fweet
potatoes, *taro*, and plantains; and that bread-fruit and yams
are rather to be efteemed rarities. Of animal food, they
can be in no want; as they have abundance of hogs, which
run, without reftraint, about the houfes; and if they eat
dogs, which is not improbable, their ftock of thefe feemed
to be very confiderable. The great number of fifhing-
hooks found amongft them, fhewed, that they derive no
inconfiderable fupply of animal food from the fea. But it
fhould feem, from their practice of falting fifh, that the
opennefs of their coaft often interrupts the bufinefs of
catching them; as it may be naturally fuppofed, that no fet
of people would ever think of preferving quantities of food
artificially, if they could depend upon a daily, regular fupply of it, in its frefh ftate. This fort of reafoning, however,
will not account for their cuftom of falting their pork, as
well as their fifh, which are preferved in gourd-fhells. The
falt, of which they ufe a great quantity for this purpofe, is

I   of

of a red colour, not very coarfe, and feems to be much the fame with what our ftragglers found at Chriftmas Ifland. It has its colour, doubtlefs, from a mixture of the mud, at the bottom of the part where it is formed; for fome of it, that had adhered in lumps, was of a fufficient whitenefs and purity.

They bake their vegetable food with heated ftones, as at the Southern Iflands; and, from the vaft quantity which we faw dreffed at one time, we fufpected, that the whole village, or, at leaft, a confiderable number of people, joined in the ufe of a common oven. We did not fee them drefs any animal food at this ifland; but Mr. Gore's party, as already mentioned, had an opportunity of fatisfying themfelves, that it was dreffed in Oneeheow in the fame fort of ovens; which leaves no doubt of this being alfo the practice in Atooi; efpecially as we met with no utenfil there, that could be applied to the purpofe of ftewing or boiling. The only artificial difh we met with, was a *taro* pudding; which, though a difagreeable mefs from its fournefs, was greedily devoured by the natives. They eat off a kind of wooden plates, or trenchers; and the women, as far as we could judge from one inftance, if reftrained from feeding at the fame difh with the men, as at Otaheite, are, at leaft, permitted to eat in the fame place near them.

Their amufements feem pretty various; for, during our fhort ftay, feveral were difcovered. The dances, at which they ufed the feathered cloaks and caps, were not feen; but from the motions which they made with their hands, on other occafions, when they fung, we could form fome judgment that they are, in fome degree at leaft, fimilar to thofe we had met with at the Southern Iflands, though not executed fo fkilfully. Neither had they, amongft them, either

flutes

flutes or reeds; and the only two musical instruments which we observed, were of an exceedingly rude kind. One of them does not produce a melody exceeding that of a child's rattle. It consists of what may be called a conic cap inverted, but scarcely hollowed at the base above a foot high, made of a coarse, sedge-like plant; the upper part of which, and the edges, are ornamented with beautiful red feathers; and to the point, or lower part, is fixed a gourd-shell, larger than the fist. Into this is put something to rattle; which is done by holding the instrument by the small part, and shaking, or rather moving it, from place to place briskly, either to different sides, or backward and forward, just before the face, striking the breast with the other hand at the same time *. The other musical instrument (if either of them deserve that name) was a hollow vessel of wood, like a platter, combined with the use of two sticks, on which one of our gentlemen saw a man performing. He held one of the sticks, about two feet long, as we do a fiddle, with one hand, and struck it with the other, which was smaller, and resembled a drum-stick, in a quicker or slower measure; at the same time beating with his foot upon the hollow vessel, that lay inverted upon the ground, and thus producing a tune, that was by no means disagreeable. This music was accompanied by the vocal performance of some women, whose song had a pleasing and tender effect.

We observed great numbers of small polished rods, about four or five feet long, somewhat thicker than the rammer of a musquet, with a tuft of long, white dog's hair fixed on the small end. These are, probably, used in their diversions. We saw a person take one of them in his hand, and,

* See Plate, No LXVII. Fig. 3.

holding

holding it up, give a fmart ftroke, till he brought it into an horizontal pofition, ftriking with the foot, on the fame fide, upon the ground, and, with his other hand, beating his breaft at the fame time. They play at bowls, with pieces of the whetftone mentioned before, of about a pound weight, fhaped fomewhat like a fmall cheefe, but rounded at the fides and edges, which are very nicely polifhed; and they have other bowls of the fame fort, made of a heavy, reddifh brown clay, neatly glazed over with a compofition of the fame colour, or of a coarfe, dark grey flate. They alfo ufe, in the manner that we throw quoits, fmall, flat, rounded pieces of the writing flate, of the diameter of the bowls, but fcarcely a quarter of an inch thick, alfo well polifhed. From thefe circumftances, one would be induced to think, that their games are rather trials of fkill than of ftrength.

In every thing manufactured by thefe people, there appears to be an uncommon degree of neatnefs and ingenuity. Their cloth, which is the principal manufacture, is made from the *morus papyrifera*; and, doubtlefs, in the fame manner as at Otaheite and Tongataboo; for we bought fome of the grooved fticks, with which it is beaten. Its texture, however, though thicker, is rather inferior to that of the cloth of either of the other places; but, in colouring or ftaining it, the people of Atooi difplay a fuperiority of tafte, by the endlefs variation of figures which they execute. One would fuppofe, on feeing a number of their pieces, that they had borrowed their patterns from fome mercer's fhop, in which the moft elegant productions of China and Europe are collected; befides fome original patterns of their own. Their colours, indeed, except the red, are not very bright; but the regularity of the figures and
ftripes

ftripes is truly furprizing; for, as far as we knew, they
have nothing like ftamps or prints, to make the impref-
fions. In what manner they produce their colours, we
had not opportunities of learning; but befides the party-
coloured forts, they have fome pieces of plain white cloth,
and others of a fingle colour, particularly dark brown and
light blue. In general, the pieces which they brought to
us, were about two feet broad, and four or five yards long,
being the form and quantity that they ufe for their common drefs, or *maro*; and even thefe we fometimes found
were compofed of pieces fewed together; an art which we
did not find to the Southward, but is ftrongly, though not
very heatly, performed here. There is alfo a particular
fort that is thin, much refembling oil-cloth; and which is
actually either oiled or foaked in fome kind of varnifh, and
feems to refift the action of water pretty well.

They fabricate a great many white mats, which are
ftrong, with many red ftripes, rhombufes, and other figures
interwoven on one fide; and often pretty large. Thefe,
probably, make a part of their drefs occafionally; for they
put them on their backs when they offered them to fale.
But they make others coarfer, plain and ftrong, which they
fpread over their floors to fleep upon.

They ftain their gourd-fhells prettily with undulated
lines, triangles, and other figures of a black colour; inftances of which we faw practifed at New Zealand. And
they feem to poffefs the art of varnifhing; for fome of
thefe ftained gourd-fhells are covered with a kind of lacker;
and on other occafions, they ufe a ftrong fize, or gluey
fubftance, to faften their things together. Their wooden
difhes and bowls, out of which they drink their *ava*, are
of the *etooa*-tree, or *cordia*, as neat, as if made in our turn-

ing-

ing-lathe, and perhaps better polifhed. And amongft their articles of handicraft, may be reckoned fmall fquare fans of mat or wicker-work, with handles tapering from them of the fame, or of wood; which are neatly wrought with fmall cords of hair, and fibres of the cocoa-nut coir, intermixed. The great variety of fifhing-hooks are ingenioufly made; fome of bone, others of wood pointed with bone, and many of pearl fhell. Of the laft, fome are like a fort that we faw at Tongataboo; and others fimply curved, as the common fort at Otaheite, as well as the wooden ones. The bones are moftly fmall, and compofed of two pieces; and all the different forts have a barb, either on the infide, like ours, or on the outfide, oppofite the fame part; but others have both, the outer one being fartheft from the point. Of this laft fort, one was procured, nine inches long, of a fingle piece of bone, which, doubtlefs, belonged to fome large fifh. The elegant form and polifh of this could not, certainly, be outdone by any European artift, even if he fhould add all his knowledge in defign, to the number and convenience of his tools. They polifh their ftones, by conftant friction, with pumice-ftone in water; and fuch of their working inftruments, or tools, as I faw, refembled thofe of the Southern Iflands. Their hatchets, or rather adzes, were exactly of the fame pattern, and either made of the fame fort of blackifh ftone, or of a clay-coloured one. They have alfo little inftruments made of a fingle fhark's tooth, fome of which are fixed to the fore-part of a dog's jaw-bone, and others to a thin wooden handle of the fame fhape; and at the other end there is a bit of ftring faftened through a fmall perforation. Thefe ferve as knives occafionally, and are, perhaps, ufed in carving.

The

The only iron tools, or rather bits of iron, feen amongft them, and which they had before our arrival, were a piece of iron hoop, about two inches long, fitted into a wooden handle *; and another edge-tool, which our people gueffed to be made of the point of a broad-fword. Their having the actual poffeffion of thefe, and their fo generally knowing the ufe of this metal, inclined fome on board to think, that we had not been the firft European vifiters of thefe iflands. But, it feems to me, that the very great furprize expreffed by them, on feeing our fhips, and their total ignorance of the ufe of fire-arms, cannot be reconciled with fuch a notion. There are many ways, by which fuch people may get pieces of iron, or acquire the knowledge of the exiftence of fuch a metal, without having ever had an immediate connection with nations that ufe it. It can hardly be doubted, that it was unknown to all the inhabitants of this fea, before Magalhaens led the way into it; for no difcoverer, immediately after his voyage, ever found any of this metal in their poffeffion; though, in the courfe of our late voyages, it has been obferved, that the ufe of it was known at feveral iflands, to which no former European fhips had ever, as far as we know, found their way. At all the places where Mendana touched, in his two voyages, it muft have been feen and left; and this would extend the knowledge of it, no doubt, to all the various iflands with which thofe, whom he had vifited, had any immediate intercourfe. It might even be carried farther; and where fpecimens of this favourite article could not be procured, defcriptions might, in fome meafure, ferve to make it known, when afterward feen. The next voyage to the Southward of the line, in

* Captain King purchafed this, and has it now in his poffeffion.

which

which any intercourse was had with the natives of this ocean, was that of Quiros, who landed at Sagittaria, the Island of Handsome People, and at Tierra del Espiritu Santo; at all which places, and at those with whom they had any communication, it must, of consequence, have been made known. To him succeeded, in this navigation, Le Maire and Schouten, whose connections with the natives commenced much farther to the Eastward, and ended at Cocos and Horn Islands. It was not surprizing, that, when I visited Tongataboo in 1773, I should find a bit of iron there, as we knew that Tasman had visited it before me; but, let us suppose, that he had never discovered the Friendly Islands, our finding iron amongst them would have occasioned much speculation; though we have mentioned before *, the method by which they had gained a renewal of their knowledge of this metal, which confirms my hypothesis. For Neeootaboo taboo, or Boscawen's Island, where Captain Wallis's ships left it, and from whence Poulaho received it, lies some degrees to the North West of Tongataboo. It is well known, that Roggewein lost one of his ships on the Pernicious Islands; which, from their situation, are, probably, not unknown to, though not frequently visited by, the inhabitants of Otaheite and the Society Islands. It is equally certain, that these last people had a knowledge of iron, and purchased it with the greatest avidity, when Captain Wallis discovered Otaheite; and this knowledge could only have been acquired, through the mediation of those neighbouring islands where it had been originally left. Indeed they acknowledge, that this was actually the case; and they have told us since, that they held it in such estimation, before Cap-

* See Vol. i. p. 370.

tain Wallis's arrival, that a Chief of Otaheite, who had got
two nails into his poffeffion, received no fmall emolument,
by letting out the ufe of thefe to his neighbours, for the
purpofe of boring holes, when their own methods failed,
or were thought too tedious *. The men of the Society
Iflands whom we found at Wateeoo, had been driven
thither, long after the knowledge and ufe of iron had
thus been introduced amongft their countrymen; and
though, probably, they had no fpecimen of it with them,
they would naturally, and with eafe, communicate at that
ifland their knowledge of this valuable material, by defcription. From the people of Wateeoo again, thofe of
Hervey's Ifland might derive that defire to poffefs fome of
it, of which we had proofs during our fhort intercourfe
with them.

The confideration of thefe facts fufficiently explains how
the knowledge of iron has been conveyed throughout this
ocean, to iflands which never have had an immediate intercourfe with Europeans; and it may eafily be conceived,
that wherever the hiftory of it only has been reported, or
a very fmall quantity of it has been left, the greater eagernefs will be fhewn by the natives to get copious fupplies
of it. The application of thefe particulars, to the inftance
now under confideration, is obvious. The people of Atooi
and Oneeheow, without having ever been vifited by Europeans before us, might have received it from intermediate

* A fimilar inftance of profitable revenue, drawn from the ufe of nails by the Chiefs
of the Caroline Iflands, is mentioned by father Cantova: " Si, par hazard, un vaiffeau
" étranger laiffe dans leurs ifles quelques vieux morceaux de fer, ils appartiennent de
" droit aux Tamoles, qui en font faire des outils, le mieux qu'il eft poffible. Ces outils
" font un fond dont le Tamole tire un revenu confiderable, car il les donne à louage, et
" ce louage fe paye affez chere." p. 314.

iflands,

iflands, lying between them and the Ladrones, which have
been frequented by the Spaniards, almoſt ever ſince the
date of Magalhaens's voyage. Or, if the diſtant Weſtern
ſituation of the Ladrones ſhould render this ſolution leſs
probable, is there not the extenſive continent of America
to windward, where the Spaniards have been ſettled for
more than two hundred years; during which long period
of time, ſhipwrecks muſt have frequently happened on its
coaſts? It cannot be thought at all extraordinary, that part
of ſuch wrecks, containing iron, ſhould, by the Eaſterly
trade wind, be, from time to time, caſt upon iſlands ſcattered about this vaſt ocean. The diſtance of Atooi from
America, is no argument againſt this ſuppoſition. But
even if it were, it would not deſtroy it. This ocean is
traverſed every year by Spaniſh ſhips; and it is obvious,
that, beſides the accident of loſing a maſt, and its appendages, caſks with iron hoops, and many other things containing iron, may be thrown, or may fall overboard, during
ſo long a paſſage, and thus find their way to land. But
theſe are not mere conjectures and poſſibilities; for one of
my people actually did ſee ſome wood in one of the houſes
at Wymoa, which he judged to be fir. It was worm-eaten,
and the natives gave him to underſtand, that it had been
driven aſhore by the waves of the ſea; and we had their
own expreſs teſtimony, that they had got the inconſiderable
ſpecimens of iron found amongſt them, from ſome place to
the Eaſtward.

From this digreſſion (if it can be called ſo), I return to the
obſervations made during our ſtay at Atooi; and ſome account muſt now be given of their canoes. Theſe, in general, are about twenty-four feet long, and have the bottom,
for the moſt part, formed of a ſingle piece or log of wood,

I i 2   hollowed

hollowed out to the thickneſs of an inch, or an inch and an
half, and brought to a point at each end. The ſides conſiſt
of three boards, each about an inch thick, and neatly fitted
and laſhed to the bottom part. The extremities, both at
head and ſtern, are a little raiſed, and both are made ſharp,
ſomewhat like a wedge; but they flatten more abruptly;
ſo that the two ſide-boards join each other, ſide by ſide, for
more than a foot. But Mr. Webber's drawing * will explain
their conſtruction more accurately than my deſcription in
words. As they are not more than fifteen or eighteen inches
broad, thoſe that go ſingle (for they ſometimes join them as
at the other iſlands), have out-riggers, which are ſhaped
and fitted with more judgment than any I had before ſeen.
They are rowed by paddles, ſuch as we had generally met
with; and ſome of them have a light triangular ſail, like
thoſe of the Friendly Iſlands, extended to a maſt and boom.
The ropes uſed for their boats, and the ſmaller cords for
their fiſhing-tackle, are ſtrong and well made.

What we ſaw of their agriculture, furniſhed ſufficient
proofs that they are not novices in that art. The vale ground
has already been mentioned as one continued plantation of
taro, and a few other things, which have all the appearance of being well attended to. The potatoe fields, and
ſpots of ſugar-cane, or plantains, on the higher grounds, are
planted with the ſame regularity; and always in ſome determinate figure; generally as a ſquare or oblong; but
neither theſe, nor the others, are incloſed with any kind of
fence, unleſs we reckon the ditches in the low grounds ſuch;
which, it is more probable, are intended to convey water
to the *taro*. The great quantity and goodneſs of theſe articles may alſo, perhaps, be as much attributed to ſkilful

* See Plates LXI. and LXV.

culture,

culture, as to natural fertility of foil, which feems better adapted to them than to bread-fruit and cocoa-nut trees; the few which we faw of thefe latter not being in a thriving ftate, which will fufficiently account for the preference given to the culture of the other articles, though more labour be required to produce them. But notwithftanding this fkill in agriculture, the general appearance of the ifland fhewed, that it was capable of much more extenfive im-provement, and of maintaining, at leaft, three times the number of the inhabitants that are at prefent upon it; for the far greater part of it, that now lies quite wafte, feemed to be as good a foil as thofe parts of it that are in cultiva-tion. We muft therefore conclude, that thefe people, from fome caufe, which we were not long enough amongft them to be able to trace, do not increafe in that proportion, which would make it neceffary to avail themfelves of the extent of their ifland, toward raifing a greater quantity of its vegeta-ble productions for their fubfiftence.

Though I did not fee a Chief of any note, there were, however, feveral, as the natives informed us, who refide upon Atooi, and to whom they proftrate themfelves as a mark of fubmiffion; which feems equivalent to the *moe, moea*, paid to the Chiefs of the Friendly Iflands, and is call-ed here *bamoea* or *moe*. Whether they were, at firft, afraid to fhew themfelves, or happened to be abfent, I cannot fay; but after I had left the ifland, one of thefe great men made his appearance, and paid a vifit to Captain Clerke on board the Difcovery. He came off in a double canoe; and, like the king of the Friendly Iflands, paid no regard to the fmall canoes that happened to lie in his way, but ran againft, or over them, without endeavouring, in the leaft, to avoid them. And it was not poffible for thefe poor people to avoid him,

him, for they could not manage their canoes; it being a neceffary mark of their fubmiffion, that they fhould lie down
till he had paffed. His attendants helped him into the
fhip, and placed him on the gang-way. Their care of him
did not ceafe then; for they ftood round him, holding each
other by the hands; nor would they fuffer any one to come
near him but Captain Clerke himfelf. He was a young
man, clothed from head to foot; and accompanied by a
young woman, fuppofed to be his wife. His name was faid
to be Tamahano. Captain Clerke made him fome fuitable
prefents; and received from him, in return, a large bowl,
fupported by two figures of men, the carving of which,
both as to the defign and the execution, fhewed fome degree of fkill. This bowl, as our people were told, ufed to
be filled with the *kava*, or *ava* (as it is called at Otaheite),
which liquor they prepare and drink here, as at the other
iflands in this ocean. Captain Clerke could not prevail
upon this great man to go below, nor to move from the
place where his attendants had firft fixed him. After ftay-
ing fome time in the fhip, he was carried again into his
canoe, and returned to the ifland, receiving the fame honours from all the natives, as when he came on board.
The next day, feveral meffages were fent to Captain Clerke,
inviting him to return the vifit afhore, and acquainting
him, that the Chief had prepared a large prefent on that
occafion. But being anxious to get to fea, and join the Refolution, the Captain did not think it advifeable to accept
of the invitation.

The very fhort and imperfect intercourfe which we had
with the natives, put it out of our power to form any accurate judgment of the mode of government eftablifhed
amongft them; but, from the general refemblance of cuftoms,

toms, and particularly from what we obferved of the honours paid to their Chiefs, it feems reafonable to believe,
that it is of the fame nature with that which prevails
throughout all the iflands we had hitherto vifited; and,
probably, their wars amongft themfelves are equally frequent. This, indeed, might be inferred from the number
of weapons which we found them poffeffed of, and from
the excellent order thefe were kept in. But we had direct
proof of the fact from their own confeffion; and, as we
underftood, thefe wars are between the different diftricts
of their own ifland, as well as between it and their neighbours of Oneeheow and Orrehoua. We need fcarcely affign
any other caufe befides this, to account for the appearance, already mentioned, of their population bearing no
proportion to the extent of their ground capable of cultivation.

Befides their fpears or lances, made of a fine chefnut-
coloured wood, beautifully polifhed, fome of which are
barbed at one end, and flattened to a point at the other,
they have a fort of weapon which we had never feen before, and not mentioned by any navigator, as ufed by the
natives of the South Sea. It is fomewhat like a dagger; in
general, about a foot and a half long, fharpened at one or
both ends, and fecured to the hand by a ftring. Its ufe is
to ftab in clofe fight; and it feems well adapted to the purpofe *. Some of thefe may be called double daggers, having
a handle in the middle, with which they are better enabled
to ftrike different ways. They have alfo bows and arrows;
but, both from their apparent fcarcity, and their flender
make, it may almoft be prefumed that they never ufe them
in battle. The knife or faw, formerly mentioned, with
which they diffect the dead bodies, may alfo be ranked

* See Plate LXVII. fig. 6.

3   amongft

amongst their weapons, as they both strike and cut with it, when closely engaged. It is a small flat wooden instrument, of an oblong shape, about a foot long, rounded at the corners, with a handle, almost like one sort of the *patoos* of New Zealand; but its edges are entirely surrounded with sharks' teeth strongly fixed to it, and pointing outward; having commonly a hole in the handle, through which passes a long string, which is wrapped several times round the wrist*. We also suspected that they use slings on some occasions; for we got some pieces of the *hæmatites*, or blood-stone, artificially made of an oval shape, divided longitudinally, with a narrow groove in the middle of the convex part. To this the person, who had one of them, applied a cord of no great thickness, but would not part with it, though he had no objection to part with the stone, which must prove fatal when thrown with any force, as it weighed a pound. We likewise saw some oval pieces of whetstone well polished, but somewhat pointed toward each end, nearly resembling in shape some stones which we had seen at New Caledonia in 1774, and used there in their slings.

What we could learn of their religious institutions, and the manner of disposing of their dead, which may, properly, be considered as closely connected, has been already mentioned. And as nothing more strongly points out the affinity between the manners of these people and of the Friendly and Society Islands, I must just mention some other circumstances to place this in a strong point of view; and, at the same time, to shew how a few of the infinite modifications of which a few leading principles are capable, may distinguish any particular nation. The people of Tongataboo inter their dead in a very decent manner, and they

* See Plate LXVII, Fig. 1.

alfo

1778.
February.

alſo inter their human ſacrifices; but they do not offer, or expoſe any other animal, or even vegetable, to their Gods, as far as we know. Thoſe of Otaheite do not inter their dead, but expoſe them to waſte by time and putrefaction, though the bones are afterward buried; and, as this is the caſe, it is very remarkable, that they ſhould inter the entire bodies of their human ſacrifices. They alſo offer other animals, and vegetables, to their Gods; but are, by no means, attentive to the ſtate of the ſacred places, where thoſe ſolemn rites are performed; moſt of their _Morais_ being in a ruinous condition, and bearing evident marks of neglect. The people of Atooi, again, inter both their common dead, and human ſacrifices, as at Tongataboo; but they reſemble thoſe of Otaheite, in the ſlovenly ſtate of their religious places, and in offering vegetables and animals to their Gods.

The _taboo_ alſo prevails in Atooi, in its full extent, and ſeemingly with much more rigour than even at Tongataboo. For the people here always aſked, with great eagerneſs and ſigns of fear to offend, whether any particular thing, which they deſired to ſee, or we were unwilling to ſhew, was _taboo_, or, as they pronounced the word, _tafoo?_ The _maia, raä,_ or forbidden articles at the Society Iſlands, though, doubtleſs, the ſame thing, did not ſeem to be ſo ſtrictly obſerved by them, except with reſpect to the dead, about whom we thought them more ſuperſtitious than any of the others, were. But theſe are circumſtances with which we are not, as yet, ſufficiently acquainted, to be deciſive about; and I ſhall only juſt obſerve, to ſhew the ſimilitude in other matters, connected with religion, that the prieſts, or _tahounas_, here, are as numerous as at the other iſlands; if we may judge, from our being able, during our ſhort ſtay, to diſtinguiſh ſeveral, ſaying their _poore_, or prayer.

VOL. II. K k But

But whatever refemblance we might difcover, in the ge-neral manners of the people of Atooi, to thofe of Otaheite, thefe, of courfe, were lefs ftriking than the coincidence of language. Indeed, the languages of both places may be faid to be almoft, word for word, the fame. It is true, that we fometimes remarked particular words to be pronounced ex-actly as we had found at New Zealand, and the Friendly Iflands; but though all the four dialects are indifputably the fame, thefe people, in general, have neither the ftrong guttural pronunciation of the former, nor a lefs degree of it, which alfo diftinguifhes the latter; and they have not only adopted the foft mode of the Otaheiteans, in avoiding harfh founds, but the whole idiom of their language; ufing not only the fame affixes and fuffixes to their words, but the fame meafure and cadence in their fongs; though in a man-ner fomewhat lefs agreeable. There feems, indeed, at firft hearing, fome difagreement, to the ear of a ftranger; but it ought to be confidered, that the people of Otaheite, from their frequent connections with the Englifh, had learnt, in fome meafure, to adapt themfelves to our fcanty knowledge of their language, by ufing not only the moft common, but even corrupted expreffions, in converfation with us; whereas, when they converfed among themfelves, and ufed the feveral parts neceffary to propriety of fpeech, they were fcarcely at all underftood by thofe amongft us, who had made the greateft proficiency in their vocabulary. A cata-logue of words was collected at Atooi, by Mr. Anderfon, who loft no opportunity of making our voyage ufeful to thofe, who amufe themfelves in tracing the migrations of the various tribes, or families, that have peopled the globe, by the moft convincing of all arguments, that drawn from affinity of language.

I

How

How fhall we account for this nation's having fpread it-felf, in fo many detached iflands, fo widely disjoined from each other, in every quarter of the Pacific Ocean! We find it, from New Zealand, in the South, as far as the Sandwich Iflands, to the North! And, in another direction, from Eafter Ifland to the Hebrides! That is, over an extent of fixty degrees of latitude, or twelve hundred leagues, North and South! And eighty-three degrees of longitude, or fixteen hundred and fixty leagues, Eaft and Weft! How much farther, in either direction, its colonies reach, is not known; but what we know already, in confequence of this and our former voyage, warrants our pronouncing it to be, though perhaps not the moft numerous, certainly, by far, the moft extenfive nation upon earth *.

Had the Sandwich Iflands been difcovered at an early period, by the Spaniards, there is little doubt that they would have taken advantage of fo excellent a fituation, and have made ufe of Atooi, or fome other of the iflands, as a refrefhing place to the fhips, that fail annually from Acapulco for Manilla. They lie almoft midway between the firft place and Guam one of the Ladrones, which is at prefent their only port in traverfing this vaft ocean; and it would not have been a week's fail out of their common route, to have touched at them; which could have been done, without running the leaft hazard of lofing the paffage, as they are fufficiently within the verge of the Eafterly trade-wind. An acquaintance with the Sandwich Iflands would have been equally favourable to our Buccaneers; who ufed fometimes to pafs from the coaft of America to the Ladrones, with a ftock of food and water fcarcely fufficient to preferve life.

* See more about the great extent of the colonies of this nation, in the Introductory Preface.

K k 2

Here

Here they might always have found plenty, and have been within a month's fure fail of the very part of California, which the Manilla fhip is obliged to make, or elfe have returned to the coaft of America, thoroughly refitted, after an abfence of two months. How happy would Lord Anfon have been, and what hardfhips would he have avoided, if he had known that there was a group of iflands, half way between America and Tinian, where all his wants could have been effectually fupplied; and in defcribing which, the elegant hiftorian of that voyage, would have prefented his reader with a more agreeable picture, than I have been able to draw in this chapter?

CHAP.

C H A P. XIII.

*Obfervations made at the Sandwich Iflands, on the Longitude,
Variation of the Compafs, and Tides.—Profecution of the
Voyage.—Remarks on the Mildnefs of the Weather, as far
as the Latitude 44° North.—Paucity of Sea Birds, in the
Northern Hemifphere.— Small Sea Animals defcribed.—
Arrival on the Coaft of America.—Appearance of the Country.—Unfavourable Winds, and boifterous Weather.—Remarks on Martin de Aguilar's River, and Juan de Fuca's
pretended Strait.—An Inlet difcovered, where the Ships anchor.—Behaviour of the Natives.*

AFTER the Difcovery had joined us, we ftood away to
the Northward, clofe hauled, with a gentle gale from
the Eaft; and nothing occurring, in this fituation, worthy
of a place in my narrative, the reader will permit me to
infert here the nautical obfervations which I had opportunities of making, relative to the iflands we had left; and
which we had been fortunate enough to add to the geography of this part of the Pacific Ocean.

The longitude of the Sandwich Iflands, was determined
by feventy-two fets of lunar obfervations; fome of which
were made while we were at anchor, in the road of
Wymoa; others, before we arrived, and after we left it,
and reduced to it, by the watch, or time-keeper. By the
mean

*1778.
February.*

Monday 2.

mean refult of thefe obfervations, the longitude of the road is — — — — 200° 13′ 0″ Eaft.

Time-keeper { Greenwich rate,   202° 0′ 0″
            { Ulietea rate   200° 21′ 0″

The latitude of the road, by the mean of } 21° 56′ 15″ North.
two meridian obfervations of the fun }

The obfervations for the variation of the compafs, did not agree very well among themfelves. It is true, they were not all made exactly in the fame fpot. The different fituations, however, could make very little difference. But the whole will be beft feen by cafting an eye on the following table.

Time.	Latitude.	Longitude.	Compafs.	Eaft Variation.	Mean Variation.
January 18th. A. M.	21° 12′	200° 41′	Gregory's 10° 10′ 10″ Knight's 9° 20′ 5″ Martin's 10° 4′ 40″		9° 51′ 38″
19th. P. M.	21° 51′	200° 20′	Knight's 10° 2′ 10″ Gregory's 11° 12′ 30″		10° 37′ 20″
28th. A. M.	21° 22′	199° 56′	Gregory's 9° 1′ 20″ Knight's 9° 1′ 25″ Martin's 10° 18′ 5″		9° 26′ 57″
28th. P. M.	21° 36′	199° 50′	Gregory's 11° 21′ 15″ Knight's 10° 40′ 0″ Martin's 11° 37′ 50″		11° 12′ 50″
Means of the above	21° 29′	200° 12′			10° 17′ 11″
On January 18th.	21° 12′	200° 41′ the North end of			

the needle dipped 42° 1′ 7″.

The tides, at the Sandwich Iflands, are fo inconfiderable, that, with the great furf which broke againft the fhore, it was hardly poffible to tell, at any time, whether we had high or low water, or whether it ebbed or flowed. On the
South

South fide of Atooi, we generally found a current fetting to the Weftward, or North Weftward. But when we were at anchor off Oneeheow, the current fet nearly North Weft and South Eaft, fix hours one way, and fix the other, and fo ftrong as to make the fhips tend, though the wind blew frefh. This was certainly a regular tide ; and, as far as I could judge, the flood came from the North Weft. 1778. February.

I now return to the progrefs of our voyage. On the 7th, being in the latitude of 29° North, and in the longitude of 200° Eaft, the wind veered to South Eaft. This enabled us to fteer North Eaft and Eaft; which courfe we continued till the 12th, when the wind had veered round by the South and Weft, to North Eaft and Eaft North Eaft. I then tacked, and ftood to the Northward, our latitude being 30° North, and our longitude 206° 15′ Eaft. Notwithftanding our advanced latitude, and its being the winter feafon, we had only begun, for a few days paft, to feel a fenfation of cold in the mornings and evenings. This is a fign of the equal and lafting influence of the fun's heat, at all feafons, to 30° on each fide the line. The difproportion is known to become very great after that. This muft be attributed, almoft entirely, to the direction of the rays of the fun, independent of the bare diftance, which is, by no means, equal to the effect. Saturday 7.

Thurfday 12.

On the 19th, being now in the latitude of 37° North, and in the longitude of 206° Eaft, the wind veered to South Eaft ; and I was enabled again to fteer to the Eaft, inclining to the North. We had, on the 25th, reached the latitude of 42° 30′, and the longitude of 219°; and then we began to meet with the rock-weed, mentioned by the writer of Lord Anfon's voyage, under the name of fea-leek, which the Manilla fhips generally fall in with. Now and then, a piece of wood Thurfday 19.

alfo

alſo appeared. But, if we had not known, that the continent of North America was not far diſtant, we might, from the few ſigns of the vicinity of land hitherto met with, have concluded, that there was none within ſome thouſand leagues of us. We had hardly ſeen a bird, or any other oceanic animal, ſince we left Sandwich Iſlands.

On the 1ſt of March, our latitude being now 44° 49′ North, and our longitude 228° Eaſt, we had one calm day. This was ſucceeded by a wind from the North, with which I ſtood to the Eaſt cloſe hauled, in order to make the land. According to the charts, it ought not to have been far from us. It was remarkable, that we ſhould ſtill carry with us ſuch moderate and mild weather, ſo far to the Northward, and ſo near the coaſt of an extenſive continent, at this time of the year. The preſent ſeaſon either muſt be uncommon for its mildneſs, or we can aſſign no reaſon, why Sir Francis Drake ſhould have met with ſuch ſevere cold, about this latitude, in the month of June *. Viſcaino, indeed, who was near the ſame place, in the depth of winter, ſays little of the cold, and ſpeaks of a ridge of ſnowy mountains, ſomewhere on the coaſt, as a thing rather remarkable †. Our ſeeing ſo few birds, in compariſon of what we met with in the ſame latitudes, to the South of the line, is another ſingular circumſtance, which muſt either proceed from a ſcàrcity of the different ſorts, or from a deficiency of places to reſt upon. From hence we may conclude, that beyond 40° in the Southern hemiſphere, the ſpecies are much more numerous, and the iſles where they inhabit alſo more plenti-

* See the account of Sir Francis's voyage, in Campbell's edition of Harris, Vol. i. p. 18. and other Collections.

† See Torquemada's Narrative of Viſcaino's Expedition, in 1602 and 1603, in the ſecond volume of Vanegas's Hiſtory of California, Engliſh tranſlation, from p. 229. to p. 308.

fully

fully fcattered about, than any where between the coaft of California and Japan, in or near that latitude.

During a calm, on the morning of the 2d, fome parts of the fea feemed covered with a kind of flime; and fome fmall fea animals were fwimming about. The moft confpicuous of which, were of the gelatinous, or *medufa* kind, almoft globular; and another fort fmaller, that had a white, or fhining appearance, and were very numerous. Some of thefe laft were taken up, and put into a glafs cup, with fome falt water, in which they appeared like fmall fcales, or bits of filver, when at reft, in a prone fituation. When they began to fwim about, which they did, with equal eafe, upon their back, fides, or belly, they emitted the brighteft colours of the moft precious gems, according to their pofition with refpect to the light. Sometimes they appeared quite pellucid, at other times affuming various tints of blue, from a pale fapphirine, to a deep violet colour; which were frequently mixed with a ruby, or opaline rednefs; and glowed with a ftrength fufficient to illuminate the veffel and water. Thefe colours appeared moft vivid, when the glafs was held to a ftrong light; and moftly vanifhed, on the fubfiding of the animals to the bottom, when they had a brownifh caft. But, with candle light, the colour was, chiefly, a beautiful, pale green, tinged with a burnifhed glofs; and, in the dark, it had a faint appearance of glowing fire. They proved to be a new fpecies of *onifcus*, and, from their properties, were, by Mr. Anderfon (to whom we owe this account of them), called *onifcus fulgens*; being, probably, an animal which has a fhare in producing fome forts of that lucid appearance, often obferved near fhips at fea, in the night. On the fame day, two large birds fettled on the water, near the fhip. One of thefe was the *procel-*

laria maxima (the *quebrantahueſſos*), and the other, which
was little more than half the ſize, ſeemed to be of the *alba-
troſs* kind. The upper part of the wings, and tip of the tail,
were black, with the reſt white; the bill yellowiſh; upon
the whole, not unlike the ſea-gull, though larger.

Friday 6.   On the 6th, at noon, being in the latitude of 44° 10′ North,
and the longitude of 234¼° Eaſt, we ſaw two ſeals, and ſeve-
Saturday 7. ral whales; and at day-break, the next morning, the long-
looked for coaſt of New Albion * was ſeen, extending from
North Eaſt to South Eaſt, diſtant ten or twelve leagues. At
noon, our latitude was 44° 33′ North, and our longitude
235° 20′ Eaſt; and the land extended from North Eaſt half
North, to South Eaſt by South, about eight leagues diſtant.
In this ſituation, we had ſeventy-three fathoms water, over
a muddy bottom, and about a league farther off found
ninety fathoms. The land appeared to be of a moderate
height, diverſified with hills and vallies, and, almoſt every
where, covered with wood. There was, however, no very
ſtriking objeĉt on any part of it, except one hill, whoſe elevated ſummit was flat. This bore Eaſt from us, at noon.
At the Northen extreme, the land formed a point, which I
called *Cape Foulweather*, from the very bad weather that
we, ſoon after, met with. I judge it to lie in the latitude of
44° 55′ North, and in the longitude of 235° 54′ Eaſt.

We had variable light airs and calms, till eight o'clock in
the evening, when a breeze ſprung up at South Weſt. With
it, I ſtood to the North Weſt, under an eaſy ſail, waiting for
Sunday 8. day-light to range along the coaſt. But at four, next morning, the wind ſhifted to North Weſt, and blew in ſqualls,
with rain. Our courſe was North Eaſt, till near ten o'clock,

* This part of the Weſt ſide of North America, was ſo named by Sir Francis
Drake.

when,

when, finding that I could make no progrefs on this tack, and feeing nothing like a harbour, I tacked, and ftood off South Weft. At this time, Cape Foulweather bore North Eaft by North, about eight leagues diftant. Toward noon, the wind veered more to the Weftward, and the weather became fair and clear; fo that we were enabled to make lunar obfervations. Having reduced all thofe that we had made fince the 19th of laft month to the prefent ones, by the time-keeper, amounting, in the whole, to feventy-two fets; their mean refult determined the longitude to be 235° 15′ 26″ Eaft, which was 14′ 11″ lefs than what the time-keeper gave. This longitude is made ufe of for fettling that of the coaft; and I have not a doubt of its being within a very few miles of the truth.

Our difficulties now began to increafe. In the evening, the wind came to the North Weft, blowing in fqualls with hail and fleet; and the weather being thick and hazy, I ftood out to fea till near noon the next day, when I tacked Monday 9. and ftood in again for the land, which made its appearance at two in the afternoon, bearing Eaft North Eaft. The wind and weather continued the fame; but, in the evening, the former veered more to the Weft, and the latter grew worfe; which made it neceffary to tack and ftand off till four the next morning, when I ventured to ftand in again.

At four in the afternoon, we faw the land, which, at Tuefday 10. fix, extended from North Eaft half Eaft, to South Eaft by South, about eight leagues diftant. In this fituation, we tacked and founded; but a line of a hundred and fixty fathoms did not reach the ground. I ftood off till midnight, then ftood in again; and, at half paft fix, we were Wednef. 11. within three leagues of the land, which extended from

L l 2 North

North by Eaſt, half Eaſt, to South, half Eaſt; each extreme about ſeven leagues diſtant. Seeing no ſigns of a harbour, and the weather being ſtill unſettled, I tacked and ſtretched off South Weſt, having then fifty-five fathoms water over a muddy bottom.

That part of the land, which we were ſo near when we tacked, is of a moderate height, though, in ſome places, it riſes higher within. It was diverſified with a great many riſing grounds and ſmall hills; many of which were entirely covered with tall, ſtraight trees; and others, which were lower, and grew in ſpots like coppices; but the interſpaces, and ſides of many of the riſing grounds, were clear. The whole, though it might make an agreeable ſummer proſpect, had now an uncomfortable appearance; as the bare grounds toward the coaſt were all covered with ſnow, which ſeemed to be of a conſiderable depth between the little hills and riſing grounds; and, in ſeveral places toward the ſea, might eaſily have been miſtaken, at a diſtance, for white cliffs. The ſnow on the riſing grounds was thinner ſpread; and farther inland, there was no appearance of any; from whence we might, perhaps, conclude, that what we ſaw toward the ſea, had fallen during the night; which was colder than any we had experienced ſince our arrival on the coaſt; and we had ſometimes a kind of ſleet. The coaſt ſeemed every where almoſt ſtraight, without any opening or inlet; and it appeared to terminate in a kind of white ſandy beach; though ſome on board thought that appearance was owing to the ſnow. Each extreme of the land that was now before us, ſeemed to ſhoot out into a point. The Northern one was the ſame which we had firſt ſeen on the 7th; and, on that account, I called it *Cape Perpetua*. It lies in the latitude of 44° 6′ North, and in the longitude

of

of 235° 52′ Eaſt. The Southern extreme before us, I named *Cape Gregory* *. Its latitude is 43° 30′, and its longitude 235° 57′ Eaſt. It is a remarkable point; the land of it riſing almoſt directly from the ſea, to a tolerable height, while that on each ſide of it is low.

I continued ſtanding off till one in the afternoon. Then I tacked, and ſtood in, hoping to have the wind off from the land in the night. But in this I was miſtaken; for at five o'clock it began to veer to the Weſt and South Weſt; which obliged me, once more, to ſtand out to ſea. At this time, Cape Perpetua bore North Eaſt by North; and the fartheſt land we could ſee to the South of Cape Gregory, bore South by Eaſt, perhaps ten or twelve leagues diſtant. If I am right in this eſtimation, its latitude will be 43° 10′, and its longitude 235° 55′ Eaſt, which is nearly the ſituation of Cape Blanco, diſcovered or ſeen by Martin d'Aguilar, on the 19th of January, 1603. It is worth obſerving, that, in the very latitude where we now were, geographers have been pleaſed to place a large entrance or ſtrait, the diſcovery of which they take upon them to aſcribe to the ſame navigator; whereas nothing more is mentioned in the account of his voyage, than his having ſeen, in this ſituation, a large river, which he would have entered, but was prevented by the currents †.

The wind, as I have obſerved, had veered to South Weſt in the evening; but it was very unſettled, and blew in ſqualls with ſnow ſhowers. In one of theſe, at midnight, it ſhifted at once to Weſt North Weſt, and ſoon increaſed to a very hard gale, with heavy ſqualls, attended with ſleet

---

* In our calendar, the 7th of March is diſtinguiſhed by the name of Perpetua M, and the 12th by that of Gregory B.

† See the Hiſtory of California. Eng. tranſ. Vol. ii. p. 292.

or

or fnow. There was no choice now ; and we were obliged to ftretch to the Southward, in order to get clear of the coaft. This was done under courfes, and two clofe-reefed topfails ; being rather more fail than the fhips could fafely bear ; but it was neceffary to carry it to avoid the more preffing danger of being forced on fhore. This gale continued till eight o'clock in the morning of the 13th ; when it abated, and I ftood in again for the land. We had been forced a confiderable way backward ; for at the time of our tacking, we were in the latitude of 42° 45′, and in the lon-gitude of 233° 30′.

The wind continued at Weft, and North Weft ; ftorms, moderate weather, and calms, fucceeding each other by
turns, till the morning of the 21ft ; when, after a few hours calm, a breeze fprung up at South Weft. This bringing with it fair weather, I fteered North Eafterly, in order to fall in with the land, beyond that part of it where we had already fo unprofitably been toffed about for the laft fort-night. In the evening, the wind veered to the Weftward ;
and, at eight o'clock, the next morning, we faw the land, extending from North Eaft to Eaft, nine leagues diftant. At this time we were in the latitude of 47° 5′ North, and in the longitude of 235° 10′ Eaft.

I continued to ftand to the North with a fine breeze at Weft, and Weft North Weft, till near feven o'clock in the evening, when I tacked to wait for day-light. At this time, we were in forty-eight fathoms water, and about four leagues from the land, which extended from North to South Eaft half Eaft, and a fmall round hill, which had the appearance of being an ifland, bore North three quar-ters Eaft, diftant fix or feven leagues, as I gueffed ; it ap-pears to be of a tolerable height, and was but juft to be
feen

seen from the deck. Between this ifland or rock, and the
Northern extreme of the land, there appeared to be a fmall
opening, which flattered us with the hopes of finding an
harbour. Thefe hopes leffened as we drew nearer; and, at
laft, we had fome reafon to think, that the opening was
clofed by low land. On this account I called the point of
land to the North of it *Cape Flattery*. It lies in the latitude
of 48° 15′ North, and in the longitude of 235° 3′ Eaft. There
is a round hill of a moderate height over it; and all the
land upon this part of the coaft is of a moderate and pretty equal height, well covered with wood, and had a very
pleafant and fertile appearance. It is in this very latitude
where we now were, that geographers have placed the pretended ftrait of Juan de Fuca. But we faw nothing like it;
nor is there the leaft probability that ever any fuch thing
exifted *.

I ftood off to the Southward till midnight, when I tacked,
and fteered to the North Weft, with a gentle breeze at South
Weft, intending to ftand in for the land as foon as day-
light fhould appear. But, by that time, we were reduced
to two courfes and clofe-reefed top-fails, having a very
hard gale, with rain, right on fhore; fo that, inftead of
running in for the land, I was glad to get an offing, or to
keep that which we had already got. The South Weft
wind was, however, but of fhort continuance; for, in the
evening, it veered again to the Weft. Thus had we perpetually ftrong Weft and North Weft winds to encounter.
Sometimes, in an evening, the wind would become moderate, and veer to the Southward; but this was always a

1778.
March.

Monday 23.

* See Michael Locke's apocryphal account of Juan de Fuca, and his pretended ftrait,
in Purchas, Vol. iii. p. 849—852. and many later Collections.

3

fure

fure prelude to a ftorm, which blew the hardeft at South
South Eaft, and was attended with rain and fleet. It feldom lafted above four or fix hours, before it was fucceeded
by another gale from the North Weft, which, generally,
brought with it fair weather. It was, by the means of thefe
Southerly blafts, that we were enabled to get to the North
Weft at all.

At length, at nine o'clock in the morning of the 29th, as
we were ftanding to the North Eaft, we again faw the land,
which, at noon, extended from North Weft by Weft, to Eaft
South Eaft, the neareft part about fix leagues diftant. Our
latitude was now 49° 29′ North, and our longitude 232° 29′
Eaft. The appearance of the country differed much from
that of the parts which we had before feen; being full of
high mountains, whofe fummits were covered with fnow.
But the valleys between them, and the grounds on the fea
coaft, high as well as low, were covered to a confiderable
breadth with high, ftraight trees, that formed a beautiful
profpect, as of one vaft foreft. The South Eaft extreme of
the land formed a low point, off which are many breakers,
occafioned by funken rocks. On this account it was called
Point Breakers. It lies in the latitude of 49° 15′ North, and
in the longitude of 233° 20′ Eaft; and the other extreme,
in about the latitude of 50°, and the longitude of 232°. I
named this laft *Woody Point.* It projects pretty much out
to the South Weft, and is high land. Between thefe two
points, the fhore forms a large bay, which I called *Hope
Bay*; hoping, from the appearance of the land, to find in it
a good harbour. The event proved, that we were not
miftaken,

As we drew nearer the coaft, we perceived the appearance of two inlets; one in the North Weft, and the other in
the

the North Eaſt corner of the bay. As I could not fetch the former, I bore up for the latter; and paſſed ſome breakers, or ſunken rocks, that lay a league or more from the ſhore. We had nineteen and twenty fathoms water half a league without them; but as ſoon as we had paſſed them, the depth increaſed to thirty, forty, and fifty fathoms, with a ſandy bottom; and farther in we found no ground with the greateſt length of line. Notwithſtanding appearances, we were not yet ſure that there were any inlets; but, as we were in a deep bay, I had reſolved to anchor, with a view to endeavour to get ſome water, of which, by this time, we were in great want. At length, as we advanced, the exiſt-ence of the inlet was no longer doubtful. At five o'clock we reached the Weſt point of it, where we were becalmed for ſome time. While in this ſituation, I ordered all the boats to be hoiſted out to tow the ſhips in. But this was hardly done, before a freſh breeze ſprung up again at North Weſt, with which we were enabled to ſtretch up into an arm of the inlet, that was obſerved by us to run into the North Eaſt. There we were again becalmed, and obliged to anchor in eighty-five fathoms water, and ſo near the ſhore as to reach it with a hawſer. The wind failed the Diſcovery before ſhe got within the arm, where ſhe anchored, and found only ſeventy fathoms.

We no ſooner drew near the inlet than we found the coaſt to be inhabited; and at the place where we were firſt becalmed, three canoes came off to the ſhip. In one of theſe were two men, in another ſix, and in the third ten. Having come pretty near us, a perſon in one of the two laſt ſtood up, and made a long harangue, inviting us to land, as we gueſſed, by his geſtures. At the ſame time, he

kept ſtrewing handfuls of feathers towards us *; and ſome
of his companions threw handfuls of a red duſt or powder
in the ſame manner. The perſon who played the orator,
wore the ſkin of ſome animal, and held, in each hand,
ſomething which rattled as he kept ſhaking it. After tiring
himſelf with his repeated exhortations, of which we did
not underſtand a word, he was quiet; and then others took
it, by turns, to ſay ſomething, though they acted their part
neither ſo long, nor with ſo much vehemence as the other.
We obſerved that two or three had their hair quite ſtrewed
over with ſmall white feathers; and others had large ones
ſtuck into different parts of the head. After the tumul-
tuous noiſe had ceaſed, they lay at a little diſtance from the
ſhip, and converſed with each other in a very eaſy manner;
nor did they ſeem to ſhew the leaſt ſurprize or diſtruſt.
Some of them, now and then, got up, and ſaid ſomething
after the manner of their firſt harangues; and one ſung a
very agreeable air, with a degree of ſoftneſs and melody
which we could not have expected; the word *haela*, being
often repeated as the burden of the ſong. The breeze
which ſoon after ſprung up, bringing us nearer to the ſhore,
the canoes began to come off in greater numbers; and we
had, at one time, thirty-two of them near the ſhip, carrying
from three to ſeven or eight perſons each, both men and
women. Several of theſe ſtood up in their canoes haran-
guing, and making geſtures after the manner of our firſt
viſiters. One canoe was remarkable for a ſingular head,
which had a bird's eye and bill, of an enormous ſize, painted

* The natives of this coaſt, twelve degrees farther South, alſo brought feathers as preſents to Sir Francis Drake on his arrival. See an account of his voyage in *Campbell's*
edit. of Harris, Vol. i. p. 18.

10   on

on it; and a perſon who was in it, who ſeemed to be a Chief, was no leſs remarkable for his uncommon appearance; having many feathers hanging from his head, and being painted in an extraordinary manner *. He held in his hand a carved bird of wood, as large as a pigeon, with which he rattled as the perſon firſt-mentioned had done; and was no leſs vociferous in his harangue, which was attended with ſome expreſſive geſtures.

Though our viſiters behaved very peaceably, and could not be ſuſpected of any hoſtile intention, we could not prevail upon any of them to come on board. They ſhewed great readineſs, however, to part with any thing they had, and took from us whatever we offered them in exchange; but were more deſirous of iron, than of any other of our articles of commerce; appearing to be perfectly acquainted with the uſe of that metal. Many of the canoes followed us to our anchoring-place; and a group of about ten or a dozen of them remained along-ſide the Reſolution moſt part of the night.

Theſe circumſtances gave us a reaſonable ground of hope, that we ſhould find this a comfortable ſtation to ſupply all our wants, and to make us forget the hardſhips and delays experienced during a conſtant ſucceſſion of adverſe winds, and boiſterous weather, almoſt ever ſince our arrival upon the coaſt of America.

* Viſcaino met with natives on the coaſt of California, while he was in the harbour of San Diego, *who were painted or beſmeared with black and white, and had their heads loaded with feathers.* *Hiſtory of California,* Vol. ii. p. 272.

A

VOYAGE

TO THE

PACIFIC OCEAN.

BOOK IV.

TRANSACTIONS AMONGST THE NATIVES OF NORTH AME-
RICA; DISCOVERIES ALONG THAT COAST AND THE EAST-
ERN EXTREMITY OF ASIA, NORTHWARD TO ICY CAPE;
AND RETURN SOUTHWARD TO THE SANDWICH ISLANDS.

CHAP. I.

The Ships enter the Sound, and moor in a Harbour.—Inter-
course with the Natives.—Articles brought to barter.—
Thefts committed.—The Observatories erected, and Carpen-
ters set to work.—Jealousy of the Inhabitants of the Sound
to prevent other Tribes having Intercourse with the Ships.—
Stormy and rainy Weather.—Progress round the Sound.—
Behaviour of the Natives at their Villages.—Their Manner
of drying Fish, &c.—Remarkable Visit from Strangers, and
introductory Ceremonies.—A second Visit to one of the Vil-
lages.—Leave to cut Grass, purchased.—The Ships sail.—
Presents given and received at parting.

THE ships having happily found so excellent shelter   1778.
in an inlet, the coasts of which appeared to be in-   March.
habited by a race of people, whose inoffensive behaviour promised a friendly intercourse, the next morn-   Monday 30.
ing,

ing, after coming to anchor, I loft no time in endeavouring to find a commodious harbour where we might ftation our-felves during our continuance in the Sound. Accordingly, I fent three armed boats, under the command of Mr. King, upon this fervice; and foon after, I went myfelf, in a fmall boat, on the fame fearch. I had very little trouble in find-ing what we wanted. On the North Weft of the arm we were now in, and not far from the fhips, I met with a con-venient fnug cove well fuited to our purpofe. Mr. King was equally fuccefsful; for he returned about noon, with an account of a ftill better harbour, which he had feen and examined, lying on the North Weft fide of the land. But as it would have required more time to carry the fhips thi-ther, than to the cove where I had been, which was imme-diately within our reach; this reafon operated to determine my choice in favour of the latter fituation. But being ap-prehenfive, that we fhould not be able to tranfport our fhips to it, and to moor them properly, before night came on, I thought it beft to remain where we were till next morn-ing; and, that no time might be loft, I employed the re-mainder of the day to fome ufeful purpofes, ordering the fails to be unbent, the top-mafts to be ftruck, and the fore-maft of the Refolution to be unrigged, in order to fix a new bib, one of the old ones being decayed.

A great many canoes, filled with the natives, were about the fhips all day; and a trade commenced betwixt us and them, which was carried on with the ftricteft honefty on both fides. The articles which they offered to fale were fkins of various animals, fuch as bears, wolves, foxes, deer, rackoons, polecats, martins; and, in particular, of the fea otters, which are found at the iflands Eaft of Kamt-fchatka. Befides the fkins in their native fhape, they alfo
brought

brought garments made of them, and another fort of clothing made of the bark of a tree, or fome plant like hemp;
weapons, fuch as bows, arrows, and fpears; fifh-hooks,
and inftruments of various kinds; wooden vizors of many
different monftrous figures; a fort of woollen ftuff, or
blanketing; bags filled with red ochre; pieces of carved
work; beads; and feveral other little ornaments of thin
brafs and iron, fhaped like a horfe-fhoe, which they hang
at their nofes; and feveral chiffels, or pieces of iron, fixed to
handles. From their poffeffing which metals, we could
infer that they had either been vifited before by fome civilized nation, or had connections with tribes on their continent, who had communication with them. But the moft
extraordinary of all the articles which they brought to the
fhips for fale, were human fkulls, and hands not yet quite
ftripped of the flefh, which they made our people plainly
underftand they had eaten; and, indeed, fome of them
had evident marks that they had been upon the fire. We
had but too much reafon to fufpect, from this circumftance, that the horrid practice of feeding on their enemies is as prevalent here, as we had found it to be at New
Zealand and other South Sea Iflands. For the various articles which they brought, they took in exchange knives,
chiffels, pieces of iron and tin, nails, looking-glaffes, buttons, or any kind of metal. Glafs beads they were not fond
of; and cloth of every fort they rejected.

We employed the next day in hauling our fhips into the
cove, where they were moored head and ftern, faftening
our hawfers to the trees on fhore. On heaving up the anchor of the Refolution, we found, notwithftanding the great
depth of water in which it was let go, that there were rocks
at the bottom. Thefe had done fome confiderable damage

to

to the cable; and the hawfers that were carried out, to warp the fhip into the cove, alfo got foul of rocks; from which it appeared that the whole bottom was ftrewed with them. The fhip being again very leaky in her upper works, I ordered the carpenters to go to work to caulk her, and to repair fuch other defects as, on examination, we might difcover.

The fame of our arrival brought a great concourfe of the natives to our fhips in the courfe of this day. We counted above a hundred canoes at one time, which might be fuppofed to contain, at an average, five perfons each; for few of them had lefs than three on board; great numbers had feven, eight, or nine; and one was manned with no lefs than feventeen. Amongft thefe vifiters, many now favoured us with their company for the firft time, which we could guefs, from their approaching the fhips with their orations and other ceremonies. If they had any diftruft or fear of us at firft, they now appeared to have laid it afide; for they came on board the fhips, and mixed with our people with the greateft freedom. We foon difcovered, by this nearer intercourfe, that they were as light-fingered as any of our friends in the iflands we had vifited in the courfe of the voyage. And they were far more dangerous thieves; for, poffeffing fharp iron inftruments, they could cut a hook from a tackle, or any other piece of iron from a rope, the inftant that our backs were turned. A large hook, weighing between twenty and thirty pounds, feveral fmaller ones, and other articles of iron, were loft in this manner. And, as to our boats, they ftripped them of every bit of iron that was worth carrying away, though we had always men left in them as a guard. They were dextrous enough in effecting their purpofes; for one fellow would contrive

to

to amufe the boat-keeper, at one end of a boat, while another was pulling out the iron-work at the other. If we miffed a thing immediately after it had been ftolen, we found little difficulty in detecting the thief, as they were ready enough to impeach one another. But the guilty perfon generally relinquifhed his prize with reluctance; and fometimes we found it neceffary to have recourfe to force.

The fhips being fecurely moored, we began our other neceffary bufinefs the next day. The obfervatories were carried afhore, and placed upon an elevated rock on one fide of the cove, clofe to the Refolution. A party of men, with an officer, was fent to cut wood, and to clear a place for the conveniency of watering. Others were employed to brew fpruce-beer, as pine trees abounded here. The forge was alfo fet up, to make the iron-work wanting for the repairs of the fore-maft. For, befides one of the bibs being defective, the larboard treftle-tree, and one of the crofs-trees were fprung.

A confiderable number of the natives vifited us daily; and, every now and then, we faw new faces. On their firft coming, they generally went through a fingular mode of introducing themfelves. They would paddle, with all their ftrength, quite round both fhips, a Chief, or other principal perfon in the canoe, ftanding up with a fpear, or fome other weapon, in his hand, and fpeaking, or rather hollowing, all the time. Sometimes the orator of the canoe would have his face covered with a mafk, reprefenting either a human vifage, or that of fome animal; and, inftead of a weapon, would hold a rattle in his hand, as before defcribed. After making this circuit round the fhips, they would come along-fide, and begin to trade without further

VOL. II.   N n   ceremony.

ceremony.   Very often, indeed, they would firſt give us a ſong, in which all in the canoe joined, with a very pleaſing harmony.

During theſe viſits, they gave us no other trouble, than to guard againſt their thieviſh tricks.   But, in the morn-
ing of the 4th, we had a ſerious alarm.   Our party on ſhore, who were employed in cutting wood, and filling water, obſerved, that the natives all around them were arming themſelves in the beſt manner they could; thoſe, who were not poſſeſſed of proper weapons, preparing ſticks, and col-lecting ſtones.   On hearing this, I thought it prudent to arm alſo; but, being determined to act upon the defenſive, I ordered all our workmen to retreat to the rock, upon which we had placed our obſervatories; leaving the natives in quiet poſſeſſion of the ground where they had aſſembled, which was within a ſtone's throw of the Reſolution's ſtern. Our fears were ill-grounded: theſe hoſtile preparations were not directed againſt us, but againſt a body of their own countrymen, who were coming to fight them; and our friends of the Sound, on obſerving our apprehenſions, uſed their beſt endeavours to convince us that this was the caſe.   We could ſee, that they had people looking out, on each point of the cove, and canoes frequently paſſed be-tween them and the main body aſſembled near the ſhips. At length, the adverſe party, in about a dozen large ca-noes, appeared off the South point of the cove, where they ſtopped, and lay drawn up in line of battle, a negociation having commenced.   Some people in canoes, in conducting the treaty, paſſed between the two parties, and there was ſome ſpeaking on both ſides.   At length, the difference, whatever it was, ſeemed to be compromiſed; but the ſtran-gers were not allowed to come along-ſide the ſhips, nor to

have

1778.
April.

have any trade or intercourfe with us. Probably we were the caufe of the quarrel; the ftrangers, perhaps, being defirous to fhare in the advantages of a trade with us; and our firft friends, the inhabitants of the Sound, being determined to engrofs us entirely to themfelves. We had proofs of this on feveral other occafions; nay, it appeared, that even thofe who lived in the Sound were not united in the fame caufe; for the weaker were frequently obliged to give way to the ftronger party, and plundered of every thing, without attempting to make the leaft refiftance.

We refumed our work in the afternoon, and, the next day, rigged the fore-maft; the head of which being rather too fmall for the cap, the carpenter went to work, to fix a piece on one fide, to fill up the vacant fpace. In cutting into the maft-head for this purpofe, and examining the ftate of it, both cheeks were found to be fo rotten, that there was no poffibility of repairing them; and it became neceffary to get the maft out, and to fix new ones upon it. It was evident, that one of the cheeks had been defective at the firft, and that the unfound part had been cut out, and a piece put in; which had not only weakened the maft-head, but had, in a great meafure, been the occafion of rotting every other part of both cheeks. Thus, when we were almoft ready to put to fea, we had all our work to do over again; and, what was ftill more provoking, an additional repair was to be undertaken, which would require fome time to be completed. But, as there was no remedy, we immediately fet about it. It was fortunate for the voyage, that thefe defects were difcovered, when we were in a place, where the materials requifite were to be procured. For, amongft the drift-wood, in the cove where the fhips lay, were fome fmall

Sunday 5.

feafoned

1778.
April.

Tuefday 7.

Wednef. 8.

feafoned trees very fit for our purpofe. One of thefe was, pitched upon; and the carpenters began, without lofs of time, to make out of it two new cheeks.

In the morning of the 7th, we got the fore-maft out, and hauled it afhore; and the carpenters of the fhips were fet to work upon it. Some parts of the lower ftanding rigging having been found to be very much decayed, as we had time now to put them in order, while the carpenters were repairing the fore-maft, I ordered a new fet of main-rigging to be fitted, and a more perfect fet of fore-rigging to be felected out of the beft parts of the old.

From the time of our putting into the Sound till now, the weather had been exceedingly fine, without either wind or rain. That comfort, at the very moment when the continuance of it would have been of moft fervice, was withdrawn. In the morning of the 8th, the wind frefhened at South Eaft, attended with thick hazy weather and rain. In the afternoon the wind increafed; and, toward the evening, it blew very hard indeed. It came, in exceffively heavy fqualls, from over the high land on the oppofite fhore, right into the cove; and, though the fhips were very well moored, put them in fome danger. Thefe tempeftuous blafts fucceeded each other pretty quick; but they were of fhort duration; and in the intervals between them we had a perfect calm. According to the old proverb, Misfortunes feldom come fingle; the mizen was now the only maft on board the Refolution that remained rigged, with its topmaft up. The former was fo defective, that it could not fupport the latter during the violence of the fqualls, but gave way at the head under the rigging. About eight o'clock the gale abated; but the rain continued with very little intermiffion for feveral days; and, that the carpenters might

might be enabled to proceed in their labours, while it prevailed, a tent was erected over the fore-maft, where they
could work with fome degree of convenience.

The bad weather which now came on, did not, however,
hinder the natives from vifiting us daily; and, in fuch circumftances, their vifits were very advantageous to us. For
they frequently brought us a tolerable fupply of fifh, when
we could not catch any ourfelves with hook and line; and
there was not a proper place near us where we could draw
a net. The fifh which they brought us were either fardines,
or what refembled them much; a fmall kind of bream;
and fometimes fmall cod.

On the 11th, notwithftanding the rainy weather, the
main-rigging was fixed and got over head; and our employment, the day after, was to take down the mizen-maft,
the head of which proved to be fo rotten, that it dropped
off while in the flings. In the evening we were vifited by
a tribe of natives whom we had never feen before; and who,
in general, were better-looking people than moft of our old
friends, fome of whom attended them. I prevailed upon
thefe vifiters to go down into the cabin for the firft time;
and obferved, that there was not a fingle object that fixed
the attention of moft of them for a moment; their countenances marking, that they looked upon all our novelties
with the utmoft indifference. This, however, was not
without exception; for a few of the company fhewed a certain degree of curiofity.

In the afternoon of the next day, I went into the woods
with a party of our men, and cut down a tree for a mizen-
maft. On the day following, it was brought to the place
where the carpenters were employed upon the fore-maft.
In the evening the wind, which had been, for fome time,

Wefterly,

Wefterly, veered to South Eaft, and increafed to a very hard gale, with rain, which continued till eight o'clock the next morning, when it abated, and veered again to the Weft.

The fore-maft being, by this time, finifhed, we hauled it along-fide; but the bad weather prevented our getting it in till the afternoon; and we fet about rigging it with the greateft expedition, while the carpenters were going on with the mizen-maft on fhore. They had made very confiderable progrefs in it on the 16th; when they difcovered that the ftick upon which they were at work was fprung, or wounded; owing, as fuppofed, to fome accident in cutting it down. So that all their labour was thrown away; and it became neceffary to get another tree out of the woods, which employed all hands above half a day. During thefe various operations, feveral of the natives, who were about the fhips, looked on with an expreffive filent furprize, which we did not expect, from their general indifference and inattention.

On the 18th, a party of ftrangers, in fix or eight canoes, came into the cove, where they remained, looking at us, for fome time; and then retired, without coming along-fide either fhip. We fuppofed, that our old friends, who were more numerous, at this time, about us, than thefe new vifiters, would not permit them to have any intercourfe with us. It was evident, upon this and feveral other occafions, that the inhabitants of the adjoining parts of the Sound engroffed us entirely to themfelves; or if, at any time, they did not hinder ftrangers from trading with us, they contrived to manage the trade for them in fuch a manner, that the price of their commodities was always kept up, while the value of ours was leffening every day. We alfo found, that many of the principal natives, who lived near us, car-

I ried

1778.
April.

ried on a trade with more diftant tribes, in the articles they had procured from us. For we obferved that they would frequently difappear for four or five days at a time, and then return with frefh cargoes of fkins and curiofities, which our people were fo paffionately fond of, that they always came to a good market. But we received moft benefit from fuch of the natives as vifited us daily. Thefe, after difpofing of all their little trifles, turned their attention to fifhing; and we never failed to partake of what they caught. We alfo got from thefe people a confiderable quantity of very good animal oil, which they had referved in bladders. In this traffic fome would attempt to cheat us, by mixing water with the oil; and, once or twice, they had the addrefs to carry their impofition fo far, as to fill their bladders with mere water, without a fingle drop of oil. It was always better to bear with thefe tricks, than to make them the foundation of a quarrel; for our articles of traffic confifted, for the moft part, of mere trifles; and yet we were put to our fhifts to find a conftant fupply even of thefe. Beads, and fuch other toys, of which I had ftill fome left, were in little eftimation. Nothing would go down with our vifiters but metal; and brafs had, by this time, fupplanted iron; being fo eagerly fought after, that before we left this place, hardly a bit of it was left in the fhips, except what belonged to our neceffary inftruments. Whole fuits of clothes were ftripped of every button; bureaus of their furniture; and copper kettles, tin cannifters, candlefticks, and the like, all went to wreck; fo that our American friends here got a greater medley and variety of things from us, than any other nation whom we had vifited in the courfe of the voyage.

After a fortnight's bad weather, the 19th proving a fair day, Sunday 19.

day, we availed ourſelves of it, to get up the top-maſts and yards; and to fix up the rigging. And, having now finiſhed moſt of our heavy work, I ſet out the next morning to take a view of the Sound. I firſt went to the Weſt point, where I found a large village, and, before it, a very ſnug harbour, in which was from nine to four fathoms water, over a bottom of fine ſand. The people of this village, who were numerous, and to moſt of whom I was well known, received me very courteouſly; every one preſſing me to go into his houſe, or rather his apartment; for ſeveral families live under the ſame roof. I did not decline the invitations; and my hoſpitable friends, whom I viſited, ſpread a mat for me to ſit down upon, and ſhewed me every other mark of civility. In moſt of the houſes were women at work, making dreſſes of the plant or bark before mentioned, which they executed exactly in the ſame manner that the New Zealanders manufacture their cloth. Others were occupied in opening ſardines. I had ſeen a large quantity of them brought on ſhore from canoes, and divided by meaſure amongſt ſeveral people, who carried them up to their houſes, where the operation of curing them by ſmoke-drying is performed. They hang them on ſmall rods; at firſt, about a foot from the fire; afterward they remove them higher and higher, to make room for others, till the rods, on which the fiſh hang, reach the top of the houſe. When they are completely dried, they are taken down and packed cloſe in bales, which they cover with mats. Thus they are kept till wanted; and they are not a diſagreeable article of food. Cod, and other large fiſh, are alſo cured in the ſame manner by them; though they ſometimes dry theſe in the open air, without fire.

From this village I proceeded up the Weſt ſide of the Sound.

1778.
April.

Sound. For about three miles, I found the fhore covered with fmall iflands, which are fo fituated as to form feveral convenient harbours, having various depths of water, from thirty to feven fathoms, with a good bottom. Two leagues within the Sound, on this Weft fide, there runs in an arm in the direction of North North Weft; and two miles farther, is another nearly in the fame direction, with a pretty large ifland before it. I had no time to examine either of thefe arms; but have reafon to believe, that they do not extend far inland, as the water was no more than brackifh at their entrances. A mile above the fecond arm, I found the remains of a village. The logs or framings of the houfes were ftanding; but the boards that had compofed their fides and roofs did not exift. Before this village were fome large fifhing wears; but I faw nobody attending them. Thefe wears were compofed of pieces of wicker-work made of fmall rods, fome clofer than others, according to the fize of the fifh intended to be caught in them. Thefe pieces of wicker-work (fome of whofe *fuperficies* are, at leaft, twenty feet by twelve), are fixed up edgewife in fhallow water, by ftrong poles or pickets, that ftand firm in the ground. Behind this ruined village is a plain of a few acres extent, covered with the largeft pine-trees that I ever faw. This was more remarkable, as the elevated ground, on moft other parts of this Weft fide of the Sound, was rather naked.

From this place, I croffed over to the other, or Eaft fide of the Sound, paffing an arm of it that runs in North North Eaft, to appearance not far. I now found, what I had before conjectured, that the land, under which the fhips lay, was an ifland; and that there were many fmaller ones lying fcattered in the Sound on the Weft fide of it. Oppofite

VOL. II.   O o   the

the North end of our large ifland, upon the main land, I obferved a village, and there I landed. The inhabitants of it were not fo polite as thofe of the other I had juft vifited. But this cold reception feemed, in a great meafure, if not entirely, owing to one furly Chief, who would not let me enter their houfes, following me wherever I went; and feveral times, by expreffive figns, marking his impatience that I fhould be gone. I attempted in vain to footh him by prefents; but though he did not refufe them, they did not alter his behaviour. Some of the young women, better pleafed with us than was their inhofpitable Chief, dreffed themfelves expeditioufly in their beft apparel, and, affembling in a body, welcomed us to their village, by joining in a fong, which was far from harfh or difagreeable.

The day being now far fpent, I proceeded for the fhips, round the North end of the large ifland; meeting, in my way, with feveral canoes laden with fardines, which had been juft caught, fomewhere in the Eaft corner of the Sound. When I got on board, I was informed, that, while I was abfent, the fhips had been vifited by fome ftrangers, in two or three large canoes, who, by figns, made our people underftand that they had come from the South Eaft, beyond the bay. They brought feveral fkins, garments, and other articles, which they bartered. But what was moft fingular, two filver table-fpoons were purchafed from them, which, from their peculiar fhape, we fuppofed to be of Spanifh manufacture. One of thefe ftrangers wore them round his neck, by way of ornament. Thefe vifiters alfo appeared to be more plentifully fupplied with iron than the inhabitants of the Sound.

The mizen-maft being finifhed, it was got in, and rigged, on the 21ft; and the carpenters were fet to work to make

3

make a new fore-top-maft, to replace the one that had been
carried away fome time before.

Next morning, about eight o'clock, we were vifited by a
number of ftrangers, in twelve or fourteen canoes. They
came into the cove from the Southward; and as foon as
they had turned the point of it, they ftopped, and lay drawn
up in a body above half an hour, about two or three hundred yards from the fhips. At firft, we thought, that they
were afraid to come nearer; but we were miftaken in this,
and they were only preparing an introductory ceremony.
On advancing toward the fhips, they all ftood up in their
canoes, and began to fing. Some of their fongs, in which
the whole body joined, were in a flow, and others in quicker
time; and they accompanied their notes with the moft regular motions of their hands; or beating in concert, with
their paddles, on the fides of the canoes; and making other
very expreffive geftures. At the end of each fong, they
remained filent a few feconds, and then began again, fometimes pronouncing the word *booee!* forcibly, as a chorus.
After entertaining us with this fpecimen of their mufic,
which we liftened to with admiration, for above half an
hour, they came along-fide the fhips, and bartered what
they had to difpofe of. Some of our old friends of the
Sound, were now found to be amongft them; and they took
the whole management of the traffic between us and the
ftrangers, much to the advantage of the latter.

Our attendance on thefe vifiters being finifhed, Captain
Clerke and I went, in the forenoon, with two boats, to the
village at the Weft point of the Sound. When I was there
before, I had obferved, that plenty of grafs grew near it;
and it was neceffary to lay in a quantity of this, as food for
the few goats and fheep which were ftill left on board. The

O o 2   inhabitants

inhabitants received us with the fame demonftrations of friendfhip which I had experienced before; and the moment we landed, I ordered fome of my people to begin their operation of cutting. I had not the leaft imagination, that the natives could make any objection to our furnifhing ourfelves with what feemed to be of no ufe to them, but was neceffary for us. However, I was miftaken; for, the moment that our men began to cut, fome of the inhabitants interpofed, and would not permit them to proceed, faying they muft " *makook*;" that is, muft firft buy it. I was now in one of the houfes; but as foon as I heard of this, I went to the field, where I found about a dozen of the natives, each of whom laid claim to fome part of the grafs that grew in this place. I bargained with them for it, and having completed the purchafe, thought that we were now at liberty to cut wherever we pleafed. But here, again, it appeared, that I was under a miftake; for the liberal manner in which I had paid the firft pretended proprietors, brought frefh demands upon me from others; fo that there did not feem to be a fingle blade of grafs, that had not a feparate owner; and fo many of them were to be fatisfied, that I very foon emptied my pockets. When they found that I really had nothing more to give, their importunities ceafed, and we were permitted to cut wherever we pleafed, and as much as we chofe to carry away.

Here I muft obferve, that I have no where, in my feveral voyages, met with any uncivilized nation, or tribe, who had fuch ftrict notions of their having a right to the exclufive property of every thing that their country produces, as the inhabitants of this Sound. At firft, they wanted our people to pay for the wood and water that they carried on board; and had I been upon the fpot, when thefe demands were

made,

made, I fhould certainly have complied with them. Our workmen, in my abfence, thought differently; for they took but little notice of fuch claims; and the natives, when they found that we were determined to pay nothing, at laft ceafed to apply. But they made a merit of neceffity; and frequently afterward, took occafion to remind us, that they had given us wood and water out of friendfhip *.

During the time I was at this village, Mr. Webber, who had attended me thither, made drawings of every thing that was curious, both within and without doors. I had alfo an opportunity of infpecting, more narrowly, the conftruction of the houfes, houfehold furniture, and utenfils, and the ftriking peculiarities of the cuftoms and modes of living of the inhabitants. Thefe fhall be defcribed in another place, in the beft manner I can, calling in to my affiftance the obfervations of Mr. Anderfon. When we had completed all our operations at this village, the natives and we parted very good friends; and we got back to the fhips in the afternoon.

The three following days were employed in getting ready to put to fea; the fails were bent; the obfervatories and in- ftruments, brewing veffels, and other things, were moved from the fhore; fome fmall fpars, for different ufes, and pieces of timber, which might be occafionally fawn into boards, were prepared and put on board; and both fhips were cleared, and put into a failing condition.

Every thing being now ready, in the morning of the

Thurfday 23.
Friday 24.
Saturday 25.

Sunday 26.

* Similar to the behaviour of the natives of Nootka, on this occafion, was that of ano- ther tribe of Indians, farther North, in latitude 57° 18′, to the Spaniards, who had pre- ceded Captain Cook only three years, in a voyage to explore the coaft of America, North- ward of California. See the journal of that voyage, writ by the fecond pilot of the fleet, and publifhed by the Honourable Mr. Daines Barrington, to whom the literary world owes fo many obligations. *Mifcellanies*, p. 505, 506.

26th,

26th, I intended to have put to fea; but both wind and tide being againft us, was obliged to wait till noon, when the South Weft wind was fucceeded by a calm; and the tide turning in our favour, we caft off the moorings, and with our boats towed the fhips out of the cove. After this, we had variable light airs and calms, till four in the afternoon, when a breeze fprung up Northerly, with very thick, hazy weather. The mercury in the barometer fell unufually low; and we had every other fore-runner of an approaching ftorm, which we had reafon to expect would be from the Southward. This made me hefitate a little, as night was at hand, whether I fhould venture to fail, or wait till the next morning. But my anxious impatience to proceed upon the voyage, and the fear of lofing this opportunity of getting out of the Sound, making a greater impreffion on my mind, than any apprehenfion of immediate danger, I determined to put to fea at all events.

Our friends, the natives, attended us, till we were almoft out of the Sound; fome on board the fhips, and others in their canoes. One of their Chiefs, who had, fome time before, attached himfelf to me, was amongft the laft who left us. Having, before he went, beftowed upon him a fmall prefent, I received in return, a beaver-fkin, of much greater value. This called upon me to make fome addition to my prefent, which pleafed him fo much, that he infifted upon my acceptance of the beaver-fkin cloak which he then wore; and of which I knew he was particularly fond. Struck with this inftance of generofity, and defirous that he fhould be no fufferer by his friendfhip to me, I prefented to him a new broad fword, with a brafs hilt; the poffeffion of which made him completely happy. He, and alfo many others of his countrymen, importuned us much to pay
them

them another vifit; and, by way of encouragement, promifed to lay in a good ftock of fkins. I make no doubt,
that whoever comes after me to this place, will find the natives prepared accordingly, with no inconfiderable fupply
of an article of trade, which, they could obferve, we were
eager to poffefs; and which we found could be purchafed
to great advantage.

Such particulars about the country, and its inhabitants, as
came to our knowledge, during our fhort ftay, and have
not been mentioned in the courfe of the narrative, will furnifh materials for the two following Chapters.

C H A P.

CHAP. II.

*The Name of the Sound, and Directions for sailing into it.—
Account of the adjacent Country.—Weather.—Climate.—
Trees.—Other vegetable Productions.—Quadrupeds, whose
Skins were brought for Sale.—Sea Animals.—Description
of a Sea Otter.—Birds.—Water Fowl.—Fish.—Shell-fish, &c.
—Reptiles.—Insects.—Stones, &c.—Persons of the Inhabi-
tants.—Their Colour.—Common Dress and Ornaments.—
Occasional Dresses, and monstrous Decorations of wooden
Masks.—Their general Dispositions.—Songs.—Musical In-
struments.—Their Eagerness to possess Iron and other Me-
tals.*

1778.
April.

ON my arrival in this inlet, I had honoured it with
the name of King George's Sound; but I afterward
found, that it is called Nootka by the natives. The entrance is situated in the East corner of Hope Bay, in the
latitude of 49° 33′ North, and in the longitude of 233° 12′
East. The East coast of that bay, all the way from Breakers
Point to the entrance of the Sound, is covered by a chain
of sunken rocks, that seemed to extend some distance from
the shore; and, near the Sound, are some islands and rocks
above water.

We enter this Sound between two rocky points, that lie
East South East, and West North West from each other, diftant between three and four miles. Within these points the
Sound widens considerably, and extends in, to the Northward,

ward, four leagues at leaft, exclufive of the feveral branches toward its bottom, the termination of which we had not an opportunity to afcertain. But, from the circumftance of finding that the water frefhened where our boats croffed their entrance, it is probable that they had almoft reached its utmoft limits. And this probability is increafed by the hills that bounded it toward the land, being covered with thick fnow, when thofe toward the fea, or where we lay, had not a fpeck remaining on them; though, in general, they were much higher. In the middle of the Sound are a number of iflands of various fizes. But the chart or fketch of the Sound, here annexed, though it has no pretenfions to accuracy, will, with all its imperfections, convey a better idea of thefe iflands, and of the figure, and the extent of the Sound, than any written defcription. The depth of water in the middle of the Sound, and even clofe home to fome parts of its fhore, is from forty-feven to ninety fathoms, and perhaps more. The harbours, and anchoring-places within its circuit, are numerous; but we had no time to furvey them. The cove in which our fhips lay is on the Eaft fide of the Sound, and on the Eaft fide of the largeft of the iflands. It is covered from the fea, but has little elfe to recommend it, being expofed to the South Eaft winds, which we found to blow with great violence; and the devaftation they make fometimes, was apparent in many places.

The land bordering upon the fea-coaft is of a middling height and level; but within the Sound, it rifes almoft every where into fteep hills, which agree in their general formation, ending in round or blunted tops, with fome fharp, though not very prominent, ridges on their fides. Some of thefe hills may be reckoned high, while others of them

are of a very moderate height; but even the higheft are intirely covered to their tops with the thickeft woods; as well
as every flat part toward the fea. There are fometimes fpots
upon the fides of fome of the hills which are bare; but they
are few, in comparifon of the whole, though they fufficiently point out the general rocky difpofition of thefe hills.
Properly fpeaking, they have no foil upon them, except a
kind of compoft, produced from rotten moffes and trees,
of the depth of two feet or more. Their foundations are,
therefore, to be confidered as nothing more than ftupendous
rocks, of a whitifh or grey caft, where they have been
expofed to the weather; but, when broken, they appeared
to be of a blueifh grey colour, like that univerfal fort which
were found at Kerguelen's Land. The rocky fhores are
a continued mafs of this; and the little coves, in the Sound,
have beaches compofed of fragments of it, with a few other
pebbles. All thefe coves are furnifhed with a great quantity of fallen wood lying in them, which is carried in by
the tide; and with rills of frefh water, fufficient for the ufe
of a fhip, which feem to be fupplied entirely from the rains,
and fogs that hover about the tops of the hills. For few
fprings can be expected in fo rocky a country, and the frefh
water found farther up the Sound, moft probably arofe
from the melting of the fnow; there being no room to fufpect, that any large river falls into the Sound, either from
ftrangers coming down it, or from any other circumftance.
The water of thefe rills is perfectly clear, and diffolves foap
eafily.

The weather, during our ftay, correfponded pretty nearly
with that which we had experienced off the coaft. That is,
when the wind was any where between North and Weft,
the weather was fine and clear; but if to the Southward of

                          Weft,

Weſt, hazy with rain. The climate, as far as we had any experience of it, is infinitely milder than that on the Eaſt coaſt of America, under the ſame parallel of latitude. The mercury in the thermometer never, even in the night, fell lower than 42°; and very often, in the day, it roſe to 60°. No ſuch thing as froſt was perceived in any of the low ground; on the contrary, vegetation had made a conſider-able progreſs; for I met with graſs that was already above a foot long.

The trees which chiefly compoſe the woods, are the Ca-nadian pine, white cypreſs, *cypreſſus thyoides*, the wild pine, with two or three other ſorts of pine leſs common. The two firſt make up almoſt two thirds of the whole; and, at a diſtance, might be miſtaken for the ſame tree; as they both run up into pointed ſpire-like tops; but they are eaſily diſtinguiſhed on coming nearer, from their colour; the cypreſs being of a much paler green, or ſhade, than the other. The trees, in general, grow with great vigour, and are all of a large ſize.

There is but little variety of other vegetable productions, though, doubtleſs, ſeveral had not yet ſprung up at the early ſeaſon when we viſited the place; and many more might be hid from the narrow ſphere of our reſearches. About the rocks, and verge of the woods, we found ſtraw-berry-plants, ſome raſberry, currant, and gooſeberry buſhes; which were all in a moſt flouriſhing ſtate; with a few ſmall black alder-trees. There are, likewiſe, a ſpecies of ſow-thiſtle; gooſe-graſs; ſome crow's-foot, which has a very fine crimſon flower; and two ſorts of *anthericum*; one with a large orange flower; and the other with a blue one. We alſo found, in theſe ſituations, ſome wild roſe-buſhes, which were juſt budding; a great quantity of young leeks, with

triangular

triangular leaves; a fmall fort of grafs; and fome water-creffes, which grow about the fides of the rills; befides great abundance of *andromeda*. Within the woods, befides two forts of underwood fhrubs unknown to us, are moffes and ferns. Of the firft of which, are feven or eight different forts; of the laft, not above three or four; and the *fpecies* of both, are moftly fuch as are common to Europe and America.

As the feafon of the year was unfavourable to our gaining much knowledge of the vegetable productions of this country, fo our own fituation while there, put it out of our power to learn much about its animals. For as the want of water made it neceffary that we fhould enter the Sound at firft, the unforefeen accidents which happened afterward, though they lengthened our ftay, were rather unfavourable to our obtaining any knowledge of this kind. The emergency of the cafe required, that every perfon fhould be conftantly employed in the neceffary bufinefs of the fhips, which was the capital object; as the feafon was advancing very faft, and the fuccefs of the voyage depended upon their diligence and alacrity in expediting the various tafks affigned to them. Hence it happened, that excurfions of every kind, either on the land, or by water, were never attempted. And as we lay in a cove on an ifland, no other animals were ever feen alive in the woods there, than two or three racoons, martins, and fquirrels. Befides thefe, fome of our people who, one day, landed on the continent, near the South Eaft fide of the entrance of the Sound, obferved the prints of a bear's feet near the fhore. The account, therefore, that we can give of the quadrupeds, is taken from the fkins which the natives brought to fell; and thefe were often fo mutilated with refpect to the diftinguifhing parts,

fuch

fuch as the paws, tails, and heads, that it was impoffible even to guefs at the animals to whom they belonged; though others were fo perfect, or, at leaft, fo well known, that they left no room to doubt about them.

Of thefe the moft common were bears, deer, foxes, and wolves. The bear-fkins were in great numbers; few of them very large; but, in general, of a fhining black colour. The deer-fkins were fcarcer, and they feem to belong to that fort called the fallow-deer by the hiftorians of Carolina; though Mr. Pennant thinks it quite a different fpecies from ours, and diftinguifhes it by the name of Virginian deer *. The foxes are in great plenty, and of feveral varieties; fome of their fkins being quite yellow, with a black tip to the tail; others of a deep or reddifh yellow, intermixed with black; and a third fort of a whitifh grey or afh-colour, alfo intermixed with black. Our people ufed to apply the name of fox or wolf indifcriminately, when the fkins were fo mutilated as to leave room for a doubt. But we got, at laft, an entire wolf's fkin with the head on; and it was grey. Befides the common fort of martin, the pine-martin is alfo here; and another, whofe fkin is of a lighter brown colour than either, with coarfer hair; but is not fo common, and is, perhaps, only a mere variety arifing from age, or fome other accidental circumftance. The ermine is alfo found at this place; but is rare and fmall; nor is the hair remarkably fine, though the animal appeared to be perfectly white, except an inch or more at the tip of the tail. The racoons and fquirrels are of the common fort; but the latter is rather fmaller than ours, and has a deeper rufty colour running along the back.

* See *Virginian deer*; Pennant's Hift. Quad. Vol. i. Nº 46; and Arctic Zool. Nº 6.

We

We were clear as to the exiftence of all the animals already mentioned; but there are two others, befides, which we could not diftinguifh with fufficient certainty. Of the firft of thefe we faw none of the fkins, but what were dreffed or tanned like leather. The natives wear them on fome occafions; and, from the fize as well as thicknefs, they were generally concluded to belong to the elk, or moufe-deer; though fome of them perhaps might belong to the buffalo. The other animal, which feems by no means rare, was gueffed to be a fpecies of the wild cat or *lynx*. The length of the fkins, without the head, which none of them had, was about two feet two inches. They are covered with a very fine wool or fur, of a very light brown or whitifh yellow colour, intermixed with long hairs, which on the back, where they are fhorteft, are blackifh; on the fides, where they are longer, of a filver white; and on the belly, where they are longeft, of the colour of the wool; but the whitifh, or filver hairs, are often fo predominant, that the whole animal acquires a caft of that kind. The tail is only three inches long, and has a black tip. The whole fkin being, by the natives, called *wanfhee*; that, moft probably, is their name for this animal. Hogs, dogs, and goats, have not as yet found their way to this place. Nor do the natives feem to have any knowledge of our brown rats, to which, when they faw them on board the fhips, they applied the name they give to fquirrels. And though they called our goats *eineetla*, this, moft probably, is their name for a young deer or fawn.

The fea animals feen off the coaft, were whales, porpoifes, and feals. The laft of thefe feem only of the common fort, judging from the fkins which we faw here; their colour being either filvery, yellowifh, plain, or fpotted, with black.

black. The porpoife is the *phocena*. I have chofen to refer
to this clafs the fea-otter, as living moftly in the water. It
might have been fufficient to have mentioned, that this
animal abounds here, as it is fully defcribed in different
books, taken from the accounts of the Ruffian adventurers
in their expeditions Eaftward from Kamtfchatka, if there
had not been a fmall difference in one that we faw. We, for
fome time, entertained doubts, whether the many fkins
which the natives brought, really belonged to this animal;
as our only reafon for being of that opinion, was founded on
the fize, colour, and finenefs of the fur; till a fhort while
before our departure, when a whole one, that had been juft
killed, was purchafed from fome ftrangers who came to
barter; and of this Mr. Webber made a drawing. It was
rather young, weighing only twenty-five pounds; of a
fhining or gloffy black colour; but many of the hairs being
tipt with white, gave it a greyifh caft at firft fight. The face,
throat, and breaft were of a yellowifh white, or very light
brown colour, which, in many of the fkins, extended the
whole length of the belly. It had fix cutting teeth in each
jaw; two of thofe of the lower jaw being very minute, and
placed without, at the bafe of the two middle ones. In thefe
circumftances, it feems to difagree with thofe found by the
Ruffians; and alfo in not having the outer toes of the hind
feet fkirted with a membrane. There feemed alfo a greater
variety in the colour of the fkins, than is mentioned by the
defcribers of the Ruffian fea-otters. Thefe changes of colour certainly take place at the different gradations of life.
The very young ones had brown hair, which was coarfe,
with very little fur underneath; but thofe of the fize of
the entire animal, which came into our poffeffion, and juft
defcribed, had a confiderable quantity of that fubftance;

and

and both in that colour and state the fea-otters feem to remain, till they have attained their full growth. After that,
they lofe the black colour, and affume a deep brown or
footy colour; but have then a greater quantity of very fine
fur, and fcarcely any long hairs. Others, which we fufpected to be ftill older, were of a chefnut brown; and a few
fkins were feen that had even acquired a perfectly yellow
colour. The fur of thefe animals, as mentioned in the
Ruffian accounts, is certainly fofter and finer than that of
any others we know of; and, therefore, the difcovery of
this part of the continent of North America, where fo valuable an article of commerce may be met with, cannot be
a matter of indifference *.

Birds, in general, are not only rare as to the different
fpecies, but very fcarce as to numbers; and thefe few are
fo fhy, that, in all probability, they are continually ha-
raffed by the natives; perhaps to eat them as food, certainly
to get poffeffion of their feathers, which they ufe as ornaments. Thofe which frequent the woods, are crows and
ravens, not at all different from our Englifh ones; a blueifh
jay or magpie; common wrens, which are the only finging bird that we heard; the Canadian, or migrating thrufh;
and a confiderable number of brown eagles, with white
heads and tails; which, though they feem principally to
frequent the coaft, come into the Sound in bad weather,
and fometimes perch upon the trees. Amongft fome other
birds, of which the natives either brought fragments, or
dried fkins, we could diftinguifh a fmall fpecies of hawk;
a heron; and the *alcyon*, or large-crefted American king-

* Mr. Coxe, on the authority of Mr. Pallas, informs us, that the old and middle-aged
fea-otters fkins are fold, at Kiachta, by the Ruffians, to the Chinefe, from 80 to 100 rubles
a fkin; that is, from 16l. to 20l. each. See *Coxe's Ruffian Difcoveries*, p. 13.

fifher.

fiſher. There are alſo ſome, which, I believe, are not mentioned, or at leaſt vary, very conſiderably, from the accounts
given of them by any writers who have treated profeſſedly
on this part of natural hiſtory. The two firſt of theſe are
ſpecies of wood-peckers. One leſs than a thruſh, of a black
colour above, with white ſpots on the wings, a crimſon
head, neck and breaſt, and a yellowiſh olive-coloured belly;
from which laſt circumſtance it might, perhaps, not improperly be called the yellow-bellied wood-pecker. The
other is a larger, and much more elegant bird, of a duſky
brown colour, on the upper part, richly waved with black,
except about the head; the belly of a reddiſh caſt, with
round black ſpots; a black ſpot on the breaſt; and the un-
der-ſide of the wings and tail of a plain ſcarlet colour,
though blackiſh above; with a crimſon ſtreak running
from the angle of the mouth, a little down the neck on
each ſide. The third and fourth, are a ſmall bird of the
finch kind, about the ſize of a linnet, of a dark duſky colour, whitiſh below, with a black head and neck, and white
bill; and a ſand-piper, of the ſize of a ſmall pigeon, of a
duſky brown colour, and white below, except the throat
and breaſt, with a broad white band acroſs the wings.
There are alſo humming-birds; which yet ſeem to differ
from the numerous ſorts of this delicate animal already
known, unleſs they be a mere variety of the *trochilus colu-
bris* of Linnæus. Theſe, perhaps, inhabit more to the
Southward, and ſpread Northward as the ſeaſon advances;
becauſe we ſaw none at firſt, though, near the time of our
departure, the natives brought them to the ſhips in great
numbers.

The birds which frequent the waters and the ſhores, are
not more numerous than the others. The quebrantahueſſos,

VOL. II.   Q q   gulls,

gulls, and shags were seen off the coast; and the two last also frequent the Sound. They are of the common sorts; the shags being our corvorant or water-crow. We saw two sorts of wild-ducks; one black, with a white head, which were in confiderable flocks; the other white, with a red bill, but of a larger fize; and the greater *lumme*, or diver, found in our northern countries. There were also seen, once or twice, some swans flying across the Sound to the North-ward; but we knew nothing of their haunts. On the shores, besides the sand-piper, described above, we found another, about the fize of a lark, which bears a great affi-nity to the burre; and a plover differing very little from our common sea-lark.

Fish are more plentiful in quantity than birds, though the variety is not very great; and yet, from several circum-ftances, it is probable, that even the variety is confiderably increased at certain seasons. The principal sorts, which we found in great numbers, are the common herring, but scarcely exceeding seven inches in length; a smaller sort, which is the same with the anchovy, or sardine, though rather larger; a white, or silver-coloured bream, and an-other of a gold-brown colour, with many narrow longitu-dinal blue ftripes. The herrings and sardines, doubtless, come in large shoals, and only at ftated seasons, as is com-mon with that sort of fish. The bream of both sorts, may be reckoned the next to these in quantity; and the full grown ones weighed, at leaft, a pound. The other fish, which are all scarce, are a small brown kind of *fculpin*, such as is found on the coast of Norway; another of a brownish red caft; froft-fish; a large one, somewhat refembling the bull-head, with a tough skin, deftitute of scales; and now and then, toward the time of our leaving the Sound, the

natives

natives brought a small brownish cod, spotted with white; and a red fish of the same size, which some of our people said they had seen in the strait of Magalhaens; besides another differing little from the hake. There are also considerable numbers of those fish called the *chimæræ*, or little sea wolves, by some; which is a-kin to, and about the size of, the *pezegallo*, or elephant-fish. Sharks, likewise, sometimes frequent the Sound; for the natives have some of their teeth in their possession; and we saw some pieces of ray, or scate, which seemed to have been pretty large. The other marine animals that ought to be mentioned here, are a small cruciated *medusa*, or blubber; star-fish, which differ somewhat from the common ones; two small sorts of crabs; and two others, which the natives brought; one of them of a thick, tough, gelatinous consistence; and the other a sort of membranaceous tube or pipe, both which are probably taken from the rocks. And we, also, purchased from them, once, a very large cuttle-fish.

There is abundance of large muscles about the rocks; many sea-ears; and we often saw shells of pretty large plain *chamæ*. The smaller sorts are some *trochi* of two species; a curious *murex*; rugged wilks; and a snail; all which are, probably, peculiar to this place; at least I do not recollect to have seen them in any country near the same latitude, in either hemisphere. There are, besides these, some small plain cockles, limpets; and some strangers, who came into the Sound, wore necklaces of a small bluish *volute*, or *panamae*. Many of the muscles are a span in length; and some having pretty large pearls; which, however, are both badly shaped and coloured. We may conclude, that there is red coral in the Sound, or somewhere upon the coast; some thick pieces, or branches, having been seen in the canoes of the natives.

Q q 2 The

The only animals of the reptile kind obferved here, and found in the woods, were brown fnakes two feet long, with whitifh ftripes on the back and fides; which are harmlefs, as we often faw the natives carry them alive in their hands; and brownifh water-lizards, with a tail exactly like that of an eel, which frequented the fmall ftanding pools about the rocks.

The infect tribe feem to be more numerous. For though the feafon, which is peculiarly fitted to their appearing abroad was only beginning, we faw four or five different forts of butterflies, none of which were uncommon; a good many humble-bees; fome of our common goofeberry moths; two or three forts of flies; a few beetles; and fome mufquitoes, which, probably, may be more numerous and troublefome in a country fo full of wood, during the Summer, though at this time they did little mifchief.

As to the mineral fubftances in this country, though we found both iron and copper here, there is little reafon to believe that either of them belong to the place. Neither were the ores of any metal feen, if we except a coarfe, red, earthy, or ochry fubftance, ufed by the natives in painting themfelves, which probably may contain a little iron; with a white and a black pigment ufed for the fame purpofe. But we did not procure fpecimens of them, and therefore cannot pofitively determine what are their component parts.

Befides the ftone or rock that conftitutes the mountains and fhores, which fometimes contains pieces of very coarfe *quartz*, we found, amongft the natives, things made of a hard black *granite*, though not remarkably compact or fine grained; a greyifh whetftone; the common oil ftone of our

carpenters,

carpenters, in coarfer and finer pieces; and fome black bits which are little inferior to the hone-ftone. The natives alfo ufe the tranfparent leafy *glimmer*, or Mufcovy glafs; a brown leafy or martial fort; and they, fometimes, brought to us pieces of rock-cryftal, tolerably tranfparent. The two firft are, probably, found near the fpot, as they feemed to be in confiderable quantities; but the latter feems to be brought from a greater diftance, or is very fcarce; for our vifiters always parted with it reluctantly. Some of the pieces were octangular, and had the appearance of being formed into that fhape by art.

The perfons of the natives are, in general, under the common ftature; but not flender in proportion, being commonly pretty full or plump, though not mufcular. Neither doth the foft flefhinefs feem ever to fwell into corpulence; and many of the older people are rather fpare, or lean. The vifage of moft of them is round and full; and fometimes, alfo, broad, with high prominent cheeks; and, above thefe, the face is frequently much depreffed, or feems fallen in quite acrofs between the temples; the nofe alfo flattening at its bafe, with pretty wide noftrils, and a rounded point. The forehead rather low; the eyes fmall, black, and rather languifhing than fparkling; the mouth round, with large round thickifh lips; the teeth tolerably equal and well fet, but not remarkably white. They have either no beards at all, which was moft commonly the cafe, or a fmall thin one upon the point of the chin; which does not arife from any natural defect of hair on that part, but from plucking it out more or lefs; for fome of them, and particularly the old men, have not only confiderable beards all over the chin, but whifkers, or muftachios; both on the upper lip, and running from thence toward the lower jaw obliquely
down-

downward *. Their eye-brows are also scanty, and always
narrow; but the hair of the head is in great abundance,

* One of the most curious singularities observable in the natural history of the human
species, is the supposed defect in the habit and temperature of the bodies of the American
Indians, exemplified in their having no beards, while they are furnished with a profusion
of hair on their heads. M. de Paw, the ingenious author of *Recherches sur les Américains*; Dr. Robertson, in his *History of America*; and, in general, the writers for whose
authority we ought to have the highest deference, adopt this as an indisputable matter of
fact. May we not be permitted to request those who espouse their sentiments, to re-
consider the question, when we can produce Captain Cook's evidence on the opposite
side, at least so far as relates to the American tribe, whom he had intercourse with at
Nootka? Nor is Captain Cook singular in his report. What he saw on the sea coast,
Captain Carver also met with amongst the American Indians far up in the country.
His words are as follow: " From minute inquiries, and a curious inspection, I am able
" to declare (however respectable I may hold the authority of these Historians in other
" points), that their assertions are erroneous, and proceeding from a want of a thorough
" knowledge of the customs of the Indians. After the age of puberty, their bodies, in
" their natural state, are covered in the same manner as those of the Europeans. The
" men, indeed, esteem a beard very unbecoming, and take great pains to get rid of it;
" nor is there any ever to be perceived on their faces, except when they grow old, and
" become inattentive to appearances.—The Naudowesses, and the remote nations, pluck
" them out with bent pieces of hard wood, formed into a kind of nippers; whilst those
" who have communication with Europeans, procure from them wire, which they
" twist into a screw or worm; applying this to the part, they press the rings together,
" and with a sudden twitch draw out all the hairs that are inclosed in them." *Carver's*
Travels, p. 224, 225. The remark made by Mr. Marsden, who also quotes Carver,
is worth attending to, that the vizor or mask of Montezuma's armour, preserved at
Brussels, has remarkably large whiskers; and that those Americans could not have imitated this ornament, unless nature had presented them with the model. From Captain
Cook's observation on the West coast of North America, combined with Carver's in
the inland parts of that continent, and confirmed by the Mexican Vizor as above, there
seems abundant reason to agree with Mr. Marsden, who thus modestly expresses himself:
" Were it not for the numerous and very respectable authorities, from which we are
" assured that the natives of America are naturally beardless, I should think that the com-
" mon opinion on that subject had been hastily adopted; and that their appearing thus at
" a mature age, was only the consequence of an early practice, similar to that observed
" among the Sumatrans. Even now, I must confess, that it would remove some small
" degree of doubt from my mind, could it be ascertained that no such custom prevails."
Marsden's History of Sumatra, p. 39, 40.

                                                          very

very coarfe and ftrong; and, without a fingle exception, black, ftraight, and lank, or hanging down over the fhoulders. The neck is fhort; the arms and body have no particular mark of beauty or elegance in their formation, but are rather clumfy; and the limbs, in all, are very fmall in proportion to the other parts, and crooked, or ill-made, with large feet badly fhaped, and projecting ankles. This laft defect feems, in a great meafure, to arife from their fitting fo much on their hams or knees, both in their canoes and houfes.

Their colour we could never pofitively determine, as their bodies were incrufted with paint and dirt; though, in particular cafes, when thefe were well rubbed off, the whitenefs of the fkin appeared almoft to equal that of Europeans; though rather of that pale effete caft which diftinguifhes thofe of our Southern nations. Their children, whofe fkins had never been ftained with paint, alfo equalled ours in whitenefs. During their youth, fome of them have no difagreeable look, if compared to the generality of the people; but this feems to be entirely owing to the particular animation attending that period of life; for, after attaining a certain age, there is hardly any diftinction. Upon the whole, a very remarkable famenefs feems to characterize the countenances of the whole nation; a dull phlegmatic want of expreffion, with very little variation, being ftrongly marked in all of them.

The women are nearly of the fame fize, colour, and form, with the men; from whom it is not eafy to diftinguifh them, as they poffefs no natural delicacies fufficient to render their perfons agreeable; and hardly any one was feen, even amongft thofe who were in the prime of life, who had the leaft pretenfions to be called handfome.

I

Their

Their common drefs is a flaxen garment, or mantle, ornamented on the upper edge by a narrow ftrip of fur, and,
at the lower edge, by fringes or taffels. It paffes under the
left arm, and is tied over the right fhoulder, by a ftring before, and one behind, near its middle; by which means
both arms are left free; and it hangs evenly, covering the
left fide, but leaving the right open, except from the loofe
part of the edges falling upon it, unlefs when the mantle
is faftened by a girdle (of coarfe matting or woollen) round
the waift, which is often done. Over this, which reaches
below the knees, is worn a fmall cloak of the fame fubftance, likewife fringed at the lower part. In fhape this refembles a round difh cover, being quite clofe, except in
the middle, where there is a hole juft large enough to admit the head; and then, refting upon the fhoulders, it covers
the arms to the elbows, and the body as far as the waift.
Their head is covered with a cap, of the figure of a truncated cone, or like a flower-pot, made of fine matting, having the top frequently ornamented with a round or pointed
knob, or bunch of leathern taffels; and there is a ftring
that paffes under the chin, to prevent its blowing off.

Befides the above drefs, which is common to both fexes,
the men frequently throw over their other garments the
fkin of a bear, wolf, or fea-otter, with the hair outward, and
tie it, as a cloak, near the upper part, wearing it fometimes
before, and fometimes behind. In rainy weather, they
throw a coarfe mat about their fhoulders. They have alfo
woollen garments, which, however, are little in ufe. The
hair is commonly worn hanging down loofe; but fome,
when they have no cap, tie it in a bunch on the crown of
the head. Their drefs, upon the whole, is convenient, and
would by no means be inelegant, were it kept clean. But
as

1778.
April.

as they rub their bodies conftantly over with a red paint, of a clayey or coarfe ochry fubftance, mixed with oil, their garments, by this means, contract a rancid offenfive fmell, and a greafy naftinefs. So that they make a very wretched dirty appearance; and what is ftill worfe, their heads and their garments fwarm with vermin, which, fo depraved is their tafte for cleanlinefs, we ufed to fee them pick off with great compofure, and eat.

Though their bodies are always covered with red paint, their faces are often ftained with a black, a brighter red, or a white colour, by way of ornament. The laft of thefe gives them a ghaftly, difgufting afpect. They alfo ftrew the brown martial *mica* upon the paint, which makes it glitter. The ears of many of them are perforated in the lobe, where they make a pretty large hole; and two others higher up on the outer edge. In thefe holes they hang bits of bone; quills fixed upon a leathern thong; fmall fhells; bunches of woollen taffels; or pieces of thin copper; which our beads could never fupplant. The *feptum* of the nofe, in many, is alfo perforated, through which they draw a piece of foft cord; and others wear, at the fame place, fmall thin pieces of iron, brafs, or copper, fhaped almoft like a horfe-fhoe, the narrow opening of which receives the *feptum*, fo as that the two points may gently pinch it; and the ornament thus hangs over the upper lip. The rings of our brafs buttons, which they eagerly purchafed, were appropriated to this ufe. About their wrifts they wear bracelets or bunches of white bugle beads, made of a conic fhelly fubftance; bunches of thongs, with taffels; or a broad black fhining horny fubftance, of one piece. And about their ancles they alfo frequently wear many folds of leathern thongs, or the finews of animals twifted to a confiderable thicknefs.

VOL. II.   R r   Thus

Thus far of their ordinary drefs and ornaments; but they have fome that feem to be ufed only on extraordinary occafions; either when they exhibit themfelves as ftrangers, in vifits of ceremony, or when they go to war. Amongft the firft may be confidered the fkins of animals, fuch as wolves or bears, tied on in the ufual manner, but ornamented at the edges with broad borders of fur, or of the woollen ftuff manufactured by them, ingenioufly wrought with various figures. Thefe are worn either feparately, or over their other common garments. On fuch occafions, the moft common head-drefs is a quantity of withe, or half beaten bark, wrapped about the head; which, at the fame time, has various large feathers, particularly thofe of eagles, ftuck in it, or is entirely covered, or, we may fay, powdered with fmall white feathers. The face, at the fame time, is varioufly painted, having its upper and lower parts of different colours, the ftrokes appearing like frefh gafhes; or it is befmeared with a kind of tallow, mixed with paint, which is afterward formed into a great variety of regular figures, and appears like carved work. Sometimes, again, the hair is feparated into fmall parcels, which are tied at intervals of about two inches, to the end, with thread; and others tie it together, behind, after our manner, and ftick branches of the *cupreffus thyoides* in it. Thus dreffed, they have a truly favage and incongruous appearance; but this is much heightened when they affume, what may be called, their monftrous decorations. Thefe confift of an endlefs variety of carved wooden mafk or vizors, applied on the face, or to the upper part of the head or forehead. Some of thefe refemble human faces, furnifhed with hair, beards, and eye-brows; others, the heads of birds, particularly of eagles and quebrantahueffos; and many, the heads of land and

fea-sea-animals, such as wolves, deer, and porpoises, and others. But, in general, these representations much exceed the natural size; and they are painted, and often strewed with pieces of the foliaceous *mica*, which makes them glitter, and serves to augment their enormous deformity. They even exceed this sometimes, and fix on the same part of the head large pieces of carved work, resembling the prow of a canoe, painted in the same manner, and projecting to a considerable distance. So fond are they of these disguises, that I have seen one of them put his head into a tin kettle he had got from us, for want of another sort of mask. Whether they use these extravagant masquerade ornaments on any particular religious occasion, or diversion; or whether they be put on to intimidate their enemies when they go to battle, by their monstrous appearance; or as decoys when they go to hunt animals, is uncertain. But it may be concluded, that, if travellers or voyagers, in an ignorant and credulous age, when many unnatural or marvellous things were supposed to exist, had seen a number of people decorated in this manner, without being able to approach so near as to be undeceived, they would readily have believed, and, in their relations, would have attempted to make others believe, that there existed a race of beings, partaking of the nature of man and beast; more especially, when, besides the heads of animals on the human shoulders, they might have seen the whole bodies of their men-monsters covered with quadrupeds' skins *.

The only dress amongst the people of Nootka, observed by us, that seems peculiarly adapted to war, is a thick leathern

---

* The reflection in the text may furnish the admirers of Herodotus, in particular, with an excellent apology for some of his wonderful tales of this sort.

mantle

mantle doubled, which, from its fize, appears to be the fkin of an elk or buffalo, tanned. This they faften on, in the common manner; and it is fo contrived, that it may reach up, and cover the breaft quite to the throat, falling, at the fame time, almoft to the heels. It is, fometimes, ingenioufly painted in different compartments; and is not only fufficiently ftrong to refift arrows; but, as they informed us by figns, even fpears cannot pierce it; fo that it may be confidered as their coat of mail, or moft complete defenfive armour. Upon the fame occafion, they fometimes wear a kind of leathern cloak, covered with rows of dried hoofs of deer, difpofed horizontally, appended by leathern thongs, covered with quills; which, when they move, make a loud rattling noife, almoft equal to that of many fmall bells. It feems doubtful, however, whether this part of their garb be intended to ftrike terror in war, or only is to be confidered as belonging to their eccentric ornaments on ceremonious occafions. For we faw one of their mufical entertainments, conducted by a man dreffed in this fort of cloak, with his mafk on, and fhaking his rattle.

Though thefe people cannot be viewed without a kind of horror, when equipped in fuch extravagant dreffes, yet, when divefted of them, and beheld in their common habit and actions, they have not the leaft appearance of ferocity in their countenances; and feem, on the contrary, as obferved already, to be of a quiet, phlegmatic, and inactive difpofition; deftitute, in fome meafure, of that degree of animation and vivacity that would render them agreeable as focial beings. If they are not referved, they are far from being loquacious; but their gravity is, perhaps, rather a confequence of the difpofition juft mentioned, than of any conviction of its propriety, or the effect of any particular

mode

mode of education. For, even in the greateft paroxyfms of their rage, they feem unable to exprefs it fufficiently, either with warmth of language, or fignificancy of geftures.

Their orations, which are made either when engaged in any altercation or difpute, or to explain their fentiments publicly on other occafions, feem little more than fhort fentences, or rather fingle words, forcibly repeated, and conftantly in one tone and degree of ftrength, accompanied only with a fingle gefture, which they ufe at every fentence, jerking their whole body a little forward, by bending the knees, their arms hanging down by their fides at the fame time.

Though there be but too much reafon, from their bringing to fale human fkulls and bones, to infer that they treat their enemies with a degree of brutal cruelty, this circumftance rather marks a general agreement of character with that of almoft every tribe of uncivilized man, in every age, and in every part of the globe, than that they are to be reproached with any charge of peculiar inhumanity. We had no reafon to judge unfavourably of their difpofition in this refpect. They feem to be a docile, courteous, good-natured people ; but, notwithftanding the predominant phlegm of their tempers, quick in refenting what they look upon as an injury ; and, like moft other paffionate people, as foon forgetting it. I never found that thefe fits of paffion went farther than the parties immediately concerned ; the fpectators not troubling themfelves about the quarrel, whether it was with any of us, or amongft their own body ; and preferving as much indifference as if they had not known any thing about it. I have often feen one of them rave and fcold, without any of his countrymen paying the leaft attention to his agitation ; and when none of us could

trace

trace the caufe, or the object of his difpleafure. In fuch
cafes they never difcover the leaft fymptom of timidity,
but feem determined, at all events, to punifh the infult.
For, even with refpect to us, they never appeared to be under the leaft apprehenfion of our fuperiority; but when
any difference happened, were juft as ready to avenge the
wrong, as amongft themfelves.

Their other paffions, efpecially their curiofity, appear in
fome meafure to lie dormant. For few expreffed any defire
to fee or examine things wholly unknown to them; and
which, to thofe truly poffeffed of that paffion, would have
appeared aftonifhing. They were always contented to procure the articles they knew and wanted, regarding every
thing elfe with great indifference; nor did our perfons, apparel, and manners, fo different from their own, or even the
extraordinary fize and conftruction of our fhips, feem to
excite admiration, or even engage attention.

One caufe of this may be their indolence, which feems
confiderable. But, on the other hand, they are certainly
not wholly unfufceptible of the tender paffions; if we may
judge from their being fo fond of mufic, which is moftly
of the grave or ferious, but truly pathetic fort. They keep
the exacteft concert in their fongs, which are often fung by
great numbers together, as thofe already mentioned, with
which they ufed to entertain us in their canoes. Thefe are
generally flow and folemn; but the mufic is not of that
confined fort found amongft many rude nations; for the
variations are very numerous and expreffive, and the cadence or melody powerfully foothing. Befides their full
concerts, fonnets of the fame grave caft were frequently
fung by fingle performers, who keep time by ftriking the
hand againft the thigh. However, the mufic was fometimes
I   varied,

varied, from its predominant folemnity of air; and there were inftances of ftanzas being fung in a more gay and lively ftrain, and even with a degree of humour.

The only inftruments of mufic (if fuch they may be called) which I faw amongft them, were a rattle; and a fmall whiftle, about an inch long, incapable of any variation, from having but one hole. They ufe the rattle when they fing; but upon what occafions they ufe the whiftle I know not, unlefs it be when they drefs themfelves like particular animals, and endeavour to imitate their howl or cry. I once faw one of them dreffed in a wolf's fkin, with the head over his own, and imitating that animal by making a fqueaking noife with one of thefe whiftles, which he had in his mouth. The rattles are, for the moft part, made in the fhape of a bird, with a few pebbles in the belly; and the tail is the handle. They have others, however, that bear rather more refemblance to a child's rattle.

In trafficking with us, fome of them would betray a knavifh difpofition, and carry off our goods without making any return. But, in general, it was otherwife; and we had abundant reafon to commend the fairnefs of their conduct. However, their eagernefs to poffefs iron and brafs, and, indeed, any kind of metal, was fo great, that few of them could refift the temptation to fteal it, whenever an opportunity offered. The inhabitants of the South Sea Iflands, as appears from a variety of inftances in the courfe of this voyage, rather than be idle, would fteal any thing that they could lay their hands upon, without ever confidering, whether it could be of ufe to them or no. The novelty of the object, with them, was a fufficient motive for their endeavouring, by any indirect means, to get poffeffion of it; which marked that, in fuch cafes, they were rather actuated

by

by a childifh curiofity, than by a difhoneft difpofition, regardlefs of the modes of fupplying real wants.   The inhabitants of Nootka, who invaded our property, cannot have
fuch apology made for them.   They were thieves in the
ftricteft fenfe of the word ; for they pilfered nothing from
us, but what they knew could be converted to the purpofes
of private utility, and had a real value according to their
eftimation of things.   And it was lucky for us, that nothing
was thought valuable by them, but the fingle articles of our
metals.   Linen, and fuch like things, were perfectly fecure from their depredations ; and we could fafely leave
them hanging out afhore all night, without watching.   The
fame principle which prompted our Nootka friends to pilfer
from us, it was natural to fuppofe, would produce a fimilar
conduct in their intercourfe with each other.   And, accordingly, we had abundant reafon to believe, that ftealing is
much practifed amongft them ; and that it chiefly gives
rife to their quarrels ; of which we faw more than one inftance.

C H A P.

ᐧC H A P. III.

Manner of building the Houſes in Nootka Sound.—Inſide of them deſcribed.—Furniture and Utenſils.—Wooden Images. —Employments of the Men.—Of the Women.—Food, animal and vegetable.—Manner of preparing it.—Weapons.—Manufactures and mechanic Arts.—Carving and Painting.— Canoes.—Implements for fiſhing and hunting.—Iron Tools. —Manner of procuring that Metal.—Remarks on their Language, and a Specimen of it.—Aſtronomical and nautical Obſervations made in Nootka Sound.

THE two towns or villages, mentioned in the courſe of my Journal, ſeem to be the only inhabited parts of the Sound. The number of inhabitants in both might be pretty exactly computed from the canoes that were about the ſhips the ſecond day after our arrival. They amounted to about a hundred; which, at a very moderate allowance, muſt, upon an average, have held five perſons each. But as there were ſcarcely any women, very old men, children, or youths amongſt them at that time, I think it will rather be rating the number of the inhabitants of the two towns too low, if we ſuppoſe they could be leſs than four times the number of our viſiters; that is, two thouſand in the whole.

The village at the entrance of the Sound ſtands on the ſide of a riſing ground, which has a pretty ſteep aſcent

1778. April.

from the beach to the verge of the wood, in which fpace it is fituated.

The houfes are difpofed in three ranges or rows, rifing gradually behind each other; the largeft being that in front, and the others lefs; befides a few ftraggling, or fingle ones, at each end. Thefe ranges are interrupted or disjoined at irregular diftances, by narrow paths, or lanes, that pafs upward; but thofe which run in the direction of the houfes, between the rows, are much broader. Though there be fome appearance of regularity in this difpofition, there is none in the fingle houfes; for each of the divifions, made by the paths, may be confidered either as one houfe, or as many; there being no regular or complete fepara- tion, either without or within, to diftinguifh them by. They are built of very long and broad planks *, refting upon the edges of each other, faftened or tied by withes of pine bark, here and there; and have only flender pofts, or ra- ther poles, at confiderable diftances, on the outfide, to which they alfo are tied; but within are fome larger poles placed aflant. The height of the fides and ends of thefe habitations, is feven or eight feet; but the back part is a little higher, by which means the planks, that compofe the roof, flant forward, and are laid on loofe, fo as to be moved about; either to be put clofe, to exclude the rain; or, in fair weather, to be feparated, to let in the light, and carry out the fmoke. They are, however, upon the whole, mi- ferable dwellings, and conftructed with little care or in- genuity. For, though the fide-planks be made to fit pretty

* The habitations of the natives, more to the North upon this coaft, where Behring's people landed in 1741, feem to refemble thofe of Nootka. Muller defcribes them thus: " Ces cabanes étoient de bois revetu de planches bien unies, et même enchantrées en " quelques endroits." Muller, *Decouvertes*, p. 255.

clofely

1778.
April.

clofely in fome places, in others they are quite open; and
there are no regular doors into them; the only way of entrance being either by a hole, where the unequal length
of the planks has accidentally left an opening; or, in
fome cafes, the planks are made to pafs a little beyond
each other, or overlap, about two feet afunder; and the
entrance is in this fpace. There are alfo holes, or win-
dows, in the fides of the houfes to look out at; but without any regularity of fhape or difpofition; and thefe have
bits of mat hung before them, to prevent the rain getting in.

On the infide, one may frequently fee from one end to
the other of thefe ranges of building without interruption. For though, in general, there be the rudiments,
or rather veftiges, of feparations on each fide, for the accommodation of different families, they are fuch as do
not intercept the fight; and often confift of no more than
pieces of plank, running from the fide toward the middle
of the houfe; fo that, if they were complete, the whole
might be compared to a long ftable, with a double range
of ftalls, and a broad paffage in the middle. Clofe to the
fides, in each of thefe parts, is a little bench of boards,
raifed five or fix inches higher than the reft of the floor,
and covered with mats, on which the family fit and fleep.
Thefe benches are commonly feven or eight feet long, and
four or five broad. In the middle of the floor, between
them, is the fire-place, which has neither hearth nor chim-
ney. In one houfe, which was in the end of a middle
range, almoft quite feparated from the reft by a high clofe
partition, and the moft regular, as to defign, of any that I
faw, there were four of thefe benches; each of which held
a fingle family, at a corner, but without any feparation by

boards;

boards; and the middle part of the houfe appeared common to them all.

Their furniture confifts chiefly of a great number of
chefts and boxes of all fizes, which are generally piled upon
each other, clofe to the fides or ends of the houfe; and
contain their fpare garments, fkins, mafks, and other
things which they fet a value upon. Some of thefe are
double, or one covers the other as a lid; others have a lid
faftened with thongs; and fome of the very large ones
have a fquare hole, or fcuttle, cut in the upper part; by
which the things are put in and taken out. They are often
painted black, ftudded with the teeth of different animals,
or carved with a kind of freeze-work, and figures of birds
or animals, as decorations. Their other domeftic utenfils
are moftly fquare and oblong pails or buckets to hold water and other things; round wooden cups and bowls; and
fmall fhallow wooden troughs, about two feet long, out of
which they eat their food; and bafkets of twigs, bags of
matting, &c. Their fifhing implements, and other things
alfo, lie or hang up in different parts of the houfe, but
without the leaft order; fo that the whole is a complete
fcene of confufion; and the only places that do not partake
of this confufion are the fleeping-benches, that have nothing on them but the mats; which are alfo cleaner, or of a
finer fort, than thofe they commonly have to fit on in their
boats.

The naftinefs and ftench of their houfes are, however, at
leaft equal to the confufion. For, as they dry their fifh
within doors, they alfo gut them there, which, with their
bones and fragments thrown down at meals, and the addition of other forts of filth, lie every where in heaps, and
are, I believe, never carried away, till it becomes trouble-

fome,

some, from their size, to walk over them. In a word, their houses are as filthy as hog-sties; every thing in and about them stinking of fish, train-oil, and smoke.

But, amidst all the filth and confusion that are found in the houses, many of them are decorated with images. These are nothing more than the trunks of very large trees, four or five feet high, set up singly, or by pairs, at the upper end of the apartment, with the front carved into a human face; the arms and hands cut out upon the sides, and variously painted; so that the whole is a truly monstrous figure. The general name of these images is *Klumma*; and the names of two particular ones, which stood abreast of each other, three or four feet asunder, in one of the houses, were *Natchkoa* and *Matseeta*. Mr. Webber's view of the inside of a Nootka house, in which these images are represented, will convey a more perfect idea of them than any description. A mat, by way of curtain, for the most part, hung before them, which the natives were not willing, at all times, to remove; and when they did unveil them, they seemed to speak of them in a very mysterious manner. It should seem that they are, at times, accustomed to make offerings to them; if we can draw this inference from their desiring us, as we interpreted their signs, to give something to these images, when they drew aside the mats that covered them *. It was natural, from these

* It should seem, that Mr. Webber was obliged to repeat his offerings pretty frequently, before he could be permitted to finish his drawing of these images. The following account is in his own words: " After having made a general view of their habitations, I fought for an inside, which might furnish me with sufficient matter to convey " a perfect idea of the mode in which these people live. Such was soon found. While " I was employed, a man approached me with a large knife in his hand, seemingly dis- " pleased, when he observed that my eyes were fixed on two representations of human " figures,

thefe circumſtances, for us to think that they were repre-
ſentatives of their gods, or ſymbols of ſome religious or
ſuperſtitious object: and yet we had proofs of the little real
eſtimation they were in; for with a ſmall quantity of iron
or braſs, I could have purchaſed all the gods (if their
images were ſuch) in the place. I did not ſee one that was
not offered to me; and I actually got two or three of the
very ſmalleſt ſort.

The chief employment of the men ſeems to be that of
fiſhing, and killing land or ſea animals, for the ſuſtenance
of their families; for we ſaw few of them doing any thing
in the houſes; whereas the women were occupied in manu-
facturing their flaxen or woollen garments, and in preparing the ſardines for drying; which they alſo carry up from
the beach in twig-baſkets, after the men have brought
them in their canoes. The women are alſo ſent in the
ſmall canoes to gather muſcles, and other ſhell-fiſh; and
perhaps on ſome other occaſions; for they manage theſe
with as much dexterity as the men; who, when in the canoes with them, ſeem to pay little attention to their ſex, by

" figures, which were placed at one end of the apartment, carved on planks, of a gigantic
" proportion, and painted after their cuſtom. However, I took as little notice of him as
" poſſible, and proceeded; to prevent which, he ſoon provided himſelf with a mat, and
" placed it in ſuch a manner as to hinder my having any longer a ſight of them. Being
" pretty certain that I could have no future opportunity to finiſh my drawing, and the
" object being too intereſting to be omitted, I conſidered that a little bribery might pro-
" bably have ſome effect. Accordingly I made an offer of a button from my coat,
" which, being of metal, I thought they would be pleaſed with. This, inſtantly, produ-
" ced the deſired effect. For the mat was removed, and I was left at liberty to proceed
" as before. Scarcely had I ſeated myſelf, and made a beginning, when he returned
" and renewed his former practice, continuing it till I had parted with every ſingle
" button; and when he ſaw that he had completely ſtripped me, I met with no farther
" obſtruction."

                                                        offering

offering to relieve them from the labour of the paddle; nor, indeed, do they treat them with any particular refpect or tendernefs in other fituations. The young men appeared to be the moft indolent or idle fet in this community; for they were eithe r fitting about, in fcattered companies, to bafk themfelves in the fun; or lay wallowing in the fand upon the beach, like a number of hogs, for the fame purpofe, without any covering. But this difregard of decency was confined to the men. The women were always properly clothed, and behaved with the utmoft propriety; juftly deferving all commendation, for a bafhfulnefs and modefty becoming their fex; but more meritorious in them, as the men feem to have no fenfe of fhame. It is impoffible, however, that we fhould have been able to obferve the exact mode of their domeftic life and employments, from a fingle vifit (as the firft was quite tranfitory) of a few hours. For it may be eafily fuppofed, that, on fuch an occafion, moft of the labour of all the inhabitants of the village would ceafe upon our arrival, and an interruption be given even to the ufual manner of appearing in their houfes, during their more remifs or fociable hours, when left to themfelves. We were much better enabled to form fome judgment of their difpofition, and, in fome meafure, even of their method of living, from the frequent vifits fo many of them paid us at our fhips, in their canoes; in which, it fhould feem, they fpend a great deal of time, at leaft in the fummer feafon. For we obferved that they not only eat and fleep frequently in them, but ftrip off their clothes, and lay themfelves along to bafk in the fun, in the fame manner as we had feen practifed at their village. Their canoes of the larger fort, are, indeed, fufficiently fpacious for that purpofe, and perfectly dry; fo that, under fhelter of a fkin, they are, except

3

in

in rainy weather, much more comfortable habitations than their houfes.

Though their food, ftrictly fpeaking, may be faid to con-fift of every thing animal or vegetable that they can pro-cure, the quantity of the latter bears an exceedingly fmall proportion to that of the former. Their greateft reliance feems to be upon the fea, as affording fifh, mufcles, and fmaller fhell-fifh, and fea-animals. Of the firft, the prin-cipal are herrings and fardines; the two fpecies of bream formerly mentioned; and fmall cod. But the herrings and fardines are not only eaten frefh, in their feafon, but like-wife ferve as ftores, which, after being dried and fmoked, are preferved by being fewed up in mats, fo as to form large bales, three or four feet fquare. It feems that the herrings alfo fupply them with another grand refource for food; which is a vaft quantity of roe, very curioufly pre-pared. It is ftrewed upon, or, as it were, incruftated about, fmall branches of the Canadian pine. They alfo prepare it upon a long narrow fea-grafs, which grows plentifully upon the rocks, under water. This *caviare*, if it may be fo called, is kept in bafkets or bags of mat, and ufed occa-fionally, being firft dipped in water. It may be confidered as the winter bread of thefe people, and has no difagree-able tafte. They alfo eat the roe of fome other fifh, which, from the fize of its grains, muft be very large; but it has a rancid tafte and fmell. It does not appear that they pre-pare any other fifh in this manner, to preferve them for any length of time. For though they fplit and dry a few of the bream and *chimæræ*, which are pretty plentiful; they do not fmoke them as the herrings and fardines.

The next article, on which they feem to depend for a large proportion of their food, is the large mufcle; great

abundance

abundance of which are found in the Sound. These are roasted in their shells, then stuck upon long wooden skewers, and taken off occasionally as wanted; being eat without any other preparation, though they often dip them in oil, as a sauce. The other marine productions, such as the smaller shell-fish, though they contribute to increase the general stock, are by no means to be looked upon as a standing or material article of their food, when compared to those just mentioned.

Of the sea-animals, the most common that we saw in use amongst them, as food, is the porpoise; the fat or rind of which, as well as the flesh, they cut in large pieces, and having dried them, as they do the herrings, eat them without any farther preparation. They also prepare a sort of broth from this animal, in its fresh state, in a singular manner, putting pieces of it in a square wooden vessel or bucket, with water, and then throwing heated stones into it. This operation they repeat till they think the contents are sufficiently stewed or seethed. They put in the fresh, and take out the other stones, with a cleft stick, which serves as tongs; the vessel being always placed near the fire, for that purpose *. This is a pretty common dish amongst them; and, from its appearance, seems to be strong, nourishing food. The oil which they procure from these and other sea-animals, is also used by them in great quantities; both supping it alone, with a large scoop or spoon, made of horn; or mixing it with other food, as sauce.

It may also be presumed that they feed upon other sea-animals, such as seals, sea-otters, and whales; not only

---

* This operation is represented by Mr. Webber, in his drawing of the inside of a Nootka house.

from the fkins of the two firft being frequent amongft
them, but from the great number of implements, of all
forts, intended to deftroy thefe different animals; which
clearly points out their dependance upon them; though
perhaps they do not catch them in great plenty at all
feafons; which feemed to be the cafe while we lay there,
as no great number of frefh fkins, or pieces of the flefh,
were feen.

The fame might, perhaps, be faid of the land-animals,
which, though doubtlefs the natives fometimes kill them,
appeared to be fcarce at this time; as we did not fee a fingle
piece of the flefh belonging to any of them; and though
their fkins be in tolerable plenty, it is probable that many
of thefe are procured by traffic from other tribes. Upon
the whole, it feems plain, from a variety of circumftances,
that thefe people procure almoft all their animal food from
the fea, if we except a few birds, of which the gulls or
fea-fowl, which they fhoot with their arrows, are the moft
material.

As the Canadian pine-branches and fea-grafs, on which
the fifh roe is ftrewed, may be confidered as their only win-
ter-vegetables; fo, as the fpring advances, they make ufe
of feveral others as they come in feafon. The moft common of thefe, which we obferved, were two forts of lilia-
ceous roots, one fimply tunicated, the other granulated
upon its furface, called *mahkatte* and *koohquoppa*, which
have a mild fweetifh tafte, and are mucilaginous, and
eaten raw. The next, which they have in great quantities, is a root called *aheita*, refembling, in tafte, our li-
quorice; and another fern root, whofe leaves were not yet
difclofed. They alfo eat, raw, another fmall, fweetifh,
infipid root, about the thicknefs of *farfaparilla*; but we

10   were

were ignorant of the plant to which it belongs; and alſo of another root, which is very large and palmated, which we ſaw them dig up near the village, and afterward eat it. It is alſo probable that, as the ſeaſon advances, they have many others, which we did not ſee. For though there be no appearance of cultivation amongſt them, there are great quantities of alder, gooſeberry and currant buſhes, whoſe fruits they may eat in their natural ſtate, as we have ſeen them eat the leaves of the laſt, and of the lilies, juſt as they were plucked from the plant. It muſt, however, be obſerved, that one of the conditions which they ſeem to require, in all food, is, that it ſhould be of the bland or leſs acrid kind; for they would not eat the leek or garlic, though they brought vaſt quantities to ſell, when they underſtood we were fond of it. Indeed, they ſeemed to have no reliſh for any of our food; and when offered ſpirituous liquors, they rejected them as ſomething unnatural and diſguſting to the palate.

Though they ſometimes eat ſmall marine-animals, in their freſh ſtate, raw, it is their common practice to roaſt or broil their food; for they are quite ignorant of our method of boiling; unleſs we allow that of preparing their porpoiſe broth is ſuch; and, indeed, their veſſels being all of wood, are quite inſufficient for this purpoſe.

Their manner of eating is exactly conſonant to the naſti-neſs of their houſes and perſons; for the troughs and plat-ters, in which they put their food, appear never to have been waſhed from the time they were firſt made, and the dirty remains of a former meal are only ſweeped away by the ſucceeding one. They alſo tear every thing ſolid, or tough, to pieces, with their hands and teeth; for though they make uſe of their knives to cut off the larger portions,

they

they have not, as yet, thought of reducing thefe to fmaller pieces and mouthfuls, by the fame means, though obvioufly more convenient and cleanly. But they feem to have no idea of cleanlinefs; for they eat the roots which they dig from the ground, without fo much as fhaking off the foil that adheres to them.

We are uncertain if they have any fet time for meals; for we have feen them eat at all hours, in their canoes. And yet, from feeing feveral meffes of the porpoife broth preparing toward noon, when we vifited the village, I fhould fufpect that they make a principal meal about that time.

Their weapons are bows and arrows, flings, fpears, fhort truncheons of bone, fomewhat like the *patoo patoo* of New Zealand, and a fmall pick-axe, not unlike the common American *tomahawk*. The fpear has generally a long point, made of bone. Some of the arrows are pointed with iron; but moft commonly their points were of indented bone. The tomahawk is a ftone, fix or eight inches long, pointed at one end, and the other end fixed into a handle of wood. This handle refembles the head and neck of the human figure; and the ftone is fixed in the mouth, fo as to reprefent an enormoufly large tongue. To make the refemblance ftill ftronger, human hair is alfo fixed to it. This weapon they call *taaweefh*, or *tfufkeeah*. They have another ftone weapon called *feeaik*, nine inches or a foot long, with a fquare point.

From the number of ftone weapons, and others, we might almoft conclude, that it is their cuftom to engage in clofe fight; and we had too convincing proofs that their wars are both frequent and bloody, from the vaft number of human fculls which they brought to fell.

Their

Their manufactures, and mechanic arts, are far more extensive and ingenious, whether we regard the design, or the execution, than could have been expected from the natural disposition of the people, and the little progress that civilization has made amongst them in other respects. The flaxen and woollen garments, with which they cover themselves, must necessarily engage their first care; and are the most material of those that can be ranked under the head of manufactures. The former of these are made of the bark of a pine-tree, beat into a hempen state. It is not spun, but, after being properly prepared, is spread upon a stick, which is fastened across to two others that stand upright. It is disposed in such a manner, that the manufacturer, who sits on her hams at this simple machine, knots it across with small plaited threads, at the distance of half an inch from each other. Though, by this method, it be not so close or firm as cloth that is woven, the bunches between the knots make it sufficiently impervious to the air, by filling the interstices; and it has the additional advantage of being softer and more pliable. The woollen garments, though probably manufactured in the same manner, have the strongest resemblance to woven cloth. But the various figures which are very artificially inserted in them, destroy the supposition of their being wrought in a loom; it being extremely unlikely, that these people should be so dexterous as to be able to finish such a complex work, unless immediately by their hands. They are of different degrees of fineness; some resembling our coarsest rugs or blankets; and others almost equal to our finest forts, or even softer, and certainly warmer. The wool, of which they are made, seems to be taken from different animals, as the fox and brown *lynx*; the last of which is by

far

far the fineft fort ; and, in its natural ftate, differs little from the colour of our coarfer wools ; but the hair, with which the animal is alfo covered, being intermixed, its appearance, when wrought, is fomewhat different. The ornamental parts or figures in thefe garments, which are difpofed with great tafte, are commonly of a different colour, being dyed, chiefly, either of a deep brown, or of a yellow ; the laft of which, when it is new, equals the beft in our carpets as to brightnefs.

To their tafte or defign in working figures upon their garments, correfponds their fondnefs for carving, in every thing they make of wood. Nothing is without a kind of freeze-work, or the figure of fome animal upon it ; but the moft general reprefentation is that of the human face, which is often cut out upon birds, and the other monftrous figures mentioned before ; and even upon their ftone and their bone weapons. The general defign of all thefe things is perfectly fufficient to convey a knowledge of the object they are intended to reprefent ; but the carving is not exe-cuted with the nicety that a dexterous artift would beftow even upon an indifferent defign. The fame, however, can-not be faid of many of the human mafks and heads ; where they fhew themfelves to be ingenious fculptors. They not only preferve, with great exactnefs, the general character of their own faces, but finifh the more minute parts, with a degree of accuracy in proportion, and neatnefs in execution. The ftrong propenfity of this people to works of this fort, is remarkable, in a vaft variety of parti-culars. Small whole human figures ; reprefentations of birds, fifh, and land and fea animals ; models of their houfe-hold utenfils and of their canoes, were found amongft them in great abundance.

The

The imitative arts being nearly allied, no wonder that, to their fkill in working figures in their garments, and carving them in wood, they fhould add that of drawing them in colours. We have fometimes feen the whole procefs of their whale-fifhery painted on the caps they wear. This, though rudely executed, ferves, at leaft, to fhew, that though there be no appearance of the knowledge of letters amongft them, they have fome notion of a method of commemorating and reprefenting actions, in a lafting way, independently of what may be recorded in their fongs and traditions. They have alfo other figures painted on fome of their things ; but it is doubtful if they ought to be confidered as fymbols, that have certain eftablifhed fignifications, or only the mere creation of fancy and caprice.

Their canoes are of a fimple ftructure ; but, to appearance, well calculated for every ufeful purpofe. Even the largeft, which carry twenty people or more, are formed of one tree. Many of them are forty feet long, feven broad, and about three deep. From the middle, toward each end, they become gradually narrower, the after-part, or ftern, ending abruptly or perpendicularly, with a fmall knob on the top ; but the fore-part is lengthened out, ftretching forward and upward, ending in a notched point or prow, confiderably higher than the fides of the canoe, which run nearly in a ftraight line. For the moft part, they are without any orna-ment ; but fome have a little carving, and are decorated by fetting feals' teeth on the furface, like ftuds ; as is the practice on their mafks and weapons. A few have, likewife, a kind of additional head or prow, like a large cut-water, which is painted with the figure of fome animal. They have no feats, nor any other fupporters, on the infide, than feveral round fticks, little thicker than a cane, placed acrofs,

at

at mid depth. They are very light, and their breadth and flatnefs enable them to fwim firmly, without an out-rigger, which none of them have; a remarkable diftinction between the navigation of all the American nations, and that of the Southern parts of the Eaft Indies, and the Iflands in the Pacific Ocean. Their paddles are fmall and light; the fhape, in fome meafure, refembling that of a large leaf, pointed at the bottom, broadeft in the middle, and gradually lofing itfelf in the fhaft, the whole being about five feet long. They have acquired great dexterity in managing thefe paddles, by conftant ufe; for fails are no part of their art of navigation.

Their implements for fifhing and hunting, which are both ingenioufly contrived, and well made, are nets, hooks and lines, harpoons, gigs, and an inftrument like an oar. This laft is about twenty feet long, four or five inches broad, and about half an inch thick. Each edge, for about two-thirds of its length (the other third being its handle), is fet with fharp bone-teeth, about two inches long. Herrings and fardines, and fuch other fmall fifh as come in fhoals, are attacked with this inftrument; which is ftruck into the fhoal, and the fifh are caught either upon, or between the teeth. Their hooks are made of bone and wood, and rather inartificially; but the harpoon, with which they ftrike the whales and leffer fea animals, fhews a great reach of contrivance. It is compofed of a piece of bone, cut into two barbs, in which is fixed the oval blade of a large mufcle fhell, in which is the point of the inftrument. To this is faftened about two or three fathoms of rope; and to throw this harpoon, they ufe a fhaft of about twelve or fifteen feet long, to which the line or rope is made faft; and to one end of which the harpoon is fixed, fo as to feparate

from

from the fhaft, and leave it floating upon the water as a buoy, when the animal darts away with the harpoon.

We can fay nothing as to the manner of their catching or killing land animals, unlefs we may fuppofe that they fhoot the fmaller forts with their arrows, and engage bears, or wolves and foxes, with their fpears. They have, indeed, feveral nets, which are probably applied to that purpofe *; as they frequently threw them over their heads, to fhew their ufe, when they brought them to us for fale. They alfo, fometimes, decoy animals, by covering themfelves with a fkin, and running about upon all fours, which they do very nimbly, as appeared from the fpecimens of their fkill, which they exhibited to us, making a kind of noife or neighing at the fame time; and, on thefe occafions, the mafks, or carved heads, as well as the real dried heads, of the different animals, are put on.

As to the materials, of which they make their various articles, it is to be obferved, that every thing of the rope kind, is formed either from thongs of fkins, and finews of animals; or from the fame flaxen fubftance of which their mantles are manufactured. The finews often appeared to be of fuch a length, that it might be prefumed they could be of no other animal than the whale. And the fame may be faid of the bones of which they make their weapons already mentioned; fuch as their bark-beating inftruments, the points of their fpears, and the barbs of their harpoons.

Their great dexterity in works of wood, may, in fome meafure, be afcribed to the affiftance they receive from iron tools. For, as far as we know, they ufe no other; at leaft,

* One of the methods of catching the fea-otter, when afhore, in Kamtfchatka, is with nets. See *Coxe's Ruffian Difcoveries*, p. 13.

we faw only one chiffel of bone. And though, originally,
their tools muft have been of different materials, it is not
improbable that many of their improvements have been
made fince they acquired a knowledge of that metal, which
now is univerfally ufed in their various wooden works.
The chiffel and the knife, are the only forms, as far as we
faw, that iron affumes amongft them.   The chiffel is a
long flat piece, fitted into a handle of wood. A ftone ferves
for a mallet, and a piece of fifh-fkin for a polifher. I have
feen fome of thefe chiffels that were eight or ten inches
long, and three or four inches broad; but, in general, they
were fmaller. The knives are of various fizes; fome very
large; and their blades are crooked, fomewhat like our
pruning-knife; but the edge is on the back or convex part.
Moft of them that we faw were about the breadth and
thicknefs of an iron hoop; and their fingular form marks
that they are not of European make. Probably, they are
imitations of their own original inftruments, ufed for the
fame purpofes. They fharpen thefe iron tools upon a
coarfe flate whetftone; and likewife keep the whole inftrument conftantly bright.

Iron, which they call *feekemaile*, (which name they alfo
give to tin, and all white metals) being familiar to thefe
people, it was very natural for us to fpeculate about the
mode of its being conveyed to them. Upon our arrival in
the Sound, they immediately difcovered a knowledge of
traffic, and an inclination for it; and we were convinced afterward, that they had not received this knowledge from a
curfory interview with any ftrangers; but, from their method, it feemed to be an eftablifhed practice, of which they
were fond, and in which they were alfo well fkilled. With
whom they carry on this traffic, may perhaps admit of

I   fome

some doubt. For though we found amongst them things doubtless of European manufacture, or at least derived from some civilized nation, such as iron and brass, it, by no means, appears that they receive them immediately from these nations. For we never observed the least sign of their having seen ships like ours before, nor of their having traded with such people. Many circumstances serve to prove this almost beyond a doubt. They were earnest in their inquiries, by signs, on our arrival, if we meant to settle amongst them; and if we came as friends: signifying, at the same time, that they gave the wood and water freely, from friendship. This not only proves, that they considered the place as entirely their property, without fearing any superiority; but the inquiry would have been an unnatural one, on a supposition that any ships had been here before; had trafficked, and supplied themselves with wood and water; and had then departed; for, in that case, they might reasonably expect we would do the same. They, indeed, expressed no marks of surprize at seeing our ships. But this, as I observed before, may be imputed to their natural indolence of temper, and want of curiosity. Nor were they even startled at the report of a musquet; till, one day, upon their endeavouring to make us sensible, that their arrows and spears could not penetrate the hide-dresses, one of our gentlemen shot a musquet ball through one of them, folded six times. At this they were so much staggered, that they plainly discovered their ignorance of the effect of fire-arms. This was very often confirmed afterward when we used them at their village, and other places, to shoot birds, the manner of which plainly confounded them; and our explanations of the use of shot and ball, were received with the most significant marks of their having no previous ideas on this matter.

Some

Some account of a Spanifh voyage to this coaft, in 1774, or 1775, had reached England before I failed; but the fore-going circumftances fufficiently prove, that thefe fhips had not been at Nootka *. Befides this, it was evident that iron was too common here; was in too many hands ; and the ufes of it were too well known, for them to have had the firft knowledge of it fo very lately ; or, indeed, at any ear-lier period, by an accidental fupply from a fhip. Doubtlefs, from the general ufe they make of this metal, it may be fuppofed to come from fome conftant fource, by way of traffic, and that not of a very late date ; for they are as dex-terous in ufing their tools as the longeft practice can make them. The moft probable way, therefore, by which we can fuppofe that they get their iron, is by trading for it with other Indian tribes, who either have immediate com-munication with European fettlements upon that continent, or receive it, perhaps, through feveral intermediate nations. The fame might be faid of the brafs and copper found amongft them.

Whether thefe things be introduced by way of Hudfon's Bay and Canada, from the Indians, who deal with our tra-ders, and fo fucceffively acrofs from one tribe to the other; or whether they be brought from the North Weftern parts of Mexico, in the fame manner; perhaps cannot be eafily determined. But it fhould feem, that not only the rude materials, but fome articles in their manufactured ftate, find their way hither. The brafs ornaments for nofes, in

---

* We now know that Captain Cook's conjecture was well founded. It appears, from the Journal of this Voyage, already referred to, that the Spaniards had intercourfe with the natives of this coaft, only in three places, in latitude 41° 7′; in latitude 47° 21′; and in latitude 57° 18′. So that they were not within two degrees of Nootka; and it is moft probable, that the people there never heard of thefe Spanifh fhips.

particular,

particular, are fo neatly made, that I am doubtful whether the Indians are capable of fabricating them. The materials certainly are European; as no American tribes have been found, who knew the method of making brafs; though copper has been commonly met with, and, from its foft-nefs, might be fafhioned into any fhape, and alfo polifhed. If our traders to Hudfon's Bay and Canada do not ufe fuch articles in their traffic with the natives, they muft have been introduced at Nootka from the quarter of Mexico, from whence, no doubt, the two filver table-fpoons, met with here, were originally derived. It is moft probable, however, that the Spaniards are not fuch eager traders, nor have formed fuch extenfive connections with the tribes North of Mexico, as to fupply them with quantities of iron, from which they can fpare fo much to the people here *.

Of the political and religious inftitutions eftablifhed amongft them, it cannot be fuppofed that we fhould learn much. This we could obferve, that there are fuch men as Chiefs, who are diftinguifhed by the name or title of *Ac-week*, and to whom the others are, in fome meafure, fub-ordinate. But, I fhould guefs, the authority of each of thefe great men extends no farther than the family to which he belongs, and who own nim as their head. Thefe *Acweeks* were not always elderly men; from which

* Though the two filver table-fpoons, found at Nootka Sound, moft probably came from the Spaniards in the South, there feems to be fufficient grounds for believing that the regular fupply of iron comes from a different quarter. It is remarkable, that the Spaniards, in 1775, found at *Puerto de la Trinidad*, in latitude 41° 7′, *arrows pointed with copper or iron, which they underftood were procured from the North*. Mr. Daines Bar-rington, in a note at this part of the Spanifh Journal, p. 20. fays, " I fhould conceive " that the copper and iron, here mentioned, muft have originally been bartered at our " forts in Hudfon's Bay."

I con-

I concluded that this title came to them by inheri-
tance.

I faw nothing that could give the leaft infight into their
notions of religion, befides the figures before mentioned,
called by them *Klumma*. Moft probably thefe were idols;
but as they frequently mentioned the word *acweek*, when
they fpoke of them, we may, perhaps, be authorized to
fuppofe that they are the images of fome of their anceftors,
whom they venerate as divinities. But all this is mere
conjecture; for we faw no act of religious homage paid to
them; nor could we gain any information, as we had
learned little more of their language, than to afk the names
of things, without being able to hold any converfation
with the natives, that might inftruct us as to their inftitutions or traditions.

In drawing up the preceding account of the people of
this Sound, I have occafionally blended Mr. Anderfon's obfervations with my own; but I owe every thing to him that
relates to their language; and the following remarks are in
his own words.

" Their language is, by no means, harfh or difagreeable,
farther than proceeds from their ufing the *k* and *h* with
more force, or pronouncing them with lefs foftnefs than we
do; and, upon the whole, it abounds rather with what we
may call labial and dental, than with guttural founds. The
fimple founds which we have not heard them ufe, and
which, confequently, may be reckoned rare, or wanting in
their language, are thofe reprefented by the letters *b, d, f,
g, r,* and *v.* But, on the other hand, they have one, which
is very frequent, and not ufed by us. It is formed, in a
particular manner, by clafhing the tongue partly againft
the roof of the mouth, with confiderable force; and may
be

be compared to a very coarfe or harfh method of lifping. It is difficult to reprefent this found by any compofition of our letters, unlefs, fomehow, from *lfztbl*. This is one of their moft ufual terminations, though we fometimes found it in the beginning of words. The next moft general termination is compofed of *tl*; and many words end with *z* and *fs*. A fpecimen or two, of each of thefe, is here put down:

Opulfztbl,	The fun.
Onulfztbl,	The moon.
Kabfheetl,	Dead.
Teefhcheetl,	To throw a ftone.
Kooomitz,	A human fcull.
Quabmifs,	Fifh roe.

They feem to take fo great a latitude in their mode of fpeaking, that I have fometimes obferved four or five different terminations of the fame word. This is a circumftance very puzzling at firft to a ftranger, and marks a great imperfection in their language.

As to the compofition of it, we can fay very little; having been fcarcely able to diftinguifh the feveral parts of fpeech. It can only be inferred, from their method of fpeaking, which is very flow and diftinct, that it has few prepofitions or conjunctions; and, as far as we could difcover, is deftitute of even a fingle interjection, to exprefs admiration or furprize. From its having few conjunctions, it may be conceived, that thefe being thought unneceffary, as being underftood, each fingle word, with them, will alfo exprefs a great deal, or comprehend feveral fimple ideas; which feems to be the cafe. But, for the fame reafon, the language will be defective in other refpects; not having words to diftinguifh or exprefs differences which really exift, and

hence

hence not fufficiently copious. This was obferved to be the cafe, in many inftances, particularly with refpect to the names of animals. The relation or affinity it may bear to other languages, either on this, or on the Afiatic continent, I have not been able fufficiently to trace, for want of proper fpecimens to compare it with, except thofe of the Efquimaux, and Indians about Hudfon's Bay; to neither of which it bears the leaft refemblance. On the other hand, from the few Mexican words I have been able to procure, there is the moft obvious agreement, in the very frequent terminations of the words in *l*, *tl*, or *z*, throughout the language *."

The large vocabulary of the Nootka language, collected by Mr. Anderfon, fhall be referved for another place +, as its infertion here would too much interrupt our narration. At prefent I only felect their numerals, for the fatisfaction of fuch of our readers as love to compare thofe of different nations, in different parts of the world :

Tfawack,	One.
Akkla,	Two.
Katfitfa,	Three.
Mo, or *Moo.*	Four.
Sochah,	Five.
Nofpo,	Six.
Atftepoo,	Seven.
Atlaquolthl,	Eight.
Tfawaquulthl,	Nine.
Haeeoo,	Ten.

* May we not, in confirmation of Mr. Anderfon's remark, obferve, that *Opulfzthl,* the Nootka name of the Sun; and *Vitziputzli,* the name of the Mexican Divinity, have no very diftant affinity in found ?

✝ It will be found at the end of the third volume.

Were

1778.
April.

Were I to affix a name to the people of Nootka, as a
diftinct nation, I would call them *Wakaſhians*; from the
word *wakaſh*, which was very frequently in their mouths.
It feemed to exprefs applaufe, approbation, and friendſhip.
For when they appeared to be fatisfied, or well pleafed with
any thing they faw, or any incident that happened, they
would, with one voice, call out *wakaſh! wakaſh!* I ſhall
take my leave of them, with remarking, that, differing fo
effentially as they certainly do, in their perfons, their cuftoms, and language, from the inhabitants of the iflands in
the Pacific Ocean, we cannot fuppofe their refpective pro-
genitors to have been united in the fame tribe, or to have
had any intimate connection, when they emigrated from
their original fettlements, into the places where we now
find their defcendants.

My account of the tranfactions in Nootka Sound would be
imperfect, without adding the aftronomical and nautical obfervations made by us, while the fhips were in that ftation.

Latitude.

The latitude of the observatory by — { Sun - - 49° 36′ 1″, 15‴
Stars { South 49 36 8, 36
North 49 36 10, 30

The mean of thefe means - 49 36 6, 47 North.

Longitude.

The longitude, by lunar obferva-tions {
Twenty fets taken on the 21ft and 23d of March } 233° 26′ 18″, 7‴
Ninety-three taken at the obfervatory — — } 233 18 6, 6
Twenty-four taken on the 1ft, 2d, and 3d of May } 233 7 16, 7

The mean of thefe means - 233 17 13, 27 Eaft.

VOL. II. X x But

But by reducing each set taken before
we arrived in the Sound, and after
we left it, by the time-keeper, and
adding them up with those made } 233° 17′ 30″, 5′
on the spot, the mean of the 137
sets will be - - - -

Longitude by the { Greenwich rate - 235° 46′ 51″, 0‴
time-keeper { Ulietea rate - - 233 59 24, 0

From the results of the last fifteen days observations of
equal altitudes of the Sun, the daily rate of the time-keeper
was losing, on mean time, 7″; and on the 16th of April, she
was too slow for mean time, by 16ʰ 0ᵐ 58″, 45. There was
found an irregularity in her rate, greater than at any time
before. It was thought proper to reject the first five days,
as the rate in them differed so much from that of the fifteen following; and even in these, each day differed from
another more than usual.

Variation of the Compass.

April 4th. { A. M. } Observatory, { 15° 57′ 48¾″ } 15° 49′ 25″ East.
{ P. M. } Mean of four needles { 15 41 2 }

5th. { A. M. } On board the ship, { 19° 50′ 49″ } 19 44 47½
17th. { P. M. } Mean of four needles { 19 38 46 }

The variation found on board the ship, ought to be taken
for the true one; not only as it agreed with what we observed at sea; but because it was found, that there was
something ashore that had a considerable effect upon the
compasses; in some places more than others. At one spot,
on the West point of the Sound, the needle was attracted
11 ¼ points from its proper direction.

10   *Inclination*

Inclination of the dipping Needle.

April 5th. On board with balanced needle	{ Marked { Unmarked	} End North } and dipping	{ 71° 26' 22½" { 71 54 22½	} 71° 40' 22½"	
The same needle at the observatory	{ Marked { Unmarked	} End North } and dipping	{ 72 3 45 { 71 56 15	} 72 0 0	
18th. Ditto - -	{ Marked { Unmarked	} End North } and dipping	{ 71 58 20 { 72 16 10	} 72 7 15	
5th. Spare needle at the observatory	{ Marked { Unmarked	} End North } and dipping	{ 72 32 30 { 73 6 0	} 72 49 15	
18th. Ditto - -	{ Marked { Unmarked	} End North } and dipping	{ 72 55 0 { 73 28 30	} 73 11 45	
22d. Spare needle on board - -	{ Marked { Unmarked	} End North } and dipping	{ 73 28 38 { 72 53 30	} 73 11 4	

Hence the mean dip, with both needles, on shore, was - 72 32 3¼
On board - - - - - 72 25 43¾

This is as near as can be expected; and shews, that whatever it was that affected the compasses, whether on board or ashore, it had no effect upon the dipping needles.

Tides.

It is high-water on the days of the new and full moon, at 12ʰ 20ᵐ. The perpendicular rise and fall, eight feet nine inches; which is to be understood of the day-tides, and those which happen two or three days after the full and new moon. The night-tides, at this time, rise near two feet higher. This was very conspicuous during the spring-tide of the full moon, which happened soon after our arrival; and it was obvious, that it would be the same in those of the new moon, though we did not remain here long enough to see the whole of its effect.

Some circumstances, that occurred daily, relating to this, deserve particular notice. In the cove where we got wood

X x 2

and

and water, was a great deal of drift-wood thrown aſhore; a part of which we had to remove, to come at the water. It often happened, that large pieces or trees, which we had removed in the day, out of the reach of the then high-water, were found, the next morning, floated again in our way; and all our ſpouts, for conveying down the water, thrown out of their places, which were immoveable during the day-tides. We alſo found, that wood, which we had ſplit up for fuel, and had depoſited beyond the reach of the day-tide, floated away during the night. Some of theſe circum-ſtances happened every night or morning, for three or four days in the height of the ſpring-tides; during which time we were obliged to attend every morning-tide, to remove the large logs out of the way of watering.

I cannot ſay, whether the flood-tide falls into the Sound from the North Weſt, South Weſt, or South Eaſt. I think it does not come from the laſt quarter; but this is only conjecture, founded upon the following obſervations: The South Eaſt gales, which we had in the Sound, were ſo far from increaſing the riſe of the tide, that they rather dimi-niſhed it; which would hardly have happened, if the flood and wind had been in the ſame direction.

CHAP.

C H A P. IV.

*A Storm, after failing from Nootka Sound.—Refolution fprings
a Leak.—Pretended Strait of Admiral de Fonte paffed
unexamined.—Progrefs along the Coaft of America.—Beering's Bay.—Kaye's Ifland.—Account of it.—The Ships come
to an Anchor.—Vifited by the Natives.—Their Behaviour.—
Fondnefs for Beads and Iron.—Attempt to plunder the Difcovery.—Refolution's Leak ftopped.—Progrefs up the Sound.
—Meffrs. Gore and Roberts fent to examine its Extent.—
Reafons againft a Paffage to the North through it.—The
Ships proceed down it, to the open Sea.*

HAVING put to fea, on the evening of the 26th, as
before related, with ftrong figns of an approaching
ftorm; thefe figns did not deceive us. We were hardly out
of the Sound, before the wind, in an inftant, fhifted from
North Eaft to South Eaft by Eaft, and increafed to a ftrong
gale, with fqualls and rain, and fo dark a fky, that we could
not fee the length of the fhip. Being apprehenfive, from
the experience I had fince our arrival on this coaft, of the
wind veering more to the South, which would put us in
danger of a lee-fhore, we got the tacks on board, and
ftretched off to the South Weft, under all the fail the fhips
could bear. Fortunately, the wind veered no farther Southerly, than South Eaft; fo that at day-light the next morning, we were quite clear of the coaft.

1778.
April.

Sunday 26.

Monday 27.

The

The Difcovery being at fome diftance aftern, I brought to, till fhe came up, and then bore away, fteering North Weft; in which direction I fuppofed the coaft to lie. The wind was at South Eaft, blew very hard, and in fqualls, with thick hazy weather. At half paft one in the afternoon, it blew a perfect hurricane; fo that I judged it highly dangerous to run any longer before it, and, therefore, brought the fhips to, with their heads to the Southward, under the forefails and mizen-ftayfails. At this time, the Refolution fprung a leak, which, at firft, alarmed us not a little. It was found to be under the ftarboard buttock; where, from the bread-room, we could both hear and fee the water rufh in; and, as we then thought, two feet under water. But in this we were happily miftaken; for it was afterward found to be even with the water-line, if not above it, when the fhip was upright. It was no fooner difcovered, than the fifh-room was found to be full of water, and the cafks in it afloat; but this was, in a great meafure, owing to the water not finding its way to the pumps through the coals that lay in the bottom of the room. For after the water was baled out, which employed us till midnight, and had found its way directly from the leak to the pumps, it appeared that one pump kept it under, which gave us no fmall fatisfaction. In the evening, the wind veered to the South, and its fury, in fome degree, ceafed. On this, we fet the main-fail, and two topfails clofe-reefed, and ftretched to the Weftward. But at eleven o'clock, the gale again increafed, and obliged us to take in the topfails, till five o'clock Tuefday 28. the next morning, when the ftorm began to abate; fo that we could bear to fet them again.

The weather now began to clear up; and, being able to fee feveral leagues round us, I fteered more to the Northward.

At

At noon, the latitude, by obfervation, was 50° 1′; longitude 229° 26′ *. I now fteered North Weft by North, with
a frefh gale at South South Eaft, and fair weather. But
at nine in the evening, it began again to blow hard, and
in fqualls with rain. With fuch weather, and the wind between South South Eaft and South Weft, I continued the
fame courfe till the 30th, at four in the morning, when I
fteered North by Weft, in order to make the land. I regretted very much indeed that I could not do it fooner, for
this obvious reafon, that we were now paffing the place
where geographers † have placed the pretended ftrait of Admiral de Fonte. For my own part, I give no credit to fuch
vague and improbable ftories, that carry their own confutation along with them. Neverthelefs, I was very defirous
of keeping the American coaft aboard, in order to clear up
this point beyond difpute. But it would have been highly
imprudent in me, to have engaged with the land in weather fo exceedingly tempeftuous, or to have loft the advantage of a fair wind, by waiting for better weather. This
fame day at noon we were in the latitude of 53° 22′, and
in the longitude of 225° 14′.

The next morning, being the 1ft of May, feeing nothing
of the land, I fteered North Eafterly, with a frefh breeze
at South South Eaft and South, with fqualls and fhowers
of rain and hail. Our latitude at noon was 54° 43′, and
our longitude 224° 44′. At feven in the evening, being
in the latitude of 55° 20′, we got fight of the land, ex-

1778.
April.

Thurfday 30.

May.
Friday 1.

---

* As in the remaining part of this Volume, the Latitude and Longitude are very
frequently fet down; the former being invariably North, and the latter Eaft, the conftant
repetition of the two words, *North* and *Eaft*, has been omitted, to avoid unneceffary
precifion.

† See De Lifle's *Carte Générale des Découvertes de l'Amiral de Fonte*, &c. Paris,
1752; and many other Maps.

tending

tending from North North Eaſt to Eaſt, or Eaſt by South,
about twelve or fourteen leagues diſtant. An hour after, I
ſteered North by Weſt; and at four the next morning, the
coaſt was ſeen from North by Weſt to South Eaſt, the
neareſt part about ſix leagues diſtant. *.

At this time the Northern point of an inlet, or what appeared to be one, bore Eaſt by South. It lies in the latitude
of 56°; and from it to the Northward, the coaſt ſeemed to
be much broken, forming bays and harbours every two or
three leagues; or elſe appearances much deceived us. At
ſix o'clock, drawing nearer the land, I ſteered North Weſt
by North, this being the direction of the coaſt; having a
freſh gale at South Eaſt, with ſome ſhowers of hail, ſnow
and ſleet. Between eleven and twelve o'clock, we paſſed a
group of ſmall iſlands lying under the main land, in the
latitude of 56° 48′; and off, or rather to the Northward of,
the South point of a large bay. An arm of this bay, in the
Northern part of it, ſeemed to extend in toward the North,
behind a round elevated mountain that lies between it and
the ſea. This mountain I called *Mount Edgcumbe*; and
the point of land that ſhoots out from it, *Cape Edgcumbe*.
The latter lies in the latitude of 57° 3′, and in the longitude
of 224° 7′; and, at noon, it bore North 20° Weſt, ſix leagues
diſtant.

* This muſt be very near that part of the American coaſt, where Tſcherikow anchored in 1741. For Muller places its latitude in 56°. Had this Ruſſian navigator
been ſo fortunate as to proceed a little farther Northward along the coaſt, he would
have found, as we now learn from Captain Cook, bays, and harbours, and iſlands,
where his ſhip might have been ſheltered, and his people protected in landing. For the
particulars of the misfortunes he met with here, two boats crews, which he ſent aſhore,
having never returned, probably cut off by the natives, ſee *Muller's Découvertes de Ruſſes*,
p. 248, 254. The Spaniards, in 1775, found two good harbours on this part of the
coaſt; that called *Guadalupe*, in latitude 57° 11′, and the other, *De los Remedios*, in latitude 57° 18′.

The

The land, except in some places close to the sea, is all of a considerable height, and hilly; but Mount Edgcumbe far out-tops all the other hills. It was wholly covered with snow; as were also all the other elevated hills; but the lower ones, and the flatter spots, bordering upon the sea, were free from it, and covered with wood.

As we advanced to the North, we found the coast from Cape Edgcumbe to trend North and North Easterly for six or seven leagues, and there form a large bay. In the entrance of that bay are some islands; for which reason I named it the *Bay of Islands*. It lies in the latitude of 57° 20′ *; and seemed to branch into several arms, one of which turned to the South, and may probably communicate with the bay on the East side of Cape Edgcumbe, and make the land of that Cape an island. At eight o'clock in the evening, the Cape bore South East, half South; the Bay of Islands North, 53° East; and another inlet, before which are also some islands, bore North, 52° East, five leagues distant. I continued to steer North North West, half West, and North West by West, as the coast trended, with a fine gale at North East, and clear weather.

At half an hour past four in the morning, on the 3d, Mount Edgcumbe bore South, 54° East; a large inlet, North, 50° East, distant six leagues; and the most advanced point of the land, to the North West, lying under a very high peaked mountain, which obtained the name of *Mount Fair Weather*, bore North, 32° West. The inlet was named *Cross Sound*, as being first seen on that day so marked in our ca-

---

* It should seem, that in this very bay, the Spaniards, in 1775, found their port which they call *De los Remedios*. The latitude is exactly the same; and their Journal mentions its *being protected by a long ridge of high islands*. See *Miscellanies by the Honourable Daines Barrington*, p. 503, 504.

lendar.

lendar. It appeared to branch in feveral arms, the largeft of which turned to the Northward. The South Eaft point of this Sound is a high promontory, which obtained the name of *Crofs Cape*. It lies in the latitude of 57° 57′, and its longitude is 223° 21′. At noon it bore South Eaft; and the point under the peaked mountain, which was called *Cape Fair Weather*, North by Weft, a quarter Weft, diftant thirteen leagues. Our latitude at this time, was 58° 17′, and our longitude 222° 14′; and we were diftant from the fhore three or four leagues. In this fituation we found the variation of the compafs to be from 24° 11′ to 26° 11′ Eaft.

Here the North Eaft wind left us, and was fucceeded by light breezes from the North Weft, which lafted for feveral days. I ftood to the South Weft, and Weft South Weft, till

eight o'clock the next morning, when we tacked, and ftood toward the fhore. At noon, the latitude was 58° 22′, and the longitude 220° 45′. Mount Fair Weather, the peaked mountain over the cape of the fame name, bore North, 63° Eaft; the fhore under it twelve leagues diftant. This mountain, which lies in the latitude of 58° 52′, and in the longitude of 222°, and five leagues inland, is the higheft of a chain, or rather a ridge, of mountains, that rife at the North Weft entrance of Crofs Sound, and extend to the North Weft, in a parallel direction with the coaft. Thefe mountains were wholly covered with fnow, from the higheft fummit down to the fea-coaft; fome few places excepted, where we could perceive trees rifing, as it were, out of the fea; and which, therefore, we fuppofed, grew on low land, or on iflands bordering upon the fhore of the continent *.

At

* According to Muller, Beering fell in with the coaft of North America, in latitude 58° 28′; and he defcribes its afpect thus: " *L'afpeĉt du pays étoit affrayant par fes hautes*
" *montagnes*

At five in the afternoon, our latitude being then 58° 53′,
and our longitude 220° 52′; the fummit of an elevated mountain appeared above the horizon, bearing North, 26° Weft; and, as was afterwards found, forty leagues diftant. We fuppofed it to be Beering's Mount St. Elias; and it ftands by that name in our chart.

This day we faw feveral whales, feals, and porpoifes; many gulls, and feveral flocks of birds, which had a black ring about the head; the tip of the tail, and upper part of the wings, with a black band; and the reft bluifh above, and white below. We alfo faw a brownifh duck, with a black or deep blue head and neck, fitting upon the water.

Having but light winds, with fome calms, we advanced flowly; fo that on the 6th at noon, we were only in the latitude of 59° 8′, and in the longitude of 220° 19′. Mount Fair Weather bore South, 63° Eaft, and Mount Elias North, 30° Weft; the neareft land about eight leagues diftant. In the direction of North, 47° Eaft from this ftation, there was the appearance of a bay, and an ifland off the South point of it that was covered with wood. It is here where I fuppofe Commodore Beering to have anchored. The latitude, which is 59° 18′, correfponds pretty well with the map of his voyage *, and the longitude is 221° Eaft. Behind the bay (which I fhall diftinguifh by the name of *Beering's Bay*, in honour of its difcoverer), or rather to the South of it, the chain of mountains before mentioned, is interrupted by a plain of a

---

" *montagnes couvertes de niege*." The chain, or ridge of mountains, covered with fnow, mentioned here by Captain Cook, in the fame latitude, exactly agrees with what Beering met with. See Muller's *Voyages et Découvertes des Ruffes*, p. 248—254.

* Probably Captain Cook means Muller's map, prefixed to his Hiftory of the Ruffian Difcoveries.

few

few leagues extent; beyond which the fight was unlimited; fo that there is either a level country or water behind
it. In the afternoon, having a few hours calm, I took this
opportunity to found, and found feventy fathoms water
over a muddy bottom. The calm was fucceeded by a light
breeze from the North, with which we ftood to the Weft-
Thurfday 7. ward; and at noon the next day, we were in the latitude of
59° 27', and the longitude of 219° 7'. In this fituation, Mount
Fair Weather bore South, 70° Eaft; Mount St. Elias, North,
half Weft; the Wefternmoft land in fight, North, 52° Weft;
and our diftance from the fhore four or five leagues; the
depth of water being eighty-two fathoms over a muddy
bottom. From this ftation we could fee a bay (circular to
appearance) under the high land, with low wood-land on
each fide of it.

We now found the coaft to trend very much to the Weft,
inclining hardly any thing to the North; and as we had the
wind moftly from the Weftward, and but little of it, our
Saturday 9. progrefs was flow. On the 9th at noon, the latitude was
59° 30', and the longitude 217°. In this fituation the neareft
land was nine leagues diftant; and Mount St. Elias bore
North, 30° Eaft, nineteen leagues diftant. This mountain
lies twelve leagues inland, in the latitude of 60° 27', and in
the longitude of 219°. It belongs to a ridge of exceedingly
high mountains, that may be reckoned a continuation of
the former; as they are only divided from them by the
plain above mentioned. They extend as far to the Weft as
the longitude of 217°; where, although they do not end,
they lofe much of their height, and become more broken
and divided.

Sunday 10. At noon on the 10th, our latitude was 59° 51' and our longitude 215° 56', being no more than three leagues from the
coaft

coaft of the continent, which extended from Eaft half North, to North Weft half Weft, as far as the eye could reach. To the Weftward of this laft direction was an ifland that extended from North, 52° Weft, to South, 85° Weft, diftant fix leagues. A point fhoots out from the main toward the North Eaft end of the ifland, bearing, at this time, North, 30° Weft, five or fix leagues diftant. This point I named *Cape Suckling*. The point of the Cape is low; but within it, is a tolerably high hill, which is disjoined from the mountains by low land; fo that, at a diftance, the Cape looks like an ifland. On the North fide of Cape Suckling is a bay that appeared to be of fome extent, and to be covered from moft winds. To this bay I had fome thoughts of going, to ftop our leak, as all our endeavours to do it at fea had proved ineffectual. With this view, I fteered for the Cape; but as we had only variable light breezes, we approached it flowly. However, before night, we were near enough to fee fome low land fpitting out from the Cape to the North Weft, fo as to cover the Eaft part of the bay from the South wind. We alfo faw fome fmall iflands in the bay, and elevated rocks between the Cape and the North Eaft end of the ifland. But ftill there appeared to be a paffage on both fides of thefe rocks; and I continued fteering for them all night, having from forty-three to twenty-feven fathoms water over a muddy bottom.

At four o'clock next morning, the wind, which had been Monday 11. moftly at North Eaft, fhifted to North. This being againft us, I gave up the defign of going within the ifland, or into the bay, as neither could be done without lofs of time. I therefore bore up for the Weft end of the ifland. The wind blew faint; and at ten o'clock it fell calm. Being not far from the ifland, I went in a boat, and landed upon it, with

a view

a view of feeing what lay on the other fide; but finding it farther to the hills than I expected, and the way being fteep and woody, I was obliged to drop the defign. At the foot of a tree, on a little eminence not far from the fhore, I left a bottle with a paper in it, on which were infcribed the names of the fhips, and the date of our difcovery. And along with it, I inclofed two filver twopenny pieces of his Majefty's coin, of the date 1772. Thefe, with many others, were furnifhed me by the Reverend Dr. Kaye *; and, as a mark of my efteem and regard for that gentleman, I named the ifland, after him, *Kaye's Ifland*. It is eleven or twelve leagues in length, in the direction of North Eaft and South Weft; but its breadth is not above a league, or a league and a half, in any part of it. The South Weft point, which lies in the latitude of 59° 49', and the longitude of 216° 58', is very remarkable, being a naked rock, elevated confiderably above the land within it. There is alfo an elevated rock lying off it, which, from fome points of view, appears like a ruined caftle. Toward the fea, the ifland terminates in a kind of bare floping cliffs, with a beach, only a few paces acrofs to their foot, of large pebble ftones, intermixed in fome places with a brownifh clayey fand, which the fea feems to depofit after rolling in, having been wafhed down from the higher parts, by the rivulets or torrents. The cliffs are compofed of a bluifh ftone or rock, in a foft or mouldering ftate, except in a few places. There are parts of the fhore interrupted by fmall vallies and gullies. In each of thefe, a rivulet or torrent rufhes down with confiderable impetuofity; though it may be fuppofed that they are only furnifhed from the fhow, and laft no longer than till it is all melted. Thefe vallies are filled with pine-trees, which

* Then Sub-almoner, and Chaplain to his Majefty, now Dean of Lincoln.

3

grow

grow down clofe to the entrance, but only to about half way up the higher or middle part of the ifland. The woody part alfo begins, every where, immediately above the cliffs, and is continued to the fame height with the former; fo that the ifland is covered, as it were, with a broad girdle of wood, fpread upon its fide, included between the top of the cliffy fhore, and the higher parts in the centre. The trees, however, are far from being of an uncommon growth; few appearing to be larger than one might grafp round with his arms, and about forty or fifty feet high; fo that the only purpofe they could anfwer for fhipping, would be to make top-gallant-mafts, and other fmall things. How far we may judge of the fize of the trees which grow on the neighbouring continent, it may be difficult to determine. But it was obferved, that none larger than thofe we faw growing, lay upon the beach amongft the drift-wood. The pine-trees feemed all of one fort; and there was neither the Canadian pine, nor cyprefs to be feen. But there were a few which appeared to be the alder, that were but fmall, and had not yet fhot forth their leaves. Upon the edges of the cliffs, and on fome floping ground, the furface was covered with a kind of turf, about half a foot thick; which feemed compofed of the common mofs; and the top, or upper part of the ifland had almoft the fame appearance as to colour; but whatever covered it feemed to be thicker. I found amongft the trees fome currant and hawberry bufhes; a fmall yellow-flowered violet; and the leaves of fome other plants not yet in flower, particularly one which Mr. Anderfon fuppofed to be the *heracleum* of Linnæus, the fweet herb, which Steller, who attended Beering, imagined the Americans here drefs for food, in the fame manner as the natives of Kamtfchatka *.

* See Muller, p. 256.

We

We faw, flying about the wood, a crow; two or three of the white-headed eagles mentioned at Nootka; and another fort full as large, which appeared alfo of the fame colour, or blacker, and had only a white breaft. This fpecies is in the LEVERIAN *Mufeum*; and defcribed by Mr. *Latham*, in his Synopfis of Birds, Vol. i. p. 33, N° 72, under the name of the *White-bellied Eagle*. In the paffage from the fhip to the fhore, we faw a great many fowls fitting upon the water, or flying about in flocks or pairs; the chief of which were a few quebrantahueffes; divers; ducks, or large peterels; gulls; fhags; and purres. The divers were of two forts; one very large, of a black colour, with a white breaft and belly; the other fmaller, and with a longer and more pointed bill, which feemed to be the common guillemot. The ducks were alfo of two forts; one brownifh, with a black or deep blue head and neck, and is perhaps the ftone duck defcribed by Steller. The others fly in larger flocks, but are fmaller than thefe, and are of a dirty black colour. The gulls were of the common fort, and thofe which fly in flocks. The fhags were large and black, with a white fpot behind the wings as they flew; but probably only the larger water corvorant. There was alfo a fingle bird feen flying about, to appearance of the gull kind, of a fnowy white colour, with black along part of the upper fide of its wings. I owe all thefe remarks to Mr. Anderfon. At the place where we landed, a fox came from the verge of the wood, and eyed us with very little emotion, walking leifurely without any figns of fear. He was of a reddifh-yellow colour, like fome of the fkins we bought at Nootka, but not of a large fize. We alfo faw two or three little feals off fhore; but no other animals or birds; nor the leaft figns of inhabitants having ever been upon the ifland.

I returned

I returned on board at half paſt two in the afternoon;
and, with a light breeze Eaſterly, ſteered for the South Weſt
point of the iſland, which we got round by eight o'clock, and
then ſtood for the Weſternmoſt land now in ſight, which, at
this time, bore North Weſt half North. On the North Weſt
ſide of the North Eaſt end of Kaye's Iſland, lies another
iſland, ſtretching South Eaſt and North Weſt about three
leagues, to within the ſame diſtance of the North Weſt
boundary of the bay above mentioned, which is diſtinguiſhed by the Name of *Comptroller's Bay.*

Next morning, at four o'clock, Kaye's Iſland was ſtill
in ſight, bearing Eaſt a quarter South. At this time, we
were about four or five leagues from the main; and
the moſt Weſtern part in ſight bore North Weſt half
North. We had now a freſh gale at Eaſt South Eaſt; and
as we advanced to the North Weſt, we raiſed land more
and more Weſterly; and, at laſt, to the Southward of
Weſt; ſo that, at noon, when the latitude was 60° 11′, and
the longitude 213° 28′, the moſt advanced land bore from
us South Weſt by Weſt half Weſt. At the ſame time, the
Eaſt point of a large inlet bore Weſt North Weſt, three
leagues diſtant.

From Comptroller's Bay to this point, which I name *Cape
Hincbingbroke,* the direction of the coaſt is nearly Eaſt and
Weſt. Beyond this, it ſeemed to incline to the Southward;
a direction ſo contrary to the modern charts founded upon
the late Ruſſian diſcoveries, that we had reaſon to expect
that, by the inlet before us, we ſhould find a paſſage to the
North; and that the land to the Weſt and South Weſt was
nothing but a group of iſlands. Add to this, that the wind
was now at South Eaſt, and we were threatened with a fog
and a ſtorm; and I wanted to get into ſome place to ſtop the

VOL. II.   Z z   leak,

leak, before we encountered another gale. These reasons induced me to steer for the inlet, which we had no sooner reached, than the weather became so foggy, that we could not see a mile before us, and it became necessary to secure the ships in some place, to wait for a clearer sky. With this view, I hauled close under Cape Hinchingbroke, and anchored before a small cove, a little within the Cape, in eight fathoms water, a clayey bottom, and about a quarter of a mile from the shore.

The boats were then hoisted out, some to sound, and others to fish. The seine was drawn in the cove; but without success, for it was torn. At some short intervals, the fog cleared away, and gave us a sight of the lands around us. The Cape bore South by West half West, one league distant; the West point of the inlet South West by West, distant five leagues; and the land on that side extended as far as West by North. Between this point and North West by West, we could see no land; and what was in the last direction seemed to be at a great distance. The Westernmost point we had in sight on the North shore, bore North North West half West, two leagues distant. Between this point, and the shore under which we were at anchor, is a bay about three leagues deep; on the South East side of which there are two or three coves, such as that before which we had anchored; and in the middle some rocky islands.

To these islands Mr. Gore was sent in a boat, in hopes of shooting some eatable birds. But he had hardly got to them, before about twenty natives made their appearance in two large canoes; on which he thought proper to return to the ships, and they followed him. They would not venture along-side, but kept at some distance, hollowing

3   aloud,

aloud, and alternately clafping and extending their arms; and, in a fhort time, began a kind of fong exactly after the manner of thofe at Nootka. Their heads were alfo powdered with feathers. One man held out a white garment, which we interpreted as a fign of friendfhip; and another ftood up in the canoe, quite naked, for almoft a quarter of an hour, with his arms ftretched out like a crofs, and motionlefs. The canoes were not conftructed of wood, as at King George's or Nootka Sound. The frame only, being flender laths, was of that fubftance; the outfide confifting of the fkins of feals, or of fuch like animals. Though we returned all their figns of friendfhip, and, by every expreffive gefture, tried to encourage them to come along-fide, we could not prevail. Some of our people repeated feveral of the common words of the Nootka language, fuch as *feekemaile*, and *mahook*; but they did not feem to underftand them. After receiving fome prefents, which were thrown to them, they retired toward that part of the fhore from whence they came; giving us to underftand by figns, that they would vifit us again the next morning. Two of them, however, each in a fmall canoe, waited upon us in the night; probably with a defign to pilfer fomething, thinking we fhould be all afleep; for they retired as foon as they found themfelves difcovered.

During the night, the wind was at South South Eaft, blowing hard and in fqualls, with rain, and very thick weather. At ten o'clock next morning, the wind became more moderate, and the weather being fomewhat clearer, we got under fail, in order to look out for fome fnug place, where we might fearch for, and ftop the leak; our prefent ftation being too much expofed for this purpofe. At firft, I propofed to have gone up the bay, before which we had an-

chored;

chored; but the clearnefs of the weather tempted me to steer to the Northward, farther up the great inlet, as being all in our way. As foon as we had paffed the North Weft point of the bay above mentioned, we found the coaft on that fide to turn fhort to the Eaftward. I did not follow it, but continued our courfe to the North, for a point of land which we faw in that direction.

The natives who vifited us the preceding evening, came off again in the morning, in five or fix canoes; but not till we were under fail; and although they followed us for fome time, they could not get up with us. Before two in the afternoon, the bad weather returned again, with fo thick a haze, that we could fee no other land befides the point juft mentioned, which we reached at half paft four, and found it to be a fmall ifland, lying about two miles from the adjacent coaft, being a point of land, on the Eaft fide of which we difcovered a fine bay, or rather harbour. To this we plied up, under reefed topfails and courfes. The wind blew ftrong at South Eaft, and in exceffively hard fqualls, with rain. At intervals, we could fee land in every direction; but in general the weather was fo foggy, that we could fee none but the fhores of the bay into which we were plying. In paffing the ifland, the depth of water was twenty-fix fathoms, with a muddy bottom. Soon after, the depth increafed to fixty and feventy fathoms, a rocky bottom; but in the entrance of the bay, the depth was from thirty to fix fathoms; the laft very near the fhore. At length, at eight o'clock, the violence of the fqualls obliged us to anchor in thirteen fathoms, before we had got fo far into the bay as I intended; but we thought ourfelves fortunate that we had already fufficiently fecured ourfelves at this hour; for the night was exceedingly ftormy.

The

The weather, bad as it was, did not hinder three of the natives from paying us a vifit. They came off in two canoes; two men in one, and one in the other; being the number each could carry. For they were built and conftructed in the fame manner with thofe of the Efquimaux; only, in the one were two holes for two men to fit in; and in the other but one. Each of thefe men had a ftick, about three feet long, with the large feathers or wing of birds tied to it. Thefe they frequently held up to us; with a view, as we guefled, to exprefs their pacific difpofition *.

The treatment thefe men met with, induced many more to vifit us, between one and two the next morning, in both great and fmall canoes. Some ventured on board the fhip; but not till fome of our people had ftepped into their boats. Amongft thofe who came on board, was a good-looking middle-aged man, whom we afterward found to be the Chief. He was clothed in a drefs made of the fea-otter's fkin; and had on his head fuch a cap as is worn by the people of King George's Sound, ornamented with fky-blue glafs beads, about the fize of a large pea. He feemed to fet a much higher value upon thefe, than upon our white glafs beads. Any fort of beads, however, appeared to be in high eftimation with thefe people; and they readily gave whatever they had in exchange for them; even their fine fea-otter fkins. But here I muft obferve, that they fet no more value upon thefe than upon other

---

* Exactly correfponding to this, was the manner of receiving Beering's people, at the Schumagin Iflands, on this coaft, in 1741. ' Muller's words are—" On fait ce que c'eft " que le *Calumet*, que les Américains feptentrionaux préfentent en figne de paix. Ceux-ci " en tenoient de pareils en main. C'étoient des bâtons avec *ailes de faucon* attachées au " bout." *Decouvertes*, p. 268.

fkins,

skins, which was also the case at King George's Sound, till our people set a higher price upon them; and even after that, the natives of both places would sooner part with a dress made of these, than with one made of the skins of wild-cats or of martins.

These people were also desirous of iron; but they wanted pieces eight or ten inches long at least, and of the breadth of three or four fingers. For they absolutely rejected small pieces. Consequently, they got but little from us; iron having, by this time, become rather a scarce article. The points of some of their spears or lances were of that metal; others were of copper; and a few of bone; of which the points of their darts, arrows, &c. were composed. I could not prevail upon the Chief to trust himself below the upper deck; nor did he and his companions remain long on board. But while we had their company, it was necessary to watch them narrowly, as they soon betrayed a thievish disposition. At length, after being about three or four hours along-side the Resolution, they all left her, and went to the Discovery; none having been there before, except one man, who, at this time, came from her, and immediately returned thither in company with the rest. When I observed this, I thought this man had met with something there, which he knew would please his countrymen better than what they met with at our ship. But in this I was mistaken, as will soon appear.

As soon as they were gone, I sent a boat to sound the head of the bay. For, as the wind was moderate, I had thoughts of laying the ship ashore, if a convenient place could be found where I might begin our operations to stop the leak. It was not long before all the Americans left the Discovery, and instead of returning to us, made

their

their way toward our boat employed as above. The officer
in her feeing this, returned to the ship, and was followed
by all the canoes. The boat's crew had no fooner come
on board, leaving in her two of their number by way of
a guard, than fome of the Americans ftepped into her.
Some prefented their fpears before the two men; others
caft loofe the rope which faftened her to the ship; and the
reft attempted to tow her away. But the inftant they faw
us preparing to oppofe them, they let her go, ftepped out
of her into their canoes, and made figns to us to lay down
our arms, having the appearance of being as perfectly
unconcerned as if they had done nothing amifs. This,
though rather a more daring attempt, was hardly equal to
what they had meditated on board the Difcovery. The
man who came and carried all his countrymen from the
Refolution to the other ship, had firft been on board of
her; where, after looking down all the hatchways, and feeing nobody but the officer of the watch, and one or two
more, he no doubt thought they might plunder her with
eafe; efpecially as she lay at fome diftance from us. It was
unqueftionably with this view, that they all repaired to her.
Several of them, without any ceremony, went on board;
drew their knives; made figns to the officer and people on
deck to keep off; and began to look about them for plunder. The firft thing they met with was the rudder of one
of the boats, which they threw over-board to thofe of their
party who had remained in the canoes. Before they had
time to find another object that pleafed their fancy, the
crew were alarmed, and began to come upon deck armed
with cutlaffes. On feeing this, the whole company of plun-
derers fneaked off into their canoes, with as much deli-
beration and indifference as they had given up the boat;
                                                      and

and they were obferved defcribing to thofe who had not
been on board, how much longer the knives of the fhip's
crew were than their own. It was at this time, that my
boat was on the founding duty; which they muft have
feen; for they proceeded directly for her, after their dif-
appointment at the Difcovery. I have not the leaft doubt,
that their vifiting us fo very early in the morning was with
a view to plunder; on a fuppofition, that they fhould find
every body afleep.

May we not, from thefe circumftances, reafonably infer,
that thefe people are unacquainted with fire-arms? For
certainly, if they had known any thing of their effect, they
never would have dared to attempt taking a boat from under a fhip's guns, in the face of above a hundred men; for
moft of my people were looking at them, at the very inftant they made the attempt. However, after all thefe
tricks, we had the good fortune to leave them as ignorant,
in this refpect, as we found them. For they neither heard
nor faw a mufquet fired, unlefs at birds.

Juft as we were going to weigh the anchor, to proceed
farther up the bay, it began to blow and to rain as hard as
before; fo that we were obliged to bear away the cable
again, and lay faft. Toward the evening, finding that the
gale did not moderate, and that it might be fome time before an opportunity offered to get higher up, I came to a
refolution to heel the fhip where we were; and, with this
view, moored her with a kedge-anchor and hawfer. In
heaving the anchor out of the boat, one of the feamen,
either through ignorance or carelefsnefs, or both, was carried over-board by the buoy-rope, and followed the anchor
to the bottom. It is remarkable, that, in this very critical
fituation, he had prefence of mind to difengage himfelf, and
come

come up to the furface of the water, where he was taken up,
with one of his legs fractured in a dangerous manner.

Early the next morning, we gave the fhip a good heel to
port, in order to come at, and ftop the leak. On ripping
off the fheathing, it was found to be in the feams, which
were very open, both in and under the wale; and, in feveral places, not a bit of oakum in them. While the carpenters were making good thefe defects, we filled all our empty
water-cafks, at a ftream hard by the fhip. The wind was
now moderate, but the weather was thick and hazy, with
rain.

The natives, who left us the preceding day, when the
bad weather came on, paid us another vifit this morning.
Thofe who came firft, were in fmall canoes; others, afterward, arrived in large boats; in one of which were twenty
women, and one man, befides children.

In the evening of the 16th, the weather cleared up; and
we then found ourfelves furrounded on every fide by land.
Our ftation was on the Eaft-fide of the Sound, in a place,
which in the chart is diftinguifhed by the name of *Snug
Corner Bay*. And a very fnug place it is. I went, accompanied by fome of the officers, to view the head of it; and
we found that it was fheltered from all winds; with a depth
of water from feven to three fathoms over a muddy bottom.
The land, near the fhore, is low; part clear, and part wooded. The clear ground was covered, two or three feet thick,
with fnow; but very little lay in the woods. The very
fummits of the neighbouring hills were covered with
wood; but thofe farther inland feemed to be naked rocks,
buried in fnow.

The leak being ftopped, and the fheathing made good
over it, at four o'clock in the morning of the 17th, we
VOL. II. 3 A weighed,

weighed, and fteered to the North-weftward, with a light
breeze at Eaft North Eaft; thinking, if there fhould be any
paffage to the North through this inlet, that it muft be in
that direction.   Soon after we were under fail, the natives,
in both great and fmall canoes, paid us another vifit, which
gave us an additional opportunity of forming a more perfect idea of their perfons, drefs, and other particulars, which
fhall be afterward defcribed. Our vifiters feemed to have no
other bufinefs, but to gratify their curiofity ; for they entered into no fort of traffic with us.   After we had got over
to the North Weft point of the arm in which we had anchored, we found that the flood-tide came into the inlet,
through the fame channel by which we had entered.   Although this circumftance did not make wholly againft a
paffage, it was, however, nothing in its favour.   After paffing the point above mentioned, we met with a good deal of
foul ground, and many funken rocks, even out in the
middle of the channel, which is here five or fix leagues
wide.   At this time the wind failed us, and was fucceeded
by calms and light airs from every direction; fo that we
had fome trouble to extricate ourfelves from the threatening danger.   At length, about one o'clock, with the affiftance of our boats, we got to an anchor, under the Eaftern
fhore, in thirteen fathoms water, and about four leagues
to the North of our laft ftation.   In the morning, the weather had been very hazy ; but it afterward cleared up, fo
as to give us a diftinct view of all the land round us, particularly to the Northward, where it feemed to clofe.   This
left us but little hopes of finding a paffage that way ; or,
indeed, in any other direction, without putting out again
to fea.

    To enable me to form a better judgment, I difpatched Mr.
                        I   Gore,

Gore, with two armed boats, to examine the Northern arm; and the mafter, with two other boats, to examine another arm that feemed to take an Eafterly direction. Late in the evening, they both returned. The Mafter reported, that the arm he had been fent to, communicated with that from which we had laft come; and that one fide of it was only formed by a group of iflands. Mr. Gore informed me, that he had feen the entrance of an arm, which, he was of opinion, extended a long way to the North Eaft; and that, probably by it, a paffage might be found. On the other hand, Mr. Roberts, one of the mates, whom I had fent with Mr. Gore to fketch out the parts they had examined, was of opinion, that they faw the head of this arm. The difagreement of thefe two opinions, and the circumftance already mentioned of the flood-tide entering the Sound from the South, rendered the exiftence of a paffage this way very doubtful. And, as the wind in the morning had become favourable for getting out to fea, I refolved to fpend no more time in fearching for a paffage in a place that promifed fo little fuccefs. Befides this, I confidered, that, if the land on the Weft fhould prove to be iflands, agreeably to the late Ruffian Difcoveries *, we could not fail of getting far enough to the North, and that in good time; provided we did not lofe the feafon in fearching places, where a paffage was not only doubtful, but improbable. We were now upward of five hundred and twenty leagues to the Weftward of any part of Baffin's, or of Hudfon's Bay. And whatever paffage there may be, it muft be, or, at leaft, part of it, muft lie to the North of latitude 72° †.

* Captain Cook feems to take his ideas of thefe from Mr. Stœhlin's map, prefixed to the Account of the Northern Archipelago; publifhed by Dr. Maty. London, 1774.

† On what evidence Captain Cook formed his judgment as to this, is mentioned in the Introduction.

Who

Who could expect to find a passage or strait of such extent?

Having thus taken my resolution, next morning at three o'clock, we weighed, and with a gentle breeze at North, proceeded to the Southward down the inlet; and met with the same broken ground, as on the preceding day. However, we soon extricated ourselves from it, and afterward never struck ground with a line of forty fathoms. Another passage into this inlet was now discovered, to the South West of that by which we came in, which enabled us to shorten our way out to sea. It is separated from the other by an island, extending eighteen leagues in the direction of North East and South West; to which I gave the name of *Montagu Island.*

In this South West channel are several islands. Those that lie in the entrance, next the open sea, are high and rocky. But those within are low ones; and being entirely free from snow, and covered with wood and verdure, on this account they were called *Green Islands.*

At two in the afternoon, the wind veered to the South West, and South West by South, which reduced us to the necessity of plying. I first stretched over to within two miles of the Eastern shore, and tacked in fifty-three fathoms water. In standing back to Montagu Island, we discovered a ledge of rocks; some above, and others under water, lying three miles within, or to the North of the Northern point of Green Islands. Afterward, some others were seen in the middle of the channel farther out than the islands. These rocks made unsafe plying in the night (though not very dark); and, for that reason, we spent it standing off and on, under Montagu Island; for the depth of water was too great to come to an anchor.

At

At day-break, the next morning, the wind came more favourable, and we fteered for the channel between Montagu Ifland and the Green Iflands, which is between two and three leagues broad, and from thirty-four to feventeen fathoms deep. We had but little wind all the day ; and, at eight o'clock in the evening, it was a dead calm ; when we anchored in twenty-one fathoms water, over a muddy bottom ; about two miles from the fhore of Montagu's Ifland. The calm continued till ten o'clock the next morning, when it was fucceeded by a fmall breeze from the North, with which we weighed ; and, by fix o'clock in the evening, we were again in the open fea, and found the coaft trending Weft by South, as far as the eye could reach.

C H A P.

CHAP. V.

*The Inlet called Prince William's Sound.—Its Extent.—Per-
sons of the Inhabitants described.—Their Dress.—Incision of
the Under-lip.—Various other Ornaments.—Their Boats.—
Weapons, fishing, and hunting Instruments.—Utensils.—
Tools.—Uses, Iron is applied to.—Food.—Language, and a
Specimen of it.—Animals.—Birds.—Fish.—Iron and Beads,
whence received.*

1778.
May.
TO the inlet, which we had now left, I gave the name
of *Prince William's Sound.* To judge of this Sound
from what we faw of it, it occupies, at leaft, a degree and
a half of latitude, and two of longitude, exclufive of the
arms or branches, the extent of which is not known. The
direction which they feemed to take, as alfo the fituation
and magnitude of the feveral iflands in and about it, will
be beft feen in the fketch, which is delineated with as
much accuracy as the fhort time and other circumftances
would allow.

The natives, who came to make us feveral vifits while
we were in the Sound, were generally not above the common height; though many of them were under it. They
were fquare, or ftrong chefted; and the moft difpropor-
tioned part of their body feemed to be their heads, which
were very large; with thick, fhort necks; and large, broad
or fpreading faces; which, upon the whole, were flat. Their
eyes, though not fmall, fcarcely bore a proportion to the
size

fize of their faces; and their nofes had full, round points, hooked, or turned up at the tip. Their teeth were broad, white, equal in fize, and evenly fet. Their hair was black, thick, ftraight and ftrong; and their beards, in general, thin, or wanting; but the hairs about the lips of thofe who have them, were ftiff or briftly, and frequently of a brown colour. And feveral of the elderly men had even large and thick, but ftraight beards.

Though, in general, they agree in the make of their perfons, and largenefs of their heads, there is a confiderable variety in their features; but very few can be faid to be of the handfome fort, though their countenance commonly indicates a confiderable fhare of vivacity, good-nature, and franknefs. And yet fome of them had an air of fullennefs and referve. Some of the women have agreeable faces; and many are eafily diftinguifhable from the men by their features, which are more delicate; but this fhould be underftood chiefly of the youngeft fort, or middle-aged. The complexion of fome of the women, and of the children, is white; but without any mixture of red. And fome of the men, who were feen naked, had rather a brownifh or fwarthy caft, which could fcarcely be the effect of any ftain; for they do not paint their bodies.

Their common drefs (for men, women, and children are clothed alike), is a kind of clofe frock, or rather robe; reaching generally to the ankles, though fometimes only to the knees. At the upper part is a hole juft fufficient to admit the head, with fleeves that reach to the wrift. Thefe frocks are made of the fkins of different animals; the moft common of which are thofe of the fea-otter, grey fox, racoon, and pine martin; with many of feal fkins; and, in general, they are worn with the hairy fide outward. Some

alfo

alfo have thefe frocks made of the fkins of fowls, with only the down remaining on them, which they glue on other fubftances. And we faw one or two woollen garments like thofe of Nootka. At the feams, where the different fkins are fewed together, they are commonly ornamented with taffels or fringes of narrow thongs, cut out of the fame fkins. A few have a kind of cape, or collar; and fome a hood; but the other is the moft common form, and feems to be their whole drefs in good weather. When it rains, they put over this another frock, ingenioufly made from the inteftines of whales, or fome other large animal, prepared fo fkilfully, as almoft to refemble our gold-beater's leaf. It is made to draw tight round the neck; its fleeves reach as low as the wrift, round which they are tied with a ftring; and its fkirts, when they are in their canoes, are drawn over the rim of the hole in which they fit; fo that no water can enter. At the fame time, it keeps the men entirely dry upward. For no water can penetrate through it, any more than through a bladder. It muft be kept continually moift or wet; otherwife it is apt to crack or break. This, as well as the common frock, made of the fkins, bears a great refemblance to the drefs of the Green-landers, as defcribed by Crantz *.

In general, they do not cover their legs, or feet; but a few have a kind of fkin ftockings, which reach half-way

---

* Crantz's Hiftory of Greenland, Vol. i. p. 136—138. The reader will find in Crantz many very ftriking inftances, in which the Greenlanders, and Americans of Prince William's Sound, refemble each other, befides thofe mentioned in this Chapter by Captain Cook. The drefs of the people of Prince William's Sound, as defcribed by Captain Cook, alfo agrees with that of the inhabitants of Schumagin's Iflands, difcovered by Beering in 1741. Muller's words are, "Leur habillement étoit de boyaux de "baleines pour le haut du corps, et de peaux de chiens-marins pour le bas." *Découvertes des Ruffes*, p. 274.

up the thigh; and scarcely any of them are without mittens for the hands, made of the skins of bears paws. Those who wear any thing on their heads, resembled, in this respect, our friends at Nootka; having high truncated conic caps, made of straw, and sometimes of wood, resembling a seal's head well painted.

The men commonly wear the hair cropt round the neck and forehead; but the women allow it to grow long; and most of them tie a small lock of it on the crown; or a few club it behind, after our manner. Both sexes have the ears perforated with several holes, about the outer and lower part of the edge, in which they hang little bunches of beads, made of the same tubulous shelly substance used for this purpose by those of Nootka. The *septum* of the nose is also perforated; through which they frequently thrust the quill-feathers of small birds, or little bending ornaments, made of the above shelly substance, strung on a stiff string or cord, three or four inches long, which give them a truly grotesque appearance. But the most uncommon and unsightly ornamental fashion, adopted by some of both sexes, is their having the under-lip slit, or cut, quite through, in the direction of the mouth, a little below the swelling part. This incision, which is made even in the sucking children, is often above two inches long; and either by its natural retraction, when the wound is fresh, or by the repetition of some artificial management, assumes the true shape of lips, and becomes so large as to admit the tongue through. This happened to be the case, when the first person having this incision was seen by one of the seamen, who called out, that the man had two mouths; and, indeed, it does not look unlike it. In this artificial mouth they stick a flat, narrow ornament, made chiefly out of a solid shell or bone, cut into

VOL. II. 3 B little

little narrow pieces, like fmall teeth, almoft down to the bafe or thickeft part, which has a fmall projecting bit at each end that fupports it when put into the divided lip; the cut part then appearing outward. Others have the lower lip only perforated into feparate holes; and then the ornament confifts of as many diftinct fhelly ftuds, whofe points are pufhed through thefe holes, and their heads appear within the lip, as another row of teeth immediately under their own.

Thefe are their native ornaments. But we found many beads of European manufacture among them, chiefly of a pale blue colour, which they hang in their ears; about their caps; or join to their lip-ornaments, which have a fmall hole drilled in each point to which they are faftened, and others to them, till they hang fometimes as low as the point of the chin. But, in this laft cafe, they cannot remove them fo eafily; for, as to their own lip-ornaments, they can take them out with their tongue, or fuck them in, at pleafure. They alfo wear bracelets of the fhelly beads, or others of a cylindrical fhape, made of a fubftance like amber; with fuch alfo as are ufed in their ears and nofes. And fo fond are they, in general, of ornament, that they ftick any thing in their perforated lip; one man appearing with two of our iron nails projecting from it like prongs; and another endeavouring to put a large brafs button into it.

The men frequently paint their faces of a bright red, and of a black colour, and fometimes of a blue, or leaden colour; but not in any regular figure; and the women, in fome meafure, endeavoured to imitate them, by puncturing or ftaining the chin with black, that comes to a point in each cheek; a practice very fimilar to which is in fafhion
amongft

amongſt the females of Greenland, as we learn from
Crantz *. Their bodies are not painted, which may be
owing to the ſcarcity of proper materials; for all the colours
which they brought to ſell in bladders, were in very ſmall
quantities. Upon the whole, I have no where ſeen ſavages
who take more pains than theſe people do, to ornament, or
rather to disfigure their perſons.

Their boats or canoes are of two ſorts; the one being
large and open, and the other ſmall and covered. I mentioned already, that in one of the large boats were twenty
women, and one man, beſides children. I attentively examined and compared the conſtruction of this, with Crantz's
deſcription of what he calls the great, or women's boat in
Greenland, and found that they were built in the ſame
manner, parts like parts, with no other difference than in
the form of the head and ſtern; particularly of the firſt,
which bears ſome reſemblance to the head of a whale. The
framing is of ſlender pieces of wood, over which the ſkins
of ſeals, or of other larger ſea-animals, are ſtretched, to
compoſe the outſide. It appeared alſo, that the ſmall canoes
of theſe people are made nearly of the ſame form, and of
the ſame materials with thoſe uſed by the Greenlanders †
and Eſquimaux; at leaſt the difference is not material.
Some of theſe, as I have before obſerved, carry two men.
They are broader in proportion to their length than thoſe
of the Eſquimaux; and the head or fore-part curves ſomewhat like the head of a violin.

The weapons, and inſtruments for fiſhing and hunting,
are the very ſame that are made uſe of by the Eſquimaux
and Greenlanders; and it is unneceſſary to be particular in
my account of them, as they are all very accurately deſcribed

* Vol. i. p. 138.   † See Crantz, Vol. i. p. 150.

by Crantz *. I did not fee a fingle one with thefe people that he has not mentioned; nor has he mentioned one that they have not. For defenfive armour they have a kind of jacket, or coat of mail, made of thin laths, bound together with finews, which makes it quite flexible, though fo clofe as not to admit an arrow or dart. It only covers the trunk of the body, and may not be improperly compared to a woman's ftays.

As none of thefe people lived in the bay where we anchored, or where any of us landed, we faw none of their habitations; and I had not time to look after them. Of their domeftic utenfils, they brought in their boats fome round and oval fhallow difhes of wood; and others of a cylindrical fhape much deeper. The fides were made of one piece, bent round, like our chip-boxes, though thick, neatly faftened with thongs, and the bottoms fixed in with fmall wooden pegs. Others were fmaller, and of a more elegant fhape, fomewhat refembling a large oval butter-boat, without a handle, but more fhallow, made from a piece of wood, or horny fubftance. Thefe laft were fometimes neatly carved. They had many little fquare bags, made of the fame gut with their outer frocks, neatly ornamented with very minute red feathers interwoven with it, in which were contained fome very fine finews, and bundles of fmall cord, made from them, moft ingenioufly plaited. They alfo brought many chequered bafkets, fo clofely wrought as to hold water; fome wooden models of their canoes; a good many little images, four or five inches long, either of wood, or ftuffed; which were covered with a bit of fur, and ornamented with pieces of fmall quill

* Vol. i. p. 146. He has alfo given a reprefentation of them on a plate there inferted.

feathers,

feathers, in imitation of their fhelly beads, with hair fixed on their heads. Whether thefe might be mere toys for children, or held in veneration, as reprefenting their deceafed friends, and applied to fome fuperftitious purpofe, we could not determine. But they have many inftruments made of two or three hoops, or concentric pieces of wood, with a crofs-bar fixed in the middle, to hold them by. To thefe are fixed a great number of dried barnacle-fhells, with threads, which ferve as a rattle, and make a loud noife, when they fhake them. This contrivance feems to be a fubftitute for the rattling-bird at Nootka; and perhaps both of them are employed on the fame occafions *.

With what tools they make their wooden utenfils, frames of boats, and other things, is uncertain; as the only one feen amongft them was a kind of ftone adze, made almoft after the manner of thofe of Otaheite, and the other iflands of the South Sea. They have a great many iron knives; fome of which are ftraight; others a little curved; and fome very fmall ones, fixed in pretty long handles, with the blades bent upward, like fome of our fhoemakers inftruments. But they have ftill knives of another fort, which are fometimes near two feet long, fhaped almoft like a dagger, with a ridge in the middle. Thefe they wear in fheaths of fkins, hung by a thong round the neck, under their robe; and they are, probably, only ufed as weapons; the other knives being apparently applied to other purpofes. Every thing they have, however, is as well and ingenioufly made, as if they were furnifhed with the moft complete tool-cheft; and their fewing, plaiting of finews,

* The rattling-ball found by Steller, who attended Beering in 1741, at no great diftance from this Sound, feems to be for a fimilar ufe. See Muller, p. 256.

and

and fmall work on their little bags, may be put in com-
petition with the moft delicate manufactures found in any
part of the known world. In fhort, confidering the otherwife uncivilized or rude ftate in which thefe people are,
their Northern fituation, amidft a country perpetually covered with fnow, and the wretched materials they have to
work with, it appears, that their invention and dexterity,
in all manual works, is at leaft equal to that of any other
nation.

The food which we faw them eat, was dried fifh, and the
flefh of fome animal, either broiled or roafted. Some of the
latter that was bought, feemed to be bear's flefh, but with a
fifhy tafte. They alfo eat the larger fort of fern root, mentioned at Nootka, either baked, or dreffed in fome other
way; and fome of our people faw them eat freely of a
fubftance which they fuppofed to be the inner part of the
pine bark. Their drink is moft probably water; for in
their boats they brought fnow in the wooden veffels, which
they fwallowed by mouthfuls. Perhaps it could be carried
with lefs trouble, in thefe open veffels, than water itfelf.
Their method of eating feems decent and cleanly; for they
always took care to feparate any dirt that might adhere to
their victuals. And though they fometimes did eat the raw
fat of fome fea animal, they cut it carefully into mouthfuls, with their fmall knives. The fame might be faid of
their perfons, which, to appearance, were always clean and
decent, without greafe or dirt; and the wooden veffels, in
which their victuals are probably put, were kept in excellent order; as well as their boats, which were neat, and free
from lumber.

Their language feems difficult to be underftood at firft;
not from any indiftinctnefs or confufion in their words and

founds,

1778.
May.

founds, but from the various fignifications they have. For they appeared to ufe the very fame word, frequently, on very different occafions; though doubtlefs this might, if our intercourfe had been of longer duration, have been found to be a miftake on our fide. The only words I could obtain, and for them I am indebted to Mr. Anderfon *, were thofe that follow; the firft of which was alfo ufed at Nootka, in the fame fenfe; though we could not trace an affinity between the two dialects in any other inftance.

Akaſhou,	*What's the name of that ?*
Namuk,	*An ornament for the ear.*
Lukluk,	*A brown ſhaggy ſkin, perhaps a bear's*
Aa,	*Yes.*
Natooneſhuk,	*The ſkin of a ſea-otter.*
Keeta,	*Give me ſomething.*
Naema,	*Give me ſomething in exchange, or barter.*
Ooonaka,	*Of, or belonging to me.—Will you barter for this that belongs to me ?*
Manaka,	
Ahleu,	*A ſpear.*
Weena, or Veena,	*Stranger—calling to one.*
Keelaſhuk,	*Guts of which they make jackets.*
Tawuk,	*Keep it.*
Amilhtoo,	*A piece of white bear's ſkin, or perhaps the hair that covered it.*
Whaehai,	*Shall I keep it ? do you give it me ?*

* We are alfo indebted to him for many remarks in this chapter, interwoven with thofe of Captain Cook, as throwing confiderable light on many parts of his journal.

Yaut,

Yaut,	*I'll go*; or *shall I go ?*
Chilke,	*One.*
Taiha,	*Two.*
Tokke,	*Three.*
(Tinke)	
Chukelo*,	*Four ?*
Koeheene,	*Five ?*
Takulai,	*Six ?*
Keichilho,	*Seven ?*
Klu, *or* Kliew,	*Eight ?*

As to the animals of this part of the continent, the fame muſt be underſtood as of thoſe at Nootka; that is, that the knowledge we have of them is entirely taken from the ſkins which the natives brought to ſell. Theſe were chiefly of ſeals; a few foxes; the whitiſh cat, or *lynx*; common and pine martins; ſmall ermines; bears; racoons; and ſea-otters. Of theſe, the moſt common were the martin, racoon, and ſea-otter ſkins, which compoſed the ordinary dreſs of the natives; but the ſkins of the firſt, which in general were of a much lighter brown than thoſe at Nootka, were far ſuperior to them in fineneſs; whereas the laſt, which, as well as the martins, were far more plentiful than at Nootka, ſeemed greatly inferior in the fineneſs and thickneſs of their fur, though they greatly exceeded them in ſize; and were almoſt all of the gloſſy black ſort, which is doubtleſs the colour moſt eſteemed in thoſe ſkins. Bear and ſeal ſkins were alſo pretty common; and the laſt were in general white, very beautifully ſpotted with black; or ſome-

---

* With regard to theſe numerals, Mr. Anderſon obſerves, that the words correſponding to ours, are not certain after paſſing *three*; and therefore he marks thoſe, about whoſe poſition he is doubtful, with a point of interrogation.

times

times fimply white; and many of the bears here were of a brown, or footy colour.

Befides thefe animals, which were all feen at Nootka, there are fome others in this place which we did not find there; fuch as, the white bear; of whofe fkins the natives brought feveral pieces, and fome entire fkins of cubs; from which their fize could not be determined. We alfo found the wolverene, or quickhatch, which had very bright colours; a larger fort of ermine than the common one, which is the fame as at Nootka, varied with a brown colour, and with fcarcely any black on its tail. The natives alfo brought the fkin of the head of fome very large animal; but it could not be pofitively determined what it was; though, from the colour and fhagginefs of the hair, and its unlikenefs to any land animal, we judged it might probably be that of the large male urfine feal, or fea-bear. But one of the moft beautiful fkins, and which feems peculiar to this place, as we never faw it before, is that of a fmall animal about ten inches long, of a brown or rufty colour on the back, with a great number of obfcure whitifh fpecks; and the fides of a blueifh afh colour, alfo with a few of thefe fpecks. The tail is not above a third of the length of its body, and is covered with hair of a whitifh colour at the edges. It is no doubt the fame with thofe called fpotted field mice, by Mr. Stæhlin *, in his fhort account of the New Northern Archipelago. But whether they be really of the moufe kind, or a fquirrel, we could not tell, for want of perfect fkins; though Mr. Anderfon was inclined to think that it is the fame animal defcribed under the name of the *Cafan* marmot, by Mr. Pennant. The number of fkins we found here, points out the great plenty of thefe feveral animals

* In his Account of Kodjak, p. 32 and 34.

juft mentioned; but it is remarkable, that we neither faw the fkins of the moofe nor of the common deer.

Of the birds mentioned at Nootka, we found here only the white-headed eagle; the fhag; the *alcyon*, or great king-fifher, which had very fine bright colours; and the hum-ming-bird, which came frequently and flew about the fhip, while at anchor; though it can fcarcely live here in the winter, which muft be very fevere. The water fowls were geefe; a fmall fort of duck, almoft like that mentioned at Kerguelen's Land; another fort which none of us knew; and fome of the black feapyes, with red bills, which we found at Van Diemen's Land, and New Zealand. Some of the people who went on fhore, killed a groufe, a fnipe, and fome plover. But though, upon the whole, the water fowls were pretty numerous, efpecially the ducks and geefe, which frequent the fhores, they were fo fhy, that it was fcarcely poffible to get within fhot; fo that we obtained a very fmall fupply of them as refrefhment. The duck men-tioned above, is as large as the common wild-duck, of a deep black colour, with a fhort pointed tail, and red feet. The bill is white, tinged with red toward the point, and has a large black fpot, almoft fquare, near its bafe, on each fide, where it is alfo enlarged or diftended. And on the forehead is a large triangular white fpot; with one ftill larger on the back part of the neck. The female has much duller colours, and none of the ornaments of the bill, except the two black fpots, which are obfcure.

There is likewife a fpecies of diver here, which feems peculiar to the place. It is about the fize of a partridge; has a fhort, black, compreffed bill; with the head and up-per part of the neck of a brown black; the reft of a deep brown, obfcurely waved with black, except the under-part,

I which

which is entirely of a blackifh caft, very minutely varied with white; the other (perhaps the female) is blacker above, and whiter below. A fmall land bird, of the finch kind, about the fize of a yellow-hammer, was alfo found; but was fufpected to be one of thofe which change their colour, with the feafon, and with their migrations. At this time, it was of a dufky brown colour, with a reddifh tail; and the fuppofed male had a large yellow fpot on the crown of the head, with fome varied black on the upper part of the neck; but the laft was on the breaft of the female.

The only fifh we got, were fome torfk and halibut, which were chiefly brought by the natives to fell; and we caught a few fculpins about the fhip; with fome purplifh ftar-fifh, that had feventeen or eighteen rays. The rocks were obferved to be almoft deftitute of fhell fifh; and the only other animal of this tribe feen, was a red crab, covered with fpines of a very large fize.

The metals we faw were copper and iron; both which, particularly the latter, were in fuch plenty, as to conftitute the points of moft of the arrows and lances. The ores, with which they painted themfelves, were a red, brittle, unctuous ochre, or iron-ore, not much unlike cinnabar in colour; a bright blue pigment, which we did not procure; and black lead. Each of thefe feems to be very fcarce, as they brought very fmall quantities of the firft and laft, and feemed to keep them with great care.

Few vegetables of any kind were feen; and the trees which chiefly grew here, were the Canadian and fpruce pine, and fome of them tolerably large.

The beads and iron found amongft thefe people, left no room to doubt, that they muft have received them from

fome civilized nation. We were pretty certain, from circumftances already mentioned, that we were the firft Europeans with whom they had ever communicated directly;
and it remains only to be decided, from what quarter they
had got our manufactures, by intermediate conveyance.
And there cannot be the leaft doubt of their having received thefe articles, through the intervention of the more inland tribes, from Hudfon's Bay, or the fettlements on the
Canadian lakes; unlefs it can be fuppofed (which however
is lefs likely) that the Ruffian traders, from Kamtfchatka,
have already extended their traffic thus far; or at leaft that
the natives of their moft Eafterly Fox Iflands communicate
along the coaft, with thofe of Prince William's Sound *.

As to the copper, thefe people feem to procure it themfelves, or at moft it paffes through few hands to them; for
they ufed to exprefs its being in a fufficient quantity amongft
them, when they offered any to barter, by pointing to their
weapons; as if to fay, that having fo much of this metal
of their own, they wanted no more.

It is, however, remarkable, if the inhabitants of this
Sound be fupplied with European articles, by way of the
intermediate traffic to the Eaft coaft, that they fhould, in

---

* There is a circumftance mentioned by Muller, in his account of Beering's voyage
to the coaft of America in 1741, which feems to decide this queftion. His people found
iron at the Schumagin Iflands, as may be fairly prefumed from the following quotation:
" Un feul homme avoit un couteau pendu à fa ceinture, qui parut fort fingulier à nos
" gens par fa figure. Il étoit long de huit pouces, et fort épais, et large à l'endroit où
" devoit être la pointe. On ne peut favoir quel étoit l'ufage de cet outil." *Découvertes
des Ruffes*, p. 274.
      If there was iron amongft the natives on this part of the American coaft, prior to the
difcovery of it by the Ruffians, and before there was any traffic with them carried on from
Kamtfchatka, what reafon can there be to make the leaft doubt of the people of Prince
William's Sound, as well as thofe of Schumagin's Iflands, having got this metal from the
only probable fource, the European fettlements on the North Eaft coaft of this continent?

return,

return, never have given to the more inland Indians any of their sea-otter skins; which would certainly have been seen, some time or other, about Hudson's Bay. But, as far as I know, that is not the case; and the only method of accounting for this, must be by taking into consideration the very great distance; which, though it might not prevent European goods coming so far, as being so uncommon, might prevent the skins, which are a common article, from passing through more than two or three different tribes, who might use them for their own clothing; and send others, which they esteemed less valuable, as being of their own animals, Eastward, till they reach the traders from Europe.

CHAP.

CHAP. VI.

Progress along the Coast.—Cape Elizabeth.—Cape St. Her-
mogenes.—Accounts of Beering's Voyage very defective.—
Point Banks.—Cape Douglas.—Cape Bede.—Mount St. Au-
gustin.—Hopes of finding a Passage up an Inlet.—The Ships
proceed up it.—Indubitable Marks of its being a River.—
Named Cook's River.—The Ships return down it.—Various
Visits from the Natives.—Lieutenant King lands, and takes
possession of the Country.—His Report.—The Resolution runs
aground on a Shoal.—Reflections on the Discovery of Cook's
River.—The considerable Tides in it accounted for.

1778.
May.

Wednes. 20.
Thursday 21.

AFTER leaving Prince William's Sound, I steered to
the South West, with a gentle breeze at North North
East; which, at four o'clock, the next morning, was succeeded by a calm; and soon after, the calm was succeeded
by a breeze from South West. This freshening, and veering to North West, we still continued to stretch to the
South West, and passed a lofty promontory; situated in the
latitude of 59° 10′, and the longitude of 207° 45′. As the
discovery of it was connected with the Princess Elizabeth's
birth-day, I named it *Cape Elizabeth*. Beyond it we could
see no land; so that, at first, we were in hopes that it was
the Western extremity of the continent; but not long after,
we saw our mistake; for fresh land appeared in sight, bearing West South West.

The

The wind, by this time, had increafed to a very ftrong gale, and forced us to a good diftance from the coaft. In the afternoon of the 22d, the gale abated; and we ftood to the Northward for Cape Elizabeth; which at noon, the next day, bore Weft, ten leagues diftant. At the fame time, a new land was feen, bearing South 77° Weft, which was fuppofed to connect Cape Elizabeth with the land we had feen to the Weftward.

The wind continued at Weft, and I ftood to the Southward till noon the next day, when we were within three leagues of the coaft which we had difcovered on the 22d. It here formed a point that bore Weft North Weft. At the fame time more land was feen extending to the Southward, as far as South South Weft; the whole being twelve or fifteen leagues diftant. On it was feen a ridge of mountains covered with fnow, extending to the North Weft, behind the firft land, which we judged to be an ifland, from the very inconfiderable quantity of fnow that lay upon it. This point of land is fituated in the latitude of 58° 15′, and in the longitude of 207° 42′; and by what I can gather from the account of Beering's voyage, and the chart that accompanies it in the Englifh edition *, I conclude, that it muft be what he called Cape St. Hermogenes. But the account of that voyage is fo very much abridged, and the chart fo extremely inaccurate, that it is hardly poffible, either by the one or by the other, or by comparing both together, to find out any one place which that navigator either faw or touched at. Were I to form a judgment of Beering's proceedings on this coaft, I fhould fuppofe that he fell in with the continent near Mount Fair-weather. But I am

* Captain Cook means Muller's; of which a tranflation had been publifhed in London fome time before he failed.

by

by no means certain, that the bay to which I have given his name, is the place where he anchored. Nor do I know, that what I called Mount St. Elias, is the same conspicuous mountain to which he gave that name. And as to his Cape St. Elias, I am entirely at a loss to pronounce where it lies.

On the North East side of Cape St. Hermogenes, the coast turned toward the North West, and appeared to be wholly unconnected with the land seen by us the preceding day. In the chart above mentioned, there is here a space, where Beering is supposed to have seen no land. This also favoured the later account published by Mr. Stæhlin, who makes Cape St. Hermogenes, and all the land that Beering discovered to the South West of it, to be a cluster of islands; placing St. Hermogenes amongst those which are destitute of wood. What we now saw, seemed to confirm this; and every circumstance inspired us with hopes of finding here a passage Northward, without being obliged to proceed any farther to the South West.

We were detained off the Cape, by variable light airs _{Monday 25.} and calms, till two o'clock the next morning, when a breeze springing up at North East, we steered North North West along the coast; and soon found the land of Cape St. Hermogenes to be an island, about six leagues in circuit, separated from the adjacent coast by a channel one league broad. A league and a half to the North of this island, lie some rocks, above water; on the North East side of which we had from thirty to twenty fathoms water.

At noon, the island of St. Hermogenes bore South half East, eight leagues distant; and the land to the North West of it, extended from South half West to near West. In this

last

laſt direction it ended in a low point, now five leagues diſtant, which was called *Point Banks*. The latitude of the ſhip, at this time, was 58° 41′, and its longitude 207° 44′. In this ſituation, the land, which was ſuppoſed to connect Cape Elizabeth with this South Weſt land, was in ſight, bearing North Weſt half North. I ſteered directly for it; and, on a nearer approach, found it to be a group of high iſlands and rocks, entirely unconnected with any other land. They obtained the name of *Barren Iſles* from their very naked appearance. Their ſituation is in the latitude of 59°, and in a line with Cape Elizabeth and Point Banks; three leagues diſtant from the former, and five from the latter.

I intended going through one of the channels that divide theſe iſlands; but meeting with a ſtrong current ſetting againſt us, I bore up, and went to the leeward of them all. Toward the evening, the weather, which had been hazy all day, cleared up, and we got ſight of a very lofty promontory, whoſe elevated ſummit, forming two exceedingly high mountains, was ſeen above the clouds. This promontory I named *Cape Douglas*, in honour of my very good friend, Dr. Douglas, canon of Windſor. It is ſituated in the latitude of 58° 56′, and in the longitude of 206° 10′; ten leagues to the Weſtward of Barren Iſles; and twelve from Point Banks, in the direction of North Weſt by Weſt half Weſt.

Between this point and Cape Douglas, the coaſt ſeemed to form a large and deep bay; which, from ſome ſmoke that had been ſeen on Point Banks, obtained the name of *Smokey Bay*.

At day-break, the next morning, being the 26th, having got to the Northward of the Barren Iſles, we diſcovered more land,

land, extending from Cape Douglas to the North. It formed a chain of mountains of vaft height; one of which,
far more confpicuous than the reft, was named *Mount
St. Auguftin.* The difcovery of this land did not difcourage us; as it was fuppofed to be wholly unconnected with
the land of Cape Elizabeth. For, in a North North Eaft
direction, the fight was unlimited by every thing but the
horizon. We alfo thought, that there was a paffage to the
North Weft, between Cape Douglas and Mount St. Auguftin. In fhort, it was imagined, that the land on our larboard, to the North of Cape Douglas, was compofed of a
group of iflands, disjoined by fo many channels, any one
of which we might make ufe of according as the wind
fhould ferve.

With thefe flattering ideas, having a frefh gale at
North North Eaft, we ftood to the North Weft, till eight
o'clock, when we clearly faw that what we had taken for
iflands were fummits of mountains, every where connected
by lower land, which the hazinefs of the horizon had
prevented us from feeing at a greater diftance. This
land was every where covered with fnow, from the tops
of the hills down to the very fea-beach; and had every
other appearance of being part of a great continent. I
was now fully perfuaded that I fhould find no paffage by
this inlet; and my perfevering in the fearch of it here, was
more to fatisfy other people, than to confirm my own
opinion.

At this time, Mount St. Auguftin bore North, 40° Weft,
three or four leagues diftant. This mountain is of a coni-
cal figure, and of very confiderable height; but it remains
undetermined whether it be an ifland or part of the continent. Finding that nothing could be done to the Weft, we
tacked,

tacked, and ftood over to Cape Elizabeth, under which we fetched at half paft five in the afternoon. On the North fide of Cape Elizabeth, between it and a lofty promontory, named *Cape Bede* *, is a bay, in the bottom of which there appeared to be two fnug harbours. We ftood well into this bay, where we might have anchored in twenty-three fathoms water; but as I had no fuch view, we tacked and ftood to the Weftward, with the wind at North, a very ftrong gale, attended by rain, and thick hazy weather.

The next morning the gale abated; but the fame weather continued till three o'clock in the afternoon, when it cleared up. Cape Douglas bore South Weft by Weft; Mount St. Auguftin Weft half South; and Cape Bede South, 15° eaft, five leagues diftant. In this fituation, the depth of water was forty fathoms, over a rocky bottom. From Cape Bede, the coaft trended North Eaft by Eaft, with a chain of mountains inland, extending in the fame direction. The land on the coaft was woody; and there feemed to be no deficiency of harbours. But what was not much in our favour, we difcovered low land in the middle of the inlet, extending from North North Eaft, to North Eaft by Eaft half Eaft. However, as this was fuppofed to be an ifland, it did not difcourage us. About this time, we got a light breeze Southerly, and I fteered to the Weftward of this low land; nothing appearing to obftruct us in that direction. Our foundings, during the night, were from thirty to twenty-five fathoms.

On the 28th in the morning, having but very little wind, and obferving the fhip to drive to the Southward, in order to ftop her, I dropped a kedge-anchor, with an eight inch

---

* In naming this, and Mount St. Auguftin, Captain Cook was directed by our Calendar.

hawfer

hawſer bent to it. But, in bringing the ſhip up, the hawſer parted near the inner end; and we loſt both it and the an-chor. For although we brought the ſhip up with one of the bowers, and ſpent moſt of the day in ſweeping for them, it was to no effect. By an obſervation, we found our ſtation to be in the latitude of 59° 51'; the low land above mentioned extended from North Eaſt to South, 75° Eaſt; the neareſt part two leagues diſtant. The land on the Weſtern ſhore was about ſeven leagues diſtant, and extended from South 35° Weſt, to North 7° Eaſt; ſo that the extent of the inlet was now reduced to three points and a half of the compaſs; that is, from North-half Eaſt, to North Eaſt. Be-tween theſe two points no land was to be ſeen. Here was a ſtrong tide ſetting to the Southward out of the inlet. It was the ebb, and ran between three and four knots in an hour; and it was low water at ten o'clock. A good deal of ſea-weed, and ſome drift-wood, were carried out with the tide. The water too had become thick like that in rivers; but we were encouraged to proceed by finding it as ſalt at low water as the ocean. The ſtrength of the flood-tide was three knots; and the ſtream ran up till four in the after-noon.

As it continued calm all day, I did not move till eight o'clock in the evening; when, with a light breeze at Eaſt, we weighed, and ſtood to the North up the inlet. We had not been long under ſail, before the wind veered to the North, increaſing to a freſh gale, and blowing in ſqualls, with rain. This did not, however, hinder us from plying up as long as the flood continued; which was till near five o'clock the next morning. We had ſoundings from thirty-five to twenty-four fathoms. In this laſt depth we anchored about two leagues from the Eaſtern ſhore, in the latitude of 60° 8';

Friday 29.

                                                     ſome

some low land, that we judged to be an island, lying under the Western shore, extended from North half West, to North West by North, distant three or four leagues.

The weather had now become fair and tolerably clear; so that we could see any land that might lie within our horizon; and in a North North East direction no land, nor any thing to obstruct our progress, was visible. But, on each side, was a ridge of mountains, rising one behind another, without the least separation. I judged it to be low water, by the shore, about ten o'clock; but the ebb ran down till near noon. The strength of it was four knots and a half; and it fell, upon a perpendicular, ten feet three inches, that is, while we lay at anchor; so that there is reason to believe this was not the greatest fall. On the Eastern shore we now saw two columns of smoke, a sure sign that there were inhabitants.

At one in the afternoon we weighed, and plied up under double-reefed top-sails and courses, having a very strong gale at North North East, nearly right down the inlet. We stretched over to the Western shore, and fetched within two leagues of the South end of the low land, or island before mentioned, under which I intended to have taken shelter till the gale should cease. But falling suddenly into twelve fathoms water, from upward of forty, and seeing the appearance of a shoal ahead, spitting out from the low land, I tacked, and stretched back to the Eastward; and anchored under that shore in nineteen fathoms water, over a bottom of small pebble stones.

Between one and two in the morning of the 30th, we weighed again with the first of the flood, the gale having, by this time, quite abated, but still continuing contrary; so that we plied up till near seven o'clock, when the tide being

being done, we anchored in nineteen fathoms, under the same shore as before. The North West part of it, forming a bluff point, bore North, 20° East, two leagues diftant; a point on the other shore oppofite to it, and nearly of the fame height, bore North, 36° Weft; our latitude, by obfervation, 60° 37'.

About noon, two canoes, with a man in each, came off to the ship, from near the place where we had feen the fmoke the preceding day. They laboured very hard in paddling acrofs the ftrong tide; and hefitated a little before they would come quite clofe; but upon figns being made to them, they approached. One of them talked a great deal to no purpofe; for we did not underftand a word he faid. He kept pointing to the fhore, which we interpreted to be an invitation to go thither. They accepted a few trifles from me, which I conveyed to them from the quartergallery. Thefe men, in every refpect, refembled the people we had met with in Prince William's Sound, as to their perfons and drefs. Their canoes were alfo of the fame conftruction. One of our vifiters had his face painted jet black, and feemed to have no beard; but the other, who was more elderly, had no paint, and a confiderable beard, with a vifage much like the common fort of the Prince William's people. There was alfo fmoke feen upon the flat Weftern fhore this day, from whence we may infer, that thefe lower fpots, and iflands, are the only inhabited places.

When the flood made, we weighed, and then the canoes left us. I ftood over to the Weftern fhore, with a frefh gale at North North Eaft, and fetched under the point above mentioned. This, with the other on the oppofite fhore, contracted the channel to the breadth of four

leagues.

leagues. Through this channel ran a prodigious tide. It looked frightful to us, who could not tell whether the agitation of the water was occasioned by the stream, or by the breaking of the waves against rocks or sands. As we met with no shoal, it was concluded to be the former; but, in the end, we found ourselves mistaken. I now kept the Western shore aboard, it appearing to be the safest. Near the shore we had a depth of thirteen fathoms; and two or three miles off, forty and upward. At eight in the evening, we anchored under a point of land which bore North East, three leagues distant, in fifteen fathoms water. Here we lay during the ebb, which ran near five knots in the hour.

Until we got thus far, the water had retained the same degree of saltness at low, as at high-water; and, at both periods, was as salt as that in the ocean. But now the marks of a river displayed themselves. The water taken up this ebb, when at the lowest, was found to be very considerably fresher, than any we had hitherto tasted; insomuch that I was convinced that we were in a large river, and not in a strait, communicating with the Northern seas. But as we had proceeded thus far, I was desirous of having stronger proofs; and, therefore, weighed with the next flood in the morning of the 31st, and plied higher up, or rather drove up with the tide; for we had but little wind.

About eight o'clock, we were visited by several of the natives, in one large, and several small canoes. The latter carried only one person each; and some had a paddle with a blade at each end, after the manner of the Esquimaux. In the large canoes were men, women, and children. Before they reached the ship, they displayed a leathern frock
upon

upon a long pole, as a fign, as we underftood it, of their peaceable intentions. This frock they conveyed into the fhip, in return for fome trifles which I gave them. I could obferve no difference between the perfons, drefs, ornaments, and boats of thefe people, and thofe of Prince William's Sound, except that the fmall canoes were rather of a lefs fize, and carried only one man. We procured from them fome of their fur, dreffes, made of the fkins of fea-otters, martins, hares, and other animals; a few of their darts; and a fmall fupply of falmon and halibut. In exchange for thefe they took old clothes, beads, and pieces of iron. We found that they were in poffeffion of large iron knives, and of fky-blue glafs beads, fuch as we had found amongft the natives of Prince William's Sound. Thefe latter they feemed to value much, and confequently thofe which we now gave them. But their inclination led them, efpecially, to afk for large pieces of iron; which metal, if I was not much miftaken, they called by the name of *goone*; though, like their neighbours in Prince William's Sound, they feemed to have many fignifications to one word. They evidently fpoke the fame language; as the words *keeta, naema, oonaka,* and a few others of the moft common we heard in that Sound, were alfo frequently ufed by this new tribe. After fpending about two hours between the one fhip and the other, they all retired to the Weftern fhore.

At nine o'clock, we came to an anchor, in fixteen fathoms water, about two leagues from the Weft fhore, and found the ebb already begun. At its greateft ftrength, it ran only three knots in the hour, and fell, upon a perpendicular, after we had anchored, twenty-one feet. The weather was mifty, with drizzling rain, and clear, by turns.

At

1778.
May.

At the clear intervals, we faw an opening between the mountains on the Eaſtern ſhore, bearing Eaſt from the ſtation of the ſhips, with low land, which we ſuppoſed to be iſlands lying between us and the main land. Low land was alſo ſeen to the Northward, that ſeemed to extend from the foot of the mountains on the one ſide, to thoſe on the other ; and, at low water, we perceived large ſhoals ſtretching out from this low land ; ſome of which were at no great diſtance from us. From theſe appearances, we were in ſome doubt whether the inlet did not take an Eaſterly direction, through the above opening ; or whether that opening was only a branch of it, and the main channel continued its Northern direction through the low land now in ſight. The continuation and direction of the chain of mountains on each ſide of it, ſtrongly indicated the probability of the latter ſuppoſition.

To determine this point, and to examine the ſhoals, I diſpatched two boats, under the command of the maſter ; and, as ſoon as the flood-tide made, followed with the ſhips : but, as it was a dead calm, and the tide ſtrong, I anchored, after driving about ten miles in an Eaſt direction. At the loweſt of the preceding ebb, the water at the ſurface, and for near a foot below it, was found to be perfectly freſh ; retaining, however, a conſiderable degree of ſaltneſs at a greater depth. Beſides this, we had now many other, and but too evident, proofs of being in a great river. Such as low ſhores ; very thick and muddy water ; large trees, and all manner of dirt and rubbiſh, floating up and down with the tide. In the afternoon, the natives, in ſeveral canoes, paid us another viſit ; and trafficked with our people for ſome time, without ever giving us reaſon to accuſe them of any act of diſhoneſty.

VOL. II.   3 E   At

At two o'clock next morning, being the 1st of June, the master returned, and reported that he found the inlet, or, rather, river, contracted to the breadth of one league, by low land on each side, through which it took a Northerly direction. He proceeded three leagues through this narrow part, which he found navigable for the largest ships, being from twenty to seventeen fathoms deep. The least water, at a proper distance from the shore and shoals, was ten fathoms; and this was before he entered the narrow part. While the ebb or stream run down, the water was perfectly fresh; but, after the flood made, it became brackish; and, toward high water, very much so, even as high up as he went. He landed upon an island, which lies between this branch and the Eastern one; and upon it saw some currant bushes, with the fruit already set; and some other fruit-trees and bushes, unknown to him. The soil appeared to be clay, mixed with sand. About three leagues beyond the extent of his search, or to the Northward of it, he observed there was another separation in the Eastern chain of mountains, through which he supposed the river took a North East direction; but it seemed rather more probable that this was only another branch, and that the main channel kept its Northern direction, between the two ridges or chains of mountains before mentioned. He found that these two ridges, as they extended to the North, inclined more and more to each other, but never appeared to close; nor was any elevated land seen between them, only low land, part woody, and part clear.

All hopes of finding a passage were now given up. But as the ebb was almost spent, and we could not return against the flood, I thought I might as well take the advantage of the latter, to get a nearer view of the Eastern branch; and,

by

by that means, finally to determine whether the low land on the East side of the river was an island, as we had supposed, or not. With this purpose in view, we weighed with the first of the flood, and, having a faint breeze at North East, stood over for the Eastern shore, with boats ahead, sounding. Our depth was from twelve to five fathoms; the bottom a hard gravel, though the water was exceedingly muddy. At eight o'clock, a fresh breeze sprung up at East, blowing in an opposite direction to our course; so that I despaired of reaching the entrance of the river, to which we were plying up, before high water. But thinking that what the ships could not do, might be done by boats, I dispatched two, under the command of Lieutenant King, to examine the tides, and to make such other observations as might give us some insight into the nature of the river.

At ten o'clock, finding the ebb begun, I anchored in nine fathoms water, over a gravelly bottom. Observing the tide to be too strong for the boats to make head against it, I made a signal for them to return on board, before they had got half way to the entrance of the river they were sent to examine, which bore from us South 80° East, three leagues distant. The principal information gained by this tide's work, was the determining that all the low land, which we had supposed to be an island or islands, was one continued tract, from the banks of the great river, to the foot of the mountains, to which it joined; and that it terminated at the South entrance of this Eastern branch, which I shall distinguish by the name of *River Turnagain*. On the North side of this river, the low land again begins, and stretches out from the foot of the mountains, down to the banks of the great river; so that, before the river Turnagain, it forms a large bay, on the South side of which we were now at an-

3 E 2   chor;

chor; and where we had from twelve to five fathoms, from half-flood to high-water.

After we had entered the bay, the flood fet ftrong into the river Turnagain; and ebb came out with ftill greater force; the water falling, while we lay at anchor, twenty feet upon a perpendicular. Thefe circumftances convinced me, that no paffage was to be expected by this fide river, any more than by the main branch. However, as the water during the ebb, though very confiderably frefher, had ftill a ftrong degree of faltnefs, it is but reafonable to fuppofe, that both thefe branches are navigable by fhips, much farther than we examined them; and that by means of this river, and its feveral branches, a very extenfive inland communication lies open. We had traced it as high as the latitude of 61° 30′, and the longitude of 210°; which is feventy leagues, or more, from its entrance, without feeing the leaft appearance of its fource.

If the difcovery of this great river *, which promifes to vie with the moft confiderable ones already known to be capable of extenfive inland navigation, fhould prove of ufe either to the prefent, or to any future age, the time we fpent in it ought to be the lefs regretted. But to us, who had a much greater object in view, the delay thus occafioned was an effential lofs. The feafon was advancing apace. We knew not how far we might have to proceed to the South; and we were now convinced, that the continent of North America extended farther to the Weft, than, from the modern moft reputable charts, we had reafon to expect. This made the exiftence of a paffage into Baffin's or Hudfon's

---

* Captain Cook having here left a blank which he had not filled up with any particular name, Lord Sandwich directed, with the greateft propriety, that it fhould be called *Cook's River*.

Bays

Bays lefs probable; or, at leaft, fhewed it to be of greater extent. It was a fatisfaction to me, however, to reflect, that, if I had not examined this very confiderable inlet, it would have been affumed, by fpeculative fabricators of geography, as a fact, that it communicated with the fea to the North, or with Baffin's or Hudfon's Bay to the Eaft; and been marked, perhaps, on future maps of the world, with greater precifion, and more certain figns of reality, than the invifible, becaufe imaginary, Straits of de Fuca, and de Fonte.

In the afternoon, I fent Mr. King again, with two armed boats, with orders to land, on the Northern point of the low land, on the South Eaft fide of the river; there to difplay the flag; to take poffeffion of the country and river, in his Majefty's name; and to bury in the ground a bottle, containing fome pieces of Englifh coin, of the year 1772, and a paper, on which was infcribed the names of our fhips, and the date of our difcovery. In the mean time, the fhips were got under fail, in order to proceed down the river. The wind ftill blew frefh, Eafterly; but a calm enfued, not long after we were under way; and the flood-tide meeting us off the point where Mr. King landed (and which thence got the name of *Point Poffeffion*), we were obliged to drop anchor in fix fathoms water, with the point bearing South, two miles diftant.

When Mr. King returned, he informed me, that as he approached the fhore, about twenty of the natives made their appearance, with their arms extended; probably, to exprefs thus their peaceable difpofition, and to fhew that they were without weapons. On Mr. King's, and the gentlemen with him, landing, with mufquets in their hands, they feemed alarmed, and made figns expreffive of their requeft to lay

them

them down. This was accordingly done; and then they
fuffered the gentlemen to walk up to them, and appeared to
be cheerful and fociable. They had with them a few pieces
of frefh falmon, and feveral dogs. Mr. Law, furgeon of the
Difcovery, who was one of the party, having bought one
of the latter, took it down toward the boat, and fhot it
dead, in their fight. This feemed to furprize them exceedingly; and, as if they did not think themfelves fafe
in fuch company, they walked away; but it was foon after
difcovered, that their fpears, and other weapons, were hid
in the bufhes clofe behind them. Mr. King alfo informed
me, that the ground was fwampy, and the foil poor, light,
and black. It produced a few trees and fhrubs; fuch
as pines, alders, birch, and willows; rofe and currant
bufhes; and a little grafs; but they faw not a fingle plant
in flower.

We weighed anchor, as foon as it was high water; and,
with a faint breeze Southerly, ftood over to the Weft fhore,
where the return of the flood obliged us to anchor early
next morning. Soon after, feveral large, and fome fmall
canoes, with natives, came off, who bartered their fkins;
after which they fold their garments, till many of them
were quite naked. Amongft others, they brought a number
of white hare or rabbit fkins; and very beautiful reddifh
ones of foxes; but there were only two or three fkins of
otters. They alfo fold us fome pieces of falmon and halibut.
They preferred iron to every thing elfe offered to them in
exchange. The lip-ornaments did not feem fo frequent
amongft them, as at Prince William's Sound; but they had
more of thofe which pafs through the nofe, and, in general,
thefe were alfo much longer. They had, however, a greater
quantity of a kind of white and red embroidered work on
                                                    fome

Tuefday 2.

some parts of their garments, and on other things, such as their quivers, and knife-cases.

At half past ten, we weighed with the first of the ebb, and having a gentle breeze at South, plied down the river; in the doing of which, by the inattention and neglect of the man at the lead, the Resolution struck, and stuck fast on a bank, that lies nearly in the middle of the river, and about two miles above the two projecting bluff points before mentioned. This bank was, no doubt, the occasion of that very strong rippling, or agitation of the stream, which we had observed when turning up the river. There was not less than twelve feet depth of water about the ship, at the lowest of the ebb; but other parts of the bank were dry. As soon as the ship came aground, I made a signal for the Discovery to anchor. She, as I afterward understood, had been near ashore on the West side of the bank. As the flood-tide came in, the ship floated off, soon after five o'clock in the afternoon, without receiving the least damage, or giving us any trouble; and, after standing over to the West shore, into deep water, we anchored to wait for the ebb, as the wind was still contrary.

We weighed again with the ebb, at ten o'clock at night; and, between four and five next morning, when the tide was finished, once more cast anchor about two miles below the bluff point, on the West shore, in nineteen fathoms water. A good many of the natives came off, when we were in this station, and attended upon us all the morning. Their company was very acceptable; for they brought with them a large quantity of very fine salmon, which they exchanged for such trifles as we had to give them. Most of it was split ready for drying; and several hundred weight of it was procured for the two ships.

In

In the afternoon, the mountains, for the firft time fince our entering the river, were clear of clouds; and we difcovered a volcano in one of thofe on the Weft fide. It is in the latitude of 60° 23′; and is the firft high mountain to the North of Mount St. Auguftin. The volcano is on that fide of it that is next the river, and not far from the fummit. It did not now make any ftriking appearance, emitting only a white fmoke, but no fire.

The wind remaining Southerly, we continued to tide it down the river; and, on the 5th, in the morning, coming to the place where we had loft our kedge-anchor, made an attempt to recover it, but without fuccefs. Before we left this place, fix canoes came off from the Eaft fhore; fome conducted by one, and others by two men. They remained at a little diftance from the fhips, viewing them, with a kind of filent furprize, at leaft half an hour, without exchanging a fingle word with us, or with one another. At length, they took courage, and came along-fide; began to barter with our people; and did not leave us till they had parted with every thing they brought with them, confifting of a few fkins and fome falmon. And here it may not be improper to remark, that all the people we had met with in this river, feemed, by every ftriking inftance of refemblance, to be of the fame nation with thofe who inhabit Prince William's Sound, but differing effentially from thofe of Nootka, or King George's Sound, both in their perfons and language. The language of thefe is rather more guttural; but, like the others, they fpeak ftrongly and diftinct, in words which feem fentences.

I have before obferved, that they are in poffeffion of iron; that is, they have the points of their fpears and knives of this metal; and fome of the former are alfo made of copper.

Their

Their fpears are like our fpontoons; and their knives, which they keep in fheaths, are of a confiderable length. Thefe, with a few glafs beads, are the only things we faw amongft them that were not of their own manufacture. I have already offered my conjectures from whence they derive their foreign articles; and fhall only add here, that, if it were probable that they found their way to them from fuch of their neighbours with whom the Ruffians may have eftablifhed a trade, I will be bold to fay, the Ruffians themfelves have never been amongft them: for if that had been the cafe, we fhould hardly have found them clothed in fuch valuable fkins as thofe of the fea-otter.

There is not the leaft doubt, that a very beneficial fur trade might be carried on with the inhabitants of this vaft coaft. But unlefs a Northern paffage fhould be found practicable, it feems rather too remote for Great Britain to receive any emolument from it. It muft, however, be obferved, that the moft valuable, or rather the only valuable fkins, I faw on this Weft fide of America, were thofe of the fea-otter. All their other fkins feemed to be of an inferior quality; particularly thofe of their foxes and martins. It muft alfo be obferved, that moft of the fkins, which we purchafed, were made up into garments. However, fome of thefe were in good condition; but others were old and ragged enough; and all of them very loufy. But as thefe poor people make no other ufe of fkins but for clothing themfelves, it cannot be fuppofed that they are at the trouble of dreffing more of them than are neceffary for this purpofe. And, perhaps, this is the chief ufe for which they kill the animals; for the fea and the rivers feem to fupply them with their principal articles of food. It would, probably, be much otherwife, were they once habituated to a

conftant trade with foreigners. This intercourfe would increafe their wants, by introducing them to an acquaintance
with new luxuries; and, in order to be enabled to purchafe
thefe, they would be more affiduous in procuring fkins,
which they would foon difcover to be the commodity moft
fought for; and a plentiful fupply of which, I make no
doubt, would be had in the country.

It will appear, from what has been faid occafionally of the
tide, that it is confiderable in this river, and contributes very
much to facilitate the navigation of it. It is high-water in
the ftream, on the days of the new and full moon, between
two and three o'clock; and the tide rifes, upon a perpendicular, between three and four fathoms. The reafon of the
tide's being greater here, than at other parts of this coaft,
is eafily accounted for. The mouth of the river being fituated in a corner of the coaft, the flood that comes from the
ocean is forced into it by both fhores, and by that means
fwells the tide to a great height. A view of the chart will
illuftrate this.

The variation of the compafs was 25° 40′ Eaft.

C H A P.

C H A P. VII.

Discoveries after leaving Cook's River.—Iſland of St. Her-
mogenes.—Cape Whitſunday.—Cape Greville.—Cape Bar-
nabàs.— Two-headed Point.— Trinity Iſland.— Beering's
Foggy Iſland.—A beautiful bird deſcribed.—Kodiak and the
Schumagin Iſlands.—A Ruſſian Letter brought on board by
a Native.— Conjectures about it.— Rock Point.—Halibut
Iſland.— A Volcano Mountain.— Providential Eſcape.—
Arrival of the Ships at Oonalaſchka.— Intercourſe with
the Natives there.—Another Ruſſian Letter.—Samgunoodha
Harbour deſcribed.

A S ſoon as the ebb tide made in our favour, we weighed, and, with a light breeze, between Weſt South Weſt, and South South Weſt, plied down the river, till the flood obliged us to anchor again. At length, about one o'clock, next morning, a freſh breeze ſprung up at Weſt, with which we got under ſail, and, at eight, paſſed the Barren Iſlands, and ſtretched away for Cape St. Hermogenes. At noon, this Cape bore South South Eaſt, eight leagues diſtant ; and the paſſage between the iſland of that name, and the main land, bore South. For this paſſage I ſteered, intending to go through it. But ſoon after the wind failed us ; and we had baffling light airs from the Eaſtward ; ſo that I gave up my deſign of carrying the ſhips between the iſland and the main.

1778.
June.
Friday 5.

Saturday 6.

3 F 2

At

At this time we faw feveral columns of fmoke on the coaft of the continent, to the Northward of the paffage; and, moft probably, they were meant as fignals to attract us thither. Here the land forms a bay, or perhaps a harbour; off the North Weft point of which lies a low, rocky ifland. There are alfo fome other iflands of the fame appearance, fcattered along the coaft, between this place and Point Banks.

At eight in the evening, the ifland of St. Hermogenes extended from South half Eaft, to South South Eaft, a quarter Eaft; and the rocks that lie on the North fide of it bore South Eaft, three miles diftant. In this fituation, we had forty fathoms water over a bottom of fand and fhells. Soon after, on putting over hooks and lines, we caught feveral halibut.

At midnight, being paft the rocks, we bore up to the Southward; and, at noon, St. Hermogenes bore North, four leagues diftant. At this time, the Southernmoft point of the main land, within or to the Weftward of St. Hermogenes, lay North half Weft, diftant five leagues. This promontory, which is fituated in the latitude of 58° 15′, and in the longitude of 207° 24′, was named, after the day, *Cape Whitfunday*. A large bay, which lies to the Weft of it, obtained the name of *Whitfuntide Bay*. The land on the Eaft fide of this bay, of which Cape Whitfunday is the Southern point, and Point Banks the Northern one, is, in all refpects, like the ifland of St. Hermogenes; feemingly deftitute of wood, and partly free from fnow. It was fuppofed to be covered with a moffy fubftance, that gave it a brownifh caft. There were fome reafons to think it was an ifland. If this be fo, the laft-mentioned bay is only the ftrait or paffage that feparates it from the main land.

Between

Between one and two in the afternoon, the wind, which had been at North Eaſt, ſhifted at once to the Southward. It was unſettled till ſix, when it fixed at South, which was the very direction of our courſe; ſo that we were obliged to ply up the coaſt. The weather was gloomy, and the air dry, but cold. We ſtood to the Eaſtward till midnight; then tacked, and ſtood in for the land; and, between ſeven and eight in the morning of the 8th, we were within four miles of it, and not more than half a league from ſome ſunken rocks, which bore Weſt South Weſt. In this ſituation we tacked in thirty-five fathoms water, the iſland of St. Hermogenes bearing North, 20° Eaſt, and the Southernmoſt land in ſight, South.

In ſtanding in for this coaſt, we croſſed the mouth of Whitſuntide Bay, and ſaw land all round the bottom of it; ſo that either the land is connected, or elſe the points lock in, one behind another. I am more inclined to think, that the former is the caſe; and that the land, Eaſt of the bay, is a part of the continent. Some ſmall iſlands lie on the Weſt of the bay. The ſea-coaſt to the Southward of it is rather low, with projecting rocky points, between which are ſmall bays or inlets. There was no wood, and but little ſnow upon the coaſt; but the mountains, which lie at ſome diſtance inland, were wholly covered with the latter. We ſtood off till noon; then tacked, and ſtood in for the land. The latitude, at this time, was 57° 52½'; Cape St. Hermogenes bore North, 30° Weſt, eight leagues diſtant; and the Southernmoſt part of the coaſt in ſight, the ſame that was ſeen before, bore South Weſt, ten leagues diſtant. The land here forms a point, which was named *Cape Greville*. It lies in the latitude of 57° 33', and in the longitude of 207° 15'; and is diſtant fifteen leagues
from

from Cape St. Hermogenes, in the direction of South, 17° Weſt.

The three following days we had almoſt conſtant miſty weather, with drizzling rain; ſo that we ſeldom had a ſight of the coaſt. The wind was South Eaſt by South, and South South Eaſt, a gentle breeze, and the air raw and cold. With this wind and weather, we continued to ply up the coaſt, making boards of ſix or eight leagues each. The depth of water was from thirty to fifty-five fathoms, over a coarſe, black ſandy bottom.

The fog clearing up, with the change of the wind to South Weſt, in the evening of the 12th, we had a ſight of the land bearing Weſt, twelve leagues diſtant. We ſtood in for it early next morning. At noon we were not above three miles from it; an elevated point, which obtained the name of *Cape Barnabas*, lying in the latitude of 57° 13′ bore North North Eaſt half Eaſt, ten miles diſtant; and the coaſt extended from North, 42° Eaſt, to Weſt South Weſt. The North Eaſt extreme was loſt in a haze; but the point to the South Weſt, whoſe elevated ſummit terminated in two round hills, on that account was called *Two-headed Point*. This part of the coaſt, in which are ſeveral ſmall bays, is compoſed of high hills and deep vallies; and in ſome places we could ſee the tops of other hills, beyond thoſe that form the coaſt; which was but little encumbered with ſnow, but had a very barren appearance. Not a tree or buſh was to be ſeen upon it; and, in general, it had a browniſh hue, probably the effect of a moſſy covering.

I continued to ply to the South Weſt by Weſt, as the coaſt trended; and, at ſix in the evening, being midway between Cape Barnabas and Two-headed Point, and two leagues from the ſhore, the depth of water was ſixty-two fathoms.

I   From

From this ftation, a low point of land made its appearance beyond Two-headed Point, bearing South, 69° Weft; and, without it, other land that had the appearance of an ifland, bore South, 59° Weft.

At noon, on the 13th, being in latitude 56° 49', Cape St. Barnabas bore North, 52° Eaft; Two-headed Point North, 14° Weft, feven or eight miles diftant; and the coaft of the continent extended as far as South, 72°¼ Weft; and the land feen the preceding evening, and fuppofed to be an ifland, now appeared like two iflands. From whatever quarter Two-headed Point was viewed, it had the appearance of being an ifland; or elfe it is a peninfula, on each fide of which the fhore forms a bay. The wind ftill continued Wefterly, a gentle breeze; the weather rather dull and cloudy, and the air fharp and dry.

We were well up with the Southernmoft land next morning, and found it to be an ifland, which was named *Trinity Ifland*. Its greateft extent is fix leagues in the direction of Eaft and Weft. Each end is elevated naked land, and in the middle it is low; fo that, at a diftance, from fome points of view, it affumes the appearance of two iflands. It lies in the latitude of 56° 36', and in the longitude of 205°; and between two and three leagues from the continent; which fpace is interfperfed with fmall iflands and rocks; but there feemed to be good paffage enough, and alfo fafe anchorage. At firft we were inclined to think, that this was Beering's *Foggy Ifland* *; but its fituation fo near the main does not fuit his chart.

At eight in the evening, we ftood in for the land, till we were within a league of the above-mentioned fmall iflands. The Wefternmoft part of the continent now in fight, being

* *Tumannoi-oftrow*, c'eft-à-dire, *L'ifle Nebuleufe*. Muller, p. 261.

a low

a low point facing Trinity Ifland, and which we called *Cape
Trinity*, now bore Weft North Weft. In this fituation,
having tacked in fifty-four fathoms water, over a bottom of
black fand, we ftood over for the ifland, intending to work
up between it and the main. The land to the Weftward of
Two-headed Point, is not fo mountainous as it is to the
North Eaft of it, nor does fo much fnow lie upon it. There
are, however, a good many hills confiderably elevated; but
they are disjoined by large tracts of flat land that appeared
to be perfectly deftitute of wood, and very barren.

As we were ftanding over toward the ifland, we met two
men in a fmall canoe, paddling from it to the main. Far
from approaching us, they feemed rather to avoid it. The
wind now began to incline to the South; and we had reafon
to expect, that it would foon be at South Eaft. Experience having taught us, that a South Eafterly wind was here
generally, if not always, accompanied by a thick fog, I
was afraid to venture through between the ifland and the
continent, left the paffage fhould not be accomplifhed before night, or before the thick weather came on; when
we fhould be obliged to anchor, and, by that means, lofe
the advantage of a fair wind. Thefe reafons induced me
to ftretch out to fea; and we paffed two or three rocky
iflots that lie near the Eaft end of Trinity Ifland. At four
in the afternoon, having weathered the ifland, we tacked,
and fteered Weft, Southerly, with a frefh gale at South
South Eaft; which, before midnight, veered to the South
Eaft; and was, as ufual, attended with mifty, drizzling,
rainy weather.

By the courfe we fteered all night, I was in hopes of falling in with the continent in the morning. And, doubtlefs,
we fhould have feen it, had the weather been, in the leaft,
clear;

clear; but the fog prevented. Seeing no land at noon, and
the gale increafing, with a thick fog and rain, I fteered Weft
North Weft, under fuch fail as we could eafily haul the
wind with; being fully fenfible of the danger of running
before a ftrong gale in a thick fog, in the vicinity of an unknown coaft. It was, however, neceffary to run fome rifk
when the wind favoured us; for clear weather, we had
found, was generally accompanied with winds from the
Weft.

Between two and three in the afternoon, land was feen
through the fog, bearing North Weft, not more than three
or four miles diftant. Upon this, we immediately hauled
up South, clofe to the wind. Soon after, the two courfes
were fplit, fo that we had others to bring to the yards; and
feveral others of our fails received confiderable damage.
At nine, the gale abated; the weather cleared up; and we
got fight of the coaft again, extending from Weft by South
to North Weft, about four or five leagues diftant. On
founding, we found a hundred fathoms water, over a muddy bottom. Soon after, the fog returned, and we faw no
more of the land all night.

At four next morning, the fog being now difperfed, we
found ourfelves in a manner furrounded by land; the continent, or what was fuppofed to be the continent, extending from Weft South Weft to North Eaft by North; and
fome elevated land bearing South Eaft half South; by eftimation eight or nine leagues diftant. The North Eaft
extreme of the main was the fame point of land that we
had fallen in with during the fog; and we named it *Foggy
Cape*. It lies in latitude 56° 31′. At this time, having had
but little wind all night, a breeze fprung up at North Weft.

With this we stood to the Southward, to make the land, seen in that direction, plainer.

At nine o'clock, we found it to be an island of about nine leagues in compaſs; lying in the latitude of 56° 10′, and in the longitude of 202° 45′; and it is diſtinguiſhed in our chart by the name of *Foggy Iſland*; having reaſon to believe, from its ſituation, that it is the ſame which had that name given to it by Beering. At the ſame time, three or four iſlands, lying before a bay, formed by the coaſt of the main land, bore North by Weſt; a point, with three or four pinnacle rocks upon it, which was called *Pinnacle Point*, bore North Weſt by Weſt; and a cluſter of ſmall iſlots, or rocks, lying about nine leagues from the coaſt, South South Eaſt.

At noon, when our latitude was 56° 9′, and our longitude 201° 45′, theſe rocks bore South, 58′ Eaſt, ten miles diſtant; Pinnacle Point, North North Weſt, diſtant ſeven leagues; the neareſt part of the main land North Weſt by Weſt, ſix leagues diſtant; and the moſt advanced land to the South Weſt, which had the appearance of being an iſland, bore Weſt, a little Southerly. In the afternoon, we had little or no wind; ſo that our progreſs was inconſiderable. At eight in the evening, the coaſt extended from South Weſt to North North Eaſt; the neareſt part about eight leagues diſtant.

On the 17th, the wind was between Weſt and North Weſt, a gentle breeze, and ſometimes almoſt calm. The weather was clear, and the air ſharp and dry. At noon, the continent extended from South Weſt to North by Eaſt; the neareſt part ſeven leagues diſtant. A large group of iſlands lying about the ſame diſtance from

3   the

the continent, extended from South 26° Weſt, to South 52° Weſt.

It was calm great part of the 18th; and the weather was clear and pleaſant. We availed ourſelves of this, by making obſervations for the longitude and variation. The latter was found to be 21° 27′ Eaſt. There can be no doubt that there is a continuation of the continent between Trinity Iſland and Foggy Cape, which the thick weather prevented us from ſeeing. For ſome diſtance to the South Weſt of that Cape, this country is more broken or rugged than any part we had yet ſeen, both with reſpect to the hills themſelves, and to the coaſt, which ſeemed full of creeks, or ſmall inlets, none of which appeared to be of any great depth. Perhaps, upon a cloſer examination, ſome of the projecting points between theſe inlets will be found to be iſlands. Every part had a very barren aſpect; and was covered with ſnow, from the ſummits of the higheſt hills, down to a very ſmall diſtance from the ſea-coaſt.

Having occaſion to ſend a boat on board the Diſcovery, one of the people in her ſhot a very beautiful bird of the awk kind. It is ſomewhat leſs than a duck, and of a black colour, except the fore-part of the head, which is white; and from above and behind each eye ariſes an elegant yellowiſh-white creſt, revolved backward as a ram's horn. The bill and feet are red. It is, perhaps, the *alca monochroa* of Steller, mentioned in the Hiſtory of Kamtſchatka *. I think the firſt of theſe birds was ſeen by us, a little to the Southward of Cape St. Hermogenes. From that time, we generally ſaw ſome of them every day; and ſometimes in large flocks. Beſides theſe, we daily ſaw moſt of the other ſea-

* P. 153. Eng. Tranſ.—The Tufted Auk. *Pennant's Arct. Zool.* ii. N° 432.

3 G 2

birds,

birds, that are commonly found in other Northern oceans; such as gulls, fhags, puffins, fheerwaters; and fometimes ducks, geefe, and fwans. And feldom a day paffed without feeing feals, whaleʃ and other large fiſh.

In the afternoon, we got a light breeze of wind Southerly, which enabled us to fteer Weſt, for the channel that appeared between the iflands and the continent; and, at day-break next morning, we were at no great diftance from it, and found feveral other iflands, within thofe already feen by us, of various extent both in height and circuit. But between thefe laft iflands, and thofe before feen, there feemed to be a clear channel, for which I fteered, being afraid to keep the coaft of the continent aboard, left we fhould miftake fome point of it for an ifland, and, by that means, be drawn into fome inlet, and lofe the advantage of the fair wind, which at this time blew.

I therefore kept along the Southernmoft chain of iflands; and at noon we were in the latitude of 55° 18′, and in the narroweft part of the channel, formed by them and thofe which lie along the continent, where it is about a league and a half, or two leagues over. The largeft ifland in this group was now on our left, and is diftinguifhed by the name of *Kodiak* ⁕, according to the information we afterward received. I left the reft of them without names. I believe them to be the fame that Beering calls Schumagin's Iflands †; or thofe iflands which he called by that name, to be a part of them; for this group is pretty extenfive. We faw iflands as far to the Southward as an ifland could be feen. They commence in the longitude of 200° 15′ Eaft; and extend a degree and a half, or two degrees, to the Weft-

⁕ See an Account of Kodiak, in Stæhlin's New Northern Archipelago, p. 30—39.
† See Muller's *Découvertes des Ruſſes*, p. 262—277.

ward.

ward. I cannot be particular; as we could not diftinguifh all the iflands from the coaft of the continent. Moft of thefe iflands are of a good height, very barren and rugged; abounding with rocks and fteep cliffs, and exhibiting other romantic appearances. There are feveral fnug bays and coves about them; ftreams of frefh water run from their elevated parts; fome drift-wood was floating around; but not a tree or bufh was to be feen growing on the land. A good deal of fnow ftill lay on many of them; and the parts of the continent, which fhewed themfelves between the innermoft iflands, were quite covered with it.

At four in the afternoon, we had paffed all the iflands that lay to the Southward of us; the Southernmoft, at this time, bearing South 3° Eaft, and the Wefternmoft point of land now in fight, South 82° Weft. For this point we fteered, and paffed between it and two or three elevated rocks that lie about a league to the Eaft of it.

Some time after we had got through this channel, in which we found forty fathoms water, the Difcovery, now two miles aftern, fired three guns, and brought to, and made the fignal to fpeak with us. This alarmed me not a little; and, as no apparent danger had been remarked in the paffage through the channel, it was apprehended that fome accident, fuch as fpringing a leak, muft have happened. A boat was immediately fent to her; and in a fhort time returned with Captain Clerke. I now learned from him, that fome natives, in three or four canoes, who had been following the fhip for fome time, at length got under his ftern. One of them then made many figns, taking off his cap, and bowing, after the manner of Europeans. A rope being handed down from the fhip, to this he faftened a fmall thin wooden cafe or box; and having delivered this

fafe,

safe, and fpoken fomething, and made fome more figns, the canoes dropped aftern, and left the Difcovery. No one on board her had any fufpicion that the box contained any thing, till after the departure of the canoes, when it was accidentally opened, and a piece of paper was found, folded up carefully, upon which fomething was written in the Ruffian language, as was fuppofed. The date 1778 was prefixed to it; and, in the body of the written note, there was a reference to the year 1776. Not learned enough to decypher the alphabet of the writer, his numerals marked fufficiently that others had preceded us in vifiting this dreary part of the globe, who were united to us by other ties befides thofe of our common nature; and the hopes of foon meeting with fome of the Ruffian traders, could not but give a fenfible fatisfaction to thofe who had, for fuch a length of time, been converfant with the favages of the Pacific Ocean, and of the continent of North America.

Captain Clerke was, at firft, of opinion, that fome Ruffians had been fhipwrecked here; and that thefe unfortunate perfons, feeing our fhips pafs, had taken this method to inform us of their fituation. Impreffed with humane fentiments, on fuch an occafion, he was defirous of our ftopping till they might have time to join us. But no fuch idea occurred to me. It feemed obvious, that if this had been the cafe, it would have been the firft ftep taken by fuch fhipwrecked perfons, in order to fecure to themfelves, and to their companions, the relief they could not but be folicitous about, to fend fome of their body off to the fhips in the canoes. For this reafon, I rather thought that the paper contained a note of information, left by fome Ruffian trader, who had lately been amongft thefe iflands, to

be

be delivered to the next of their countrymen who fhould arrive; and that the natives, feeing our fhips pafs, and fuppofing us to be Ruffians, had refolved to bring off the note, thinking it might induce us to ftop. Fully convinced of this, I did not ftay to inquire any farther into the matter; but made fail, and ftood away to the Weftward, along the coaft: perhaps I fhould fay along the iflands; for we could not pronounce, with certainty, whether the neareft land, within us, was continent or iflands. If not the latter, 'the coaft here forms fome tolerably large and deep bays.

We continued to run all night with a gentle breeze at North Eaft; and, at two o'clock next morning, fome breakers were feen within us, at the diftance of two miles. Two hours after, others were feen ahead; and, on our larboard bow, and between us and the land, they were innumerable. We did but juft clear them, by holding a South courfe. Thefe breakers were occafioned by rocks; fome of which were above water. They extend feven leagues from the land; and are very dangerous, efpecially in thick weather, to which this coaft feems much fubject. At noon, we had juft got on their outfide; and, by obfervation, we were in the latitude of 54° 44', and in the longitude of 198°. The neareft land, being an elevated bluff point, which was called *Rock Point*, bore North, feven or eight leagues diftant; the Wefternmoft part of the main, or what was fuppofed to be the main, bore North 80° Weft; and a round hill, without, which was found to be an ifland, and was called *Halibut-head*, bore South 65° Weft, thirteen leagues diftant.

On the 21ft at noon, having made but little progrefs, on account of faint winds and calms, Halibut-head, which lies in the latitude of 54° 27', and in the longitude of 197°, bore
North

North 24° Weſt; and the iſland on which it is, and called *Halibut Iſland*, extended from North by Eaſt, to North Weſt by Weſt, two leagues diſtant. This iſland is ſeven or eight leagues in circuit; and, except the head, the land of it is low and very barren. There are ſeveral ſmall iſlands near it, all of the ſame appearance; but there ſeemed to be a paſſage between them and the main, two or three leagues broad.

The rocks and breakers, before mentioned, forced us ſo far from the continent, that we had but a diſtant view of the coaſt between Rock Point and Halibut Iſland. Over this and the adjoining iſlands we could ſee the main land covered with ſnow; but, particularly, ſome hills, whoſe elevated tops were ſeen, towering above the clouds, to a moſt ſtupendous height. The moſt South Weſterly of theſe hills was diſcovered to have a *volcano*, which conti-nually threw up vaſt columns of black ſmoke. It ſtands not far from the coaſt; and in the latitude of 54° 48′, and the longitude of 195° 45′. It is alſo remarkable, from its figure, which is a complete cone; and the *volcano* is at the very ſummit. We ſeldom ſaw this (or indeed any other of theſe mountains) wholly clear of clouds. At times, both baſe and ſummit would be clear; when a narrow cloud, ſometimes two or three, one above another, would embrace the middle, like a girdle; which, with the co-lumn of ſmoke, riſing perpendicular to a great height out of its top, and ſpreading before the wind into a tail of vaſt length, made a very picturesque appearance. It may be worth remarking, that the wind, at the height to which the ſmoke of this *volcano* reached, moved ſometimes in a direction contrary to what it did at ſea, even when it blew a freſh gale.

In

1778.
June.

In the afternoon, having three hours calm, our people caught upward of a hundred halibuts, some of which weighed a hundred pounds, and none less than twenty pounds. This was a very seasonable refreshment to us. In the height of our fishing, which was in thirty-five fathoms water, and three or four miles from the shore, a small canoe, conducted by one man, came to us from the large island. On approaching the ship, he took off his cap, and bowed, as the other had done, who visited the Discovery the preceding day. It was evident, that the Russians must have a communication and traffic with these people; not only from their acquired politeness, but from the note before mentioned. But we had now a fresh proof of it; for our present visiter wore a pair of green cloth breeches, and a jacket of black cloth, or stuff, under the gut-shirt or frock of his own country. He had nothing to barter, except a grey fox skin, and some fishing implements or harpoons; the heads of the shafts of which, for the length of a foot, or more, were neatly made of bone, as thick as a walking-cane, and carved. He had with him a bladder, full of something, which we supposed to be oil; for he opened it, took a mouthful, and then fastened it again.

His canoe was of the same make with those we had seen before; but rather smaller. He used the double-bladed paddle, as did also those who had visited the Discovery. In his size and features, he exactly resembled those we saw in Prince William's Sound, and in the Great River; but he was quite free from paint of any kind; and had the perforation of his lip made in an oblique direction, without any ornament in it. He did not seem to understand any of the words commonly used by our visiters in the Sound, when repeated to him. But, perhaps, our faulty pronunciation, rather than his ignorance of the dialect, may be inferred from this.

The weather was cloudy and hazy, with, now and then,
funshine, till the afternoon of the 22d, when the wind came round to the South East, and, as usual, brought thick rainy weather. Before the fog came on, no part of the main land was in sight, except the *volcano*, and another mountain close by it. I continued to steer West till seven in the evening, when, being apprehensive of falling in with the land in thick weather, we hauled the wind to the Southward, till two o'clock next morning, and then bore away again West. We made but little progress, having the wind variable, and but little of it, till at last it fixed in the Wes-tern board, and at five in the afternoon, having a gleam of funshine, we saw land bearing North 59° West, appearing in hillocks like islands.

At six in the morning of the 24th, we got a sight of the continent; and, at nine it was seen extending from North East by East, to South West by West, half West; the nearest part about four leagues distant. The land to the South West proved to be islands; the same that had been seen the pre-ceding evening. But the other was a continuation of the continent, without any islands to obstruct our view of it. In the evening, being about four leagues from the shore, in forty-two fathoms water, having little or no wind, we had recourse to our hooks and lines; but only two or three small cod were caught.

The next morning we got a breeze Easterly; and, what was uncommon, with this wind, clear weather; so that we not only saw the *volcano*, but other mountains, both to the East and West of it, and all the coast of the main land under them, much plainer than at any time before. It extended
from

1778.
June.

from North East by North, to North West half West, where it seemed to terminate. Between this point and the islands without it, there appeared a large opening, for which I steered, till we raised land beyond it. This land, although we did not perceive that it joined the continent, made a passage through the opening very doubtful. It also made it doubtful, whether the land which we saw to the South West, was insular or continental; and, if the latter, it was obvious that the opening would be a deep bay or inlet, from which, if once we entered it with an Easterly wind, it would not be so easy to get out. Not caring, therefore, to trust too much to appearances, I steered to the Southward. Having thus got without all the land in sight, I then steered West, in which direction the islands lay; for such we found this land to be.

By eight o'clock we had passed three of them, all of a good height. More of them were now seen to the Westward; the South Westernmost part of them bearing West North West. The weather, in the afternoon, became gloomy, and at length turned to a mist; and the wind blew fresh at East. I therefore, at ten at night, hauled the wind to the Southward till day-break, when we resumed our course to the West. Friday 26.

Day-light availed us little; for the weather was so thick, that we could not see a hundred yards before us; but as the wind was now moderate, I ventured to run. At half past four, we were alarmed at hearing the sound of breakers on our larboard bow. On heaving the lead, we found twenty-eight fathoms water; and the next cast, twenty-five. I immediately brought the ship to, with her head to the Northward, and anchored in this last depth, over a bottom of coarse sand; calling to the Discovery, she being close by us, to anchor also.

A few

A few hours after, the fog having cleared away a little, it appeared that we had escaped very imminent danger. We found ourselves three quarters of a mile from the North East side of an island, which extended from South by West half West, to North by East half East, each extreme about a league distant. Two elevated rocks, the one bearing South by East, and the other East by South, were about half a league each from us, and about the same distance from each other. There were several breakers about them; and yet Providence had, in the dark, conducted the ships through, between these rocks, which I should not have ventured in a clear day, and to such an anchoring-place, that I could not have chosen a better.

Finding ourselves so near land, I sent a boat to examine what it produced. In the afternoon she returned; and the officer, who commanded her, reported, that it produced some tolerably good grass, and several other small plants; one of which was like purslain, and eat very well, either in soups, or as a sallad. There was no appearance of shrubs or trees; but on the beach were a few pieces of drift-wood. It was judged to be low water between ten and eleven o'clock; and we found, where we lay at anchor, that the flood-tide came from the East or South East.

In the night, the wind blew fresh at South; but was more moderate toward the morning, and the fog partly dispersed. Having weighed at seven o'clock, we steered to the Northward, between the island under which we had anchored, and another small one near it. The channel is not above a mile broad; and before we were through it, the wind failed, and we were obliged to anchor in thirty-four fathoms water. We had now land in every direction. That to the South, extended to the South West, in a ridge

of

of mountains; but our fight could not determine whether it
compofed one or more iflands. We afterward found it to be
only one ifland, and known by the name of *Oonalafhka*. Between it, and the land to the North, which had the appearance of being a group of iflands, there feemed to be a channel, in the direction of North Weft by North. On a point,
which bore Weft from the fhip, three quarters of a mile
diftant, were feveral natives, and their habitations. To this
place we faw them tow in two whales, which we fuppofed
they had juft killed. A few of them, now and then, came
off to the fhips, and bartered a few trifling things with
our people; but never remained above a quarter of an hour
at a time. On the contrary, they rather feemed fhy; and
yet, we could judge that they were no ftrangers to veffels,
in fome degree, like ours. They behaved with a degree of
politenefs uncommon to favage tribes.

At one o'clock in the afternoon, having a light breeze at
North Eaft, and the tide of flood in our favour, we weighed,
and fteered for the channel above mentioned, in hopes, after we were through, of finding the land trend away to
the Northward, or, at leaft, a paffage out to fea, to the Weft.
For we fuppofed ourfelves, as it really happened, to be
amongft iflands, and not in an inlet of the continent. We
had not been long under fail, before the wind veered to the
North, which obliged us to ply. The foundings were from
forty to twenty-feven fathoms, over a bottom of fand and
mud. In the evening, the ebb making againft us, we anchored about three leagues from our laft ftation, with the
paffage bearing North Weft.

At day-break the next morning, we weighed, with a Sunday 28.
light breeze at South, which carried us up to the paffage,
when it was fucceeded by variable light airs from all directions.

I

rections.   But as there run a rapid tide in our favour, the Refolution got through before the ebb made.   The Difcovery was not fo fortunate.   She was carried back, got into the race ; and had fome trouble to get clear of it.   As foon as we were through, the land, on one fide, was found to trend Weft and South Weft ; and that on the other fide to trend North.   This gave us great reafon to hope, that the continent had here taken a new direction, which was much in our favour.   Being in want of water, and perceiving that we run fome rifk of driving about in a rapid tide, without wind to govern the fhip, I ftood for a harbour, lying on the South fide of the paffage ; but we were very foon driven paft it ; and, to prevent being forced back through the paffage, came to an anchor in twenty-eight fathoms water, pretty near the Southern fhore, out of the reach of the ftrong tide.   And yet, even here, we found it to run full five knots and a half in the hour.

While we lay here, feveral of the natives came off to us, each in a canoe ; and bartered a few fifhing implements for tobacco.   One of them, a young man, overfet his canoe, while along-fide of one of our boats.   Our people caught hold of him ; but the canoe went adrift, and, being picked up by another, was carried afhore.   The youth, by this accident, was obliged to come into the fhip ; and he went down into my cabin, upon the firft invitation, without expreffing the leaft reluctance, or uneafinefs.   His drefs was an upper garment, like a fhirt, made of the large gut of fome fea-animal, probably the whale ; and an under garment of the fame fhape, made of the fkins of birds, dreffed with the feathers on, and neatly fewed together ; the feathered fide being worn next his fkin.   It was mended, or patched, with pieces of filk-ftuff ; and his cap was
                                                    ornamented

ornamented with two or three forts of glafs beads. His own clothes being wet, I gave him others, in which he dreffed himfelf, with as much eafe as I could have done. From his behaviour, and that of fome others, we were convinced that thefe people were no ftrangers to Europeans, and to fome of their cuftoms. But there was fomething in our fhips that greatly excited their curiofity; for fuch as could not come off in canoes, affembled on the neighbouring hills to look at them.

At low water, having weighed and towed the fhip into the harbour, we anchored there in nine fathoms water, over a bottom of fand and mud. The Difcovery got in foon after. A launch was now fent for water; and a boat to draw the feine; but we caught only four trout, and a few other fmall fifh.

Soon after we anchored, a native of the ifland brought on board fuch another note as had been given to Captain Clerke. He prefented it to me; but it was written in the Ruffian language, which, as already obferved, none of us could read. As it could be of no ufe to me, and might be of confequence to others, I returned it to the bearer, and difmiffed him with a few prefents; for which he expreffed his thanks, by making feveral low bows as he retired.

In walking, next day, along the fhore, I met with a Monday 29. group of natives of both fexes, feated on the grafs, at a repaft, confifting of raw fifh, which they feemed to eat with as much relifh as we fhould a turbot, ferved up with the richeft fauce. By the evening, we had completed our water, and made fuch obfervations as the time and weather would permit. I have taken notice of the rapidity of the tide without the harbour; but it was inconfiderable within. It was low water at noon; and high water at half paft fix

in

in the evening; and the water rofe, upon a perpendicular, three feet four inches; but there were marks of its fometimes rifing a foot higher.

Thick fogs, and a contrary wind, detained us till the 2d of July; which afforded an opportunity of acquiring fome knowledge of the country and of its inhabitants. The refult of our obfervations will be mentioned in another place. At prefent I fhall only defcribe the harbour.

It is called, by the natives, *Samganoodha*; and is fituated on the North fide of Oonalafhka, in the latitude of 53° 55′, in the longitude of 193° 30′; and in the ftrait, or paffage, that feparates this ifland from thofe that lie to the North of it, and whofe pofition before the harbour fhelters it from the winds that blow from that quarter. It runs in, South by Weft, about four miles, and is about a mile broad at the entrance; narrowing toward the head, where its breadth is not above a quarter of a mile, and where fhips can lie land-locked, in feven, fix, and four fathoms water. Great plenty of good water may be eafily got; but not a fingle ftick of wood of any fize.

C H A P.

CHAP. VIII.

Progress Northward, after leaving Oonalashka.—The Islands Oonella and Acootan.—Ooneemak.—Shallowness of the Water along the Coast.—Bristol Bay.—Round Island.—Calm Point.—Cape Newenham.—Lieutenant Williamson lands, and his Report.—Bristol Bay, and its Extent.—The Ships obliged to return, on account of Shoals.—Natives come off to the Ships.—Death of Mr. Anderson; his Character; and Island named after him.—Point Rodney.—Sledge Island, and Remarks on landing there.—King's Island.— Cape Prince of Wales, the Western Extreme of America. Course Westward.—Anchor in a Bay on the Coast of Asia.

HAVING put to sea with a light breeze, at South South East, we steered to the North, meeting with nothing to obstruct us in this course. For, as I observed before, the Island of Oonalashka, on the one side, trended South West; and, on the other, no land was to be seen in a direction more Northerly than North East; the whole of which land was a continuation of the same group of islands which we had fallen in with on the 25th of June. That which lies before Samganoodha, and forms the North East side of the passage through which we came, is called *Oonella*, and is about seven leagues in circumference. Another island, to the North East of it, is called *Acootan*, which is considerably larger than Oonella, and hath in it some very high

1778.
July.
Thursday 2.

VOL. II.   3 I   mountains,

mountains, which were covered with snow. It appeared, that we might have gone very safely between these two islands and the continent, the South West point of which opened off the North East point of Acootan, in the direction of North, 60° East; and which proved to be the same point of land we had seen when we quitted the coast of the continent, on the 25th of June, to go without the islands. It is called by the people of these parts *Oonemak*, and lies in the latitude of 54° 30′, and in the longitude of 192° 30′. Over the cape, which, of itself, is high land, is a round elevated mountain, at this time entirely covered with snow.

At six in the evening, this mountain bore East, 2° North; and at eight we had no land in sight. Concluding, therefore, that the coast of the continent had now taken a North Easterly direction, I ventured to steer the same course till

Friday 3. one o'clock next morning, when the watch on deck thought they saw land ahead. Upon this we wore, and stood to the South West for two hours, and then resumed our course to the East North East.

At six o'clock, land was seen ahead, bearing South East, about five leagues distant. As we advanced, we raised more and more land, all connected, and seemingly in the direction of our course. At noon, it extended from South South West to East; the nearest part five or six leagues distant. Our latitude, at this time, was 55° 21′, and our longitude 195° 18′. This coast is on the North West side of the *volcano* mountain; so that we must have seen it, if the weather had been tolerably clear.

At six in the evening, after having run eight leagues upon an East by North course from noon, we sounded, and found forty-eight fathoms, over a bottom of black sand.

fand. Being at this time four leagues from the land, the
Eaftern part in fight bore Eaft South Eaft, and appeared as a high round hummock, feemingly detached from the main.

Having continued to fteer Eaft North Eaft all night, at eight in the morning of the 4th, the coaft was feen from South South Weft to Eaft by South; and at times we could fee high land, covered with fnow, behind it. Soon after, it fell calm, and being in thirty fathoms water, we put over hooks and lines, and caught a good number of fine cod-fifh. At noon, having now a breeze from the Eaft, and the weather being clear, we found ourfelves fix leagues from the land, which extended from South by Weft to Eaft by South. The hummock, feen the preceding evening, bore South Weft by South, ten leagues diftant. Our latitude was now 55° 50′, and our longitude 197° 3′. A great hollow fwell from Weft South Weft, affured us, that there was no main land near, in that direction. I ftood to the North till fix in the afternoon, when the wind having veered to South Eaft, enabled us to fteer Eaft North Eaft. The coaft lay in this direction, and, at noon the next day, was about four leagues diftant.

On the 6th and 7th, the wind being Northerly, we made
but little progrefs. At eight in the evening of the latter, we were in nineteen fathoms water, and about three or four leagues from the coaft, which, on the 8th, extended from South South Weft to Eaft by North, and was all low land, with a ridge of mountains behind it, covered with fnow. It is probable, that this low coaft extends, fome diftance, to the South Weft; and that fuch places as we fometimes took for inlets or bays, are only vallies between the mountains.

On

On the morning of the 9th, with a breeze at North West, we steered East by North, to get nearer the coast. At noon, we were in the latitude of 57° 49′, and in the longitude of 201° 33′, and about two leagues from the land, which extended from South by East to East North East; being all a low coast, with points shooting out in some places, which, from the deck, appeared like islands; but, from the masthead, low land was seen to connect them. In this situation, the depth of water was fifteen fathoms, the bottom a fine black sand.

As we had advanced to the North East, we had found the depth of water gradually decreasing, and the coast trending more and more Northerly. But the ridge of mountains behind it, continued to lie in the same direction as those more Westerly; so that the extent of the low land, between the foot of the mountains and the sea coast, insensibly increased. Both high and low grounds were perfectly destitute of wood; but seemed to be covered with a green turf, except the mountains, which were covered with snow. Continuing to steer along the coast, with a gentle breeze Westerly, the water gradually shoaled from fifteen to ten fathoms, though we were at the distance of eight or ten miles from the shore. At eight in the evening, an elevated mountain, which had been in sight for some time, bore South East by East, twenty-one leagues distant. Some other mountains, belonging to the same chain, and much farther distant, bore East 3° North. The coast extended as far as North East half North, where it seemed to terminate in a point, beyond which we hoped and expected, that it would take a more Easterly direction. But soon after, we discovered low land, extending from behind this point, as far as North West by West, where it was lost in the horizon;

horizon; and behind it was high land, that appeared in detached hills.

Thus the fine profpect we had of getting to the North vanifhed in a moment. I ftood on till nine o'clock, for fo long it was light, and then the point above mentioned, bore North Eaft half Eaft, about three miles diftant. Behind this point is a river, the entrance of which feemed to be a mile broad; but I can fay nothing as to its depth. The water appeared difcoloured, as upon fhoals, but a calm would have given it the fame afpect. It feemed to have a wind-ing direction, through the great flat that lies between the chain of mountains to the South Eaft, and the hills to the North Weft. It muft abound with falmon, as we faw many leaping in the fea before the entrance; and fome were found in the maws of cod which we had caught. The entrance of this river, diftinguifhed by the name of *Briftol River*, lies in the latitude of 58° 27', and in the longitude of 201° 55'.

Having fpent the night in making fhort boards; at day-break on the morning of the 10th, we made fail to the Weft South Weft, with a gentle breeze at North Eaft. At eleven o'clock, we thought the coaft to the North Weft ter-minated in a point, bearing North Weft by Weft; and as we had now deepened the water from nine to fourteen fathoms, I fteered for the point, ordering the Difcovery to keep ahead. But before fhe had run a mile, fhe made a fignal for fhoal water. At that inftant, we had the depth of feven fathoms; and before we could get the fhip's head the other way, had lefs than five; but the Difcovery had lefs than four.

We ftood back to the North Eaft, three or four miles.; but finding there was a ftrong tide or current fetting to the Weft

Weft South Weft, that is toward the fhoal, we anchored in ten fathoms, over a bottom of fine fand. Two hours after we had anchored, the water had fallen two feet and upward; which proved, that it was the tide of ebb that came from the river above mentioned. We alfo examined fome of the water which we had taken up, and found that it was not half fo falt as common fea water. This furnifhed another proof, that we were before a large river.

At four in the afternoon, the wind fhifting to South Weft, we weighed and ftood to the Southward, with boats ahead founding; and paffed over the South end of the fhoal, in fix fathoms water. We then got into thirteen and fifteen; in which laft depth we anchored, at half paft eight; fome part of the chain of mountains, on the South Eaft fhore, in fight, bearing South Eaft half South; and the Wefternmoft land on the other fhore, North Weft. We had, in the courfe of the day, feen high land, bearing North, 60° Weft, by eftimation twelve leagues diftant.

Saturday 11. Having weighed next morning, at two o'clock, with a light breeze at South Weft by Weft, we plied to windward till nine; when judging the flood tide to be now made againft us, we came to an anchor in twenty-four fathoms. We lay here till one, when the fog, which had prevailed this morning, difperfing, and the tide making in our favour, we weighed, and plied to the South Weft. In the evening, the wind was very variable, and we had fome thunder. We had heard none before, fince our arrival upon the coaft; and this was at a great diftance.

Sunday 12. The wind having fettled again in the South Weft quarter, in the morning of the 12th, we ftood to the North Weft, and at ten faw the continent. At noon, it extended from North Eaft by North, to North North Weft a quarter

3   Weft;

Weſt; and an elevated hill bore North North Weſt, ten leagues diſtant. This proved to be an iſland, which, from its figure, obtained the name of *Round Iſland*. It lies in the latitude of 58° 37′, and in the longitude of 200° 6′, and ſeven miles from the continent. In the evening at nine, having ſtood to the Northward to within three leagues of the ſhore, we tacked in fourteen fathoms water; the extremes of the coaſt bearing Eaſt South Eaſt half Eaſt, and Weſt. The wind veering to the North Weſt, enabled us to make a good ſtretch along ſhore, till two o'clock in the morning, when we got all at once into ſix fathoms water, being at this time two leagues from the ſhore. After edging off a little, our depth gradually increaſed, and at noon we had twenty fathoms, when the latitude was 58° 13′, and the longitude 199°. Round Iſland bore North, 5° Eaſt; and the Weſt extreme of the coaſt North, 16° Weſt, ſeven leagues diſtant. It is an elevated point, which obtained the name of *Calm Point*, from our having calm weather when off it. To the North Weſt of Round Iſland are two or three hillocks, that appeared like iſlands; and it is poſſible they may be ſuch; for we had but a diſtant view of the coaſt in this place.

During the 14th and 15th, our progreſs was ſlow, having little wind, and ſometimes ſo thick a fog, that we could not ſee the length of the ſhip. The ſoundings were from fourteen to twenty-ſix fathoms; and we had tolerable ſucceſs in fiſhing, catching cod, and now and then a few flat fiſh. At five in the morning of the 16th, the fog having cleared up, we found ourſelves nearer the land than we expected. Calm Point bore North, 72° Eaſt, and a point eight leagues from it, in the direction of Weſt, bore North, 3° Eaſt, three miles diſtant. Between theſe two points, the coaſt

Monday 13.

Tueſday 14.
Wedneſ. 15.

Thurſday 16.

coaſt forms a bay, in ſome parts of which the land was hardly viſible from the maſt-head. There is alſo a bay on the North Weſt ſide of this laſt point, between it and an elevated promontory, which, at this time, bore North, 36° Weſt, ſixteen miles diſtant. At nine, I ſent Lieutenant Williamſon to this promontory, with orders to land, and ſee what direction the coaſt took beyond it, and what the country produced; for, from the ſhips, it had but a barren appearance. We found here the flood-tide ſetting ſtrongly to the North Weſt along the coaſt. At noon it was high-water, and we anchored in twenty-four fathoms, four leagues diſtant from the ſhore. At five in the afternoon, the tide making in our favour, we weighed, and drove with it; for there was no wind.

Soon after Mr. Williamſon returned, and reported, that he had landed on the point, and, having climbed the higheſt hill, found, that the fartheſt part of the coaſt in ſight bore nearly North. He took poſſeſſion of the country in his Majeſty's name, and left on the hill a bottle, in which was inſcribed, on a piece of paper, the names of the ſhips, and the date of the diſcovery. The promontory, to which he gave the name of *Cape Newenham*, is a rocky point, of tolerable height, ſituated in the latitude of 58° 42′, and in the longitude of 197° 36′. Over, or within it, are two elevated hills, riſing one behind the other. The innermoſt, or Eaſternmoſt, is the higheſt. The country, as far as Mr. Williamſon could ſee, produces neither tree nor ſhrub. The hills are naked; but on the lower grounds grew graſs, and other plants, very few of which were in flower. He ſaw no other animal but a doe and her fawn; and a dead ſea-horſe, or cow, upon the beach. Of theſe animals we had lately ſeen a great many.

As

1778.
July.

As the coast takes a Northerly direction from Cape Newenham, that Cape fixes the Northern limit of the great bay and gulph, lying before the river Briftol, which, in honour of the admiral Earl of Briftol, was named *Briftol Bay*. Cape *Ooneemak* is the South limit of this bay; and is diftant eighty-two leagues from Cape Newenham, in the direction of South South Weft.

About eight in the evening, a light breeze fpringing up, which fixed at South South Eaft, we fteered North Weft, and North North Weft, round Cape Newenham, which, at noon next day, bore South by Eaft, diftant four Friday 17. leagues. At this time the moft advanced land to the Northward bore North, 30° Eaft; our depth of water was feventeen fathoms; and the neareft fhore 3 ½ leagues diftant. We had but little wind all the afternoon; fo that, at ten at night, we had only made three leagues upon a North courfe.

We fteered North by Weft till eight the next morning, Saturday 18. when, our depth of water decreafing fuddenly to five and feven fathoms, we brought to, till a boat from each fhip was fent ahead to found, and then fteered North Eaft after them; and at noon we had deepened the water to feventeen fathoms. At this time, Cape Newenham bore South, 9° Eaft, diftant eleven or twelve leagues; the North Eaft extreme of the land in fight North, 66° Eaft; and the neareft fhore about four or five leagues diftant. Our latitude, by obfervation, was 59° 16′.

Between this latitude and Cape Newenham, the coaft is compofed of hills, and low land, and appeared to form feveral bays. A little before one o'clock, the boats ahead made the fignal for meeting with fhoal water. It feems they had only two fathoms; and, at the fame time, the

VOL. II.   3 K   fhips

ships were in six fathoms. By hauling a little more to the Northward, we continued in much the same depth till between five and six o'clock, when the boats meeting with less and less water, I made the signal to the Discovery, she being then ahead, to anchor, which we did soon after. In bringing our ship up, the cable parted at the clinch, which obliged us to come to with the other anchor. We rode in six fathoms water, a sandy bottom, and about four or five leagues from the main-land; Cape Newenham bearing South, seventeen leagues distant. The fartheft hills we could see to the North, bore North East by East; but there was low land stretching out from the high land, as far as North by East. Without this was a shoal of sand and stones, that was dry at half ebb.

I had sent the two Masters, each in a boat, to found between this shoal and the coast. On their return, they reported, that there was a channel, in which they found six and seven fathoms water; but that it was narrow and intricate. At low water, we made an attempt to get a hawser round the lost anchor; but did not succeed then. However, being determined not to leave it behind me, as long as there was a probability of recovering it, I persevered in my endeavours; and at last succeeded in the evening of the 20th.

While we were thus employed, I ordered Captain Clerke to send his Master in a boat to look for a passage in the South West quarter. He did so; but no channel was to be found in that direction; nor did there appear to be any way to get clear of these shoals, but to return by the track which had brought us in. For, although by following the channel we were in, we might probably have got farther down the coast; and though possibly this channel might have

have led us at laſt to the North, clear of the ſhoals, ſtill the attempt would have been attended with vaſt riſk; and if we ſhould not have ſucceeded, there would have been a conſiderable loſs of time that could ill be ſpared. Theſe reaſons induced me to return by the way in which we came; and ſo get without the ſhoals.

A number of lunar obſervations made by Mr. King and myſelf, on this, and the four preceding days, and all reduced to the ſhip's preſent ſtation, gave the longitude, 197° 45′ 48″

By the time-keeper it was - - - 197 26 48
Our latitude was - - - - - 59 37 30
Variation by the } A. M. 23° 34′ 3″ }
  mean of three } P. M. 22 19 40 } mean 22 56 51 Eaſt.
  compaſſes,

The Northernmoſt part of the coaſt that we could ſee from this ſtation, I judged to lie in the latitude of 60°. It ſeemed to form a low point, which obtained the name of *Shoal Neſs*.

The tide of flood ſets to the North, and the ebb to the South. It riſes and falls, upon a perpendicular, five or ſix feet; and I reckon it to be high-water, on the full and change days, at eight o'clock.

Having weighed at three in the morning on the 21ſt, with a light breeze at North North Weſt, we ſteered back to the Southward, having three boats ahead to direct us. But, notwithſtanding this precaution, we found more difficulty in returning than we had in advancing; and at laſt were obliged to anchor, to avoid running upon a ſhoal, which had only a depth of five feet. While we lay here, twenty-ſeven men of the country, each in a canoe, came off to the ſhips, which they approached with great caution; hollowing and opening their arms as they advanced. This,

Tueſday 21.

3 K 2 we

we underſtood, was to expreſs their pacific intentions.
At length ſome approached near enough to receive a
few trifles that were thrown to them. This encouraged
the reſt to venture along-ſide; and a traffic preſently
commenced between them and our people; who got
dreſſes of ſkins, bows, arrows, darts, wooden veſſels, &c.;
our viſiters taking in exchange for theſe whatever was offered them. They ſeemed to be the ſame ſort of people
that we had of late met with all along this coaſt; wore the
ſame kind of ornaments in their lips and noſes; but were
far more dirty, and not ſo well clothed. They appeared to
be wholly unacquainted with people like us; they knew
not the uſe of tobacco; nor was any foreign article ſeen
in their poſſeſſion, unleſs a knife may be looked upon as
ſuch. This, indeed, was only a piece of common iron
fitted in a wooden handle, ſo as to anſwer the purpoſe of
a knife. They, however, knew the value and uſe of this
inſtrument ſo well, that it ſeemed to be the only article
they wiſhed for. Moſt of them had their hair ſhaved or cut
ſhort off, leaving only a few locks behind, or on one ſide.
For a covering for the head they wore a hood of ſkins,
and a bonnet which appeared to be of wood. One part of
their dreſs, which we got from them, was a kind of
girdle, very neatly made of ſkin, with trappings depend-
ing from it, and paſſing between the legs, ſo as to conceal the adjoining parts. By the uſe of ſuch a girdle, it
ſhould ſeem that they ſometimes go naked, even in this
high latitude; for they hardly wear it under their other
clothing.

The canoes were made of ſkins, like all the others we
had lately ſeen; only with this difference, that theſe were
broader, and the hole in which the man ſits was wider,

than

than in any I had before met with. Our boats returning from founding feemed to alarm them, fo that they
all left us fooner than probably they would otherwise have
done.

It was the 22d in the evening before we got clear of thefe
fhoals, and then I durft not venture to fteer to the Weftward
in the night, but fpent it off Cape Newenham; and at day-
break, next morning, fteered to the North Weft, ordering
the Difcovery to lead. Before we had run two leagues, our
depth of water decreafed to fix fathoms. Fearing, if we
continued this courfe, that we fhould find lefs and lefs water, I hauled to the Southward; the wind being at Eaft, a
frefh breeze. This courfe brought us gradually into eighteen fathoms, and, having that depth, I ventured to fteer
a little Wefterly; and afterward Weft, when we at laft found
twenty-fix fathoms water.

On the 24th at noon we were, by obfervation, in the latitude of 58° 7', and in the longitude of 194° 22'. Three
leagues to the Weftward of this ftation we had twenty-eight
fathoms water, and then fteered Weft North Weft, the water gradually deepening to thirty-four fathoms. I would
have fteered more Northerly, but the wind having veered
in that direction, I could not.

The 25th in the evening, having a very thick fog, and
but little wind, we dropped anchor in thirty fathoms water.
Our latitude was now 58° 29', and our longitude 191° 37'.
At fix, the next morning, the weather clearing up a little,
we weighed, and, with a fmall breeze at Eaft, fteered North;
our foundings being from twenty-eight to twenty-five fathoms. After running nine leagues upon this courfe, the
wind returned back to the North, which obliged us to fteer
more Wefterly.

The

1778.
July.
Tuefday 28.

The weather continued, for the moft part, foggy, till toward noon on the 28th, when we had a few hours clear fun-fhine; during which we made feveral lunar obfervations. The mean refult of them, reduced to noon, when the latitude was 59° 55′, gave 190° 6′ longitude; and the time-keeper gave 189° 59′. The variation of the compafs was 18° 40′ Eaft. Continuing our Wefterly courfe, the water having now deepened to thirty-fix fathoms, at four

Wednef. 29.

o'clock next morning we difcovered land, bearing North Weft by Weft, fix leagues diftant. We ftood toward it till half paft ten, when we tacked in twenty-four fathoms water; being, at this time, a league from the land, which bore North North Weft. It was the South Eaft extremity, and formed a perpendicular cliff of confiderable height; on which account it was called *Point Upright*, and lies in the latitude of 60° 17′, and in the longitude of 187° 30′. More land was feen to the Weftward of the Point; and, at a clear interval, we faw another elevated portion of land, in the direction of Weft by South; and this feemed to be entirely feparated from the other. Here we met with an incredible number of birds, all of the awk kind before defcribed.

We had baffling light winds all the afternoon, fo that we made but little progrefs; and the weather was not clear enough to enable us to determine the extent of the land before us. We fuppofed it to be one of the many iflands laid down by Mr. Stæhlin in his map of the New Northern Archipelago; and we expected every moment to fee more of them.

Thurfday 30.

At four in the afternoon of the 30th, Point Upright bore North Weft by North, fix leagues diftant. About this time, a light breeze fpringing up at North North Weft,
we

we ftood to the North Eaft till four o'clock next morning, when the wind veering to the Eaftward, we tacked, and ftood to the North Weft. Soon after the wind came to South Eaft; and we fteered North Eaft by North; which courfe we continued, with foundings from thirty-five to twenty fathoms, till next day at noon. At this time we were in the latitude of 60° 58′, and in the longitude of 191°. The wind now veering to North Eaft, I firft made a ftretch of ten leagues to the North Weft; and then, feeing no land in that direction, I ftood back to the Eaftward about fifteen leagues, and met with nothing but pieces of drift-wood. The foundings were from twenty-two to nineteen fathoms.

Variable, light winds, with fhowers of rain, prevailed all the 2d; but fixing in the South Eaft quarter, in the morning of the 3d, we refumed our courfe to the Northward. At noon we were, by obfervation, in the latitude of 62° 34′, our longitude was 192°; and our depth of water fixteen fathoms.

Mr. Anderfon, my furgeon, who had been lingering under a confumption for more than twelve months, expired between three and four this afternoon. He was a fenfible young man, an agreeable companion, well fkilled in his own profeffion; and had acquired confiderable knowledge in other branches of fcience. The reader of this Journal will have obferved how ufeful an affiftant I had found him in the courfe of the voyage; and had it pleafed God to have fpared his life, the Public, I make no doubt, might have received from him fuch communications, on various parts of the natural hiftory of the feveral places we vifited, as would have abundantly fhewn, that he was not unworthy of this commendation.

10

commendation *. Soon after he had breathed his laft, land was feen to the Weftward, twelve leagues diftant. It was fuppofed to be an ifland; and, to perpetuate the memory of the deceafed, for whom I had a very great regard, I named it *Anderfon's Ifland*. The next day, I removed Mr. Law, the furgeon of the Difcovery, into the Refolution, and appointed Mr. Samuel, the Surgeon's firft mate of the Refolution, to be Surgeon of the Difcovery.

Tuefday 4. On the 4th, at three in the afternoon, land was feen, extending from North North Eaft to North Weft. We ftood on toward it till four o'clock, when, being four or five miles from it, we tacked; and, foon after, the wind falling, we anchored in thirteen fathoms water, over a fandy bottom; being about two leagues from the land, and, by our reckoning, in the latitude of 64° 27′, and in the longitude of 194° 18′. At intervals, we could fee the coaft extending from Eaft to North Weft, and a pretty high ifland, bearing Weft by North, three leagues diftant.

The land before us, which we fuppofed to be the continent of America, appeared low next the fea; but, inland, it fwelled into hills, which rife, one behind another, to a confiderable height. It had a greenifh hue, but feemed deftitute of wood, and free from fhow. While we lay at anchor, we found that the flood-tide came from the Eaft, and fet to the Weft, till between ten and eleven o'clock. From that time, till two the next morning, the ftream fet to the Eaftward, and the water fell three feet. The flood ran both ftronger and longer than the ebb; from which I concluded, that, befides the tide, there was a Wefterly current.

* Mr. Anderfon's Journal feems to have been difcontinued for about two months before his death; the laft date in his MSS. being of the 3d of June.

Art

At ten in the morning of the 5th, with the wind at South Weſt, we ran down, and anchored between the iſland and the continent, in ſeven fathoms water. Soon after, I landed upon the iſland, accompanied by Mr. King and ſome others of the officers. I hoped to have had from it a view of the coaſt and ſea to the Weſtward; but the fog was ſo thick in that direction, that the proſpect was not more extenſive than from the ſhip. The coaſt of the continent ſeemed to take a turn to the Northward, at a low point named *Point Rodney*, which bore from the iſland North Weſt half Weſt, three or four leagues diſtant; but the high land, which took a more Northerly direction, was ſeen a great way farther.

This iſland, which was named *Sledge Iſland*, and lies in the latitude of 64° 30′, and in the longitude of 193° 57′, is about four leagues in circuit. The ſurface of the ground is com-poſed chiefly of large looſe ſtones, that are, in many places, covered with moſs and other vegetables, of which there were above twenty or thirty different ſorts, and moſt of them in flower. But I ſaw neither ſhrub nor tree, either upon the iſland, or on the continent. On a ſmall low ſpot, near the beach where we landed, was a good deal of wild purſlain, peaſe, long-wort, &c.; ſome of which we took on board for the pot. We ſaw one fox; a few plovers, and ſome other ſmall birds; and we met with ſome decayed huts that were partly built below ground. People had lately been on the iſland; and it is pretty clear, that they frequently viſit it for ſome purpoſe or other, as there was a beaten path from the one end to the other. We found, a little way from the ſhore where we landed, a ſledge, which occaſioned this name being given to the iſland. It ſeemed to be ſuch a one as the Ruſſians in Kamtſchatka make uſe of to convey goods from place to place, over the ice or ſnow. It was ten feet long, twenty inches broad; and had a kind of rail-work on each ſide, and was ſhod with bone. The conſtruction of it was admirable, and all the parts neatly put together; ſome with wooden pins, but moſtly with thongs or laſhings of whale-bone, which made me think it was entirely the workmanſhip of the natives.

Thurſday 6. At three o'clock the next morning, we weighed, and proceeded to the North Weſtward, with a light Southerly breeze. We had an opportunity to obſerve the ſun's meridian altitude for the latitude; and to get altitudes, both in the forenoon and afternoon, to obtain the longitude by the time-keeper. As we had but little wind, and variable withal, we advanced but ſlowly; and, at eight in the evening, finding the ſhips ſettle faſt toward the land into ſhoal water, I anchored in ſeven fathoms, about two leagues from the coaſt. Sledge Iſland bore South, 51°Eaſt, ten leagues diſtant; and was ſeen over the South point of the main land.

Soon after we had anchored, the weather, which had been miſty, clearing up, we ſaw high land extending from North, 40° Eaſt, to North, 30° Weſt, apparently disjoined from the coaſt, under which we were at anchor, which ſeemed to trend away North Eaſt. At the ſame time, an iſland was ſeen bearing North, 81° Weſt, eight or nine leagues diſtant. It appeared to have no great extent, and was named *King's Iſland*. We rode here till eight o'clock,

Friday 7. next morning, when we weighed, and ſtood to the North Weſt. The weather clearing up toward the evening, we got ſight of the North Weſt land, extending from North by Weſt, to North Weſt by North, diſtant about three leagues. We ſpent the night making ſhort boards, the weather being miſty and rainy, with little wind; and, between four

Saturday 8. and five of the morning of the 8th, we had again a ſight
of

of the North Weft land; and, foon after, on account of a
calm, and a current driving us toward the fhore, we found it neceffary to anchor in twelve fathoms water, about two miles from the coaft. Over the Weftern extreme is an elevated peaked hill, fituated in latitude 65° 36′, and in longitude 192° 18′. A breeze at North Eaft fpringing up at eight o'clock, we weighed, and ftood to the South Eaft, in hopes of finding a paffage between the coaft on which we had anchored on the 6th in the evening, and this North Weft land. But we foon got into feven fathoms water, and difcovered low land connecting the two coafts, and the high land behind it.

Being now fatisfied that the whole was a continued coaft, I tacked, and ftood away for its North Weft part, and came to an anchor under it in feventeen fathoms water. The weather, at this time, was very thick with rain; but, at four next morning, it cleared up, fo that we could fee the land about us. A high fteep rock or ifland bore Weft by South; another ifland to the North of it, and much larger, bore Weft by North; the peaked hill above mentioned, South Eaft by Eaft; and the point under it, South, 32° Eaft. Under this hill lies fome low land, ftretching out toward the North Weft, the extreme point of which bore North Eaft by Eaft, about three miles diftant. Over, and beyond it, fome high land was feen, fuppofed to be a continuation of the continent.

This point of land, which I named *Cape Prince of Wales*, is the more remarkable, by being the Weftern extremity of all America hitherto known. It is fituated in the latitude of 65° 46′, and in the longitude of 191° 45′. The obfervations by which both were determined, though made in fight of it, were liable to fome fmall error, on account of

3 L 2 the

the hazineſs of the weather. We thought we ſaw ſome people upon the coaſt; and probably we were not miſtaken, as ſome elevations, like ſtages, and others like huts, were ſeen at the ſame place. We ſaw the ſame things on the continent within Sledge Iſland, and on ſome other parts of the coaſt.

It was calm till eight o'clock in the morning, when a faint breeze at North ſpringing up, we weighed. But we had ſcarcely got our ſails ſet, when it began to blow and rain very hard, with miſty weather. The wind and current, being in contrary directions, raiſed ſuch a ſea, that it frequently broke into the ſhip. We had a few minutes ſunſhine at noon; and from the obſervation then obtained, we fixed the above-mentioned latitude.

Having plied to windward till two in the afternoon, with little effect, I bore up for the iſland we had ſeen to the Weſtward, propoſing to come to an anchor under it till the gale ſhould ceaſe. But on getting to this land, we found it compoſed of two ſmall iſlands, each not above three or four leagues in circuit; and conſequently they could afford us little ſhelter. Inſtead of anchoring, therefore, we continued to ſtretch to the Weſtward; and, at eight o'clock, land was ſeen in that direction, extending from North North Weſt, to Weſt by South, the neareſt part ſix leagues diſtant. I ſtood on till ten, and then made a board to the Eaſtward, in order to ſpend the night.

Monday 10.
At day-break in the morning of the 10th, we reſumed our courſe to the Weſt for the land we had ſeen the preceding evening. At eleven minutes after ſeven, when the longitude, by the time-keeper, was 189° 24′, it extended from South, 72° Weſt, to North, 41° Eaſt. Between the South Weſt extreme, and a point which bore Weſt, two leagues diſtant,

tant, the fhore forms a large bay, in which we anchored at ten o'clock in the forenoon, about two miles from the North fhore, in ten fathoms water, over a gravelly bottom. The South point of the bay bore South, 58° Weft; the North point North, 43° Eaft; the bottom of the bay North, 60° Weft, two or three leagues diftant; and the two iflands we had paffed the preceding day, North, 72° Eaft, diftant fourteen leagues.

1778.
Auguft.

C H A P.

CHAP. IX.

Behaviour of the Natives, the Tfchutfki, on feeing the Ships.
—Interview with fome of them.—Their Weapons.—Per-
fons.—Ornaments.—Clothing.—Winter and Summer Ha-
bitations.—The Ships crofs the Strait, to the Coaft of Ame-
rica.—Progrefs Northward.—Cape Mulgrave.—Appear-
ance of Fields of Ice.—Situation of Icy Cape.—The Sea
blocked up with Ice.—Sea-horfes killed, and ufed as Provi-
fions.—Thefe Animals defcribed.—Dimenfions of one of
them.—Cape Lifburne.—Fruitlefs Attempts to get through
the Ice, at a Diftance from the Coaft.—Obfervations on the
Formation of this Ice.—Arrival on the Coaft of Afia.—Cape
North.—The Profecution of the Voyage deferred to the en-
fuing Year.

1778.
Auguft.

Monday 10.

A S we were ftanding into this bay, we perceived on the
North fhore a village, and fome people, whom the
fight of the fhips feemed to have thrown into confufion, or
fear. We could plainly fee perfons running up the country with burdens upon their backs. At thefe habitations I
propofed to land ; and, accordingly, went with three armed
boats, accompanied by fome of the officers. About thirty
or forty men, each armed with a fpontoon, a bow, and arrows, ftood drawn up on a rifing ground clofe by the village.
As we drew near, three of them came down toward the fhore,
and were fo polite as to take off their caps, and to make

I   us us low bows. We returned the civility; but this did not inſpire them with ſufficient confidence to wait for our landing; for the moment we put the boats aſhore, they retired. I followed them alone, without any thing in my hand; and by ſigns and geſtures prevailed on them to ſtop, and to receive ſome trifling preſents. In return for theſe, they gave me two fox-ſkins, and a couple of ſea-horſe teeth. I cannot ſay whether they or I made the firſt preſent; for it appeared to me that they had brought down with them theſe things for this very purpoſe; and that they would have given them to me, even though I had made no return.

They ſeemed very fearful and cautious; expreſſing their deſire, by ſigns, that no more of our people ſhould be permitted to come up. On my laying my hand on the ſhoulder of one of them, he ſtarted back ſeveral paces. In proportion as I advanced, they retreated backward; always in the attitude of being ready to make uſe of their ſpears; while thoſe on the riſing ground ſtood ready to ſupport them with their arrows. Inſenſibly, myſelf, and two or three of my companions, got in amongſt them. A few beads diſtributed to thoſe about us, ſoon created a kind of confidence; ſo that they were not alarmed when a few more of our people joined us; and, by degrees, a ſort of traffic between us commenced. In exchange for knives, beads, tobacco, and other articles, they gave us ſome of their clothing, and a few arrows. But nothing that we had to offer could induce them to part with a ſpear, or a bow. Theſe they held in conſtant readineſs, never once quitting them, except at one time, when four or five perſons laid theirs down, while they gave us a ſong and a dance. And even then, they placed them in ſuch a manner, that they could lay hold of them

in

in an inftant; and, for their fecurity, they defired us to fit
down.

The arrows were pointed either with bone or ftone; but
very few of them had barbs; and fome had a round blunt
point. What ufe thefe may be applied to, I cannot fay;
unlefs it be to kill fmall animals, without damaging the
fkin. The bows were fuch as we had feen on the American coaft, and like thofe ufed by the Efquimaux. The
fpears, or fpontoons, were of iron or fteel, and of European
or Afiatic workmanfhip; in which no little pains had been
taken to ornament them with carving, and inlayings of
brafs, and of a white metal. Thofe who ftood ready with
bows and arrows in their hands, had the fpear flung over
their right fhoulder by a leathern ftrap. A leathern quiver,
flung over their left fhoulder, contained arrows; and fome
of thefe quivers were extremely beautiful; being made of
red leather, on which was very neat embroidery, and other
ornaments.

Several other things, and, in particular, their clothing,
fhewed that they were poffeffed of a degree of ingenuity, far
furpaffing what one could expect to find amongft fo Northern a people. All the Americans we had feen, fince our
arrival on that coaft, were rather low of ftature, with round
chubby faces, and high cheek-bones. The people we now
were amongft, far from refembling them, had long vifages,
and were ftout and well made. In fhort, they appeared to
be a quite different nation. We faw neither women, nor
children of either fex; nor any aged, except one man, who
was bald-headed; and he was the only one who carried no
arms. The others feemed to be picked men, and rather under than above the middle age. The old man had a black
mark acrofs his face, which I did not fee in any others.

All

All of them had their ears bored; and fome had glafs beads hanging to them. Thefe were the only fixed ornaments we faw about them; for they wear none to the lips. This is another thing in which they differ from the Americans we had lately feen.

Their clothing confifted of a cap, a frock, a pair of breeches, a pair of boots, and a pair of gloves, all made of leather, or of the fkins of deer, dogs, feals, &c, and extremely well dreffed; fome with the hair or fur on; but others without it. The caps were made to fit the head very clofe; and befides thefe caps, which moft of them wore, we got from them fome hoods, made of fkins of dogs, that were large enough to cover both head and fhoulders. Their hair feemed to be black; but their heads were either fhaved, or the hair cut clofe off; and none of them wore any beard. Of the few articles which they got from us, knives and tobacco were what they valued moft.

We found the village compofed both of their fummer and their winter habitations. The latter are exactly like a vault, the floor of which is funk a little below the furface of the earth. One of them, which I examined, was of an oval form, about twenty feet long, and twelve or more high. The framing was compofed of wood, and the ribs of whales, difpofed in a judicious manner, and bound together with fmaller materials of the fame fort. Over this framing is laid a covering of ftrong coarfe grafs; and that again is covered with earth; fo that, on the outfide, the houfe looks like a little hillock, fupported by a wall of ftone, three or four feet high, which is built round the two fides, and one end. At the other end, the earth is raifed floping, to walk up to the entrance, which is by a hole in the top of the roof over that end. The floor was boarded, and under it a kind of cellar, in which I saw nothing but water. And at the end of each houfe was a vaulted room, which I took to be a ftore-room. Thefe ftore-rooms communicated with the houfe, by a dark paffage; and with the open air, by a hole in the roof, which was even with the ground one walked upon; but they cannot be faid to be wholly under ground; for one end reached to the edge of the hill, along which they were made, and which was built up with ftone. Over it ftood a kind of fentry-box, or tower, compofed of the large bones of large fifh.

The fummer huts were pretty large and circular, being brought to a point at the top. The framing was of flight poles, and bones, covered with the fkins of fea-animals. I examined the infide of one. There was a fire-place, juft within the door, where lay a few wooden veffels, all very dirty. Their bed-places were clofe to the fide, and took up about half the circuit. Some privacy feemed to be ob-ferved; for there were feveral partitions made with fkins. The bed and bedding were of deer-fkins; and moft of them were dry and clean.

About the habitations were erected feveral ftages, ten or twelve feet high; fuch as we had obferved on fome parts of the American coaft. They were wholly compofed of bones; and feemed intended for drying their fifh and fkins, which were thus placed beyond the reach of their dogs, of which they had a great many. Thefe dogs are of the fox kind, rather large, and of different colours, with long foft hair like wool. They are, probably, ufed in drawing their fledges in winter. For fledges they have, as I faw a good many laid up in one of the winter huts. It is alfo not im-probable, that dogs may conftitute a part of their food. Several lay dead, that had been killed that morning.

The

The canoes of thefe people are of the fame fort with thofe of the Northern Americans; fome, both of the large and of the fmall ones, being feen lying in a creek under the village.

By the large fifh-bones, and of other fea-animals, it appeared that the fea fupplied them with the greateft part of their fubfiftence. The country appeared to be exceedingly barren; yielding neither tree nor fhrub, that we could fee. At fome diftance Weftward, we obferved a ridge of mountains covered with fnow, that had lately fallen.

At firft, we fuppofed this land to be a part of the ifland of Alafchka, laid down in Mr. Stæhlin's map before mentioned. But from the figure of the coaft, the fituation of the oppofite fhore of America, and from the longitude, we foon began to think that it was, more probably, the country of the Tfchutfki, or the Eaftern extremity of Afia, explored by Beering in 1728. But to have admitted this, without farther examination, I muft have pronounced Mr. Stæhlin's map, and his account of the new Northern Archipelago, to be either exceedingly erroneous, even in latitude, or elfe to be a mere fiction; a judgment which I had no right to pafs upon a publication fo refpectably vouched, without producing the cleareft proofs.

After a ftay of between two and three hours, with thefe people, we returned to our fhips; and, foon after, the wind veering to the South, we weighed anchor, ftood out of the bay, and fteered to the North Eaft, between the coaft and the two iflands. The next day, at noon, the former extended from South 80° Weft, to North 84° Weft; the latter bore South 40° Weft; and the peaked mountain, over Cape Prince of Wales, bore South 36° Eaft; with land extending from it

3 M 2

as

as far as South 75° Eaft. The latitude of the fhip was 66° 51′ ; the longitude 191° 19′ ; our depth of water twenty-eight fathoms ; and our pofition nearly in the middle of the channel between the two coafts, each being feven leagues diftant.

From this ftation we fteered Eaft, in order to get nearer the American coaft. In this courfe the water fhoaled gradually, and there being little wind, and all our endeavours to increafe our depth failing, I was obliged at laft to drop anchor in fix fathoms ; the only remedy we had left to prevent the fhips driving into lefs. The neareft part of the Weftern land bore Weft, twelve leagues diftant ; the peaked hill over Cape Prince of Wales, South 16° Weft ; and the Northernmoft part of the American continent in fight, Eaft South Eaft, the neareft part about four leagues diftant. After we had anchored, I fent a boat to found, and the water was found to fhoal gradually toward the land. While we lay at anchor, which was from fix to nine in the evening, we found little or no current ; nor could we perceive that the water either rofe or fell.

A breeze of wind fpringing up at North, we weighed, and ftood to the Weftward, which courfe foon brought us
into deep water ; and, during the 12th, we plied to the North, both coafts being in fight ; but we kept neareft to that of America.

At four in the afternoon of the 13th, a breeze fpringing up at South, I fteered North Eaft by North, till four o'clock
next morning, when, feeing no land, we directed our courfe Eaft by North ; and between nine and ten, land, fuppofed to be a continuation of the continent, appeared. It extended from Eaft by South to Eaft by North ; and, foon after, we faw more land, bearing North by Eaft. Coming pretty fuddenly

denly into thirteen fathoms water, at two in the afternoon, we made a trip off till four, when we ſtood in again
for the land; which was ſeen, ſoon after, extending from
North to South Eaſt; the neareſt part three or four leagues
diſtant. The coaſt here forms a point, named *Point Mulgrave*, which lies in the latitude of 67° 45′; and in the
longitude of 194° 51′. The land appeared very low next
the ſea; but, a little back, it riſes into hills of a moderate
height. The whole was free from ſnow; and, to appearance, deſtitute of wood. I now tacked, and bore away
North Weſt by Weſt; but, ſoon after, thick weather with
rain coming on, and the wind increaſing, I hauled more to
the Weſt.

Next morning, at two o'clock, the wind veered to South
Weſt by South, and blew a ſtrong gale, which abated at
noon; and the ſun ſhining out, we found ourſelves, by obſervation, in the latitude of 68° 18′. I now ſteered North
Eaſt, till ſix o'clock the next morning, when I ſteered two
points more Eaſterly. In this run we met with ſeveral ſea-
horſes, and flights of birds; ſome like ſand-larks, and others
no bigger than hedge-ſparrows. Some ſhags were alſo
ſeen; ſo that we judged ourſelves to be not far from land.
But as we had a thick fog, we could not expect to ſee any;
and, as the wind blew ſtrong, it was not prudent to continue
a courſe which was moſt likely to bring us to it. From
the noon of this day, to ſix o'clock in the morning of the
following, I ſteered Eaſt by North; which courſe brought
us into ſixteen fathoms water. I now ſteered North Eaſt by
Eaſt, thinking, by this courſe, to deepen our water. But,
in the ſpace of ſix leagues, it ſhoaled to eleven fathoms;
which made me think it proper to haul cloſe to the wind,
that now blew at Weſt. Toward noon, both ſun and moon
were

were ſeen clearly at intervals, and we got ſome flying obſervations for the longitude; which, reduced to noon, when
the latitude was 70° 33′, gave 197° 41′. The time-keeper,
for the ſame time, gave 198°; and the variation was
35° 1′ 22″ Eaſt. We had, afterward, reaſon to believe, that
the obſerved longitude was within a very few miles of the
truth.

Some time before noon, we perceived a brightneſs in
the Northern horizon, like that reflected from ice, commonly called the blink. It was little noticed, from a ſuppoſition that it was improbable we ſhould meet with ice ſo
ſoon. And yet, the ſharpneſs of the air, and gloomineſs of
the weather, for two or three days paſt, ſeemed to indicate
ſome ſudden change. About an hour after, the ſight of a
large field of ice, left us no longer in doubt about the cauſe
of the brightneſs of the horizon. At half paſt two, we
tacked, cloſe to the edge of the ice, in twenty-two fathoms
water, being then in the latitude of 70° 41′; not being able
to ſtand on any farther. For the ice was quite impenetra-
ble, and extended from Weſt by South, to Eaſt by North, as
far as the eye could reach. Here were abundance of ſea-
horſes; ſome in the water; but far more upon the ice. I
had thoughts of hoiſting out the boats to kill ſome; but
the wind freſhening, I gave up the deſign; and continued to ply to the Southward, or rather to the Weſtward;
for the wind came from that quarter.

Tueſday 18.   We gained nothing; for, on the 18th at noon, our latitude was 70° 44′; and we were near five leagues farther
to the Eaſtward. We were, at this time, cloſe to the
edge of the ice, which was as compact as a wall; and
ſeemed to be ten or twelve feet high at leaſt. But, farther
North, it appeared much higher. Its ſurface was extremely
rugged;

3

rugged; and, here and there, we faw upon it pools of water.

We now ftood to the Southward; and, after running fix leagues, fhoaled the water to feven fathoms; but it foon deepened to nine fathoms. At this time, the weather, which had been hazy, clearing up a little, we faw land extending from South to South Eaft by Eaft, about three or four miles diftant. The Eaftern extreme forms a point, which was much encumbered with ice; for which rea-fon it obtained the name of *Icy Cape*. Its latitude is 70° 29', and its longitude 198° 20'. The other extreme of the land was loft in the horizon; fo that there can be no doubt of its being a continuation of the American continent. The Difcovery being about a mile aftern, and to leeward, found lefs water than we did; and tacking on that account, I was obliged to tack alfo, to prevent feparation.

Our fituation was now more and more critical. We were in fhoal water, upon a lee fhore; and the main body of the ice to windward, driving down upon us. It was evident, that if we remained much longer between it and the land, it would force us afhore; unlefs it fhould happen to take the ground before us. It feemed nearly to join the land to leeward; and the only direction that was open, was to the South Weft. After making a fhort board to the Northward, I made the fignal for the Difcovery to tack, and tacked myfelf at the fame time. The wind proved rather favourable; fo that we lay up South Weft, and South Weft by Weft.

At eight in the morning of the 19th, the wind veer-ing back to Weft, I tacked to the Northward; and, at noon, the latitude was 70° 6', and the longitude 196° 42'. In this fituation, we had a good deal of drift-ice about us;

us; and the main ice was about two leagues to the North. At half paſt one, we got in with the edge of it. It was not ſo compact as that which we had ſeen to the North-ward; but it was too cloſe, and in too large pieces, to attempt forcing the ſhips through it. On the ice lay a prodigious number of ſea-horſes; and, as we were in want of freſh proviſions, the boats from each ſhip were ſent to get ſome.

By ſeven o'clock in the evening, we had received, on board the Reſolution, nine of theſe animals; which, till now, we had ſuppoſed to be ſea-cows; ſo that we were not a little diſappointed, eſpecially ſome of the ſeamen, who, for the novelty of the thing, had been feaſting their eyes for ſome days paſt. Nor would they have been diſappointed now, nor have known the difference, if we had not happened to have one or two on board, who had been in Greenland, and declared what animals theſe were, and that no one ever eat of them. But, notwithſtanding this, we lived upon them as long as they laſted; and there were few on board who did not prefer them to our ſalt meat.

The fat, at firſt, is as ſweet as marrow; but in a few days it grows rancid, unleſs it be ſalted; in which ſtate, it will keep much longer. The lean fleſh is coarſe, black, and has rather a ſtrong taſte; and the heart is nearly as well taſted as that of a bullock. The fat, when melted, yields a good deal of oil, which burns very well in lamps; and their hides, which are very thick, were very uſeful about our rigging. The teeth, or tuſks, of moſt of them were, at this time, very ſmall; even ſome of the largeſt and oldeſt of theſe animals, had them not exceeding ſix inches in length. From this we concluded, that they had lately ſhed their old teeth.

They

They lie, in herds of many hundreds, upon the ice; huddling one over the other like ſwine; and roar or bray very loud; ſo that, in the night, or in foggy weather, they gave us notice of the vicinity of the ice, before we could ſee it. We never found the whole herd aſleep; ſome being always upon the watch. Theſe, on the approach of the boat, would wake thoſe next to them; and the alarm being thus gradually communicated, the whole herd would be awake preſently. But they were ſeldom in a hurry to get away, till after they had been once fired at. Then they would tumble one over the other, into the ſea, in the utmoſt confuſion. And, if we did not, at the firſt diſcharge, kill thoſe we fired at, we generally loſt them, though mortally wounded. They did not appear to us to be that dangerous animal ſome authors have deſcribed; not even when attacked. They are rather more ſo, to appearance, than in reality. Vaſt numbers of them would follow, and come cloſe up to the boats. But the flaſh of a muſquet in the pan, or even the bare pointing of one at them, would ſend them down in an inſtant. The female will defend the young one to the very laſt, and at the expence of her own life, whether in the water, or upon the ice. Nor will the young one quit the dam, though ſhe be dead; ſo that, if you kill one, you are ſure of the other. The dam, when in the water, holds the young one between her fore-fins.

Mr. Pennant, in his *Synopſis Quadr*. p. 335*, has given a very good deſcription of this animal under the name of *Arctic Walrus*; but I have no where ſeen a good drawing

---

* Mr. Pennant, ſince Captain Cook wrote this, has deſcribed this animal in a new work, which he calls *Arctic Zoology*, now ready for publication. We have been favoured with his obliging communications on this, and other particulars; and, therefore, refer the reader to the *Arctic Zoology*, N° 72.

of one. Why they should be called sea-horses, is hard to say; unless the word be a corruption of the Russian name *Morse*; for they have not the least resemblance of a horse. This is, without doubt, the same animal that is found in the Gulph of St. Laurence, and there called Sea-cow. It is certainly more like a cow than a horse; but this likeness consists in nothing but the snout. In short, it is an animal like a seal; but incomparably larger. The dimensions and weight of one, which was none of the largest, were as follows:

		Feet.	Inches.
Length from the snout to the tail		9	4
Length of the neck, from the snout to the shoulder-bone		2	6
Height of the shoulder		5	0
Length of the fins { Fore		2	4
{ Hind		2	6
Breadth of the fins { Fore		1	2½
{ Hind		2	0
Snout { Breadth		0	5½
{ Depth		1	3
Circumference of the neck close to the ears		2	7
Circumference of the body at the shoulder		7	10
Circumference near the hind fins		5	6
From the snout to the eyes		0	7

	lb.
Weight of the carcase, without the head, skin, or entrails	854
Head	41½
Skin	205

I could not find out what these animals feed upon. There was nothing in the maws of those we killed.

It is worth obſerving, that for ſome days before this date, we had frequently ſeen flocks of ducks flying to the Southward. They were of two ſorts, the one much larger than the other. The largeſt were of a brown colour; and, of the ſmall ſort, either the duck or drake was black and white, and the other brown. Some ſaid they ſaw geeſe alſo. Does not this indicate that there muſt be land to the North; where theſe birds find ſhelter, in the proper ſeaſon, to breed, and from whence they were now returning to a warmer climate?

By the time that we had got our ſea-horſes on board, we were, in a manner, ſurrounded with the ice; and had no way left to clear it, but by ſtanding to the Southward; which was done till three o'clock next morning, with a gentle breeze Weſterly; and, for the moſt part, thick, foggy weather. The ſoundings were from twelve to fifteen fathoms. We then tacked, and ſtood to the North till ten o'clock; when the wind veering to the Northward, we directed our courſe to the Weſt South Weſt and Weſt. At two in the afternoon, we fell in with the main ice; along the edge of which we kept; being partly directed by the roaring of the ſea-horſes; for we had a very thick fog. Thus we continued ſailing till near midnight, when we got in amongſt the looſe ice, and heard the ſurge of the ſea upon the main ice.

The fog being very thick, and the wind Eaſterly, I now hauled to the Southward; and, at ten o'clock the next morn- ing, the fog clearing away, we ſaw the continent of America, extending from South by Eaſt, to Eaſt by South; and at noon, from South Weſt half South, to Eaſt; the neareſt part five leagues diſtant. At this time we were in the latitude of 69° 32′, and in the longitude of 195° 48′; and as the main

ice

ice was at no great diftance from us, it is evident, that it now covered a part of the fea, which, but a few days before, had been clear; and that it extended farther to the South, than where we firft fell in with it. It muft not be under-ftood, that I fuppofed any part of this ice which we had feen, to be fixed; on the contrary, I am well affured, that the whole was a moveable mafs.

Having but little wind, in the afternoon, I fent the Mafter in a boat, to try if there was any current; but he found none. I continued to fteer in for the American land, until eight o'clock, in order to get a nearer view of it, and to look for a harbour; but feeing nothing like one, I ftood again to the North, with a light breeze Wefterly. At this time, the coaft extended from South Weft to Eaft; the neareft part four or five leagues diftant. The Southern extreme feemed to form a point, which was named *Cape Lifburne*. It lies in the latitude of 69° 5′, and in the longitude of 194° 42′, and appeared to be pretty high land, even down to the fea. But there may be low land under it, which we might not fee, being not lefs than ten leagues from it. Every where elfe, as we advanced Northward, we had found a low coaft, from which the land rifes to a middle height. The coaft now before us was without fnow, except in one or two places; and had a greenifh hue. But we could not perceive any wood upon it.

On the 22d, the wind was Southerly, and the weather moftly foggy, with fome intervals of funfhine. At eight in the evening it fell calm, which continued till midnight, when we heard the furge of the fea againft the ice, and had feveral loofe pieces about us. A light breeze now fprung up at North Eaft; and, as the fog was very thick, I fteered to the Southward, to clear the ice. At eight o'clock next morning,

morning, the fog diſperſed, and I hauled to the Weſtward. For finding that I could not get to the North near the coaſt, on account of the ice, I reſolved to try what could be done at a diſtance from it; and as the wind ſeemed to be ſettled at North, I thought it a good opportunity.

As we advanced to the Weſt, the water deepened gradually to twenty-eight fathoms, which was the moſt we had. With the Northerly wind the air was raw, ſharp, and cold; and we had fogs, ſunſhine, ſhowers of ſnow and ſleet, by turns. At ten in the morning of the 26th, we fell in with the ice. At noon, it extended from North Weſt to Eaſt by North, and appeared to be thick and compact. At this time, we were, by obſervation, in the latitude 69° 36′, and in the longitude of 184°; ſo that it now appeared we had no better proſpect of getting to the North here, than nearer the ſhore.

I continued to ſtand to the Weſtward, till five in the afternoon, when we were in a manner embayed by the ice, which appeared high, and very cloſe in the North Weſt and North Eaſt quarters, with a great deal of looſe ice about the edge of the main field. At this time, we had baffling light winds; but it ſoon fixed at South, and increaſed to a freſh gale, with ſhowers of rain. We got the tack aboard, and ſtretched to the Eaſtward; this being the only direction in which the ſea was clear of ice.

At four in the morning of the 27th, we tacked and ſtood to the Weſt, and at ſeven in the evening we were cloſe in with the edge of the ice, which lay Eaſt North Eaſt, and Weſt South Weſt, as far each way as the eye could reach. Having but little wind, I went with the boats, to examine the ſtate of the ice. I found it conſiſting of looſe pieces, of various extent, and ſo cloſe together, that I could hardly

enter

enter the outer edge with a boat; and it was as impoſſible for the ſhips to enter it, as if it had been ſo many rocks. I took particular notice, that it was all pure tranſparent ice, except the upper ſurface, which was a little porous. It appeared to be entirely compoſed of frozen ſnow, and to have been all formed at ſea. For, ſetting aſide the improbability, or rather impoſſibility, of ſuch huge maſſes floating out of rivers, in which there is hardly water for a boat, none of the productions of the land were found incorporated, or fixed in it; which muſt have unavoidably been the caſe, had it been formed in rivers, either great or ſmall. The pieces of ice that formed the outer edge of the field, were from forty or fifty yards in extent, to four or five; and I judged, that the larger pieces reached thirty feet, or more, under the ſurface of the water. It alſo appeared to me very improbable, that this ice could have been the production of the preceding winter alone. I ſhould ſuppoſe it rather to have been the production of a great many winters. Nor was it leſs improbable, according to my judgment, that the little that remained of the ſummer, could deſtroy the tenth part of what now ſubſiſted of this maſs; for the ſun had already exerted upon it the full influence of his rays. Indeed I am of opinion, that the ſun contributes very little toward reducing theſe great maſſes. For although that luminary is a conſiderable while above the horizon, it ſeldom ſhines out for more than a few hours at a time; and often is not ſeen for ſeveral days in ſucceſſion. It is the wind, or rather the waves raiſed by the wind, that brings down the bulk of theſe enormous maſſes, by grinding one piece againſt another, and by undermining and waſhing away thoſe parts that lie expoſed to the ſurge of the ſea. This was evident, from our obſerving, that the upper ſurface of many pieces

had

had been partly wafhed away, while the bafe or under part remained firm for feveral fathoms round that which appeared above water, exactly like a fhoal round an elevated rock. We meafured the depth of water upon one, and found it to be fifteen feet; fo that the fhips might have failed over it. If I had not meafured this depth, I would not have believed, that there was a fufficient weight of ice above the furface, to have funk the other fo much below it. Thus it may happen, that more ice is deftroyed in one ftormy feafon, than is formed in feveral winters, and an endlefs accumulation is prevented. But that there is always a remaining ftore, every one who has been upon the fpot will conclude, and none but clofet-ftudying philofophers will difpute.

A thick fog, which came on while I was thus employed with the boats, haftened me aboard, rather fooner than I could have wifhed, with one fea-horfe to each fhip. We had killed more, but could not wait to bring them with us. The number of thefe animals, on all the ice that we had feen, is almoft incredible. We fpent the night ftanding off and on, amongft the drift ice; and at nine o'clock the next morning, the fog having partly difperfed, boats from each fhip were fent for fea-horfes. For, by this time, our people began to relifh them, and thofe we had procured before were all confumed. At noon, our latitude was 69° 17′, our longitude 183°; the variation, by the morning azimuths, 25° 56′ Eaft; and the depth of water twenty-five fathoms. At two o'clock, having got on board as much marine beef as was thought neceffary, and the wind frefhening at South South Eaft, we took on board the boats, and ftretched to the South Weft. But not being able to weather the ice upon this tack, or to go through it, we made a board to the Eaft,

till

till eight o'clock, then refumed our courfe to the South Weft, and before midnight were obliged to tack again, on account of the ice. Soon after, the wind fhifted to the North Weft, blowing a ftiff gale, and we ftretched to the South Weft, clofe hauled.

In the morning of the 29th, we faw the main ice to the Northward, and not long after, land, bearing South Weft by Weft. Prefently after this, more land fhewed itfelf, bearing Weft. It fhewed itfelf in two hills like iflands, but afterward the whole appeared connected. As we approached the land, the depth of water decreafed very faft; fo that at noon, when we tacked, we had only eight fathoms; being three miles from the coaft, which extended from South, 30° Eaft, to North, 60° Weft. This laft extreme terminated in a bluff point, being one of the hills above mentioned.

! The weather at this time was very hazy, with drizzling rain; but foon after it cleared; efpecially to the Southward, Weftward, and Northward. This enabled us to have a pretty good view of the coaft; which, in every refpect, is like the oppofite one of America; that is, low land next the fea, with elevated land farther back. It was perfectly deftitute of wood, and even fnow; but was, probably, covered with a moffy fubftance, that gave it a brownifh caft. In the low ground lying between the high land and the fea, was a lake, extending to the South Eaft, farther than we could fee. As we ftood off, the Wefternmoft of the two hills before mentioned came open off the bluff point, in the direction of North Weft. It had the appearance of being an ifland; but it might be joined to the other by low land, though we did not fee it. And if fo, there is a two-fold point, with a bay between them. This point, which is

steep

fteep and rocky, was named *Cape North*. Its fituation is nearly in the latitude of 68° 56′, and in the longitude of 180° 51′. The coaſt beyond it muſt take a very Weſterly di-. rection; for we could fee no land to the Northward of it, though the horizon was there pretty clear. Being defirous of feeing more of the coaſt to the Weſtward, we tacked again, at two o'clock in the afternoon, thinking we could weather Cape North. But finding we could not, the wind freſhening, a thick fog coming on, with much fnow, and being fearful of the ice coming down upon us, I gave up the defign I had formed of plying to the Weſtward, and ftood off ſhore again.

The feafon was now ſo far advanced, and the time when the froſt is expected to fet in ſo near at hand, that I did not think it confiſtent with prudence, to make any farther attempts to find a paſſage into the Atlantic this year, in any direction; ſo little was the profpect of fucceeding. My attention was now directed toward finding out fome place where we might fupply ourfelves with wood and water; and the object uppermoſt in my thoughts was, how I ſhould fpend the winter, ſo as to make fome improvements in geography and navigation, and, at the fame time, be in a condition to return to the North, in farther fearch of a paſſage, the enfuing fummer.

CHAP. X.

Return from Cape North, along the Coast of Asia.—Views of the Country.—Burney's Island.—Cape Serdze Kamen, the Northern Limit of Beering's Voyage.—Pass the East Cape of Asia.—Description and Situation of it.—Observations on Muller.—The Tschutski.—Bay of Saint Laurence.—Two other Bays, and Habitations of the Natives.—Beering's Cape Tschukotskoi.—Beering's Position of this Coast accurate.—Island of Saint Laurence.—Pass to the American Coast.—Cape Darby.—Bald Head.—Cape Denbigh, on a Peninsula.—Besborough Island.—Wood and Water procured.—Visits from the Natives.—Their Persons and Habitations.—Produce of the Country.—Marks that the Peninsula had formerly been surrounded by the Sea.—Lieutenant King's Report.—Norton Sound.—Lunar Observations there.—Staeblin's Map proved to be erroneous.—Plan of future Operations.

1778.
August.

Saturday 29.

AFTER having stood off till we got into eighteen fathoms water, I bore up to the Eastward, along the coast, which, by this time, it was pretty certain, could only be the continent of Asia. As the wind blew fresh, with a very heavy fall of snow, and a thick mist, it was necessary to proceed with great caution. I therefore brought to, for a few hours in the night.

I   At

At day-break, on the 30th, we made fail, and fteered fuch a courfe as I thought would bring us in with the land; being in a great meafure guided by the lead. For the weather was as thick as ever, and it fnowed inceffantly. At ten, we got fight of the coaft, bearing South Weft, four miles diftant; and prefently after, having fhoaled the water to feven fathoms, we hauled off. At this time, a very low point, or fpit, bore South South Weft, two or three miles diftant; to the Eaft of which there appeared to be a narrow channel, leading into fome water that we faw over the point. Probably, the lake before mentioned communicates here with the fea.

1778.
Auguft.
Sunday 30.

At noon, the mift difperfing for a fhort interval, we had a tolerably good view of the coaft, which extended from South Eaft to North Weft by Weft. Some parts appeared higher than others; but in general it was very low, with high land farther up the country. The whole was now covered with fnow, which had lately fallen, quite down to the fea. I continued to range along the coaft, at two leagues diftance, till ten at night, when we hauled off; but we refumed our courfe next morning, foon after day-break, when we got fight of the coaft again, extending from Weft to South Eaft by South. At eight, the Eaftern part bore South, and proved to be an ifland; which at noon bore South Weft half South, four or five miles diftant. It is about four or five miles in circuit, of a middling height, with a fteep, rocky coaft, fituated about three leagues from the main, in the latitude of 67° 45′, and diftinguifhed in the chart by the name of *Burney's Ifland*.

Monday 31.

The inland country hereabout is full of hills; fome of which are of a confiderable height. The land was covered with fnow, except a few fpots upon the fea-coaft, which

3 O 2   ftill

ſtill continued low, but leſs ſo than farther Weſtward. For the two preceding days, the mean height of the mercury in the thermometer had been very little above the freezing point, and often below it ; ſo that the water, in the veſſels upon the deck, was frequently covered with a ſheet of ice.

I continued to ſteer South South Eaſt, nearly in the direction of the coaſt, till five in the afternoon, when land was ſeen bearing South, 50° Eaſt, which we preſently found to be a continuation of the coaſt, and hauled up for it. Being abreaſt of the Eaſtern land, at ten at night, and in doubts of weathering it, we tacked, and made a board to the Weſtward, till paſt one the next morning, when we ſtood again to the Eaſt, and found that it was as much as we could do to keep our diſtance from the coaſt, the wind being exceedingly unſettled, varying continually from North to North Eaſt. At half an hour paſt eight, the Eaſtern extreme above mentioned bore South by Eaſt, ſix or ſeven miles diſtant. At the ſame time, a head-land appeared in ſight, bearing Eaſt by South, half South ; and, ſoon after, we could trace the whole coaſt lying between them, and a ſmall iſland at ſome diſtance from it.

The coaſt ſeemed to form ſeveral rocky points, connected by a low ſhore, without the leaſt appearance of a harbour. At ſome diſtance from the ſea, the low land appeared to ſwell into a number of hills. The higheſt of theſe were covered with ſnow ; and in other reſpects, the whole country ſeemed naked. At ſeven in the evening, two points of land, at ſome diſtance beyond the Eaſtern head, opened off it in the direction of South, 37° Eaſt. I was now well aſſured, of what I had believed before, that this was the country of the Tſchutſki, or the North Eaſt coaſt of Aſia;

and

and that thus far Beering proceeded in 1728; that is, to this head, which Muller fays is called *Serdze Kamen*, on account of a rock upon it, fhaped like a heart. But I conceive, that Mr. Muller's knowledge of the geography of thefe parts is very imperfect. There are many elevated rocks upon this Cape, and poffibly fome one or other of them may have the fhape of a heart. It is a pretty lofty promontory, with a fteep rocky cliff facing the fea; and lies in the latitude of 67° 3′, and in the longitude of 188° 11′. To the Eaftward of it, the coaft is high and bold; but to the Weftward it is low, and trends North North Weft, and North Weft by Weft; which is nearly its direction all the way to Cape North. The foundings are every where the fame at the fame diftance from the fhore, which is alfo the cafe on the oppofite fhore of America. The greateft depth we found in ranging along it was twenty-three fathoms. And, in the night, or in foggy weather, the foundings are no bad guide in failing along either of thefe fhores.

At eight o'clock in the morning of the 2d, the moft advanced land to the South Eaft, bore South, 25° Eaft; and from this point of view had the appearance of being an ifland. But the thick fnow fhowers, which fucceeded one another pretty faft, and fettled upon the land, hid great part of the coaft at this time from our fight. Soon after, the fun, whofe face we had not feen for near five days, broke out at the intervals between the fhowers; and, in fome meafure, freed the coaft from the fog, fo that we had a fight of it, and found the whole to be connected. The wind ftill continued at North, the air was cold, and the mercury in the thermometer never rofe above 35°, and was fometimes as low as 30°. At noon the obferved latitude

Wednef. 2.

was

was 66° 37', Cape Serdze Kamen bore North, 52° Weſt, thirteen leagues diſtant; the Southernmoſt point of land in ſight South, 41° Eaſt; the neareſt part of the coaſt two leagues diſtant; and our depth of water twenty-two fathoms.

We had now fair weather and ſunſhine; and as we ranged along the coaſt, at the diſtance of four miles, we ſaw ſeveral of the inhabitants, and ſome of their habitations, which looked like little hillocks of earth. In the evening we paſſed the *Eaſtern Cape*, or the point above mentioned; from which the coaſt changes its direction, and trends South Weſt. It is the ſame point of land which we had paſſed on the 11th of Auguſt. They who believed implicitly in Mr. Stæhlin's map, then thought it the Eaſt point of his iſland Alaſchka; but we had, by this time, ſatisfied ourſelves, that it is no other than the Eaſtern promontory of Aſia; and probably the proper *Tſchukotſkoi Noſs*, though the promontory, to which Beering gave that name, is farther to the South Weſt.

Though Mr. Muller, in his map of the Ruſſian Diſcoveries, places the Tſchukotſkoi Noſs nearly in 75° of latitude, and extends it ſomewhat to the Eaſtward of this Cape, it appears to me, that he had no good authority for ſo doing. Indeed his own accounts, or rather Deſhneff's *, of the diſtance between the Noſs, and the river Anadir, cannot be reconciled with this very Northerly poſition. But as I hope to viſit theſe parts again, I ſhall leave the diſcuſſion of this point till then. In the mean time, I muſt conclude, as

* Avec le vent le plus favorable, on peut aller par mer de cette pointe (des Tſchuktſchis), juſqu'à l'Anadir en trois fois 24 heures ; & par terre le chemin ne peut guère être plus long.—Muller, p. 13.

Beering

Beering did before me, that this is the moft Eaftern point
of Afia. It is a peninfula of confiderable height, joined to
the continent by a very low, and, to appearance, narrow
neck of land. It fhews a fteep rocky cliff next the fea; and
off the very point are fome rocks like fpires. It is fituated
in the latitude of 66° 6′, and in the longitude of 190° 22′;
and is diftant from Cape Prince of Wales, on the American
coaft, thirteen leagues, in the direction of North, 53° Weft.
The land about this promontory is compofed of hills and
vallies. The former terminate at the fea in fteep rocky
points, and the latter in low fhores. The hills feemed to be
naked rocks; but the vallies had a greenifh hue, but deftitute of tree or fhrub.

After paffing the Cape, I fteered South Weft half Weft,
for the Northern point of St. Laurence Bay, in which we
had anchored on the 10th of laft month. We reached it by
eight o'clock next morning, and faw fome of the inhabitants at the place where I had feen them before, as well as
feveral others on the oppofite fide of the bay. None of
them, however, attempted to come off to us; which feemed
a little extraordinary, as the weather was favourable enough;
and thofe whom we had lately vifited had no reafon, that I
know of, to diflike our company. Thefe people muft be
the Tfchutfki; a nation that, at the time Mr. Muller wrote,
the Ruffians had not been able to conquer. And, from
the whole of their conduct with us, it appears that they
have not, as yet, brought them under fubjection; though
it is obvious that they muft have a trade with the Ruffians,
either directly, or by means of fome neighbouring nation;
as we cannot otherwife account for their being in poffeffion of the fpontoons, in particular, of which we took
notice.

This

This Bay of *St. Laurence* * is, at leaft, five leagues broad at the entrance, and four leagues deep, narrowing toward the bottom, where it appeared to be tolerably well fheltered from the fea-winds, provided there be a fufficient depth of water for fhips. I did not wait to examine it, although I was very defirous of finding an harbour in thofe parts, to which I might refort next fpring. But I wanted one where wood might be got, and I knew that none was to be found here. From the South point of this bay, which lies in the latitude of 65° 30′, the coaft trends Weft by South, for about nine leagues, and there forms a deep bay, or river; or elfe the land there is fo low that we could not fee it.

At one in the afternoon, in the direction of our courfe, we faw what was firft taken for a rock; but it proved to be a dead whale, which fome natives of the Afiatic coaft had killed, and were towing afhore. They feemed to conceal themfelves behind the fifh to avoid being feen by us. This was unneceffary; for we purfued our courfe, without taking any notice of them.

Friday 4. At day-break on the 4th, I hauled to the North Weft, in order to get a nearer view of the inlet feen the preceding day; but the wind, foon after, veering to that direction, I gave up the defign; and, fteering to the Southward along the coaft, paft two bays, each about two leagues deep. The Northernmoft lies before a hill, which is remarkable by being rounder than any other upon the coaft. And there is an ifland lying before the other. It may be doubted, whether there be a fufficient depth for fhips in either of thefe bays, as we always met with fhoal water, when we edged

_____

* Captain Cook gives it this name, having anchored in it on St. Laurence's day, Auguft 10. It is remarkable, that Beering failed paft this very place on the 10th of Auguft 1728; on which account, the neighbouring ifland was named by him after the fame Saint.

in

in for the fhore. The country here is exceedingly hilly and naked. In feveral places on the low ground, next the fea, were the dwellings of the natives; and near all of them were erected ftages of bones, fuch as before defcribed. Thefe may be feen at a great diftance, on account of their whitenefs.

At noon the latitude was 64° 38′, and the longitude 188° 15′; the Southernmoft point of the main in fight bore South, 48° Weft; and the neareft fhore about three or four leagues diftant. By this time, the wind had veered again to the North, and blew a gentle breeze. The weather was clear, and the air cold. I did not follow the direction of the coaft, as I found that it took a Wefterly direction toward the Gulf of Anadir, into which I had no inducement to go, but fteered to the Southward, in order to get a fight of the Ifland of St. Laurence, difcovered by Beering; which accordingly fhewed itfelf, and, at eight o'clock in the evening, it bore South, 20° Eaft; by eftimation, eleven leagues diftant. At the fame time, the Southernmoft point of the main land bore South, 83° Weft, diftant twelve leagues. I take this to be the point which Beering calls the Eaft Point of Suchotfki, or *Cape Tfchukotfkoi*; a name which he gave it, and with propriety, becaufe it was from this part of the coaft that the natives came off to him, who called themfelves of the nation of the Tfchutfki. I make its latitude to be 64° 13′, and its longitude 186° 36′.

In juftice to the memory of Beering, I muft fay, that he has delineated the coaft very well, and fixed the latitude and longitude of the points better than could be expected from the methods he had to go by. This judgment is not formed from Mr. Muller's account of the voyage, or the chart prefixed to his book; but from Dr. Campbell's account of it in his edition of Harris's Collection *, and a map thereto annexed, which is both more circumftantial and accurate than that of Mr. Muller.

The more I was convinced of my being now upon the coaft of Afia, the more I was at a lofs to reconcile Mr. Stæhlin's map of the New Northern Archipelago with my obfervations; and I had no way to account for the great difference, but by fuppofing, that I had miftaken fome part of what he calls the Ifland of Alafchka for the American continent, and had miffed the channel that feparates them. Admitting even this, there would ftill have been a confiderable difference. It was with me a matter of fome confequence, to clear up this point the prefent feafon, that I might have but one objeĉt in view the next. And, as thefe Northern ifles are reprefented by him as abounding with wood, I was in hopes, if I fhould find them, of getting a fupply of that article, which we now began to be in great want of on board.

With thefe views, I fteered over for the American coaft; and, at five in the afternoon, the next day, faw land bearing South three quarters Eaft, which we took to be Anderfon's Ifland, or fome other land near it, and therefore did not wait to examine it. On the 6th, at four in the morning, we got fight of the American coaft near Sledge Ifland; and at fix, the fame evening, this ifland bore North, 6° Eaft, ten leagues diftant; and the Eafternmoft land in fight North, 49° Eaft. If any part of what I had fuppofed to be American coaft, could poffibly be the ifland of Alafchka, it was that now before us; and in that cafe, I muft have miffed the channel between it and the main, by fteering to

Saturday 5.

Sunday 6.

* Vol. ii. p. 1016, &c.

the

the Weft, inftead of the Eaft, after we firft fell in with it.
I was not, therefore, at a lofs where to go, in order to clear
up thefe doubts.

At eight in the evening of the 7th, we had got clofe in
with the land, Sledge Ifland bearing North 85° Weft, eight
or nine leagues diftant; and the Eaftern part of the coaft
North 70° Eaft, with high land in the direction of Eaft by
North, feemingly at a great diftance beyond the point. At
this time we faw a light afhore; and two canoes, filled with
people, coming off toward us. I brought to, that they might
have time to come up. But it was to no purpofe; for, re-
fifting all the figns of friendfhip we could exhibit, they kept
at the diftance of a quarter of a mile; fo that we left them,
and purfued our courfe along the coaft.

At one in the morning of the 8th, finding the water fhoal
pretty faft, we dropped anchor in ten fathoms, where we lay
until day-light, and then refumed our courfe along the coaft,
which we found to trend Eaft, and Eaft half South. At feven in the evening, we were abreaft of a point, lying in
the latitude of 64° 21', and in the longitude of 197°; beyond
which the coaft takes a more Northerly direction. At eight,
this point, which obtained the name of *Cape Darby*, bore
South 62° Weft; the Northernmoft land in fight, North
32° Eaft; and the neareft fhore three miles diftant. In this
fituation we anchored in thirteen fathoms water, over a
muddy bottom.

Next morning, at day-break, we weighed, and failed
along the coaft. Two iflands, as we fuppofed them to be,
were at that time feen; the one bearing South 70° Eaft, and
the other Eaft. Soon after, we found ourfelves upon a coaft
covered with wood; an agreeable fight, to which, of late,
we had not been accuftomed. As we advanced to the North,

3 P 2

we

we raifed land in the direction of North Eaft half North; which proved to be a continuation of the coaft we were upon. We alfo faw high land over the iflands, feemingly at a good diftance beyond them. This was thought to be the continent, and the other land the ifland of Alafchka. But it was already doubtful, whether we fhould find a paffage between them; for the water fhoaled infenfibly as we advanced farther to the North. In this fituation, two boats were fent to found before the fhips; and I ordered the Difcovery to lead, keeping nearly in the mid channel, between the coaft on our larboard, and the Northernmoft ifland on our ftarboard. Thus we proceeded till three in the afternoon; when, having paffed the ifland, we had not more than three fathoms and an half of water; and the Refolution, at one time, brought the mud up from the bottom. More water was not to be found in any part of the channel; for, with the fhips and boats, we had tried it from fide to fide.

I therefore thought it high time to return; efpecially as the wind was in fuch a quarter that we muft ply back. But what I dreaded moft was the wind increafing, and raifing the fea into waves, fo as to put the fhips in danger of ftriking. At this time, a head land on the Weft fhore, which is diftinguifhed by the name of *Bald Head*, bore North by Weft, one league diftant. The coaft beyond it extended as far as North Eaft by North, where it feemed to end in a point; behind which the coaft of the high land, feen over the iflands, ftretched itfelf; and fome thought they could trace where it joined. On the Weft fide of Bald Head, the fhore forms a bay, in the bottom of which is a low beach, where we faw a number of huts or habitations of the natives.

Having

Having continued to ply back all night, by day-break the next morning we had got into ſix fathoms water. At nine o'clock, being about a league from the Weſt ſhore, I took two boats, and landed, attended by Mr. King, to ſeek wood and water. We landed where the coaſt projects out into a bluff head, compoſed of perpendicular *ſtrata* of a rock of a dark blue colour, mixed with quartz and glimmer. There joins to the beach a narrow border of land, now covered with long graſs, and where we met with ſome *angelica*. Beyond this, the ground riſes abruptly. At the top of this elevation, we found a heath, abounding with a variety of berries; and further on, the country was level, and thinly covered with ſmall ſpruce trees; and birch and willows no bigger than broom ſtuff. We obſerved tracks of deer and foxes on the beach; on which alſo lay a great quantity of drift-wood; and there was no want of freſh water. I returned on board, with an intention to bring the ſhips to an anchor here; but the wind then veering to North Eaſt, which blew rather on this ſhore, I ſtretched over to the oppoſite one, in the expectation of finding wood there alſo, and anchored at eight o'clock in the evening, under the South end of the Northernmoſt iſland: ſo we then ſuppoſed it to be; but, next morning, we found it to be a peninſula, united to the continent by a low neck of land, on each ſide of which the coaſt forms a bay. We plied into the Southernmoſt, and about noon anchored in five fathoms water, over a bottom of mud; the point of the peninſula, which obtained the name of *Cape Denbigh*, bearing North 68° Weſt, three miles diſtant.

Several people were ſeen upon the peninſula; and one man came off in a ſmall canoe. I gave him a knife, and a few beads, with which he ſeemed well pleaſed. Having

made

made figns to him to bring us fomething to eat, he immediately left us, and paddled toward the fhore. But meeting another man coming off, who happened to have two
dried falmon, he got them from him; and on returning to
the fhip, would give them to nobody but me. Some of our
people thought that he afked for me under the name of *Ca-
pitane*; but in this they were probably miftaken. He knew
who had given him the knife and beads, but I do not fee
how he could know that I was the Captain. Others of the
natives, foon after, came off, and exchanged a few dry fifh,
for fuch trifles as they could get, or we had to give them.
They were moft defirous of knives; and they had no diflike
to tobacco.

After dinner, Lieutenant Gore was fent to the peninfula,
to fee if wood and water were there to be got; or rather
water; for the whole beach round the bay feemed to be covered with drift-wood. At the fame time, a boat was fent
from each fhip, to found round the bay; and, at three in
the afternoon, the wind frefhening at North Eaft, we
weighed, in order to work farther in. But it was foon
found to be impoffible, on account of the fhoals, which extended quite round the bay, to the diftance of two or three
miles from the fhore; as the officers, who had been fent to
found, reported. We, therefore, kept ftanding off and on
with the fhips, waiting for Mr. Gore, who returned about
eight o'clock, with the launch laden with wood.

He reported, that there was but little frefh water; and
that wood was difficult to be got at, by reafon of the boats
grounding at fome diftance from the beach. This being the
cafe, I ftood back to the other fhore; and, at eight o'clock
the next morning, fent all the boats, and a party of men,
with an officer, to get wood from the place where I had
landed

landed two days before. We continued, for a while, to
ftand on and off with the ſhips; but, at length, came to an anchor in one-fourth leſs than five fathoms, half a league from the coaſt, the South point of which bore South 26° Weſt; and Bald Head, North 60° Eaſt, nine leagues diſtant. Cape Denbigh bore South 72° Eaſt, twenty-ſix miles diſtant; and the iſland under the Eaſt ſhore, to the Southward of Cape Denbigh, named *Beſborough Iſland*, South 52° Eaſt, fifteen leagues diſtant.

As this was a very open road, and conſequently not a ſafe ſtation, I reſolved not to wait to complete water, as that would require ſome time; but only to ſupply the ſhips with wood, and then to go in ſearch of a more convenient place for the other article. We took off the drift-wood that lay upon the beach; and as the wind blew along ſhore, the boats could ſail both ways, which enabled us to make great diſpatch.

In the afternoon, I went aſhore, and walked a little into the country; which, where there was no wood, was covered with heath and other plants, ſome of which produce berries in abundance. All the berries were ripe; the hurtle-berries too much ſo; and hardly a ſingle plant was in flower. The underwood, ſuch as birch, willows, and alders, rendered it very troubleſome walking amongſt the trees, which were all ſpruce, and none of them above ſix or eight inches in diameter. But we found ſome lying upon the beach, more than twice this ſize. All the drift-wood in theſe Northern parts was fir. I ſaw not a ſtick of any other ſort.

Next day, a family of the natives came near to the place where we were taking off wood. I know not how many there were at firſt; but I ſaw only the huſband, the wife, and

and their child; and a fourth perfon who bore the human fhape, and that was all; for he was the moft deformed cripple I had ever feen or heard of. The other man was almoft blind; and neither he, nor his wife, were fuch good-looking people as we had fometimes feen amongft the natives of this coaft. The under-lips of both were bored; and they had in their poffeffion fome fuch glafs beads as I had met with before amongft their neighbours. But iron was their beloved article. For four knives, which we had made out of an old iron hoop, I got from them near four hundred pounds weight of fifh, which they had caught on this or the preceding day. Some were trout, and the reft were, in fize and tafte, fomewhat between a mullet and a herring. I gave the child, who was a girl, a few beads; on which the mother burft into tears, then the father, then the cripple, and, at laft, to complete the concert, the girl herfelf. But this mufic continued not long *. Before night, we had got
the

* Captain King has communicated the following account of his interview with the fame family. " On the 12th, while I attended the wooding party, a canoe full of natives approached us; and, beckoning them to land, an elderly man and woman came on fhore. I gave the woman a fmall knife, making her underftand, that I would give her a much larger one for fome fifh. She made figns to me to follow her. I had proceeded with them about a mile, when the man, in croffing a ftony beach, fell down, and cut his foot very much. This made me ftop; upon which the woman pointed to the man's eyes, which, I obferved, were covered with a thick, white film. He afterward kept clofe to his wife, who apprized him of the obftacles in his way. The woman had a little child on her back, covered with the hood of her jacket: and which I took for a bundle, till I heard it cry. At about two miles diftance we came to their open fkin boat, which was turned on its fide, the convex part toward the wind, and ferved for their houfe. I was now made to perform a fingular operation on the man's eyes. Firft, I was directed to hold my breath; afterward, to breathe on the difeafed eyes; and next, to fpit on them. The woman then took both my hands, and preffing them to his ftomach, held them there for fome time, while fhe related fome calamitous hiftory of her family; pointing fometimes to her hufband, fometimes to a frightful cripple belonging to the family, and
fometimes

the fhips amply fupplied with wood; and had carried on board about twelve tons of water to each.

On the 14th, a party of men were fent on fhore to cut brooms, which we were in want of, and the branches of fpruce-trees for brewing beer. Toward noon, every body was taken on board; for the wind, frefhening, had raifed fuch a furf on the beach, that the boats could not continue to land without great difficulty. Some doubts being ftill entertained, whether the coaft we were now upon belonged to an ifland, or the American continent; and the fhallownefs of the water putting it out of our power to determine this with our fhips, I fent Lieutenant King, with two boats under his command, to make fuch fearches as might leave no room for a variety of opinions on the fubject *. Next day, the fhips removed over to the bay, which is

fometimes to her child. I purchafed all the fifh they had, confifting of very fine falmon, falmon-trout, and mullet; which were delivered moft faithfully to the man I fent for them. The man was about five feet two inches high, and well made; his colour, of a light copper; his hair black and fhort, and with little beard. He had two holes in his underlip, but no ornaments in them. The woman was fhort and fquat, with a plump round face; wore a deer-fkin jacket with a large hood; and had on wide boots. The teeth of both were black, and feemed as if they had been filed down level with the gums. The woman was punctured from the lip to the chin."

* Captain King has been fo good as to communicate his inftructions on this occafion, and the particulars of the fatigue he underwent, in carrying them into execution:

" You are to proceed to the Northward as far as the extreme point we faw on Wed-
" nefday laft, or a little further, if you think it neceffary; land there, and endeavour, from
" the heights, to difcover whether the land you are then upon, fuppofed to be the ifland
" of Alafchka, is really an ifland, or joins to the land on the Eaft, fuppofed to be the con-
" tinent of America. If the former, you are to fatisfy yourfelf with the depth of
" water in the channel between them, and which way the flood-tide comes. But if you
" find the two lands connected, lofe no time in founding; but make the beft of your way
" back to the fhip, which you will find at anchor near the point of land we anchored
" under on Friday laft. If you perceive any likelihood of a change of weather for the

is on the South Eaſt ſide of Cape Denbigh, where we anchored in the afternoon. Soon after, a few of the natives
came off in their ſmall canoes, and bartered ſome dried ſal-
mon for ſuch trifles as our people had to give them.

" worſe, you are, in that caſe, to return to the ſhip, although you have not performed the
" ſervice you are ſent upon. And, at any rate, you are not to remain longer upon it.
" than four or five days ; but the ſooner it is done the better. If any unforeſeen, or un-
" avoidable accident, ſhould force the ſhips off the coaſt, ſo that they cannot return at a
" reaſonable time, the rendezvous is at the harbour of Samganoodha ; that is, the place
" where we laſt completed our water."

" J A M E S   C O O K."

" *To Lieutenant King.*"

" Our cutter being hoiſted out, and the ſignal made for the Diſcovery's, at eight at
night, on the 14th, we ſet out. It was a little unlucky, that the boats crews had been much
fatigued during the whole day in bringing things from the ſhore. They pulled ſtoutly,
without reſt or intermiſſion, toward the land, till one o'clock in the morning of the 15th.
I wanted much to have got cloſe to it, to have had the advantage of the wind, which had
very regularly, in the evening, blown from the land, and in the day-time down the Sound,
from the North North Eaſt, and was contrary to our courſe ; but the men were, at this
time, too much fatigued to preſs them farther. We, therefore, ſet our ſails, and ſtood
acroſs the bay, which the coaſt forms to the Weſt of Baldhead, and ſteered for it. But,
as I expected, by three o'clock, the wind headed us ; and, as it was in vain to endeavour
to fetch Baldhead with our ſails, we again took to the oars. The Diſcovery's boat (being a
heavy king's-built cutter, while ours was one from Deal) had, in the night-time, detained
us very much, and now we ſoon pulled out of ſight of her ; nor would I wait, being in
great hopes to reach the extreme point that was in ſight, time enough to aſcend the heights
before dark, as the weather was at this time remarkably clear and fine ; and we could ſee
to a great diſtance. By two o'clock we had got within two miles of Baldhead, under the
lee of the high land, and in ſmooth water ; but, at the moment our object was nearly attained, all the men, but two, were ſo overcome with fatigue and ſleep, that my utmoſt endeavours to make them put on were ineffectual. They, at length, dropped their oars,
quite exhauſted, and fell aſleep in the bottom of the boat. Indeed, conſidering that they
had ſet out fatigued, and had now been ſixteen hours, out of the eighteen ſince they left
the ſhip, pulling in a poppling ſea, it was no wonder that their ſtrength and ſpirits ſhould
be worn out for want of ſleep and refreſhments. The two gentlemen, who were with
me, and myſelf, were now obliged to lay hold of the oars ; and, by a little after three, we
landed between the Baldhead and a projecting point to the Eaſtward."

At

At day-break, on the 16th, nine men, each in his canoe, paid us a vifit. They approached the fhip with fome caution; and evidently came with no other view than to gratify their curiofity. They drew up abreaft of each other, under our ftern, and gave us a fong; while one of their number beat upon a kind of drum, and another made a thoufand antic motions with his hands and body. There was, however, nothing favage, either in the fong, or in the geftures that accompanied it. None of us could perceive any difference between thefe people, either as to their fize or features, and thofe whom we had met with on every other part of the coaft, King George's Sound excepted. Their clothing, which confifted principally of deer-fkins, was made after the fame fafhion; and they obferved the cuftom of boring their under-lips, and fixing ornaments to them.

The dwellings of thefe people were feated clofe to the beach. They confift fimply of a floping roof, without any fide-walls, compofed of logs, and covered with grafs and earth. The floor is alfo laid with logs; the entrance is at one end; the fire-place juft within it; and a fmall hole is made near the door to let out the fmoke.

After breakfaft, a party of men were fent to the peninfula for brooms and fpruce. At the fame time, half the remainder of the people in each fhip had leave to go and pick berries. Thefe returned on board at noon, when the other half went on the fame errand. The berries to be got here were wild currant-berries, hurtle-berries, partridge-berries, and heath-berries. I alfo went afhore myfelf, and walked over part of the peninfula. In feveral places there was very good grafs; and I hardly faw a fpot, on which fome vegetable was not growing. The low land which

connects

connects this peninfula with the continent, is full of narrow creeks; and abounds with ponds of water, fome of which were already frozen over. There were a great many geefe and buftards; but fo fhy, that it was not poffible to get within mufket-fhot of them. We alfo met with fome fnipes; and on the high ground were partridges of two forts. Where there was any wood, mufquitoes were in plenty. Some of the officers, who travelled farther than I did, met with a few of the natives of both fexes, who treated them with civility.

It appeared to me, that this peninfula muft have been an ifland in remote times; for there were marks of the fea having flowed over the ifthmus. And, even now, it appeared to be kept out by a bank of fand, ftones, and wood thrown up by the waves. By this bank it was evident, that the land was here encroaching upon the fea, and it was eafy to trace its gradual formation.

About feven in the evening, Mr. King returned from his expedition; and reported, that he proceeded with the boats about three or four leagues farther than the fhips had been able to go; that he then landed on the Weft fide; that, from the heights, he could fee the two coafts join, and the inlet to terminate in a fmall river or creek, before which were banks of fand or mud; and every where fhoal water. The land too, was low and fwampy for fome diftance to the Northward; then it fwelled into hills; and the complete junction of thofe, on each fide of the inlet, was eafily traced.

From the elevated fpot on which Mr. King furveyed the Sound, he could diftinguifh many extenfive vallies, with rivers running through them, well wooded, and bounded by hills of a gentle afcent and moderate height. One of thefe
rivers

rivers to the North Weft appeared to be confiderable; and, from its direction, he was inclined to think, that it emptied itfelf into the fea at the head of the bay. Some of his people, who penetrated beyond this into the country, found the trees larger, the farther they advanced.

In honour of Sir Fletcher Norton*, Speaker of the Houfe of Commons, and Mr. King's near relation, I named this inlet *Norton Sound*. It extends to the Northward as far as the latitude of 64° 55′. The bay, in which we were now at anchor, lies on the South Eaft fide of it; and is called by the natives *Chacktoole*. It is but an indifferent ftation; being expofed to the South and South Weft winds. Nor is there a harbour in all this Sound. But we were fo fortunate as to have the wind from the North and North Eaft all the time, with remarkable fine weather. This gave us an opportunity to make no lefs than feventy-feven fets of lunar obfervations, between the 6th and 17th inclufive. The mean refult of thefe made the longitude of the anchoring-place, on the Weft fide of the Sound, to be - 197° 13′

Latitude - - - - - -	64	31
Variation of the compafs - - -	25	45 Eaft.
Dip of the needle - - - -	76	25

Of the tides it was obferved, that the night-flood rofe about two or three feet, and that the day-flood was hardly perceivable.

Having now fully fatisfied myfelf, that Mr. Stæhlin's map muft be erroneous; and, having reftored the American continent to that fpace which he had occupied with his imaginary ifland of Alafchka, it was high time to think of leaving thefe Northern regions, and to retire to fome place during the winter, where I might procure refrefhments for

* Now Lord Grantley.

my

my people, and a fmall fupply of provifions. Petropaulowfka, or the harbour of St. Peter and St. Paul, in Kamtfchatka, did not appear likely to furnifh either the one or
the other, for fo large a number of men. I had, befides,
other reafons for not repairing thither at this time. The
firft, and on which all the others depended, was the great
diflike I had to lie inactive for fix or feven months; which
would have been the neceffary confequence of wintering in
any of thefe Northern parts. No place was fo conveniently
within our reach, where we could expect to have our wants
relieved, as the Sandwich Iflands. To them, therefore, I
determined to proceed. But before this could be carried
into execution, a fupply of water was neceffary. With this
view, I refolved to fearch the American coaft for a harbour,
by proceeding along it to the Southward, and thus endeavour to connect the furvey of this part of it, with that lying immediately to the North of Cape Newenham. If I
failed in finding a harbour there, my plan was then to
proceed to Samganoodha, which was fixed upon as our
place of rendezvous, in cafe of feparation.

CHAP.

C H A P. XI.

Difcoveries after leaving Norton Sound.—Stuart's Ifland.— Cape Stephens. — Point Shallow-Water. — Shoals on the American Coaft. — Clerke's Ifland.—Gore's Ifland.—Pinnacle Ifland.—Arrival at Oonalafhka.—Intercourfe with the Natives and Ruffian Traders. — Charts of the Ruffian Difcoveries, communicated by Mr. Ifmyloff.—Their Errors pointed out.—Situation of the Iflands vifited by the Ruffians. —Account of their Settlement at Oonalafhka.—Of the Natives of the Ifland.—Their Perfons.—Drefs.—Ornaments.— Food. — Houfes and domeftic Utenfils. — Manufactures. — Manner of producing Fire.—Canoes.—Fifhing and Hunting Implements.—Fifhes, and Sea Animals.—Sea and Water Fowls, and Land Birds.—Land Animals, and Vegetables.— Manner of burying the Dead.—Refemblance of the Natives on this Side of America to the Greenlanders and Efquimaux.—Tides.—Obfervations for determining the Longitude of Oonalafhka.

HAVING weighed, on the 17th in the morning, with a light breeze at Eaft, we fteered to the Southward, and attempted to pafs within Befborough Ifland; but, though it lies fix or feven miles from the continent, were prevented, by meeting with fhoal water. As we had but little wind all the day, it was dark before we paffed the ifland; and the night was fpent under an eafy fail.

1778.
September.
Thurfday 17.

I   We

We refumed our courfe, at day-break on the 18th, along the coaft. At noon, we had no more than five fathoms water. At this time the latitude was 63° 37′. Befborough Ifland now bore North 42° Eaft; the Southernmoft land in fight, which proved alfo to be an ifland, South 66° Weft; the paffage between it and the main, South 40° Weft; and the neareft land about two miles diftant. I continued to fteer for this paffage, until the boats, which were ahead, made the fignal for having no more than three fathoms water. On this we hauled without the ifland; and made the fignal for the Refolution's boat to keep between the fhips and the fhore.

This ifland, which obtained the name of *Stuart's Ifland*, lies in the latitude of 63° 35′, and feventeen leagues from Cape Denbigh, in the direction of South 27° Weft. It is fix or feven leagues in circuit. Some parts of it are of a middling height; but, in general, it is low; with fome rocks lying off the Weftern part. The coaft of the continent is, for the moft part, low land; but we faw high land up the country. It forms a point, oppofite the ifland, which was named Cape *Stephens*, and lies in latitude 63° 33′, and in longitude 197° 41′. Some drift-wood was feen upon the fhores, both of the ifland and of the continent; but not a tree was perceived growing upon either. One might anchor, upon occafion, between the North Eaft fide of this ifland and the continent, in a depth of five fathoms, fheltered from Wefterly, Southerly, and Eafterly winds. But this ftation would be wholly expofed to the Northerly winds, the land, in that direction, being at too great a diftance to afford any fecurity. Before we reached Stuart's Ifland, we paffed two fmall iflands, lying between us and the main; and as we ranged along the coaft, feveral people appeared

-upon

upon the fhore, and, by figns, feemed to invite us to ap‑ proach them.

As foon as we were without the ifland, we fteered South by Weft, for the Southernmoft point of the continent in fight, till eight o'clock in the evening, when, having fhoal‑ ed the water from fix fathoms to lefs than four, I tacked, and ftood to the Northward, into five fathoms, and then fpent the night plying off and on. At the time we tacked, the Southernmoft point of land, the fame which is men‑ tioned above, and was named *Point Shallow-Water*, bore South half Eaft, feven leagues diftant.

We refumed our courfe to the Southward at day-break next morning; but fhoal water obliged us to haul more to the Weftward. At length, we got fo far advanced upon the bank, that we could not hold a North North Weft courfe, meeting fometimes with only four fathoms. The wind blowing frefh at Eaft North Eaft, it was high time to look for deep water, and to quit a coaft, upon which we could no longer navigate with any degree of fafety. I therefore hauled the wind to the Northward, and gradually deepened the water to eight fathoms. At the time we hauled the wind, we were at leaft twelve leagues from the continent, and nine to the Weftward of Stuart's Ifland. No land was feen to the Southward of Point Shallow-Water, which I judge to lie in the latitude of 63°. So that between this latitude, and Shoal Nefs, in latitude 60°, the coaft is entirely unexplored. Probably, it is acceffible only to boats, or very fmall veffels; or, at leaft, if there be channels for large vef‑ fels, it would require fome time to find them; and I am of opinion, that they muft be looked for near the coaft. From the maft head, the fea within us appeared to be chequered with fhoals; the water was very much difcoloured and muddy;

muddy; and confiderably frefher than at any of the places
where we had lately anchored. From this I inferred, that
a confiderable river runs into the fea, in this unknown
part.

As foon as we got into eight fathoms water, I fteered to
the Weftward, and afterward more Southerly, for the land
Sunday 20. difcovered on the 5th, which, at noon the next day, bore
South Weft by Weft, ten or eleven leagues diftant. At this
time we had a frefh gale at North, with fhowers of hail
and fnow at intervals, and a pretty high fea; fo that we
got clear of the fhoals but juft in time. As I now found
that the land before us lay too far to the Weftward to be
Anderfon's Ifland, I named it *Clerke's Ifland*. It lies in the
latitude of 63° 15′, and in the longitude of 190° 30′. It
feemed to be a pretty large ifland, in which are four or
more hills, all connected by low ground; fo that, at a
diftance, it looks like a group of iflands. Near its Eaft part
lies a fmall ifland remarkable by having upon it three elevated rocks. Not only the greater ifland, but this fmall
fpot was inhabited.

We got up to the Northern point of Clerke's Ifland about
fix o'clock, and having ranged along its coaft till dark,
Monday 21. brought to during the night. At day-break, next morning,
we ftood in again for the coaft, and continued to range
along it, in fearch of a harbour, till noon; when, feeing no
likelihood of fucceeding, I left it, and fteered South South
Weft, for the land which we had difcovered on the 29th of
July; having a frefh gale at North, with fhowers of fleet
and fnow. I remarked, that as foon as we opened the
channel which feparates the two continents, cloudy weather, with fnow fhowers immediately commenced; whereas, all the time we were in Norton Sound, we had, with

10   the

the fame wind, clear weather. Might not this be occafioned by the mountains to the North of that place attracting the vapours, and hindering them to proceed any farther?

At day-break in the morning of the 23d, the land above mentioned appeared in fight, bearing South Weft, fix or seven leagues diftant. From this point of view, it refembled a group of iflands; but it proved to be but one, of thirty miles in extent, in the direction of North Weft and South Eaft; the South Eaft end being Cape Upright, already taken notice of. The ifland is but narrow; efpecially at the low necks of land that connect the hills. I afterward found, that it was wholly unknown to the Ruffians; and therefore, confidering it as a difcovery of our own, I named it *Gore's Ifland*. It appeared to be barren, and without inhabitants; at leaft we faw none. Nor did we fee fo many birds about it, as when we firft difcovered it. But we faw fome fea-otters; an animal which we had not met with to the North of this latitude. Four leagues from Cape Upright, in the direction of South, 72° Weft, lies a fmall ifland, whofe elevated fummit terminates in feveral pinnacle rocks. On this account it was named *Pinnacle Ifland*. At two in the afternoon, after paffing Cape Upright, I fteered South Eaft by South, for Samganoodha, with a gentle breeze at North North Weft, being refolved to fpend no more time in fearching for a harbour amongft iflands, which I now began to fufpect had no exiftence; at leaft, not in the latitude and longitude where modern map-makers have thought proper to place them. In the evening of the 24th, the wind veered to South Weft and South, and increafed to a frefh gale.

We continued to ftretch to the Eaftward, till eight o'clock

3 R 2

in the morning of the 25th, when, in the latitude of 58° 32′,
and in the longitude of 191° 10′, we tacked and ftood to the
Weft; and foon after, the gale increafing, we were reduced
to two courfes, and clofe-reefed main top-fail. Not long
after, the Refolution fprung a leak, under the ftarboard
buttock, which filled the fpirit-room with water, before it
was difcovered; and it was fo confiderable as to keep one
pump conftantly employed. We durft not put the fhip
upon the other tack, for fear of getting upon the fhoals
that lie to the North Weft of Cape Newenham; but continued ftanding to the Weft, till fix in the evening of the

26th, when we wore and ftood to the Eaftward; and then
the leak no longer troubled us. This proved, that it was
above the water line; which was no fmall fatisfaction. The
gale was now over; but the wind remained at South and
South Weft for fome days longer.

At length, on the 2d of October, at day-break, we faw
the ifland of Oonalafhka, bearing South Eaft. But as this
was to us a new point of view, and the land was obfcured
by a thick haze, we were not fure of our fituation till noon,
when the obferved latitude determined it. As all harbours
were alike to me, provided they were equally fafe and convenient, I hauled into a bay, that lies ten miles to the Weftward of Samganoodha, known by the name of *Egoochfhac*;
but we found very deep water; fo that we were glad to get
out again. The natives, many of whom lived here, vifited
us at different times, bringing with them dried falmon, and
other fifh, which they exchanged with the feamen for tobacco. But a few days before, every ounce of tobacco that
was in the fhip had been diftributed among them; and the
quantity was not half fufficient to anfwer their demands.
Notwithftanding this, fo improvident a creature is an Englifh

lifh failor, that they were as profufe in making their bargains, as if we had now arrived at a port in Virginia; by
which means, in lefs then eight and forty hours, the value
of this article of barter was lowered above a thoufand
per cent.

At one o'clock in the afternoon of the 3d, we anchored
in Samganoodha Harbour; and the next morning the carpenters of both fhips were fet to work to rip off the fheathing of and under the wale, on the ftarboard fide abaft.
Many of the feams were found quite open; fo that it was
no wonder that fo much water had found its way into the
fhip. While we lay here, we cleared the fifh and fpirit
rooms, and the after-hold; difpofing things in fuch a manner, that in cafe we fhould happen to have any more leaks
of the fame nature, the water might find its way to the
pumps. And befides this work, and completing our water,
we cleared the fore-hold to the very bottom, and took in a
quantity of ballaft.

The vegetables which we had met with, when we were
here before, were now moftly in a ftate of decay; fo that
we were but little benefited by the great quantities of berries every where found afhore. In order to avail ourfelves
as much as poffible of this ufeful refrefhment, one third
of the people, by turns, had leave to go and pick them.
Confiderable quantities of them were alfo procured from
the natives. If there were any feeds of the fcurvy, in
either fhip, thefe berries, and the ufe of fpruce beer,
which they had to drink every other day, effectually eradi-
cated them.

We alfo got plenty of fifh; at firft, moftly falmon, both
frefh and dried, which the natives brought us. Some of
the frefh falmon was in high perfection; but there was one
fort,

fort, which we called hook-nofed, from the figure of its head, that was but indifferent. We drew the feine feveral times, at the head of the bay ; and caught a good many falmon trout, and once a halibut that weighed two hundred and fifty-four pounds. The fifhery failing, we had recourfe to hooks and lines. A boat was fent out every morning ; and feldom returned without eight or ten halibut ; which was more than fufficent to ferve all our people. The halibut were excellent, and there were few who did not prefer them to falmon. Thus we not only procured a fupply of fifh for prefent confumption, but had fome to carry with us to fea. This enabled us to make a confiderable faving of our provifions, which was an object of no fmall importance.

Thurfday 8.   On the 8th, I received by the hands of an Oonalafhka man, named Derramoufhk, a very fingular prefent, confidering the place. It was a rye loaf, or rather a pye made in the form of a loaf, for it inclofed fome falmon, highly feafoned with pepper. This man had the like prefent for Captain Clerke, and a note for each of us, written in a character which none of us could read. It was natural to fuppofe, that this prefent was from fome Ruffians now in our neighbourhood ; and therefore we fent, by the fame hand, to thefe our unknown friends, a few bottles of rum, wine, and porter ; which we thought would be as acceptable as any thing we had befides ; and we foon knew that in this we had not been miftaken. I alfo fent along with Derramoufhk, Corporal Lediard of the marines, an intelligent man, in order to gain fome farther information, with orders, that if he met with any Ruffians, he fhould endeavour to make them underftand, that we were Englifh, the friends and allies of their nation.

On

On the 10th, Lediard returned with three Ruffian feamen, or furriers; who, with fome others, refided at Egoochfhac, where they had a dwelling-houfe, fome ftore-houfes, and a floop of about thirty tons burthen. One of thefe men was either Mafter or Mate of this veffel; another of them wrote a very good hand, and underftood figures; and they were all three well-behaved intelligent men, and very ready to give me all the information I could defire. But for want of an interpreter, we had fome difficulty to underftand each other. They appeared to have a thorough knowledge of the attempts that had been made by their countrymen to navigate the Frozen Ocean, and of the difcoveries which had been made from Kamtfchatka, by Beering, Tfcherikoff, and Spangberg. But they feemed to know no more of Lieutenant Syndo *, or Synd, than his name. Nor had they the leaft idea what part of the world Mr. Staehlin's map referred to, when it was laid before them. When I pointed out Kamtfchatka, and fome other known places, upon that map, they afked, whether I had feen the iflands there laid down; and on my anfwering in the negative, one of them put his finger upon a part of this map, where a number of iflands are reprefented, and faid, that he had cruifed there for land, but never could find any. I then laid before them my own chart; and found that they were ftrangers to every part of the American coaft, except what lies oppofite this ifland. One of thefe men faid, that he had been with Beering, in his American voyage; but muft then have been very young, for he had not now, at the diftance of thirty-feven years, the appearance of being aged. Never was there greater refpect paid to the memory of any diftinguifhed

* See the little that is known of Synd's voyage, accompanied with a chart, in Mr. Coxe's Ruffian Difcoveries, p. 300.

perſon, than by theſe men to that of Beering. The trade in which they are engaged is very beneficial; and its being undertaken and extended to the Eaſtward of Kamtſchatka, was the immediate conſequence of the ſecond voyage of that able navigator, whoſe misfortunes proved to be the ſource of much private advantage to individuals, and of public utility to the Ruſſian nation. And yet, if his diſtreſſes had not accidentally carried him to die in the iſland which bears his name, and from whence the miſerable remnant of his ſhip's crew brought back ſufficient ſpecimens of its valuable furs, probably the Ruſſians never would have undertaken any future voyages, which could lead them to make diſcoveries in this ſea, toward the coaſt of America. Indeed, after his time, government ſeems to have paid leſs attention to this; and we owe what diſcoveries have been ſince made, principally to the enterpriſing ſpirit of private traders, encouraged, however, by the ſuperintending care of the Court of Peterſburg. The three Ruſſians having remained

Sunday 11. with me all night, viſited Captain Clerke next morning; and then left us, very well ſatisfied with the reception they had met with; promiſing to return in a few days, and to bring with them a chart of the iſlands lying between Oonalaſhka and Kamtſchatka.

Wedneſ. 14. On the 14th, in the evening, while Mr. Webber and I were at a village at a ſmall diſtance from Samganoodha, a Ruſſian landed there, who, I found, was the principal perſon amongſt his countrymen in this and the neighbouring iſlands. His name was Eraſim Gregorioff Sin Iſmyloff. He arrived in a canoe carrying three perſons, attended by twenty or thirty other canoes, each conducted by one man. I took notice, that the firſt thing they did, after landing, was to make a ſmall tent for Iſmyloff, of materials which they

brought

brought with them; and then they made others for themfelves, of their canoes and paddles, which they covered
with grafs; fo that the people of the village were at no
trouble to find them lodging. Ifmyloff having invited us
into his tent, fet before us fome dried falmon and berries;
which, I was fatisfied, was the beft cheer he had. He appeared to be a fenfible intelligent man; and I felt no fmall
mortification in not being able to converfe with him, unlefs
by figns, affifted by figures, and other characters; which
however were a very great help. I defired to fee him on
board the next day; and accordingly he came, with all his
attendants. Indeed, he had moved into our neighbourhood,
for the exprefs purpofe of waiting upon us.

I was in hopes to have had by him, the chart which his
three countrymen had promifed; but I was difappointed.
However, he affured me I fhould have it; and he kept his
word. I found that he was very well acquainted with the
geography of thefe parts, and with all the difcoveries that
had been made in them by the Ruffians. On feeing the
modern maps, he at once pointed out their errors. He told
me, he had accompanied Lieutenant Syndo, or Synd as he
called him, in his expedition to the North; and, according to his account, they did not proceed farther than the
Tfchukotfkoi Nos, or rather than the bay of St. Laurence;
for he pointed on our chart to the very place where I landed.
From thence, he faid, they went to an ifland in latitude 63°,
upon which they did not land, nor could he tell me its
name. But I fhould guefs it to be the fame to which I gave
the name of Clerke's Ifland. To what place Synd went
after that, or in what manner he fpent the two years, during which, as Ifmyloff faid, his refearches lafted, he either
could not or would not inform us. Perhaps he did not com-

prehend our inquiries about this; and yet, in almost every
other thing, we could make him understand us. This created a suspicion, that he had not really been in that expedition, notwithstanding his affertion.

Both Ismyloff and the others affirmed, that they knew
nothing of the continent of America to the Northward; and
that neither Lieutenant Synd, nor any other Russian, had
ever feen it of late. They call it by the fame name which
Mr. Stæhlin gives to his great island; that is, Alafchka.
Stachtan Nitada, as it is called in the modern maps, is a
name quite unknown to thefe people, natives of the islands
as well as Russians; but both of them know it by the name
of America. From what we could gather from Ismyloff
and his countrymen, the Russians have made feveral attempts to get a footing upon that part of this continent that
lies contiguous to Oonalafhka and the adjoining islands, but
have always been repulfed by the natives; whom they defcribe as a very treacherous people. They mentioned two
or three Captains, or Chief men, who had been murdered
by them; and fome of the Russians fhewed us wounds
which, they faid, they had received there.

Some other information, which we got from Ismyloff, is
worth recording, whether true or falfe. He told us, that in
the year 1773, an expedition had been made into the Frozen
Sea in fledges, over the ice, to three large islands that lie
oppofite the mouth of the river Kovyma. We were in fome
doubt, whether he did not mean the fame expedition of
which Muller gives an account *; and yet he wrote down
the

---

* The lateft expedition of this kind, taken notice of by Muller, was in 1724. But
in juftice to Mr. Ismyloff, it may be proper to mention, which is done on the authority of
a MS. communicated by Mr. Pennant, and the fubftance of which has been publifhed by
Mr.

the year, and marked the iflands on the chart. But a voyage which he himfelf had performed, engaged our attention more than any other. He faid, that on the 12th of
May 1771, he failed from Bolfcheretzk, in a Ruffian veffel,
to one of the Kuril iflands, named Mareekan, in the latitude
of 47°, where there is a harbour, and a Ruffian fettlement.
From this ifland, he proceeded to Japan, where he feems
to have made but a fhort ftay. For when the Japanefe came
to know that he and his companions were chriftians, they
made figns for them to be 'gone; but did not, fo far as we
could underftand him, offer any infult or force. From
Japan, he got to Canton; and from thence to France, in a
French fhip. From France, he travelled to Peterfburg; and
was afterward fent out again to Kamtfchatka. What became of the veffel in which he firft embarked, we could
not learn; nor what was the principal object of the voyage.
His not being able to fpeak one word of French, made this
ftory a little fufpicious. He did not even know the name
of any one of the moft common things that muft have been
in ufe every day, while he was on board the fhip, and in
France. And yet he feemed clear as to the times of his
arriving at the different places, and of his leaving them,
which he put down in writing.

The next morning, he would fain have made me a prefent of a fea-otter fkin, which, he faid, was worth eighty
roubles at Kamtfchatka. However, I thought proper to decline it; but I accepted of fome dried fifh, and feveral baf-

Mr. Coxe, that, fo late as 1768, the Governor of Siberia fent three young officers over the
ice, in fledges, to the iflands oppofite the mouth of the Kovyma. There feems no reafon for
not fuppofing, that a fubfequent expedition of this fort might alfo be undertaken in 1773.
Mr. Coxe, p. 324, places the expedition on fledges in 1764; but Mr. Pennant's MS.
may be depended upon.

kets

kets of the lily, or *faranne* root, which is defcribed at large in the Hiftory of Kamtfchatka *. In the afternoon, Mr. If-myloff, after dining with Captain Clerke, left us with all his retinue, promifing to return in a few days. Accordingly, on the 19th, he made us another vifit, and brought with him the charts before mentioned, which he allowed me to copy; and the contents of which furnifh matter for the following obfervations.

Monday 19.

There were two of them, both manufcripts, and bearing every mark of authenticity. The firft comprehended the *Penfchinfkian Sea*; the coaft of Tartary, as low as the latitude of 41°; the Kuril iflands; and the peninfula of Kamtfchatka. Since this map had been made, Wawfeelee Irkeechoff, Captain of the fleet, explored, in 1758, the coaft of Tartary, from Okotfk, and the river Amur, to Japan, or 41° of latitude. Mr. Ifmyloff alfo informed us, that great part of the fea-coaft of the peninfula of Kamtfchatka had been corrected by himfelf; and defcribed the inftrument he made ufe of, which muft have been a *theodolite*. He alfo informed us, that there were only two harbours fit for fhipping, on all the Eaft coaft of Kamtfchatka, viz. the bay of *Awat-fka*, and the river *Olutora*, in the bottom of the Gulf of the fame name; that there was not a fingle harbour upon its Weft coaft; and that *Yamfk* was the only one on all the Weft fide of the Penfchinfkian Sea, except Okotfk, till we come to the river Amur. The Kuril Iflands afford only one harbour; and that is on the North Eaft fide of Mareekan, in the latitude of 47½°; where, as I have before obferved, the Ruffians have a fettlement.

The fecond chart was, to me, the moft interefting; for it comprehended all the Difcoveries made by the Ruffians to

* Englifh Tranflation, p. 83, 84.

the

the Eaftward of Kamtfchatka, toward America; which, if we exclude the voyage of Beering and Tfcherikoff, will amount to little or nothing. The part of the American coaft, with which the latter fell in, is marked in this chart, between the latitude of 58° and 58½° and 75° of longitude from Okotfk, or 218½° from Greenwich; and the place where the former anchored, in 59½° of latitude, and 63½° of longitude from Okotfk, or 207° from Greenwich. To fay nothing of the longitude, which may be erroneous from many caufes, the latitude of the coaft, difcovered by thefe two navigators, efpecially the part of it difcovered by Tfcherikoff, differs confiderably from the account publifhed by Mr. Muller, and his chart. Indeed, whether Muller's chart, or this now produced by Mr. Ifmyloff, be moft erroneous in this refpect, it may be hard to determine; though it is not now a point worth difcuffing. But the iflands that lie difperfed between 52° and 55° of latitude, in the fpace between Kamtfchatka and America, deferve fome notice. According to Mr. Ifmyloff's account, neither the number nor the fituation of thefe iflands is well afcertained. He ftruck out about one third of them, affuring me they had no exiftence; and he altered the fituation of others confiderably; which, he faid, was neceffary, from his own obfervations. And there was no reafon to doubt about this. As thefe iflands lie all nearly under the fame parallel, different navigators, being mifled by their different reckonings, might eafily miftake one ifland, or group of iflands, for another; and fancy they had made a new difcovery, when they had only found old ones in a different pofition from that affigned to them by their former vifiters.

The iflands of St. Macarius, St. Stephen, St. Theodore, St. Abraham, Seduction Ifland, and fome others, which are

to

to be found in Mr. Muller's chart, had no place in this now produced to us; nay, both Mr. Ifmyloff, and the others, affured me, that they had been feveral times fought for in vain. And yet it is difficult to believe, how Mr. Muller, from whom fubfequent map-makers have adopted them, could place them in his chart without fome authority. Relying, however, on the teftimony of thefe people, whom I thought competent witneffes, I have left them out of my chart; and made fuch corrections amongft the other iflands as I was told was neceffary. I found there was wanting another correction; for the difference of longitude, between the Bay of Awatfka, and the harbour of Samganoodha, according to aftronomical obfervations, made at thefe two places, is greater by five degrees and a half, than it is by the chart. This error I have fuppofed to be infufed throughout the whole, though it may not be fo in reality. There was alfo an error in the latitude of fome places; but this hardly exceeded a quarter of a degree.

I fhall now give fome account of the iflands; beginning with thofe that lie neareft to Kamtfchatka, and reckoning the longitude from the harbour of Petropaulowfka, in the Bay of Awatfka. The firft is *Beering's Ifland*, in 55° of latitude, and 6° of longitude. Ten leagues from the South end of this, in the direction of Eaft by South, or Eaft South Eaft, lies *Maidenoi Oftroff*, or the Copper Ifland. The next ifland is *Atakou*, laid down in 52° 45′ of latitude, and in 15° or 16° of longitude. This ifland is about eighteen leagues in extent, in the direction of Eaft and Weft; and feems to be the fame land which Beering fell in with, and named *Mount St. John*. But there are no iflands about it, except two inconfiderable ones, lying three or four leagues from the Eaft end, in the direction of Eaft North Eaft.

3

We

1778.
October.

We next come to a group, confifting of fix or more iflands; two of which, *Atghka* and *Amluk* are tolerably large; and in each of them is a good harbour. The middle of this group lies in the latitude of 52° 30′, and 28° of longitude from Awatíka; and its extent, Eaft and Weft, is four degrees. Thefe are the ifles that Mr. Ifmyloff faid were to be removed four degrees to the Eaft, which is here done. And in the fituation they have in my chart, was a group, confifting of ten fmall iflands, which, I was told, were wholly to be ftruck out; and alfo two iflands lying between them and the group to which Oonalafhka belongs. In the place of thefe two, an ifland called Amoghta (which in the chart was fituated in the latitude of 51° 45′, and 4° of longitude to the Weft) was brought.

Nothing more need be faid to fhew how erroneous the fituation of many of thefe iflands may be; and for which I am in nowife accountable. But the pofition of the largeft group, of which Oonalafhka is one of the principal iflands, and the only one in which there is a harbour, is not liable to any fuch errors. Moft of thefe iflands were feen by us; and confequently their latitude and longitude were pretty exactly determined; particularly the harbour of Samganoodha in Oonalafhka, which muft be looked upon as a fixed point. This group of iflands may be faid to extend as far as Halibut Ifles, which are forty leagues from Oonalafhka toward the Eaft North Eaft. Within thefe ifles, a paffage was marked in Ifmyloff's chart, communicating with Briftol Bay; which converts about fifteen leagues of the coaft, that I had fuppofed to belong to the continent, into an ifland, diftinguifhed by the name of *Ooneemak*. This paffage might eafily efcape us, as we were informed that it
is

is very narrow, fhallow, and only to be navigated through with boats, or very fmall veffels.

It appeared by the chart, as well as by the teftimony of Ifmyloff and the other Ruffians, that this is as far as their countrymen have made any difcoveries, or have extended themfelves, fince Beering's time. They all faid, that no Ruffians had fettled themfelves fo far to the Eaft as the place where the natives gave the note to Captain Clerke; which Mr. Ifmyloff, to whom I delivered it, on perufing it, faid, had been written at Oomanak. It was, however, from him that we got the name of *Kodiak* *, the largeft of Schumagin's Iflands; for it had no name upon the chart produced by him. The names of all the other iflands were taken from it, and we wrote them down as pronounced by him. He faid, they were all fuch as the natives themfelves called their iflands by; but, if fo, fome of the names feem to have been ftrangely altered. It is worth obferving, that no names were put to the iflands which Ifmyloff told us were to be ftruck out of the chart; and I confidered this as fome confirmation that they have no exiftence.

I have already obferved, that the American continent is here called, by the Ruffians, as well as by the iflanders, Alafchka; which name, though it properly belong only to the country adjoining to Oonemak, is ufed by them when fpeaking of the American continent in general, which they know perfectly well to be a great land.

This is all the information I got from thefe people, relating to the geography of this part of the world; and I have reafon to believe that this was all the information they were

---

* A Ruffian fhip had been at Kodiak, in 1776; as appears from a MS. obligingly communicated by Mr. Pennant.

able

able to give. For they affured me, over and over again, that they knew of no other iflands, befides thofe which were laid down upon this chart; and that no Ruffian had ever feen any part of the continent of America to the Northward, except that which lies oppofite the country of the Tfchutfkis.

If Mr. Stæhlin was not grofsly impofed upon, what could induce him to publifh a map fo fingularly erroneous; and in which many of thefe iflands are jumbled together in regular confufion, without the leaft regard to truth? And yet, he is pleafed to call it *a very accurate little map* *. Indeed, it is a map to which the moft illiterate of his illiterate feafaring countrymen would have been afhamed to fet his name.

Mr. Ifmyloff remained with us till the 21ft, in the evening, when he took his final leave. To his care I intrufted a letter to the Lords Commiffioners of the Admiralty; in which was inclofed a chart of all the Northern coafts I had vifited. He faid there would be an opportunity of fending it to Kamtfchatka, or Okotfk, the enfuing fpring; and that it would be at Peterfburg the following winter. He gave me a letter to Major Behm, Governor of Kamtfchatka, who refides at Bolfcheretfk; and another to the commanding Officer at Petropaulowfka. Mr. Ifmyloff feemed to have abilities that might entitle him to a higher ftation in life, than that in which we found him. He was tolerably well verfed in aftronomy, and in the moft ufeful branches of the mathematics. I made him a prefent of an Hadley's octant; and though, probably, it was the firft he had ever feen, he made himfelf acquainted, in a very fhort time, with moft of the ufes to which that inftrument can be applied.

* Stæhlin's New Northern Archipelago, p. 15.

VOL. II. 3 T In

In the morning of the 22d, we made an attempt to get to fea, with the wind at South Eaft, which mifcarried. The following afternoon, we were vifited by one Jacob Ivanovitch Sopofnicoff, a Ruffian, who commanded a boat, or fmall veffel, at Oomanak. This man had a great fhare of modefty; and would drink no ftrong liquor, of which the reft of his countrymen, whom we had met with here, were immoderately fond. He feemed to know more accurately what fupplies could be got at the harbour of Petropaulowfka, and the price of the different articles, than Mr. Ifmyloff. But, by all accounts, every thing we fhould want at that place was very fcarce, and bore a high price. Flour, for inftance, was from three to five roubles the pood *; and deer, from three to five roubles each. This man told us that he was to be at Petropaulowfka in May next; and, as I underftood, was to have the charge of my letter. He feemed to be exceedingly defirous of having fome token from me to carry to Major Behm; and, to gratify him, I fent a fmall fpying-glafs.

After we became acquainted with thefe Ruffians, fome of our gentlemen, at different times, vifited their fettlement on the ifland; where they always met with a hearty welcome. This fettlement confifted of a dwelling-houfe, and two ftorehoufes. And, befides the Ruffians, there was a number of the Kamtfchadales, and of the natives, as fervants, or flaves, to the former. Some others of the natives, who feemed independent of the Ruffians, lived at the fame place. Such of them as belonged to the Ruffians were all males; and they are taken, or, perhaps, purchafed from their parents when young. There was, at this time, about twenty of thefe, who could be looked upon in no other light than as children.

* 36 lb.

They

They all live in the fame houfe; the Ruffians at the upper end, the Kamtfchadales in the middle; and the natives at the lower end; where is fixed a large boiler for preparing their food, which confifts chiefly of what the fea produces, with the addition of wild roots and berries. There is little difference between the firft and laft table, befides what is produced by cookery, in which the Ruffians have the art to make indifferent things palatable. I have eat whale's flefh of their dreffing, which I thought very good; and they made a kind of pan-pudding of falmon roe, beaten up fine, and fried, that is no bad *fuccedaneum* for bread. They may, now and then, tafte real bread, or have a difh in which flour is an ingredient; but this can only be an occafional luxury. If we except the juice of berries, which they fip at their meals, they have no other liquor befides pure water; and it feems to be very happy for them that they have nothing ftronger.

As the ifland fupplies them with food, fo it does, in a great meafure, with clothing. This confifts chiefly of fkins, and is, perhaps, the beft they could have. The upper garment is made like our waggoner's frock, and reaches as low as the knee. Befides this, they wear a waiftcoat or two, a pair of breeches; a fur cap; and a pair of boots, the foles and upper leathers of which are of Ruffian leather; but the legs are made of fome kind of ftrong gut. Their two Chiefs, Ifmyloff and Ivanovitch, wore each a calico frock; and they, as well as fome others, had fhirts, which were of filk. Thefe, perhaps, were the only part of their drefs not made amongft themfelves.

There are Ruffians fettled, upon all the principal iflands between Oonalafhka and Kamtfchatka, for the fole purpofe of collecting furs. Their great object is the fea beaver or otter.

3 T 2

otter. I never heard them inquire after any other animal; though thofe, whofe fkins are of inferior value, are alfo made part of their cargoes. I never thought to afk how long they have had a fettlement upon Oonalafhka, and the neighbouring ifles; but, to judge from the great fubjection the natives are under, this cannot be of a very late date*. All thefe furriers are relieved, from time to time, by others. Thofe we met with arrived here from Okotfk, in 1776, and are to return in 1781; fo that their ftay at the ifland will be four years at leaft.

It is now time to give fome account of the native inhabitants. To all appearance, they are the moft peaceable, inoffenfive people, I ever met with. And, as to honefty, they might ferve as a pattern to the moft civilized nation upon earth. But, from what I faw of their neighbours, with whom the Ruffians have no connection, I doubt whether this was their original difpofition; and rather think that it has been the confequence of their prefent ftate of fubjection. Indeed, if fome of our gentlemen did not mifunderftand the Ruffians, they had been obliged to make fome fevere examples †, before they could bring the iflanders into any order. If there were feverities inflicted at firft, the beft apology for them is, that they have produced the happieft confequences; and, at prefent, the greateft harmony fubfifts between the two nations. The natives have their own Chiefs in each ifland, and feem to enjoy liberty and property unmolefted. But whether or no they are tributaries to the Ruffians, we

---

* The Ruffians began to frequent Oonalafhka in 1762. See *Coxe's Ruffian Difcoveries*, ch. viii. p. 80.

† See the particulars of hoftilities between the Ruffians and natives, in Coxe, as cited above.

could

could never find out. There was fome reafon to think that they are.

Thefe people are rather low of ftature, but plump and well fhaped; with rather fhort necks; fwarthy chubby faces; black eyes; fmall beards; and long, ftraight, black hair; which the men wear loofe behind, and cut before, but the women tie up in a bunch.

Their drefs has been occafionally mentioned. Both fexes wear the fame in fafhion; the only difference is in the materials. The women's frock is made of feal fkin; and that of the men, of the fkins of birds; both reaching below the knee. This is the whole drefs of the women. But, over the frock, the men wear another made of gut, which refifts water; and has a hood to it, which draws over the head. Some of them wear boots; and all of them have a kind of oval fnouted cap, made of wood, with a rim to admit the head. Thefe caps are dyed with green and other colours; and round the upper part of the rim, are ftuck the long briftles of fome fea-animal, on which are ftrung glafs beads; and on the front is a fmall image or two made of bone.

They make ufe of no paint; but the women punɛture their faces flightly; and both men and women bore the under-lip, to which they fix pieces of bone. But it is as uncommon, at Oonalafhka, to fee a man with this ornament, as to fee a woman without it. Some fix beads to the upper lip, under the noftrils; and all of them hang ornaments in their ears.

Their food confifts of fifh, fea-animals, birds, roots, and berries; and even of fea-weed. They dry large quantities of fifh in fummer; which they lay up in fmall huts for winter ufe; and, probably, they preferve roots and berries for

for the fame time of fcarcity. They eat almoft every thing raw. Boiling and broiling were the only methods of cookery that I faw them make ufe of; and the firft was probably learnt from the Ruffians. Some have got little brafs kettles; and thofe who have not, make one of a flat ftone, with fides of clay, not unlike a ftanding pye.

I was once prefent, when the Chief of Oonalafhka made his dinner of the raw head of a large halibut, juft caught. Before any was given to the Chief, two of his fervants eat the gills, without any other dreffing, befides fqueezing out the flime. This done, one of them cut off the head of the fifh, took it to the fea and wafhed it; then came with it, and fat down by the Chief; firft pulling up fome grafs, upon a part of which the head was laid, and the reft was ftrewed before the Chief. He then cut large pieces of the cheeks, and laid thefe within the reach of the great man, who fwallowed them with as much fatisfaction as we fhould do raw oyfters. When he had done, the remains of the head were cut in pieces, and given to the attendants, who tore off the meat with their teeth, and gnawed the bones like fo many dogs.

As thefe people ufe no paint, they are not fo dirty in their perfons as the favages who thus befmear themfelves; but they are full as loufy and filthy in their houfes. Their method of building is as follows : They dig, in the ground, an oblong fquare pit, the length of which feldom exceeds fifty feet, and the breadth twenty; but in general the dimenfions are fmaller. Over this excavation they form the roof of wood which the fea throws afhore. This roof is covered firft with grafs, and then with earth; fo that the outward appearance is like a dunghill. In the middle of the roof, toward each end, is left a fquare opening,

ing, by which the light is admitted; one of thefe openings being for this purpofe only, and the other being alfo ufed to go in and out by, with the help of a ladder, or rather a poft, with fteps cut in it *. In fome houfes there is another entrance below; but this is not common. Round the fides and ends of the huts, the families (for feveral are lodged together) have their feparate apartments, where they fleep, and fit at work; not upon benches, but in a kind of concave trench, which is dug all round the infide of the houfe, and covered with mats; fo that this part is kept tolerably decent. But the middle of the houfe, which is common to all the families, is far otherwife. For, although it be covered with dry grafs, it is a receptacle for dirt of every kind, and the place for the urine trough; the ftench of which is not mended by raw hides, or leather being almoft continually fteeped in it. Behind and over the trench, are placed the few effects they are poffeffed of; fuch as their clothing, mats, and fkins.

Their houfehold furniture confifts of bowls, fpoons, buckets, piggins or cans, matted bafkets, and perhaps a Ruffian kettle or pot. All thefe utenfils are very neatly made, and well formed; and yet we faw no other tools among them but the knife and the hatchet; that is, a fmall flat piece of iron, made like an adze, by fitting it into a crooked wooden handle. Thefe were the only inftruments we met with there, made of iron. For although the Ruffians live amongft them, we found much lefs of

* Mr. Coxe's defcription of the habitations of the natives of Oonalafhka, and the other Fox Iflands, in general, agrees with Captain Cook's. See *Ruffian Difcoveries*, p. 149. See alfo *Hiftoire des différens Peuples foumis à la Domination des Ruffes*, par M. Levefque, Tom. I. p. 40, 41.

this

this metal in their poſſeſſion, than we had met with in the poſſeſſion of other tribes on the American continent, who had never ſeen, nor perhaps had any intercourſe with the Ruſſians. Probably, a few beads, a little tobacco, and ſnuff, purchaſe all they have to ſpare. There are few, if any of them, that do not both ſmoke, and chew tobacco, and take ſnuff; a luxury that bids fair to keep them always poor.

They did not ſeem to wiſh for more iron, or to want any other inſtruments, except ſewing needles, their own being made of bone. With theſe they not only ſew their canoes, and make their clothes, but alſo very curious embroidery. Inſtead of thread, they uſe the fibres of ſinews, which they ſplit to the thickneſs which each ſort of work requires. All ſewing is performed by the women. They are the taylors, ſhoemakers, and boat-builders, or boat-coverers; for the men, moſt probably, conſtruct the frame of wood over which the ſkins are ſewed. They make mats and baſkets of graſs, that are both beautiful and ſtrong. Indeed, there is a neatneſs and perfection in moſt of their work, that ſhews they neither want ingenuity nor perſeverance.

I ſaw not a fire-place in any one of their houſes. They are lighted, as well as heated, by lamps; which are ſimple, and yet anſwer the purpoſe very well. They are made of a flat ſtone, hollowed on one ſide like a plate, and about the ſame ſize, or rather larger. In the hollow part they put the oil, mixed with a little dry graſs, which ſerves the purpoſe of a wick. Both men and women frequently warm their bodies over one of theſe lamps, by placing it between their legs, under their garments, and ſitting thus over it for a few minutes.

They

They produce fire both by collifion and by attrition; the former by ftriking two ftones one againft another; on one of which a good deal of brimftone is firft rubbed. The latter method is with two pieces of wood; one of which is a ftick of about eighteen inches in length, and the other a flat piece. The pointed end of the ftick they prefs upon the other, whirling it nimbly round as a drill; thus producing fire in a few minutes. This method is common in many parts of the world. It is practifed by the Kamtfchadales, by thefe people, by the Greenlanders, by the Brazilians, by the Otaheiteans, by the New Hollanders; and probably by many other nations. Yet fome learned and ingenious men have founded an argument on this cuftom to prove, that this and that nation are of the fame extraction. But accidental agreements, in a few particular inftances, will not authorife fuch a conclufion; nor will a difagreement, either in manners or cuftoms, between two different nations, of courfe, prove that they are of different extraction. I could fupport this opinion by many inftances befides the one juft mentioned.

No fuch thing as an offenfive or even defenfive weapon was feen amongft the natives of Oonalafhka. We cannot fuppofe that the Ruffians found them in fuch a defencelefs ftate; it is more probable that, for their own fecurity, they have difarmed them. Political reafons too may have induced the Ruffians not to allow thefe iflanders to have any large canoes; for it is difficult to believe they had none fuch originally, as we found them amongft all their neighbours. However, we faw none here but one or two belonging to the Ruffians. The canoes made ufe of by the natives are the fmalleft we had any where feen upon the American coaft; though built after the fame manner, with

VOL. II. 3 U fome

some little difference in the conſtruction. The ſtern of
theſe terminates a little abruptly; the head is forked; the
upper point of the fork projecting without the under one,
which is even with the ſurface of the water. Why they
ſhould thus conſtruct them is difficult to conceive; for the
fork is apt to catch hold of every thing that comes in the
way; to prevent which, they fix a piece of ſmall ſtick from
point to point. In other reſpects, their canoes are built
after the manner of thoſe uſed by the Greenlanders and
Eſquimaux; the framing being of ſlender laths, and the
covering of ſeal-ſkins. They are about twelve feet long;
a foot and a half broad in the middle; and twelve or fourteen inches deep. Upon occaſion, they can carry two perſons; one of whom is ſtretched at full length in the canoe;
and the other ſits in the ſeat, or round hole, which is nearly
in the middle. Round this hole is a rim or hoop of wood,
about which is ſewed gut-ſkin, that can be drawn together,
or opened like a purſe, with leathern thongs fitted to the
outer edge. The man ſeats himſelf in this place; draws
the ſkin tight round his body over his gut frock, and
brings the ends of the thongs, or purſe-ſtring, over the
ſhoulder to keep it in its place. The ſleeves of his frock
are tied tight round his wriſts; and it being cloſe round
his neck, and the hood drawn over his head, where it is
confined by his cap, water can ſcarcely penetrate either to
his body, or into the canoe. If any ſhould, however, in-
ſinuate itſelf, the boatman carries a piece of ſpunge, with
which he dries it up. He uſes the double-bladed paddle,
which is held with both hands in the middle, ſtriking the
water with a quick regular motion, firſt on one ſide and
then on the other. By this means the canoe is impelled
at a great rate, and in a direction as ſtraight as a line can

I   be

be drawn. In failing from Egoochfhak to Samganoodha, two or three canoes kept way with the fhip, though fhe was going at the rate of feven miles an hour.

Their fifhing and hunting implements lie ready upon the canoes, under ftraps fixed for the purpofe. They are all made, in great perfection, of wood and bone; and differ very little from thofe ufed by the Greenlanders, as they are defcribed by Crantz. The only difference is in the point of the miffile dart; which, in fome we faw here, is not above an inch long; whereas Crantz fays, that thofe of the Greenlanders are a foot and a half in length. Indeed, thefe darts, as well as fome others of their inftruments, are fo curious, that they deferve a particular defcription; but, as many of them were brought away on board the fhips, this can be done, at any time, if thought neceffary. Thefe people are very expert in ftriking fifh, both in the fea, and in rivers. They alfo make ufe of hooks and lines, nets and wears. The hooks are compofed of bone, and the lines of finews.

The fifhes which are common to other northern feas, are found here; fuch as whales, grampuffes, porpoifes, fword-fifh, halibut, cod, falmon, trout, foals, flat-fifh; feveral other forts of fmall fifh; and there may be many more that we had no opportunity of feeing. Halibut and falmon feem to be in the greateft plenty; and on them the inhabitants of thefe ifles fubfift chiefly; at leaft, they were the only fort of fifh, except a few cod, which we obferved to be laid up for their winter ftore. To the North of 60°, the fea is, in a manner, deftitute of fmall fifh of every kind; but then whales are more numerous.

Seals, and that whole tribe of fea-animals, are not fo numerous as in many other feas. Nor can this be thought

3 U 2   ftrange,

ftrange, fince there is hardly any part of the coaft, on either continent, nor any of the iflands lying between them, that is not inhabited, and whofe inhabitants hunt thefe animals for their food and clothing. Sea-horfes are, indeed, in prodigious numbers about the ice; and the fea-otter is, I believe, no where found but in this fea. We fometimes faw an animal, with a head like a feal's, that blew after the manner of whales. It was larger than a feal, and its colour was white, with fome dark fpots. Probably this was the fea-cow, or *manati*.

I think I may venture to affert, that fea and water fowls are neither in fuch numbers, nor in fuch variety, as with us in the northern parts of the Atlantic Ocean. There are fome, however, here, that I do not remember to have feen any where elfe; particularly the *alca monochroa* of Steller, before mentioned; and a black and white duck, which I conceive to be different from the ftone-duck defcribed by Krafcheninicoff *. All the other birds feen by us are mentioned by this author, except fome that we met with near the ice; and moft, if not all of thefe, are defcribed by Martin in his voyage to Greenland. It is a little extraordinary, that penguins, which are common in many parts of the world, fhould not be found in this fea. Albatroffes too are fo very fcarce, that I cannot help thinking that this is not their proper climate.

The few land-birds that we met with are the fame with thofe in Europe; but there may be many others which we had no opportunity of knowing. A very beautiful bird was fhot in the woods at Norton Sound; which, I am told, is fometimes found in England, and known by the name of chatterer. Our people met with other fmall birds there,

* Hiftory of Kamtfchatka. Eng. Tranf. p. 160.

but

but in no great variety and abundance; such as the wood-pecker, the bullfinch, the yellow finch, and a small bird called a tit-mouse.

As our excursions and observations were confined wholly to the sea-coast, it is not to be expected, that we could know much of the animals or vegetables of the country. Except musquitoes, there are few other insects; nor reptiles, that I saw, but lizards. There are no deer upon Oonalashka, or upon any other of the islands. Nor have they any domestic animals; not even dogs. Foxes and weasels were the only quadrupeds we saw; but they told us, that they had hares also, and the *marmottas* mentioned by Krascheninicoff *. Hence it is evident, that the sea and rivers supply the greatest share of food to the inhabitants. They are also obliged to the sea for all the wood made use of for building, and other necessary purposes; for not a stick grows upon any of the islands, nor upon the adjacent coast of the continent.

The learned tell us, that the seeds of plants are, by various means, conveyed from one part of the world to another; even to islands in the midst of great oceans, and far remote from any other land. How comes it to pass, that there are no trees growing on this part of the continent of America, nor any of the islands lying near it? They are certainly as well situated for receiving seeds, by all the various ways I have heard of, as any of those coasts are that abound in wood. May not nature have denied to some soil the power of raising trees, without the assistance of art? As to the drift-wood, upon the shores of the islands, I have no doubt that it comes from America. For although there may be none on the neighbouring coast, enough may grow

* History of Kamtschatka, p. 99.

farther

farther up the country, which torrents in the spring may break loose, and bring down to the sea. And not a little may be conveyed from the woody coasts, though they lie at a greater distance.

There are a great variety of plants at Oonalashka; and most of them were in flower the latter end of June. Several of them are such as we find in Europe, and in other parts of America, particularly in Newfoundland; and others of them, which are also met with in Kamtschatka, are eat by the natives both there and here. Of these, Krascheninicoff has given us descriptions. The principal one is the *saranne*, or lily root; which is about the size of a root of garlick, round, made up of a number of small cloves, and grains like groats. When boiled, it is somewhat like saloop; the taste is not disagreeable, and we found means to make some good dishes with it. It does not seem to be in great plenty; for we got none but what Ismyloff gave us.

We must reckon amongst the food of the natives, some other wild roots; the stalk of a plant resembling *angelica*; and berries of several different sorts; such as brambleberries; cranberries; hurtle-berries; heath-berries; a small red berry, which, in Newfoundland, is called partridge-berry; and another brown berry, unknown to us. This has somewhat of the taste of a sloe, but is unlike it in every other respect. It is very astringent, if eaten in any quantity. Brandy might be distilled from it. Captain Clerke attempted to preserve some; but they fermented, and became as strong as if they had been steeped in spirits.

There were a few other plants, which we found serviceable, but are not made use of by either Russians or natives.
Such

Such as wild purflain; pea-tops; a kind of fcurvy-grafs; creffes, and fome others. All thefe, we found very palatable, dreffed either in foups or in fallads. On the low ground, and in the vallies, is plenty of grafs, which grows very thick, and to a great length. I am of opinion, that cattle might fubfift at Oonalafhka all the year round, without being houfed. And the foil, in many places, feemed capable of producing grain, roots, and vegetables. But, at prefent, the Ruffian traders, and the natives, feem fatisfied with what nature brings forth.

Native fulphur was feen amongft the inhabitants of the ifland; but I had no opportunity of learning where they got it. We found alfo ochre; a ftone that gives a purple colour; and another that gives a very good green. It may be doubted, whether this laft is known. In its natural ftate, it is of a greyifh green colour, coarfe and heavy. It eafily diffolves in oil; but when put into water, it entirely lofes its properties. It feemed to be fcarce in Oonalafhka; but we were told, that it was in greater plenty on the ifland Oonemak. As to the ftones about the fhore and hills, I faw nothing in them that was uncommon.

The people of Oonalafhka bury their dead on the fummits of hills, and raife a little hillock over the grave. In a walk into the country, one of the natives, who attended me, pointed out feveral of thefe receptacles of the dead. There was one of them, by the fide of the road leading from the harbour to the village, over which was raifed a heap of ftones. It was obferved, that every one who paffed it, added one to it. I faw in the country feveral ftone hillocks, that feemed to have been raifed by art. Many of them were apparently of great antiquity.

What their notions are of the Deity, and of a future ftate,

I know

I know not. I am equally unacquainted with their diverfions; nothing having been feen that could give us an infight into either.

They are remarkably cheerful and friendly amongft each other; and always behaved with great civility to us. The Ruffians told us, that they never had any connections with their women, becaufe they were not Chriftians. Our people were not fo fcrupulous; and fome of them had reafon to repent that the females of Oonalafhka encouraged their addreffes without any referve; for their health fuffered by a diftemper that is not unknown here. The natives of this ifland are alfo fubject to the cancer, or a complaint like it, which thofe whom it attacks, are very careful to conceal. They do not feem to be long-lived. I no where faw a perfon, man or woman, whom I could fuppofe to be fixty years of age; and but very few who appeared to be above fifty. Probably their hard way of living may be the means of fhortening their days.

I have frequently had occafion to mention, from the time of our arrival in Prince William's Sound, how remarkably the natives, on this North Weft fide of America, refemble the Greenlanders and Efquimaux, in various particulars of perfon, drefs, weapons, canoes, and the like. However, I was much lefs ftruck with this, than with the affinity which we found fubfifting between the dialects of the Greenlanders and Efquimaux, and thofe of Norton's Sound and Oonalafhka. This will appear from a table of correfponding words, which I put together, and will be inferted in the courfe of this work *. It muft be obferved, however, with regard to the words which we collected on this fide of America, that too much ftrefs is not to be laid upon their being

* It will be found, amongft other vocabularies, at the end of the third volume.

accurately

accurately reprefented; for, after Mr. Anderfon's death, we had few who took much pains about fuch matters; and I have frequently found, that the fame words written down by two or more perfons, from the mouth of the fame native, on being compared together, differed not a little. But ftill, enough is certain, to warrant this judgment, that there is great reafon to believe, that all thefe nations are of the fame extraction; and if fo, there can be little doubt of there being a Northern communication of fome fort, by fea, between this Weft fide of America and the Eaft fide, through Baffin's Bay; which communication, however, may be effectually fhut up againft fhips, by ice, and other impediments. Such, at leaft, was my opinion at this time.

I fhall now quit thefe Northern regions, with a few particulars relative to the tides and currents upon the coaft, and an account of the aftronomical obfervations made by us in Samganoodha Harbour.

The tide is no where confiderable but in the great river *.

The flood comes from the South or South Eaft, every where following the direction of the coaft to the North Weftward. Between Norton Sound and Cape Prince of Wales, we found a current fetting to the North Weft, particularly off the Cape, and within Sledge Ifland.. But this current extended only a little way from the coaft; nor was it either confiftent or uniform. To the North of Cape Prince of Wales, we found neither tide nor current, either on the American or on the Afiatic coaft, though feveral times looked for. This gave rife to an opinion entertained by fome on board our fhips, that the two coafts were con-

* Cook's River.

nected, either by land or by ice; which opinion received
some strength, by our never having any hollow waves from
the North, and by our seeing ice almost the whole way
acrofs.

The following are the refults of the feveral obfervations
made afhore, during our ftay in the harbour of Samganoodha.

The latitude, by the mean of feveral ob- ferved meridian altitudes of the fun -		53° 5′ 0″
The lon- gitude	By the mean of twenty fets of lunar obfervations, with the fun Eaft of the moon	193 47 45
	By the mean of fourteen fets, with the fun and ftars Weft of the moon	193 11 45
	The mean of thefe - -	193 29 45
	The longitude affumed - -	193 30 0

By the mean of equal altitudes of the fun,
taken on the 12th, 14th, 17th, and 21ft,
the time-keeper was found to be lofing
on mean time 8″, 8 each day ; and, on
the laft of thefe days, was too flow for
mean time 13ʰ 46ᵐ 43′, 98. Hence the
time-keeper muft have been too flow,
on the 4th, the day after our arrival, by
13ʰ 44ᵐ 26′, 62 ; and the longitude, by
Greenwich rate, will be 13ʰ 23ᵐ 53′, 8 - 200 58 27
By king George's (or Nootka) Sound rate,
12ʰ 56ᵐ 40′, 4   -   -   -   - 194 10 6
The 30th of June, the time-keeper, by
the fame rate, gave   -   - 193 12 0

The

The error of the time-keeper, at that
    time, was   -   -   -   0° 18′ 0″ Weſt.

At this time, its error was   -   -   0 40 6 Eaſt.

The error of the time-keeper, between
    our leaving Samganoodha, and our re-
    turn to it again, was   -   -   0 58 6

On the 12th of October, the variation ⎰ A. M. 20° 17′ 2″ ⎱ Mean 19° 59′ 15″ Eaſt.
By the mean of three compaſſes,   ⎱ P. M. 19 41 27 ⎰

Dip of the needle ⎰ Unmarked end ⎱ Dipping, face Eaſt ⎰ 68° 45′ ⎱ Face ⎰ 69° 30′
                ⎱ Marked end ⎰   ⎱ 69 55 ⎰ Weſt ⎱ 69 17

Mean of the dip of the North end of the needle 69° 21′ 45″.

CHAP.

CHAP. XII.

1778.
October.

Monday 26.

IN the morning of Monday the 26th, we put to ſea from Samganoodha Harbour; and, as the wind was Southerly, ſtood away to the Weſtward.

My intention was now to proceed to Sandwich Iſlands, there to ſpend a few of the winter months, in caſe we ſhould meet with the neceſſary refreſhments, and then to direct our courſe to Kamtſchatka, ſo as to endeavour to be there by the middle of May, the enſuing ſummer. In

confequence

consequence of this resolution, I gave Captain Clerke orders how to proceed, in case of separation; appointing Sandwich Iflands for the first place of rendezvous, and the harbour of Petropaulowska, in Kamtschatka, for the second.

Soon after we were out of the harbour, the wind veered to the South East and East South East, which, by the evening, carried us as far as the Western part of Oonalashka, where we got the wind at South. With this we stretched to the Westward, till seven o'clock the next morning, when we wore, and stood to the East. The wind, by this time, had increased in such a manner as to reduce us to our three courses. It blew in very heavy squalls, attended with rain, hail, and snow.

At nine o'clock in the morning of the 28th, the island of Oonalashka bore South East, four leagues distant. We then wore and stood to the Westward. The strength of the gale was now over, and toward evening the little wind that blew insensibly veered round to the East, where it continued but a short time before it got to North East, and increased to a very hard gale with rain. I steered first to the Southward; and as the wind inclined to the North and North West, I steered more Westerly.

On the 29th, at half past six in the morning, we saw land extending from East by South to South by West, supposed to be the island Amoghta. At eight, finding that we could not weather the island, as the wind had now veered to the Westward, I gave over plying, and bore away for Oonalashka, with a view of going to the Northward and Eastward of that island, not daring to attempt a passage to the South East of it, in so hard a gale of wind. At the time we bore away, the land extended from East by South half
South

South to South South Weſt, four leagues diſtant. The longitude by the time-keeper was 191° 17′, and the latitude
53° 38′. This will give a very different ſituation to this
iſland from that aſſigned to it upon the Ruſſian map. But it
muſt be remembered, that this is one of the iſlands which
Mr. Iſmyloff ſaid was wrong placed. Indeed it is a doubt
if this be Amoghta *; for after Iſmyloff had made the correction, no land appeared upon the map in this latitude ;
but, as I have obſerved before, we muſt not look for accuracy in this chart.

At eleven o'clock, as we were ſteering to the North Eaſt,
we diſcovered an elevated rock, like a tower, bearing North
North Eaſt half Eaſt, four leagues diſtant. It lies in the
latitude of 53° 57′, and in the longitude of 191° 2′, and hath
no place in the Ruſſian map †. We muſt have paſſed very
near it in the night. We could judge of its ſteepneſs from
this circumſtance, that the ſea, which now run very high,
broke no where but againſt it. At three in the afternoon,
after getting a ſight of Oonalaſhka, we ſhortened ſail, and
hauled the wind, not having time to get through the paſ-

ſage before night. At day-break the next morning, we
bore away under courſes, and cloſe-reefed top-ſails, having
a very hard gale at Weſt North Weſt, with heavy ſqualls,
attended with ſnow. At noon, we were in the middle of

---

* On the chart of Krenitzen's and Levaſheff's voyage, in 1768 and 1769, which we
find in Mr. Coxe's book, p. 251. an iſland called Amuekta, is laid down, not very far
from the place aſſigned to Amoghta by Captain Cook.

† Though this rock had no place in the Ruſſian map produced by Iſmyloff, it has a
place in the chart of Krenitzen's and Levaſheff's voyage, above referred to. That chart
alſo agrees with Captain Cook's, as to the general poſition of this group of iſlands. The
ſingularly indented ſhores of the iſland of Oonalaſhka are repreſented in both charts much
alike. Theſe circumſtances are worth attending to, as the more modern Ruſſian maps
of this Archipelago are ſo wonderfully erroneous.

the

the ftrait, between Oonalafhka, and Oonella, the harbour of Samganoodha bearing South South Eaft, one league diftant. At three in the afternoon, being through the ftrait, and clear of the ifles, Cape Providence bearing Weft South Weft, two or three leagues diftant, we fteered to the Southward, under double reefed top-fails and courfes, with the wind at Weft North Weft, a ftrong gale, and fair weather.

On Monday, the 2d of November, the wind veered to the Southward; and, before night, blew a violent ftorm, which obliged us to bring to. The Difcovery fired feveral guns, which we anfwered; but without knowing on what occafion they were fired. At eight o'clock, we loft fight of her, and did not fee her again till eight the next morning. At ten, fhe joined us; and, as the height of the gale was now over, and the wind had veered back to Weft North Weft, we made fail, and refumed our courfe to the Southward.

The 6th, in the evening, being in the latitude of 42° 12', and in the longitude of 201° 26', the variation was 17° 15' Eaft. The next morning, our latitude being 41° 20', and our longitude 202°, a fhag, or cormorant, flew feveral times round the fhip. As thefe birds are feldom, if ever, known to fly far out of fight of land, I judged that fome was not far diftant. However, we could fee none. In the afternoon, there being but little wind, Captain Clerke came on board, and informed me of a melancholy accident that happened on board his fhip, the fecond night after we left Samganoodha. The main tack gave way, killed one man, and wounded the boatfwain, and two or three more. In addition to this misfortune, I now learned, that, on the evening of the 2d, his fails and rigging received confidera-

I   ble

1778.
November.

ble damage ; and that the guns which he fired were the
fignal to bring to.

Sunday 8.   On the 8th, the wind was at North ; a gentle breeze, with
Monday 9. clear weather. On the 9th, in the latitude of 39 ⅓ °, we had
eight hours calm. This was fucceeded by the wind from
the South, attended with fair weather. Availing ourfelves
of this, as many of our people as could handle a needle,
were fet to work to repair the fails ; and the carpenters were
employed to put the boats in order.

Thurfday 12.   On the 12th at noon, being then in the latitude of 38° 14′,
and in the longitude of 206° 17′, the wind returned back to
Sunday 15. the Northward ; and, on the 15th, in the latitude of 33° 30′,
it veered to the Eaft. At this time, we faw a tropic bird,
and a dolphin ; the firft that we had obferved during the
Tuefday 17. paffage. On the 17th, the wind veered to the Southward,
Thurfday 19. where it continued till the afternoon of the 19th, when a
fquall of wind and rain brought it at once round by the
Weft to the North. This was in the latitude of 32° 26′, and
in the longitude of 207° 30′.

The wind prefently increafed to a very ftrong gale, attended with rain, fo as to bring us under double-reefed
top-fails. In lowering down the main top-fail to reef it,
the wind tore it quite out of the foot rope ; and it was
fplit in feveral other parts. This fail had only been
brought to the yard the day before, after having had a
Friday 20. repair. The next morning, we got another top-fail to
the yard. This gale proved to be the forerunner of the
trade-wind, which in latitude 25° veered to Eaft, and Eaft
South Eaft.

'I continued to fteer to the Southward, till day-light in
Wednef. 25. the morning of the 25th, at which time we were in the
latitude of 20° 55′. I now fpread the fhips, and fteered
                                                         to

to the Weſt. In the evening, we joined; and at midnight brought to. At day-break, next morning, land was ſeen extending from South South Eaſt to Weſt. We made ſail, and ſtood for it. At eight, it extended from South Eaſt half South, to Weſt; the neareſt part two leagues diſtant. It was ſuppoſed that we ſaw the extent of the land to the Eaſt, but not to the Weſt. We were now ſatisfied, that the group of the Sandwich Iſlands had been only imperfectly diſcovered; as thoſe of them which we had viſited in our progreſs Northward, all lie to the leeward of our preſent ſtation.

In the country was an elevated ſaddle hill, whoſe ſummit appeared above the clouds. From this hill, the land fell in a gentle ſlope, and terminated in a ſteep rocky coaſt, againſt which the ſea broke in a dreadful ſurf. Finding that we could not weather the iſland, I bore up, and ranged along the coaſt to the Weſtward. It was not long before we ſaw people on ſeveral parts of the ſhore, and ſome houſes and plantations. The country ſeemed to be both well wooded and watered; and running ſtreams were ſeen falling into the ſea in various places.

As it was of the laſt importance to procure a ſupply of proviſions at theſe iſlands; and experience having taught me that I could have no chance to ſucceed in this, if a free trade with the natives were to be allowed; that is, if it were left to every man's diſcretion to trade for what he pleaſed, and in the manner he pleaſed; for this ſubſtantial reaſon, I now publiſhed an order, prohibiting all perſons from trading, except ſuch as ſhould be appointed by me and Captain Clerke; and even theſe were enjoined to trade only for proviſions and refreſhments. Women were alſo forbidden to be admitted into the ſhips,

A VOYAGE TO

except under certain reftrictions. But the evil I meant to prevent, by this regulation, I foon found, had already got amongft them.

At noon, the coaft extended from South 81° Eaft, to North 56° Weft; a low flat, like an ifthmus, bore South 42° Weft; the neareft fhore three or four miles diftant; the latitude was 20° 59´; and the longitude 203° 50´. Seeing fome canoes coming off to us, I brought to. As foon as they got along-fide, many of the people, who conducted them, came into the fhip, without the leaft hefitation. We found them to be of the fame nation with the inhabitants of the iflands more to leeward, which we had already vifited; and, if we did not miftake them, they knew of our having been there. Indeed, it rather appeared too evident; for thefe people had got amongft them the venereal diftemper; and, as yet, I knew of no other way of its reaching them, but by an intercourfe with their neighbours fince our leaving them.

We got from our vifiters a quantity of cuttle-fifh, for nails and pieces of iron. They brought very little fruit and roots; but told us that they had plenty of them on their ifland, as alfo hogs and fowls. In the evening, the horizon being clear to the Weftward, we judged the Wefternmoft land in fight to be an ifland, feparated from that off which we now were. Having no doubt that the people would return to the fhips next day, with the produce of their
Friday 27. country, I kept plying off all night, and in the morning ftood clofe in fhore. At firft, only a few of the natives vifited us; but, toward noon, we had the company of a good many, who brought with them bread-fruit, potatoes, tarro, or eddy roots, a few plantains, and fmall pigs; all of which they exchanged for nails and iron tools. Indeed, we had
nothing

nothing elfe to give them. We continued trading with
them till four o'clock in the afternoon, when, having difpofed of all their cargoes, and not feeming inclined to fetch
more, we made fail, and ftood off fhore.

While we were lying to, though the wind blew frefh, I
obferved that the fhips drifted to the Eaft. Confequently,
there muft have been a current fetting in that direction.
This encouraged me to ply to windward, with a view to
get round the Eaft end of the ifland, and fo have the
whole lee-fide before us. In the afternoon of the 30th,
being off the North Eaft end of the ifland, feveral canoes
came off to the fhips. Moft of thefe belonged to a Chief
named Terreeoboo, who came in one of them. He made
me a prefent of two or three fmall pigs; and we got, by
barter, from the other people, a little fruit. After a ftay of
about two hours, they all left us, except fix or eight of
their company, who chofe to remain on board. A double
failing canoe came, foon after, to attend upon them; which
we towed aftern all night. In the evening, we difcovered
another ifland to windward, which the natives call *Owhyhee*.
The name of that, off which we had been for fome days,
we were alfo told, is *Mowee*.

On the 1ft of December, at eight in the morning, Owhyhee extended from South 22° Eaft, to South 12° Weft; and
Mowee from North 41° to North 83° Weft. Finding that we
could fetch Owhyhee, I ftood for it; and our vifiters from
Mowee not choofing to accompany us, embarked in their
canoe, and went afhore. At feven in the evening, we were
clofe up with the North fide of Owhyhee; where we fpent
the night, ftanding off and on.

In the morning of the 2d, we were furprized to fee the fummits of the mountains on Owhyhee covered with

3 Y 2   fnow.

snow. They did not appear to be of any extraordinary height; and yet, in some places, the snow seemed to be of a considerable depth, and to have lain there some time. As we drew near the shore, some of the natives came off to us. They were a little shy at first; but we soon enticed some of them on board; and at last prevailed upon them to return to the island, and bring off what we wanted. Soon after these reached the shore, we had company enough; and few coming empty-handed, we got a tolerable supply of small pigs, fruit, and roots. We continued trading with them till six in the evening; when we made sail, and stood off, with a view of plying to windward round the island.

Friday 4. In the evening of the 4th, we observed an eclipse of the moon. Mr. King made use of a night-telescope, a circular aperture being placed at the object end, about one-third of the size of the common aperture. I observed with the telescope of one of Ramsden's sextants; which, I think, answers this purpose as well as any other. The following times are the means, as observed by us both.

6ʰ 3′ 25″ beginning of the eclipse ⎱ Longitude ⎰ 204° 40′ 45″
8 27 25 end of the eclipse ⎰ ⎱ 204 25 15

Mean - - - - - - 204 35 0

The penumbra was visible, at least ten minutes before the beginning, and after the end of the eclipse. I measured the uneclipsed part of the moon, with one of Ramsden's sextants, several times before, at, and after the middle of the eclipse; but did not get the time of the middle so near as might have been effected by this method. Indeed these observations were

were made only as an experiment, without aiming at much nicety. I alfo meafured moftly one way; whereas I ought to have brought alternately the reflected and direct images to contrary fides, with refpect to each other; reading the numbers off the quadrant, in one cafe, to the left of the beginning of the divifions; and, in the other cafe, to the right hand of the fame. It is evident, that half the fum of thefe two numbers muft be the true meafurement, independent of the error of the quadrant; and this is the method that I would recommend.

But I am well affured, that it might have been obferved much nearer; and that this method may be ufeful when neither the beginning nor end of an eclipfe can be obferved, which may often happen.

Immediately after the eclipfe was over, we obferved the diftance of each limb of the moon from *Pollux* and *α Arietis*; the one being to the Eaft, and the other to the Weft. An opportunity to obferve, under all thefe circumftances, feldom happens; but when it does, it ought not to be omitted; as, in this cafe, the local errors to which thefe obfervations are liable, deftroy each other; which, in all other cafes, would require the obfervations of a whole moon. The following are the refults of thefe obfervations:

Myfelf with	*α Arietis* -	204° 22' 07"	mean	204° 21' 5"
	Pollux -	204 20 4		
Mr. King with	*α Arietis* -	204 27 45	mean	204 18 29
	Pollux -	204 9 12		
Mean of the two means	-	- - -	-	204 19 47
The time-keeper, at 4ʰ 30', to which time all the lunar obfervations are reduced -				204 04 45

The

The current which I have mentioned, as setting to the Eastward, had now ceased; for we gained but little by plying. On the 6th, in the evening, being about five leagues farther up the coast, and near the shore, we had some traffic with the natives. But, as it had furnished only a trifling supply, I stood in again the next morning, when we had a considerable number of visiters; and we lay to, trading with them till two in the afternoon. By that time, we had procured pork, fruit, and roots, sufficient for four or five days. We then made sail, and continued to ply to windward.

Having procured a quantity of sugar-cane; and having, upon a trial, made but a few days before, found that a strong decoction of it produced a very palatable beer, I ordered some more to be brewed, for our general use. But when the cask was now broached, not one of my crew would even so much as taste it. As I had no motive in preparing this beverage, but to save our spirit for a colder climate, I gave myself no trouble, either by exerting authority, or by having recourse to persuasion, to prevail upon them to drink it; knowing that there was no danger of the scurvy, so long as we could get a plentiful supply of other vegetables. But, that I might not be disappointed in my views, I gave orders that no grog should be served in either ship. I myself, and the officers, continued to make use of this sugar-cane beer, whenever we could get materials for brewing it. A few hops, of which we had some on board, improved it much. It has the taste of new malt beer; and I believe no one will doubt of its being very wholesome. And yet my inconsiderate crew alleged that it was injurious to their health.

They had no better reason to support a resolution, which
they

they took on our firſt arrival in King George's Sound, not to
drink the ſpruce-beer made there. But, whether from a
conſideration that it was not the firſt time of their being required to uſe that liquor, or from ſome other reaſon, they
did not attempt to carry their purpoſe into actual execution; and I had never heard of it till now, when they renewed their ignorant oppoſition to my beſt endeavours to ſerve
them. Every innovation whatever, on board a ſhip, though
ever ſo much to the advantage of ſeamen, is ſure to meet
with their higheſt diſapprobation. Both portable ſoup, and
four krout, were, at firſt, condemned as ſtuff unfit for human beings. Few commanders have introduced into their
ſhips more novelties, as uſeful varieties of food and drink,
than I have done. Indeed few commanders have had the
ſame opportunities of trying ſuch experiments, or been
driven to the ſame neceſſity of trying them. It has, however, been, in a great meaſure, owing to various little devi-
ations from eſtabliſhed practice, that I have been able to
preſerve my people, generally ſpeaking, from that dreadful
diſtemper, the ſcurvy, which has perhaps deſtroyed more of
our ſailors, in their peaceful voyages, than have fallen by
the enemy in military expeditions.

I kept at ſome diſtance from the coaſt, till the 13th, when
I ſtood in again, ſix leagues farther to windward than we
had as yet reached; and, after having ſome trade with the
natives who viſited us, returned to ſea. I ſhould have got
near the ſhore again on the 15th, for a ſupply of fruit or
roots, but the wind happening to be at South Eaſt by South,
and South South Eaſt, I thought this a good time to ſtretch
to the Eaſtward, in order to get round, or, at leaſt, to get a
ſight of the South Eaſt end of the iſland. The wind continued at South Eaſt by South, moſt part of the 16th. It was

3

variable

variable between South and Eaſt on the 17th; and on the 18th, it was continually veering from one quarter to ano-ther; blowing, ſometimes, in hard ſqualls; and, at other times, calm, with thunder, lightning and rain. In the afternoon, we had the wind Weſterly for a few hours; but in the evening it ſhifted to Eaſt by South, and we ſtood to the Southward, cloſe hauled, under an eaſy ſail, as the Diſ-covery was at ſome diſtance aſtern. At this time the South Eaſt point of the iſland bore South Weſt by South, about five leagues diſtant; and I made no doubt that I ſhould be able to weather it. But at one o'clock, next morning, it fell calm, and we were left to the mercy of a North Eaſterly ſwell, which impelled us faſt toward the land; ſo that, long before day-break, we ſaw lights upon the ſhore, which was not more than a league diſtant. The night was dark, with thunder, lightning, and rain.

At three o'clock, the calm was ſucceeded by a breeze from the South Eaſt by Eaſt, blowing in ſqualls, with rain. We ſtood to the North Eaſt, thinking it the beſt tack to clear the coaſt; but, if it had been day-light, we ſhould have choſen the other. At day-break, the coaſt was ſeen extending from North by Weſt, to South Weſt by Weſt; a dreadful ſurf breaking upon the ſhore, which was not more than half a league diſtant. It was evident that we had been in the moſt imminent danger. Nor were we yet in ſafety, the wind veering more Eaſterly; ſo that, for ſome time, we did but juſt keep our diſtance from the coaſt. What made our ſituation more alarming, was the leach-rope of the main top-ſail giving way; which was the occaſion of the ſail's being rent in two; and the two top-gallant ſails gave way in the ſame manner, though not half worn out. By taking a fa-vourable opportunity, we ſoon got others to the yards; and then

then we left the land aftern. The Difcovery, by being at fome diftance to the North, was never near the land; nor did we fee her till eight o'clock.

On this occafion, I cannot help obferving, that I have always found, that the bolt-ropes to our fails have not been of fufficient ftrength or fubftance. This, at different times, has been the fource of infinite trouble and vexation; and of much expence of canvas, ruined by their giving way. I wifh alfo, that I did not think there is room for remarking, that the cordage and canvas, and indeed all the other ftores made ufe of in the navy, are not of equal goodnefs with thofe, in general, ufed in the merchant fervice.

It feems to be a very prevalent opinion, amongft naval officers of all ranks, that the king's ftores are better than any others, and that no fhips are fo well fitted out as thofe of the navy. Undoubtedly they are in the right, as to the quantity, but, I fear, not as to the quality of the ftores. This, indeed, is feldom tried; for things are generally condemned, or converted to fome other ufe, by fuch time as they are half worn out. It is only on fuch voyages as ours, that we have an opportunity of making the trial; as our fituation makes it neceffary to wear every thing to the very utmoft *.

* Captain Cook may, in part, be right in his comparifon of fome cordage ufed in the King's fervice, with what is ufed in that of the merchants; efpecially in time of war, when part of the cordage wanted in the navy is, from neceffity, made by contract. But it is well known, that there is no better cordage than what is made in the King's yards. This explanation of the preceding paragraph has been fubjoined, on the authority of a naval officer of diftinguifhed rank, and great profeffional ability, who has, at the fame time, recommended it as a neceffary precaution, that fhips fitted out on voyages of difcovery, fhould be furnifhed with no cordage but what is made in the King's yards; and, indeed, that every article of their ftore, of every kind, fhould be the beft that can be made.

As soon as day-light appeared, the natives afhore difplayed a white flag, which we conceived to be a fignal of peace and friendfhip. Some of them ventured out after us; but the wind frefhening, and it not being fafe to wait, they were foon left aftern.

In the afternoon, after making another attempt to weather the Eaftern extreme, which failed, I gave it up, and run down to the Difcovery. Indeed, it was of no confequence to get round the ifland; for we had feen its extent to the South Eaft, which was the thing I aimed at; and, according to the information which we had got from the natives, there is no other ifland to the windward of this. However, as we were fo near the South Eaft end of it, and as the leaft fhift of wind, in our favour, would ferve to carry us round, I did not wholly give up the idea of weathering it; and therefore continued to ply.

Sunday 20. . On the 20th, at noon, this South Eaft point bore South, three leagues diftant; the fnowy hills Weft North Weft; and we were about four miles from the neareft fhore. In the afternoon, fome of the natives came off in their canoes, bringing with them a few pigs and plantains. The latter were very acceptable, having had no vegetables for fome days; but the fupply we now received was fo inconfiderable, being barely fufficient for one day, that I ftood in Monday 21. again the next morning, till within three or four miles of the land, where we were met by a number of canoes, laden with provifions. We brought to, and continued trading with the people in them, till four in the afternoon; when, having got a pretty good fupply, we made fail, and ftretched off to the Northward.

. I had never met with a behaviour fo free from referve and fufpicion, in my intercourfe with any tribes of favages,

as we experienced in the people of this ifland. It was very
common for them to fend up into the fhip the feveral articles they brought off for barter; afterward, they would
come in themfelves, and make their bargains on the quar-
ter-deck. The people of Otaheite, even after our repeated
vifits, do not care to put fo much confidence in us. I infer
from this, that thofe of Owhyhee muft be more faithful in
their dealings with one another, than the inhabitants of
Otaheite are. For, if little faith were obferved amongft
themfelves, they would not be fo ready to truft ftrangers.
It is alfo to be obferved, to their honour, that they had
never once attempted to cheat us in exchanges, nor to
commit a theft. They underftand trading as well as moft
people; and feemed to comprehend clearly the reafon of
our plying upon the coaft. For, though they brought off
provifions in great plenty, particularly pigs, yet they kept
up their price; and, rather than difpofe of them for lefs
than they thought they were worth, would take them
afhore again.

On the 22d, at eight in the morning, we tacked to the   Tuefday 22.
Southward with a frefh breeze at Eaft by North. At noon,
the latitude was 20° 28′ 30″; and the fnowy peak bore South
Weft half South. We had a good view of it the preceding
day, and the quantity of fnow feemed to have increafed,
and to extend lower down the hill. I ftood to the South
Eaft till midnight, then tacked to the North till four in the
morning, when we returned to the South Eaft tack; and, as   Wednef. 23.
the wind was at North Eaft by Eaft, we had hopes of weathering the ifland. We fhould have fucceeded, if the wind
had not died away, and left us to the mercy of a great fwell,
which carried us faft toward the land, which was not two
leagues diftant. At length, we got our head off, and fome

light puffs of wind, which came with fhowers of rain, put us out of danger. While we lay, as it were, becalmed, feveral of the iflanders came off with hogs, fowls, fruit, and roots. Out of one canoe we got a goofe; which was about the fize of a Mufcovy duck. Its plumage was dark grey, and the bill and legs black.

At four in the afternoon, after purchafing every thing that the natives had brought off, which was full as much as we had occafion for, we made fail, and ftretched to the North, with the wind at Eaft North Eaft. At midnight, we tacked, and ftood to the South Eaft. Upon a fuppofition that the Difcovery would fee us tack, the fignal was omitted; but fhe did not fee us, as we afterward found, and continued ftanding to the North; for, at day-light next

morning, fhe was not in fight. At this time, the weather being hazy, we could not fee far; fo that it was poffible the Difcovery might be following us; and, being paft the North Eaft part of the ifland, I was tempted to ftand on, till, by the wind veering to North Eaft, we could not weather the land upon the other tack. Confequently we could not ftand to the North, to join, or look for, the Difcovery. At noon, we were, by obfervation, in the latitude of 19° 55′, and in the longitude of 205° 3′; the South Eaft point of the ifland bore South by Eaft a quarter Eaft, fix leagues diftant; the other extreme bore North, 60° Weft; and we were two leagues from the neareft fhore. At fix in the evening, the Southernmoft extreme of the ifland bore South Weft, the neareft fhore feven or eight miles diftant; fo that we had now fucceeded in getting to the windward of the ifland, which we had aimed at with fo much perfeverance.

The Difcovery, however, was not yet to be feen. But the

the wind, as we had it, being very favourable for her to follow us, I concluded, that it would not be long before she joined us. I therefore kept cruizing off this South Eaft point of the ifland, which lies in the latitude of 19° 34', and in the longitude of 205° 6', till I was fatisfied that Captain Clerke could not join me here. I now conjectured, that he had not been able to weather the North Eaft part of the ifland, and had gone to leeward in order to meet me that way.

As I generally kept from five to ten leagues from the land, no canoes, except one, came off to us till the 28th; when we were vifited by a dozen or fourteen. The people who conducted them, brought, as ufual, the produce of the ifland. I was very forry that they had taken the trouble to come fo far. For we could not trade with them, our old ftock not being, as yet, confumed; and we had found, by late experience, that the hogs could not be kept alive, nor the roots preferved from putrefaction, many days. However, I intended not to leave this part of the ifland before I got a fupply; as it would not be eafy to return to it again, in cafe it fhould be found neceffary.

We began to be in want on the 30th; and I would have ftood in near the fhore, but was prevented by a calm; but a breeze fpringing up, at midnight, from South and South Weft, we were enabled to ftand in for the land at day-break. At ten o'clock in the morning, we were met by the iflanders with fruit and roots; but, in all the canoes, were only three fmall pigs. Our not having bought thofe which had been lately brought off, may be fuppofed to be the reafon of this very fcanty fupply. We brought to for the purpofes of trade; but, foon after, our marketing was interrupted by a very hard rain; and, befides, we were rather too far from
the

the fhore. Nor durft I go nearer; for I could not depend upon the wind's remaining where it was for a moment; the fwell alfo being high, and fetting obliquely upon the fhore, againft which it broke in a frightful furf. In the evening the weather mended; the night was clear, and it was fpent in making fhort boards.

Before day-break, the atmofphere was again loaded with heavy clouds; and the new year was ufhered in with very hard rain, which continued, at intervals, till paft ten o'clock. The wind was Southerly; a light breeze, with fome calms. When the rain ceafed the fky cleared, and the breeze frefhened. Being, at this time, about five miles from the land, feveral canoes arrived with fruit and roots; and, at laft, fome hogs were brought off. We lay to, trading with them till three o'clock in the afternoon; when, having a tolerable fupply, we made fail, with a view of proceeding to the North Weft, or lee-fide of the ifland, to look for the Difcovery. It was neceffary, however, the wind being at South, to ftretch firft to the Eaftward, till midnight, when the wind came more favourable, and we went upon the other tack. For feveral days paft, both wind and weather had been exceedingly unfettled; and there fell a great deal of rain.

The three following days were fpent in running down the South Eaft fide of the ifland. For, during the nights, we ftood off and on; and part of each day was employed in lying-to, in order to furnifh an opportunity to the natives of trading with us. They fometimes came on board, while we were five leagues from the fhore. But, whether from a fear of lofing their goods in the fea, or from the uncertainty of a market, they never brought much with them. The principal article procured was falt, which was extremely good.

On

On the 5th in the morning, we paffed the South point of the ifland, which lies in the latitude of 18° 54′; and beyond it we found the coaft to trend North, 60° Weft. On this point ftands a pretty large village, the inhabitants of which thronged off to the fhip with hogs and women. It was not poffible to keep the latter from coming on board; and no women, I ever met with, were lefs referved. Indeed, it appeared to me, that they vifited us with no other view, than to make a furrender of their perfons. As I had now got a quantity of falt, I purchafed no hogs but fuch as were fit for falting; refufing all that were under fize. However, we could feldom get any above fifty or fixty pounds weight. It was happy for us, that we had ftill fome vegetables on board; for we now received few fuch productions. Indeed, this part of the country, from its appearance, did not feem capable of affording them. Marks of its having been laid wafte by the explofion of a *volcano*, every where prefented themfelves; and though we had, as yet, feen nothing like one upon the ifland, the devaftation that it had made, in this neighbourhood, was vifible to the naked eye.

This part of the coaft is fheltered from the reigning winds; but we could find no bottom to anchor upon; a line of an hundred and fixty fathoms not reaching it, within the diftance of half a mile from the fhore. The iflanders having all left us, toward the evening, we ran a few miles down the coaft; and then fpent the night ftanding off and on.

The next morning, the natives vifited us again, bringing with them the fame articles of commerce as before. Being now near the fhore, I fent Mr. Bligh, the Mafter, in a boat, to found the coaft, with orders to land, and to look for frefh water.

water. Upon his return, he reported, that, at two cables lengths from the fhore, he had found no foundings with a line of one hundred and fixty fathoms; that, when he landed, he found no ftream or fpring, but only rain-water, depofited in holes upon the rocks; and even that was brackifh from the fpray of the fea; and that the furface of the country was entirely compofed of flags and afhes, with a few plants here and there interfperfed. Between ten and eleven, we faw with pleafure the Difcovery coming round the South point of the ifland; and, at one in the afternoon, fhe joined us. Captain Clerke then coming on board, informed me, that he had cruifed four or five days where we were feparated, and then plied round the Eaft fide of the ifland; but that, meeting with unfavourable winds, he had been carried to fome diftance from the coaft. He had one of the iflanders on board all this time: who had remained there from choice, and had refufed to quit the fhip, though opportunities had offered.

Thurfday 7.

Having fpent the night ftanding off and on, we ftood in again the next morning, and when we were about a league from the fhore, many of the natives vifited us. At noon, the obferved latitude was 19° 1′, and the longitude, by the time-keeper, was 203° 26′; the ifland extending from South, 74° Eaft, to North, 13° Weft; the neareft part two leagues diftant.

Friday 8.

At day-break on the 8th, we found that the currents, during the night, which we fpent in plying, had carried us back confiderably to windward; fo that we were now off the South Weft point of the ifland. There we brought to, in order to give the natives an opportunity of trading with us. At noon our obferved latitude was 19° 1′, and our longitude, by the time-keeper, was 203° 13′; the South Weft point

point of the ifland bearing North, 30° Eaft; two miles diftant.

We fpent the night as ufual, ftanding off and on. It happened, that four men and ten women who had come on board the preceding day, ftill remained with us. As I did not like the company of the latter, I ftood in fhore toward noon, principally with a view to get them out of the fhip; and fome canoes coming off, I took that opportunity of fending away our guefts.

We had light airs from North Weft and South Weft, and calms, till eleven in the morning of the 10th, when the wind frefhened at Weft North Weft, which, with a ftrong current fetting to the South Eaft, fo much retarded us, that, in the evening, between feven and eight o'clock, the South point of the ifland bore North, 10¼° Weft, four leagues diftant. The South fnowy hill now bore North, 1½° Eaft.

At four in the morning of the 11th, the wind having fixed at Weft, I ftood in for the land, in order to get fome refrefhments. As we drew near the fhore, the natives began to come off. We lay to, or ftood on and off, trading with them all the day; but got a very fcanty fupply at laft. Many canoes vifited us, whofe people had not a fingle thing to barter; which convinced us, that this part of the ifland muft be very poor, and that we had already got all that they could fpare. We fpent the 12th, plying off and on, with a frefh gale at Weft. A mile from the fhore, and to the North Eaft of the South point of the ifland, having tried foundings, we found ground at fifty-five fathoms depth; the bottom a fine fand. At five in the evening, we ftood to the South Weft, with the wind at Weft North Weft; and foon after midnight we had a calm.

At eight o'clock next morning, having got a fmall breeze

at South South Eaſt, we ſteered to the North North Weſt, in for the land. Soon after, a few canoes came along-ſide with ſome hogs, but without any vegetables, which articles we moſt wanted. We had now made ſome progreſs; for at noon the South point of the iſland bore South, 86½° Eaſt; the South Weſt point North, 13° Weſt; the neareſt ſhore two leagues diſtant; latitude, by obſervation, 18° 56′, and our longitude, by the time-keeper, 203° 40′. We had got the length of the South Weſt point of the iſland in the evening; but the wind now veering to the Weſtward and Northward, during the night we loſt all that we had gained. Next

Thurſday 14. morning, being ſtill off the South Weſt point of the iſland, ſome canoes came off; but they brought nothing that we were in want of. We had now neither fruit nor roots, and were under a neceſſity of making uſe of ſome of our ſea-proviſions. At length, ſome canoes from the Northward brought us a ſmall ſupply of hogs and roots.

Friday 15. We had variable light airs next to a calm, the following day, till five in the afternoon, when a ſmall breeze at Eaſt North Eaſt ſpringing up, we were at laſt enabled to ſteer along ſhore to the Northward. The weather being fine, we had plenty of company this day, and abundance of every thing. Many of our viſiters remained with us on board all night, and we towed their canoes aſtern.

Saturday 16. At day-break on the 16th, ſeeing the appearance of a bay, I ſent Mr. Bligh, with a boat from each ſhip, to examine it, being at this time three leagues off. Canoes now began to arrive from all parts; ſo that before ten o'clock, there were not fewer than a thouſand about the two ſhips, moſt of them crowded with people, and well laden with hogs and other productions of the iſland. We had the moſt ſatisfying proof of their friendly intentions; for we did not ſee a
single

single person who had with him a weapon of any sort.
Trade and curiosity alone had brought them off. Among such numbers as we had, at times, on board, it is no wonder that some should betray a thievish disposition. One of our visiters took out of the ship a boat's rudder. He was discovered; but too late to recover it. I thought this a good opportunity to shew these people the use of fire-arms; and two or three musquets, and as many four-pounders, were fired over the canoe which carried off the rudder. As it was not intended that any of the shot should take effect, the surrounding multitude of natives seemed rather more surprized than frightened.

In the evening Mr. Bligh returned, and reported, that he had found a bay in which was good anchorage, and fresh water in a situation tolerably easy to be come at. Into this bay I resolved to carry the ships, there to refit, and supply ourselves with every refreshment that the place could afford. As night approached, the greater part of our visiters retired to the shore; but numbers of them requested our permission to sleep on board. Curiosity was not the only motive, at least with some; for, the next morning, several things were missing, which determined me not to entertain so many another night.

At eleven o'clock in the forenoon, we anchored in the bay (which is called by the natives *Karakakooa*), in thirteen fathoms water, over a sandy bottom, and about a quarter of a mile from the North East shore. In this situation, the South point of the bay bore South by West; and the North point West half North. We moored with the stream-anchor and cable, to the Northward, unbent the sails, and struck yards and top-masts. The ships continued to be much crowded with natives, and were surrounded by a multitude

of

of canoes. I had no where, in the courſe of my voyages,
ſeen ſo numerous a body of people aſſembled at one place.
For, beſides thoſe who had come off to us in canoes, all the
ſhore of the bay was covered with ſpectators, and many
hundreds were ſwimming round the ſhips like ſhoals of
fiſh. We could not but be ſtruck with the ſingularity of
this ſcene; and perhaps there were few on board who now
lamented our having failed in our endeavours to find a
Northern paſſage homeward, laſt ſummer. To this diſap-
pointment we owed our having it in our power to reviſit the
Sandwich Iſlands, and to enrich our voyage with a diſcovery
which, though the laſt, ſeemed, in many reſpects, to be the
moſt important that had hitherto been made by Europeans,
throughout the extent of the Pacific Ocean.

[☞ *Here Captain Cook's journal ends. The remaining tranſactions
of the voyage are related by Captain King, in the third Volume.*]

END OF THE SECOND VOLUME.

Printed in the USA
CPSIA information can be obtained
at www.ICGtesting.com
LVHW090846141024
793746LV00001B/31

9 783861 950462